Copyright © 2024

All rights reserved. No part of this publication may be reproduced, distributed, or transmitted in any form or by any means, including photocopying, recording, or other electronic or mechanical methods, without the prior written permission of the publisher, except in the case of brief quotations embodied in critical reviews and certain other noncommercial uses permitted by copyright law.

Disclosure: This study guide is intended for educational purposes only and does not guarantee success on any examination. The content provided is based on general information available at the time of creation and may not reflect the most current exam format, content, or requirements.
Users of this study guide acknowledge that:

Exam formats, content, and requirements may change without notice.
This guide is not a substitute for official exam materials or courses provided by authorized examination bodies.
The creators and distributors of this guide are not responsible for any errors, omissions, or outdated information.
Success on any examination depends on multiple factors, including individual preparation, understanding of the subject matter, and test-taking skills.
This guide does not replace professional advice or guidance from qualified instructors or institutions.

By using this study guide, you agree that the creators and distributors shall not be held liable for any damages or losses resulting from its use. Users are encouraged to verify information with official sources and seek additional resources as needed.
All rights reserved. No part of this study guide may be reproduced, distributed, or transmitted in any form without prior written permission from the copyright holder.

Table of Contents

INTRO..4

Math Section..8

Reading Comprehension Section..................................32

Practice Test Section..45

INTRO:

The sun has barely risen, casting a soft golden hue over the construction site. The air is thick with the sounds of a new day: the hum of machinery warming up, the clink of metal tools being organized, and the muffled chatter of workers preparing for their tasks ahead. Among them is an apprentice electrician, standing at the edge of the site, boots firmly planted on the cold earth, tool belt slung over their shoulder. The nerves are undeniable—today is their first day on the job. But so is the excitement. They've worked hard to get here, and this is the moment they've been waiting for.

Their mentor, a seasoned journeyman with years of experience, steps up beside them. There's no formal introduction needed, just a firm handshake and a nod that says, "You're part of the team now." Over the next hours, the apprentice watches carefully, learning how to run conduit, wire circuits, and interpret complex diagrams with precision. Each lesson is a transfer of knowledge that's been passed down through generations of electricians. The camaraderie builds as skills are sharpened and confidence grows. What starts as anxiety slowly transforms into pride. Every outlet installed, every circuit completed, is a step towards mastering the craft.

But before this day ever arrived, there was one essential hurdle that every aspiring electrician must face: passing the IBEW Aptitude Test. It's the gateway to this world of opportunity, the first step toward joining the ranks of skilled union electricians who power industries and build the infrastructure that makes modern life possible. As you read this, imagine yourself on that job site, confident and competent, working side by side with professionals on cutting-edge projects. The tools in your hands, the power running through the circuits you install, the sense of accomplishment knowing that you're a part of something bigger.

To get there, you'll need to conquer the challenge of the IBEW Aptitude Test. This study guide is designed to help you do exactly that. Inside, you'll find the resources you need to strengthen your math and reading comprehension skills, two critical areas tested on the exam. These aren't just academic exercises—they directly relate to real-world tasks like calculating electrical loads, interpreting technical documents, and ensuring that every job meets safety standards. With dedication, focus, and the right preparation, you can overcome this test and step confidently into a rewarding career where every day brings new challenges and achievements. This is your journey, and it starts here. Let's get to work.

The IBEW Aptitude Test is a crucial step for anyone aspiring to join an electrician apprenticeship through the International Brotherhood of Electrical Workers. This test is designed to assess your foundational skills in mathematics and reading comprehension—skills that are critical for success in the electrical trade. Passing the test is not just about securing a spot in the apprenticeship program; it's about proving that you have the essential problem-solving and analytical abilities to thrive in a challenging, hands-on career.

Test Structure and Content
The IBEW Aptitude Test is divided into two main sections: **Math** and **Reading Comprehension**. Both sections are designed to evaluate your ability to perform tasks and think critically in ways that directly apply to electrical work. You'll need to demonstrate not only a solid understanding of basic principles but also the ability to apply those principles in real-world scenarios, which is why preparation is key.

Math Section
The Math section consists of **33 questions** and covers a range of topics related to algebra, functions, number series, and practical math applications. You'll have **46 minutes** to complete this portion, which means managing your time wisely is essential.

1. **Algebra**: Algebra forms the foundation of many electrical calculations. Expect questions that require solving for variables, simplifying equations, and working with inequalities. You'll encounter linear equations (e.g., solving for x in 5x+3=185x + 3 = 185x+3=18) as well as systems of equations that mimic the kinds of problem-solving electricians use in their daily work, such as calculating load capacities or determining wire sizes.
2. **Functions and Graphs**: Functions are a critical component of electrical formulas, such as determining the relationship between voltage, current, and resistance. You may see questions that require interpreting and

analyzing graphs—skills you'll need when working with load curves or power distribution diagrams. Understanding how changes in one variable affect another is key here.

3. **Number Series**: These questions test your ability to recognize patterns and sequences, a skill useful for problem-solving on the job. For instance, understanding how a pattern progresses can mirror recognizing trends in electrical loads or power fluctuations in a system.
4. **Practical Applications in Electrical Work**: You'll also encounter math problems that directly relate to what electricians do. This might include calculating circuit resistance using Ohm's Law, determining power usage, or figuring out voltage drops over long distances. Understanding how to apply these formulas is essential when working on real electrical installations.

Real-World Example: Consider a scenario where you need to calculate the resistance of a circuit given a voltage of 120V and a current of 10A. Using Ohm's Law ($R = V/I$), the correct answer is $R = 12\Omega$. These are the types of questions that blend math with practical electrical knowledge.

Reading Comprehension Section

The Reading Comprehension section consists of **36 questions** and gives you **51 minutes** to complete it. This part of the test measures your ability to read, understand, and analyze written information, a vital skill for electricians who need to interpret technical documents, safety protocols, and installation manuals.

1. **Variety of Passages**: The passages on this section are diverse. They range from general topics to technical descriptions, which may include safety guidelines or procedural instructions typical in the electrical field. You'll need to demonstrate that you can extract key information from both types of text.
2. **Identifying Main Ideas**: You'll face questions that ask you to identify the main idea or purpose of a passage. This is crucial because electricians must often cut through dense technical language to find the core message—whether it's understanding a safety regulation or determining the best method for wiring a system.
3. **Making Inferences**: Inference questions require you to go beyond the literal information in the text and make logical deductions based on the details provided. For example, a passage might describe the potential consequences of using an incorrect wire gauge. You'll need to infer the risks involved, such as fire hazards or system failures, even if they aren't explicitly mentioned.
4. **Understanding Technical Vocabulary**: You'll encounter questions that test your understanding of specialized vocabulary. While the test doesn't require advanced electrical knowledge, it's important to have a solid grasp of common technical terms. For example, you might be asked to define "conductor" in the context of electricity, where it refers to a material that allows the flow of electrical current.

Real-World Example: You may read a passage describing the process of grounding electrical circuits. The questions could ask you to identify the main safety benefits of grounding or to infer what might happen if the grounding is not properly implemented.

Test Format, Time Limits, and Scoring System

- **Math Section**: 33 questions, 46 minutes.
- **Reading Comprehension Section**: 36 questions, 51 minutes.

The total test time is around **97 minutes**, which means time management is crucial. There is no penalty for guessing, so it's important to answer every question, even if you're unsure of an answer.

The exact **scoring system** for the IBEW Aptitude Test isn't publicly available, but it is believed to use a standard scoring model where your performance is compared to that of other test-takers. While there isn't a defined "cutoff score" published by IBEW, local apprenticeship programs generally set their own thresholds for what constitutes a passing score. However, it's commonly understood that performing well in both sections is crucial to being a competitive applicant.

Minimum Passing Score and Its Role in the Selection Process

The minimum passing score is determined by the local IBEW apprenticeship committees, and your score will factor heavily into the overall apprenticeship selection process. In addition to your test score, factors like an interview and past work experience are often considered. However, the test score is typically a deciding factor—performing well can increase your chances of moving forward in the selection process.

Scoring high on both sections is critical because it demonstrates a balanced skill set. Apprenticeships are competitive, and your aptitude test results provide a direct measure of your ability to handle the technical and cognitive demands of the job. Scoring well can significantly improve your standing against other candidates.

Importance of Thorough Preparation

Thorough preparation is essential for success. The IBEW Aptitude Test isn't just a formality; it's the first step toward a rewarding career as a union electrician. This study guide is specifically designed to equip you with the skills needed to excel in both sections of the exam. Whether you're brushing up on algebraic equations or practicing reading technical documents, the strategies and practice materials in this guide will prepare you to handle the test with confidence. With this guide, you'll develop a deep understanding of math principles that apply directly to electrical work—like calculating voltage drop or circuit resistance. You'll also sharpen your ability to read and interpret complex texts, a skill that electricians use daily when working with blueprints, electrical codes, and installation guides.

The path to becoming a skilled electrician starts with mastering this test. With dedication and consistent effort, you can overcome the challenge and open the door to a fulfilling career in a high-demand field that powers homes, industries, and entire communities.

Test-Taking Strategies for the IBEW Aptitude Test

Preparation in the Days Before the Test

Proper rest is crucial for optimal cognitive function. Aim for 7-9 hours of sleep each night in the week leading up to the exam. Establish a consistent sleep schedule to regulate your body's internal clock.

Nutrition plays a key role in mental acuity. Focus on balanced meals rich in protein, complex carbohydrates, and omega-3 fatty acids. Avoid heavy, greasy foods that can lead to sluggishness. On test day, eat a light, nutritious breakfast to fuel your brain without causing discomfort.

Manage stress through regular exercise, deep breathing exercises, or meditation. Find what works best for you and incorporate it into your daily routine. Remember, some nervous energy is normal and can actually enhance performance when channeled properly.

Math Section Strategies

Time management is critical in the math section. Allocate about 1 minute per question, leaving a few minutes at the end for review. If a problem is taking too long, mark it and move on. You can always return to it if time permits.

When faced with multiple-choice questions, use elimination techniques. Look for obviously incorrect answers and cross them out. This increases your odds of selecting the correct answer, even if you're not entirely sure.

For complex problems, jot down key information and equations before solving. This organized approach helps prevent careless errors and saves time in the long run.

After solving a problem, quickly check your work by plugging your answer back into the original equation or estimating if the result seems reasonable.

Reading Comprehension Tactics

Active reading is essential for efficient comprehension. Skim the questions before reading the passage to know what information to look for. As you read, underline or circle key words, dates, and concepts.

Identify the main idea of each paragraph quickly. Often, it's stated in the first or last sentence. This skill helps you navigate the passage and locate relevant information faster.

For questions about specific details, scan the passage using keywords from the question. This targeted approach saves time compared to re-reading the entire text.

When dealing with inference questions, look for clues in the passage that support your answer. Remember, the correct response will be based on information provided, not your personal opinion.

General Test-Taking Tips

Pace yourself consistently throughout the test. If you finish a section early, use the extra time to review your answers.

Don't get bogged down on difficult questions. Mark them and return later if time allows. Sometimes, information in later questions can help you solve earlier problems.

Manage test anxiety by taking deep breaths and reminding yourself that you're well-prepared. If you feel overwhelmed, close your eyes for a moment and visualize a calm, confident state of mind.

Effective Use of This Study Guide

Create a study schedule that works with your daily routine. Consistency is key. Even 30 minutes of focused study each day is more effective than cramming for hours right before the test.

Take practice tests under timed conditions to simulate the real exam environment. This helps build stamina and improves time management skills.

Review incorrect answers thoroughly. Understand why you made the mistake and how to avoid similar errors in the future.

Mindset and Motivation

Approach the test with a growth mindset. View it as an opportunity to showcase your skills and knowledge, not as an insurmountable challenge.

Visualize success. Picture yourself confidently working through the test and achieving a high score. This positive imagery can boost your performance on test day.

Remember, your diligent preparation using this guide has equipped you with the knowledge and strategies needed to excel. Trust in your abilities and approach the test with confidence. You've put in the work – now it's time to demonstrate your capabilities and take the next step in your IBEW career journey.

Math Section

Linear Equations in Electrical Applications

Linear equations form the backbone of many electrical calculations. In its simplest form, a linear equation is expressed as ax + b = c, where 'a' and 'b' are constants, 'x' is the variable, and 'c' is the result.

Solving Linear Equations

Let's walk through solving a linear equation with variables on both sides:

$3x + 4 = 2x - 7$

1. Isolate variable terms on one side and constants on the other: $3x - 2x = -7 - 4$
2. Simplify: $x = -11$
3. Check your answer by substituting it back into the original equation: $3(-11) + 4 = 2(-11) - 7$ -33 + 4 = -22 - 7 -29 = -29 (equation balances)

This process is crucial when analyzing circuits with multiple components or when troubleshooting complex electrical systems.

Slope and Y-Intercept in Electrical Circuits

In the context of electrical circuits, the slope-intercept form ($y = mx + b$) of a linear equation takes on special significance.

Consider Ohm's Law: $V = IR$

Here, voltage (V) is analogous to 'y', current (I) to 'x', and resistance (R) to the slope 'm'. The y-intercept 'b' is zero in this case, indicating that with no current, there's no voltage drop across a resistor.

Practical Application:

Imagine a circuit with a 5Ω resistor. The equation becomes:

$V = 5I$

If we plot this on a graph, the slope (5) represents the resistance. A steeper slope indicates higher resistance, while a gentler slope suggests lower resistance.

In more complex circuits, the y-intercept might not be zero. For instance, in a circuit with a battery and a resistor in series:

$V = IR + E$

Where E is the battery voltage. Here, E represents the y-intercept, the voltage when no current flows.

Understanding these relationships helps electricians:

1. Predict system behavior under varying conditions
2. Troubleshoot issues by identifying unexpected deviations from the linear relationship
3. Design circuits to meet specific voltage or current requirements

By mastering linear equations, you're equipping yourself with a powerful tool for analyzing and manipulating electrical systems, a skill that's indispensable in the IBEW field.

Graphing Linear Equations: Slope-Intercept Form

Linear equations in slope-intercept form are expressed as $y = mx + b$, where: m = slope (rate of change) b = y-intercept (where the line crosses the y-axis) x and y = coordinates of any point on the line

To graph a linear equation:

1. Plot the y-intercept (0, b) on the y-axis
2. Use the slope to find a second point
3. Draw a line through these two points

Finding x and y intercepts:

- Y-intercept: Set $x = 0$ and solve for y
- X-intercept: Set $y = 0$ and solve for x

In electrical systems:

- Open circuit: Infinite resistance, represented by a vertical line (x = constant)
- Short circuit: Zero resistance, represented by a horizontal line (y = constant)

Example: $y = 2x + 3$ Y-intercept: (0, 3) X-intercept: $0 = 2x + 3$, $x = -1.5$ Plot (0, 3) and (-1.5, 0), then connect the points

Electricians use graphed equations to visualize voltage drop:

Voltage Drop Equation: V = IR Graph: y = mx, where y = voltage drop, m = current, x = resistance
Example: Current = 10A, Resistance range: 0-5Ω Graph points: (0,0), (1,10), (2,20), (3,30), (4,40), (5,50)
This linear graph shows how voltage drop increases with resistance. Electricians can quickly estimate voltage drop for different conductor lengths or gauge sizes by referencing the graph.
Practical application: An electrician needs to determine the maximum length of 12 AWG wire for a 20A circuit with a 3% voltage drop limit on a 120V system.
1. Calculate maximum allowed voltage drop: 120V × 0.03 = 3.6V
2. Use wire resistance: 1.588Ω per 1000 ft for 12 AWG
3. Graph the equation: y = 20x, where y = voltage drop, x = resistance
4. Find the x-value (resistance) when y = 3.6V
5. Convert resistance to length

By graphing this relationship, electricians can visually determine the maximum wire length that meets code requirements, ensuring efficient and safe installations.

Systems of Equations in Electrical Calculations
Systems of equations are fundamental in solving complex electrical problems, especially when dealing with multiple circuit branches or components. These systems allow electricians to analyze interconnected variables simultaneously, providing a comprehensive understanding of circuit behavior.
Solving Systems of Equations
Let's explore two primary methods for solving systems: substitution and elimination.
Substitution Method: Consider the system: x + 2y = 10 3x - y = 5
1. Isolate x in the first equation: x = 10 - 2y
2. Substitute this expression into the second equation: 3(10 - 2y) - y = 5
3. Solve for y: 30 - 6y - y = 5 30 - 7y = 5 -7y = -25 y = 25/7
4. Substitute y back into x = 10 - 2y to find x: x = 10 - 2(25/7) = 20/7

Elimination Method: Using the same system: x + 2y = 10 3x - y = 5
1. Multiply the first equation by 3 and the second by 1: 3x + 6y = 30 3x - y = 5
2. Subtract the second equation from the first: 7y = 25
3. Solve for y: y = 25/7
4. Substitute y into either original equation to find x: x + 2(25/7) = 10 x = 10 - 50/7 = 20/7

Both methods yield the same result: x = 20/7, y = 25/7.
Practical Application: Branch Circuit Analysis
Word Problem: An electrical panel supplies two branch circuits. Circuit A has a resistance of 20Ω and operates at 120V. Circuit B has a resistance of 30Ω and operates at 240V. Determine the current flow in each circuit.
Let's solve this using a system of equations:
Let I_1 be the current in Circuit A and I_2 be the current in Circuit B.
According to Ohm's Law: For Circuit A: $20I_1 = 120$ For Circuit B: $30I_2 = 240$
Simplifying: $I_1 = 6$ $I_2 = 8$
Therefore, Circuit A carries 6 amperes, and Circuit B carries 8 amperes.
This problem demonstrates how systems of equations can efficiently solve multi-circuit scenarios. In more complex situations, you might encounter systems with more variables, requiring advanced techniques like matrix methods.
Understanding systems of equations empowers electricians to:
1. Analyze parallel and series circuits simultaneously
2. Balance load distribution across multiple branches
3. Optimize power distribution in complex electrical systems

Mastering these mathematical tools enhances your ability to design, troubleshoot, and maintain electrical systems efficiently. As you progress in your IBEW career, you'll find these skills invaluable for tackling increasingly complex electrical challenges.

Quadratic Equations in Electrical Power Calculations
Quadratic equations take the form $ax^2 + bx + c = 0$, where $a \neq 0$. In electrical engineering, these equations often appear in power calculations and circuit analysis.

Factoring Quadratic Expressions: To factor $x^2 + 5x + 6$:
1. Identify two numbers that multiply to give 6 and add up to 5
2. These numbers are 2 and 3
3. Rewrite the expression: $x^2 + 2x + 3x + 6$
4. Group terms: $(x^2 + 2x) + (3x + 6)$
5. Factor out common terms: $x(x + 2) + 3(x + 2)$
6. Factor out $(x + 2)$: $(x + 2)(x + 3)$

The roots of this equation are $x = -2$ and $x = -3$.

Quadratic Formula: For equations that can't be easily factored, use the quadratic formula: $x = [-b \pm \sqrt{b^2 - 4ac}] / (2a)$

Example in Electrical Engineering: Calculate the resonant frequency of an RLC circuit with L = 50mH, C = 10μF.

The resonant frequency formula is: $f = 1 / (2\pi\sqrt{LC})$

Squaring both sides to create a quadratic in f: $f^2 = 1 / (4\pi^2 LC)$

Substituting values: $f^2 = 1 / (4\pi^2 * 50 \cdot 10^{-3} * 10 \cdot 10^{-6})$ $f^2 = 202,642.37$

To solve: $f = \pm\sqrt{202,642.37}$ $f \approx \pm 450.16$ Hz

We take the positive root as frequency is always positive.

Practical Application: An electrician needs to determine the time at which current in an RLC circuit reaches its peak value. The current equation is: $i(t) = 10e^{-50t} - 10e^{-150t}$

To find the peak, we differentiate and set to zero: $di/dt = -500e^{-50t} + 1500e^{-150t} = 0$

This leads to a quadratic in e^{-50t}: $3e^{-100t} - 1 = 0$

Let $u = e^{-50t}$: $3u^2 - 1 = 0$

Using the quadratic formula: $u = [0 \pm \sqrt{0^2 - 4(3)(-1)}] / (2*3)$ $u = \pm 1/\sqrt{3}$

Taking the positive root and solving for t: $e^{-50t} = 1/\sqrt{3}$ $t = -\ln(1/\sqrt{3}) / 50 \approx 0.0073$ seconds

This calculation helps the electrician predict and measure the peak current time, crucial for testing and calibrating protection devices in the circuit.

By mastering quadratic equations, electricians can solve complex problems involving resonance, power factor correction, and transient analysis, enhancing their ability to design and troubleshoot efficient electrical systems.

Exponents and Radicals in Electrical Calculations

Exponents play a crucial role in electrical calculations, particularly when dealing with power relationships and alternating current (AC) circuits. Understanding exponent laws and radical expressions is essential for efficient problem-solving in the electrical field.

Exponents and Their Laws

An exponent indicates how many times a base number is multiplied by itself. For instance, $2^3 = 2 \times 2 \times 2 = 8$.

Key exponent laws:
1. Product Rule: $x^a \times x^b = x^{(a+b)}$
2. Quotient Rule: $x^a \div x^b = x^{(a-b)}$
3. Power of a Power Rule: $(x^a)^b = x^{(ab)}$
4. Zero Exponent Rule: $x^0 = 1$ (for $x \neq 0$)
5. Negative Exponent Rule: $x^{(-a)} = 1 / x^a$

Application in Watt's Law

Watt's Law, expressed as $P = V^2 / R$, illustrates the relationship between power (P), voltage (V), and resistance (R). The squared voltage term demonstrates a key application of exponents in electrical calculations.

Example: Calculate the power dissipated in a 100Ω resistor with 12V applied across it.

$P = V^2 / R$ $P = 12^2 / 100$ $P = 144 / 100$ $P = 1.44$ watts

This calculation showcases how exponents directly impact power calculations in electrical circuits.

Simplifying Radical Expressions

Radicals are the inverse operation of exponents. The square root of a number is that number raised to the 1/2 power. Similarly, the cube root is that number raised to the 1/3 power.

Key rules for simplifying radicals:
1. $\sqrt{a \times b} = \sqrt{a} \times \sqrt{b}$
2. $\sqrt{a / b} = \sqrt{a} / \sqrt{b}$ (for $b > 0$)
3. $\sqrt{a^n} = a^{(n/2)}$ (for even n)

4. $\sqrt[3]{a^n} = a^{(n/3)}$ (for cube roots)

Application in AC Circuits: RMS Values

In AC circuits, we often work with root mean square (RMS) values. The RMS value of an AC voltage or current is the equivalent DC value that would produce the same heating effect.

For a sinusoidal waveform: $V_{RMS} = V_{peak} / \sqrt{2} \approx 0.707 \times V_{peak}$

Example: Calculate the RMS voltage of an AC signal with a peak voltage of 170V.

$V_{RMS} = 170V / \sqrt{2}$ $V_{RMS} = 170V \times (1/\sqrt{2})$ $V_{RMS} = 170V \times \sqrt{(1/2)}$ $V_{RMS} = 170V \times 0.707$ $V_{RMS} \approx 120.19V$

This calculation demonstrates how radical expressions are integral to AC circuit analysis.

Practical Applications:
1. Power Factor Correction: In AC circuits, power factor (PF) is often expressed as cos θ. When working with power triangles, you might encounter expressions like:

True Power = Apparent Power × $\sqrt{(1 - \sin^2\theta)}$

This involves simplifying a radical expression to determine the relationship between different power types in an AC circuit.

2. Impedance Calculations: In AC circuits with both resistance (R) and reactance (X), the impedance (Z) is calculated using:

$Z = \sqrt{(R^2 + X^2)}$

Understanding how to simplify this radical expression is crucial for analyzing AC circuit behavior.

3. Harmonics Analysis: When dealing with non-sinusoidal waveforms, you'll often need to calculate the Total Harmonic Distortion (THD):

$THD = \sqrt{(V_2^2 + V_3^2 + V_4^2 + ...)} / V_1$

Where V_1 is the fundamental voltage and V_2, V_3, etc., are harmonic voltages. This calculation requires a solid grasp of both exponents and radicals.

Mastering exponents and radicals allows electricians to:
- Efficiently calculate power consumption and dissipation
- Accurately analyze AC circuit behavior
- Troubleshoot power quality issues related to harmonics

As you progress in your IBEW career, these mathematical tools will become second nature, enabling you to tackle complex electrical problems with confidence and precision.

Rational Expressions in Electrical Calculations

Rational expressions are fractions where both numerator and denominator are polynomials. In electrical engineering, these expressions frequently appear in calculations involving parallel circuits and complex networks.

Parallel Resistor Formula: $1/R_{total} = 1/R1 + 1/R2 + ... + 1/Rn$

This formula is a prime example of rational expressions in electrical calculations.

Operations with Rational Expressions:
1. Addition/Subtraction: Find a common denominator, then add/subtract numerators.

Example: Combining two parallel resistors $1/R_{total} = 1/R1 + 1/R2$ $1/R_{total} = 1/6 + 1/12$ $1/R_{total} = 2/12 + 1/12 = 3/12 = 1/4$

$R_{total} = 4\Omega$

2. Multiplication: Multiply numerators and denominators separately, then simplify.

Example: Power calculation in a circuit $P = V^2 / R$ If V = 12V and R = 3Ω $P = (12^2) / 3 = 144 / 3 = 48W$

3. Division: Invert the second fraction and multiply.

Example: Voltage divider calculation $V_{out} = (R2 / (R1 + R2)) * V_{in}$ If R1 = 1kΩ, R2 = 3kΩ, V_{in} = 12V $V_{out} = (3 / (1 + 3)) * 12 = (3/4) * 12 = 9V$

Simplifying Complex Fractions:

Complex fractions are fractions that contain fractions in the numerator or denominator. They often arise in network calculations.

Method: Multiply both numerator and denominator by the LCD of all internal fractions.

Example: Simplify the complex fraction representing the total resistance of this network:

$R_{total} = 1 / (1/R1 + 1/(R2 + R3))$

Let R1 = 6Ω, R2 = 4Ω, R3 = 2Ω

R_total = 1 / (1/6 + 1/(4 + 2)) = 1 / (1/6 + 1/6) = 1 / (2/6) = 6/2 = 3Ω

Practice Problems:
1. Simplify the following expression representing a voltage divider network: (R2 / (R1 + R2)) / (R3 / (R3 + R4)) Where R1 = 2kΩ, R2 = 6kΩ, R3 = 3kΩ, R4 = 1kΩ
2. In a parallel RLC circuit, the total impedance is given by: 1/Z = 1/R + 1/(XL - XC) If R = 50Ω, XL = 100Ω, and XC = 25Ω, calculate Z.
3. A complex network has the following equivalent resistance: R_eq = 1 / (1/R1 + 1/(R2 + 1/(1/R3 + 1/R4))) Simplify this expression if R1 = R2 = R3 = R4 = 10Ω

Solutions:
1. (6 / (2 + 6)) / (3 / (3 + 1)) = (3/4) / (3/4) = 1
2. 1/Z = 1/50 + 1/(100 - 25) = 1/50 + 1/75 = 3/150 + 2/150 = 5/150 Z = 150/5 = 30Ω
3. R_eq = 1 / (1/10 + 1/(10 + 1/(1/10 + 1/10))) = 1 / (1/10 + 1/(10 + 1/(2/10))) = 1 / (1/10 + 1/(10 + 5)) = 1 / (1/10 + 1/15) = 1 / (3/30 + 2/30) = 1 / (5/30) = 30/5 = 6Ω

These problems demonstrate how rational expressions are integral to solving complex electrical network problems. Mastering these techniques allows electricians to analyze and design circuits more effectively, leading to more efficient and reliable electrical systems.

Function Notation in Electrical Contexts

Function notation provides a powerful tool for representing relationships between variables in electrical systems. It allows for clear, concise expression of complex electrical concepts and facilitates the analysis of interconnected circuit elements.

Basics of Function Notation

A function $f(x)$ represents a relationship where each input x corresponds to exactly one output. In electrical contexts, we often use variables like V (voltage), I (current), R (resistance), and P (power) instead of x and y.

Interpreting Function Notation

Consider the function $f(I) = RI^2$. This function represents the power dissipated in a resistor with resistance R when a current I flows through it.

Here:
- $f(I)$ represents the output (power)
- I is the input variable (current)
- R is a parameter (resistance)

Evaluating Functions

To evaluate a function, we substitute a specific value for the input variable.

Example 1: Power Dissipation in a Resistor Given $f(I) = RI^2$, where R = 10Ω, evaluate $f(3)$.

$f(3) = 10 \times 3^2 = 10 \times 9 = 90$ watts

This tells us that when 3 amperes flow through a 10Ω resistor, it dissipates 90 watts of power.

Example 2: Voltage Drop Across a Resistor Let $g(I) = RI$ represent the voltage drop across a resistor. If R = 5Ω, evaluate $g(2.5)$.

$g(2.5) = 5 \times 2.5 = 12.5$ volts

This indicates that when 2.5 amperes flow through a 5Ω resistor, the voltage drop is 12.5 volts.

Function Composition

Function composition involves applying one function to the result of another. This concept is particularly useful when analyzing multi-stage electrical systems.

Example: Voltage Transformation and Power Calculation

Consider a scenario with a step-down transformer followed by a resistive load. We'll use two functions:
1. $t(V) = 0.1V$ (transformer function that reduces voltage to 10%)
2. $p(V) = V^2 / R$ (power dissipation function, assuming R = 100Ω)

To find the power dissipated in the resistor given an input voltage of 1000V, we compose these functions:

$p(t(V)) = (t(V))^2 / R$

Evaluating step-by-step:
1. $t(1000) = 0.1 \times 1000 = 100V$
2. $p(100) = 100^2 / 100 = 100W$

Therefore, p(t(1000)) = 100 watts

This composition tells us that when 1000V is input to the transformer, the resulting 100V across the 100Ω resistor dissipates 100 watts of power.

Practical Applications

1. Circuit Analysis: Functions can represent the behavior of circuit elements. For instance, the current through a diode might be expressed as:

$I(V) = I_s(e^{(V/V_t)} - 1)$

Where I_s is the reverse saturation current and V_t is the thermal voltage.

2. Filter Design: The frequency response of a low-pass RC filter can be represented as:

$H(f) = 1 / \sqrt{(1 + (f/f_c)^2)}$

Where f_c is the cutoff frequency. This function helps in analyzing how the filter attenuates different frequencies.

3. Power Factor Correction: The power factor of a circuit can be expressed as a function of the phase angle:

$PF(\theta) = \cos(\theta)$

This function is crucial in understanding and improving the efficiency of AC power systems.

4. Transformer Efficiency: The efficiency of a transformer can be represented as a function of the load:

$\eta(P\_out) = P\_out / (P\_out + P\_core + P\_copper)$

Where P_core represents core losses and P_copper represents copper losses.

Mastering function notation enables electricians to:

- Model complex electrical systems concisely
- Analyze the behavior of circuits under varying conditions
- Predict system responses to different inputs
- Optimize electrical designs for efficiency and performance

As you progress in your IBEW career, proficiency with function notation will enhance your ability to tackle sophisticated electrical problems, design advanced systems, and communicate complex concepts effectively with colleagues and clients.

Identifying Patterns in Number Sequences for Electrical Applications

Pattern recognition is a crucial skill for electricians, enabling them to anticipate trends in electrical measurements, load calculations, and component specifications. Let's explore this concept through various electrical contexts.

Arithmetic Sequences in Electrical Applications:

An arithmetic sequence has a constant difference between consecutive terms. In electrical work, these sequences often appear in standardized ratings and measurements.

Wire Gauge Sizes (AWG): 4, 2, 1, 1/0, 2/0, 3/0, 4/0

While not immediately apparent, this sequence follows a pattern. The numeric value decreases by 2 for each step until reaching 1, then switches to a different notation. The cross-sectional area approximately doubles with each step. To calculate the next term in the sequence:

1. Identify the pattern: Area doubles each step
2. Convert to square millimeters: 4 AWG ≈ 21.2 mm² 2 AWG ≈ 33.6 mm² 1 AWG ≈ 42.4 mm² 1/0 AWG ≈ 53.5 mm² 2/0 AWG ≈ 67.4 mm² 3/0 AWG ≈ 85.0 mm² 4/0 AWG ≈ 107.2 mm²

The next term would be approximately 134.8 mm², corresponding to 250 kcmil.

Circuit Breaker Ratings: 15A, 20A, 30A, 40A, 50A, 60A

This sequence follows an arithmetic progression with varying differences: 15 to 20: +5 20 to 30: +10 30 to 40: +10 40 to 50: +10 50 to 60: +10

The next terms would likely be 70A, 80A, 100A, following the pattern of 10A increments, with larger jumps for higher ratings.

Recognizing Trends in Electrical Measurements:

Voltage Drop Across a Wire: Measure voltage drop at 10-foot intervals on a long run: 0.2V, 0.4V, 0.6V, 0.8V, 1.0V

Pattern: Constant increase of 0.2V per 10 feet Next term prediction: 1.2V at 60 feet

This linear pattern indicates consistent resistance per unit length. Deviations might suggest wire damage or connection issues.

Load Calculation Sequence: Analyze power consumption data for a building over 6 hours: 2kW, 2.5kW, 3.2kW, 4.1kW, 5.2kW, 6.5kW

This sequence doesn't have a constant difference, but there's a clear increasing trend. Calculate the rate of increase: 0.5kW, 0.7kW, 0.9kW, 1.1kW, 1.3kW

The rate of increase is itself increasing by 0.2kW each hour. Predicted next term: 6.5kW + 1.5kW = 8kW

This accelerating pattern might indicate the startup of additional equipment or increased occupancy. Recognizing this trend allows for proactive load management.

Practice Problems:
1. Fuse ratings follow the sequence: 5A, 10A, 15A, 20A, 25A, 30A What are the next two terms in this sequence?
2. A motor's current draw during startup is measured every 0.5 seconds: 80A, 65A, 52A, 41A, 32A, 25A Identify the pattern and predict the current at 3.5 seconds after startup.
3. LED light output (in lumens) increases with applied voltage: 800, 1000, 1250, 1550, 1900 If this pattern continues, what would be the expected output at the next voltage step?

Solutions:
1. The fuse rating sequence increases by 5A each step. Next two terms: 35A, 40A
2. The current is decreasing by approximately 20% each 0.5-second interval. 80 * 0.8 = 64 64 * 0.8 = 51.2 51.2 * 0.8 = 40.96 40.96 * 0.8 = 32.768 32.768 * 0.8 = 26.2144 26.2144 * 0.8 = 20.97 (rounded to 21A) Predicted current at 3.5 seconds: approximately 21A
3. The light output is increasing by 25% each step. 1900 * 1.25 = 2375 lumens Expected output at the next voltage step: 2375 lumens

Recognizing these patterns allows electricians to:
- Anticipate equipment behavior
- Identify potential issues before they become critical
- Make informed decisions about system design and capacity planning
- Troubleshoot more effectively by recognizing deviations from expected patterns

By honing pattern recognition skills, electricians can work more efficiently, improve safety, and optimize electrical system performance.

Geometric Sequences in Electrical Systems

Geometric sequences are series of numbers where each term after the first is found by multiplying the previous term by a fixed, non-zero number called the common ratio. In electrical systems, these sequences often appear in harmonic analysis, multistage circuits, and exponential growth or decay scenarios.

General Form: $a, ar, ar^2, ar^3, ..., ar^{n-1}$

Where: a = first term r = common ratio n = position of term

The nth term of a geometric sequence is given by: $a_n = a * r^{n-1}$

Sum of n terms of a geometric sequence: $S_n = a(1 - r^n) / (1 - r)$ (for $r \neq 1$) $S_n = na$ (for r = 1)

Applications in Electrical Systems:
1. Harmonic Frequencies: In power systems, harmonic frequencies form a geometric sequence. The fundamental frequency (usually 50 or 60 Hz) is multiplied by integers to produce harmonics.

$f_n = f_1 * n$ Where f_1 is the fundamental frequency and n is the harmonic order.

2. Multistage Amplifiers: In cascaded amplifier stages, if each stage has the same gain, the overall gain forms a geometric sequence.

$G_{total} = G^n$ Where G is the gain of each stage and n is the number of stages.

3. RC Circuit Discharge: The voltage across a capacitor during discharge follows a geometric sequence when sampled at fixed time intervals.

$V(t) = V_0 * e^{-t/RC}$ Where V_0 is initial voltage, R is resistance, and C is capacitance.

Practice Problems:
1. Harmonic Analysis: A power system has a fundamental frequency of 60 Hz. Calculate the frequency of the 5th harmonic.

Solution: a = 60 Hz r = 1 (multiply by 1 each time to get the next harmonic) n = 5 $a_5 = 60 * 1^{(5-1)} = 60 * 5 = 300$ Hz

2. Multistage Amplifier: An amplifier consists of 3 stages, each with a gain of 4. Calculate the overall gain.

Solution: a = 4 (gain of first stage) r = 1 (each stage has the same gain) n = 3 (number of stages) G_total = 4 * 1^(3-1) = 4 * 3 = 64

3. Voltage Divider: A voltage divider consists of 4 identical resistors in series. If the input voltage is 16V, find the voltage after each resistor, assuming they form a geometric sequence.

Solution: We need to find r such that: 16 * r³ = 1 (voltage after last resistor is 1/16 of input) r³ = 1/16 r = (1/16)^(1/3) ≈ 0.5

Now we can find the voltages: V_1 = 16V V_2 = 16 * 0.5 = 8V V_3 = 16 * 0.5² = 4V V_4 = 16 * 0.5³ = 2V

4. Capacitor Discharge: A capacitor discharges through a resistor. The voltage readings taken every millisecond form a geometric sequence: 100V, 90V, 81V. What will be the voltage after 5 ms?

Solution: a = 100V r = 90/100 = 0.9 n = 5 + 1 = 6 (5 ms after initial reading)
V_5 = 100 * 0.9^(6-1) ≈ 59.05V

5. Sum of Harmonics: In a power system, the amplitudes of the first 5 odd harmonics form a geometric sequence with first term 100V and common ratio 0.3. Calculate the sum of these amplitudes.

Solution: a = 100V r = 0.3 n = 5
S_5 = 100 * (1 - 0.3^5) / (1 - 0.3) = 100 * (1 - 0.00243) / 0.7 ≈ 142.51V

These problems demonstrate how geometric sequences apply to various electrical scenarios. Understanding these concepts allows electricians to:

- Analyze harmonic content in power systems
- Design and troubleshoot multistage amplifiers
- Predict voltage distributions in complex circuits
- Model capacitor discharge behavior
- Calculate cumulative effects of harmonics

Mastering geometric sequences enhances your ability to analyze and design electrical systems, particularly those involving repetitive structures or exponential behavior. This knowledge is invaluable for advanced circuit analysis, power quality assessment, and signal processing applications in your IBEW career.

Reading and Interpreting Line Graphs in Electrical Engineering

Line graphs are fundamental tools for visualizing relationships between variables in electrical systems. Understanding how to extract information from these graphs is crucial for analyzing component behavior and system performance.

Basic Elements of a Line Graph:

- X-axis: Usually represents the independent variable
- Y-axis: Typically shows the dependent variable
- Data points: Plotted values connecting to form lines
- Slope: Indicates rate of change between variables

Voltage-Current (V-I) Characteristics:

1. Resistor V-I Curve: X-axis: Current (I) Y-axis: Voltage (V)

For an ideal resistor, the V-I curve is a straight line passing through the origin. Slope = ΔV / ΔI = Resistance (R)

To calculate resistance:

1. Choose two points on the line: (I1, V1) and (I2, V2)
2. R = (V2 - V1) / (I2 - I1)

Example: Point 1: (2A, 6V) Point 2: (5A, 15V) R = (15V - 6V) / (5A - 2A) = 9V / 3A = 3Ω

2. Diode V-I Curve: X-axis: Voltage (V) Y-axis: Current (I)

Key features:

- Knee voltage: Point where current begins to flow significantly
- Reverse breakdown voltage: Sharp increase in reverse current

Extracting information:

- Forward voltage drop: Voltage at which current starts flowing (typically 0.6-0.7V for silicon diodes)
- Reverse saturation current: Small current flow in reverse bias before breakdown

3. **Transistor Characteristic Curves:** Common-Emitter Configuration: X-axis: Collector-Emitter Voltage (VCE) Y-axis: Collector Current (IC) Multiple curves for different Base Currents (IB)

Interpreting the graph:
- Active region: Linear portion of curves
- Saturation region: Curves flatten out
- Cutoff region: Near-zero collector current

Extracting β (current gain):
1. Choose a point in the active region
2. β = ΔIC / ΔIB

Example: At VCE = 5V: IB1 = 20μA, IC1 = 2mA IB2 = 40μA, IC2 = 4mA β = (4mA - 2mA) / (40μA - 20μA) = 100

4. **Transformer Magnetization Curve:** X-axis: Magnetizing force (H) Y-axis: Magnetic flux density (B)

Key features:
- Saturation point: B stops increasing significantly with H
- Remanence: Residual B when H returns to zero
- Coercivity: Reverse H required to bring B to zero

Interpreting the curve:
- Steeper initial slope indicates higher permeability
- Wider hysteresis loop suggests higher core losses

Practical Applications:
1. **Power Supply Load Regulation:** X-axis: Load Current Y-axis: Output Voltage

Interpreting the graph:
- Ideal: Horizontal line (constant voltage regardless of current)
- Real: Slight downward slope

Calculate load regulation: % Regulation = [(VNL - VFL) / VFL] × 100 Where VNL = No-load voltage, VFL = Full-load voltage

2. **Solar Panel V-I Curve:** X-axis: Voltage Y-axis: Current

Key points:
- Short-circuit current (ISC): Current at zero voltage
- Open-circuit voltage (VOC): Voltage at zero current
- Maximum power point (MPP): Point where V × I is highest

Extracting information:
- Fill Factor = (VMPP × IMPP) / (VOC × ISC)
- Efficiency = (VMPP × IMPP) / (Incident light power)

3. **Motor Torque-Speed Curve:** X-axis: Speed (RPM) Y-axis: Torque

Interpreting the graph:
- Starting torque: Torque at zero speed
- Breakdown torque: Maximum torque point
- Full-load torque: Rated operating point

Analyze motor performance:
- Speed regulation = (No-load speed - Full-load speed) / Full-load speed
- Torque reserve = (Breakdown torque - Full-load torque) / Full-load torque

Practice Exercise:

Given a V-I curve for an unknown component:

Points on the curve: (1V, 0.1mA), (2V, 0.5mA), (3V, 2mA), (4V, 8mA)
1. Is this likely a linear or non-linear component?
2. If it's non-linear, what type of component might it be?
3. Calculate the dynamic resistance at 3V.

Solution:
1. Non-linear component (current doesn't increase proportionally with voltage)

2. Likely a semiconductor diode (exponential increase in current)
3. Dynamic resistance at 3V: R = ΔV / ΔI = (4V - 2V) / (8mA - 0.5mA) ≈ 266Ω

Mastering the interpretation of line graphs enables electricians to:
- Troubleshoot circuits more effectively
- Predict component behavior under various conditions
- Optimize system designs for efficiency and performance
- Identify potential issues before they lead to failures

By developing this skill, electricians enhance their ability to make data-driven decisions and improve overall system reliability.

Interpreting Bar Graphs for Electrical Power Consumption

Bar graphs provide a visual representation of data, making them invaluable tools for analyzing power consumption patterns across various electrical appliances. Let's explore how to interpret these graphs and extract meaningful insights for energy management.

Sample Scenario: Imagine a bar graph showing the average daily power consumption of different appliances in a residential setting. Each bar represents an appliance, with its height indicating the kilowatt-hours (kWh) consumed per day.

Appliance Power Consumption (kWh/day):
1. Refrigerator: 1.5 kWh
2. Air Conditioner: 8.0 kWh
3. Water Heater: 4.5 kWh
4. Lighting: 2.0 kWh
5. Television: 0.5 kWh
6. Washing Machine: 1.0 kWh

Interpreting the Graph:
1. Identifying High Consumers: The tallest bars represent the appliances consuming the most energy. In this case, the air conditioner stands out as the highest consumer at 8.0 kWh/day.
2. Comparing Relative Consumption: The height difference between bars allows for quick comparisons. For instance, the air conditioner consumes about 16 times more energy than the television daily.
3. Grouping Similar Consumers: Appliances with similar bar heights can be grouped for analysis. The refrigerator and washing machine have comparable consumption levels.

Calculations and Analysis:
1. Total Energy Usage: To calculate the total daily energy consumption, sum the values for all appliances:
Total = 1.5 + 8.0 + 4.5 + 2.0 + 0.5 + 1.0 = 17.5 kWh/day
2. Percentage of Total Consumption: To find what percentage each appliance contributes to the total:
Air Conditioner: (8.0 / 17.5) × 100 ≈ 45.7% Water Heater: (4.5 / 17.5) × 100 ≈ 25.7% Lighting: (2.0 / 17.5) × 100 ≈ 11.4% Refrigerator: (1.5 / 17.5) × 100 ≈ 8.6% Washing Machine: (1.0 / 17.5) × 100 ≈ 5.7% Television: (0.5 / 17.5) × 100 ≈ 2.9%
3. Identifying Peak Demand Periods: While this single graph doesn't show time-of-day usage, we can infer potential peak periods:
- The air conditioner likely contributes to afternoon peak demand during hot days.
- Lighting might spike during evening hours.
- The water heater could contribute to morning and evening peaks.
4. Energy Saving Opportunities: Focus on the tallest bars for the most significant energy-saving potential:
- Adjusting the air conditioner's temperature by 1-2 degrees could yield substantial savings.
- Upgrading to a more efficient water heater could reduce the second-largest consumption source.
5. Baseload vs. Variable Load:
- Baseload: Refrigerator runs constantly, representing about 1.5 kWh of consistent daily usage.
- Variable Load: Air conditioner, lighting, and other appliances fluctuate based on usage patterns and external factors like weather.

6. Monthly Projection: To estimate monthly consumption, multiply the daily total by 30:

17.5 kWh/day × 30 days = 525 kWh/month

7. Cost Analysis: Assuming an electricity rate of $0.12 per kWh:

Monthly Cost = 525 kWh × $0.12/kWh = $63.00

Practical Applications:
1. Load Balancing: Understanding which appliances consume the most power helps in distributing loads across different circuits to prevent overloading.
2. Circuit Design: When designing home electrical systems, knowledge of typical appliance consumption helps in sizing circuits and selecting appropriate wire gauges.
3. Energy Audits: These graphs are essential tools for conducting energy audits, allowing electricians to quickly identify areas for potential energy savings.
4. Customer Education: Electricians can use these visual representations to educate homeowners about their energy usage patterns and suggest energy-saving strategies.
5. Troubleshooting: Unusual spikes in energy consumption for specific appliances can indicate malfunctions or inefficiencies, guiding troubleshooting efforts.

Mastering the interpretation of power consumption bar graphs enables electricians to:
- Provide valuable energy management advice to clients
- Design more efficient electrical systems
- Identify and resolve issues related to excessive power consumption
- Contribute to overall energy conservation efforts

As an IBEW professional, your ability to analyze and explain these graphs will enhance your value in both residential and commercial electrical work, positioning you as an expert in energy efficiency and electrical system optimization.

Pie Charts in Electrical Engineering

Pie charts are circular diagrams divided into sectors, each representing a proportion of the whole. In electrical engineering, they're particularly useful for visualizing load distribution, power factor correction capacities, and energy consumption patterns.

Key Components of a Pie Chart:
1. Sectors: Wedge-shaped portions representing data categories
2. Labels: Descriptions of each sector
3. Percentages: Numerical representation of each sector's proportion
4. Legend: Color-coded key explaining what each sector represents

Using Pie Charts in Electrical Applications:
1. Power Factor Correction Capacities:

A pie chart can show the distribution of capacitor banks in a power factor correction system:

Example: Total Capacity: 500 kVAR
- 25% : 125 kVAR (fixed)
- 15% : 75 kVAR (1st step)
- 20% : 100 kVAR (2nd step)
- 40% : 200 kVAR (3rd step)

This visual representation helps quickly assess the system's flexibility in adjusting power factor under varying load conditions.

2. Distribution of Electrical Loads:

Pie chart showing energy consumption in a commercial building:

Total Load: 1000 kW
- 40% : HVAC (400 kW)
- 30% : Lighting (300 kW)
- 15% : Office Equipment (150 kW)
- 10% : Elevators (100 kW)
- 5% : Miscellaneous (50 kW)

This breakdown helps identify areas for potential energy savings and guides load management strategies.
3. Energy Source Mix:

Pie chart depicting the sources of electrical energy for a facility:
Total Energy: 10,000 MWh/year

- 45% : Grid Supply (4,500 MWh)
- 30% : Solar PV (3,000 MWh)
- 15% : Wind Turbines (1,500 MWh)
- 10% : Backup Generators (1,000 MWh)

This visualization aids in assessing renewable energy integration and backup power adequacy.

Calculating Percentages and Actual Values:

To calculate percentage: (Sector Value / Total Value) × 100 = Percentage

To calculate actual value from percentage: (Percentage × Total Value) / 100 = Actual Value

Practice Problems:
1. A facility's main distribution panel has the following circuit breaker configuration:
    - 3 × 100A breakers
    - 2 × 60A breakers
    - 5 × 20A breakers
    - 8 × 15A breakers

Create a pie chart showing the distribution of breaker ratings. Calculate the percentage for each rating.

2. An energy audit reveals the following annual consumption for a small factory: Total: 500,000 kWh
    - Production Equipment: 250,000 kWh
    - Lighting: 75,000 kWh
    - HVAC: 100,000 kWh
    - Office Equipment: Remaining kWh

Draw a pie chart, calculate percentages, and determine the Office Equipment consumption.

3. A power quality meter shows the following harmonic distribution:
    - Fundamental (60 Hz): 100A
    - 3rd Harmonic: 15A
    - 5th Harmonic: 10A
    - 7th Harmonic: 5A
    - Higher Order Harmonics: 2A

Create a pie chart of harmonic content. Calculate the Total Harmonic Distortion (THD).

Solutions:
1. Circuit Breaker Configuration: Total Amperage: (3 × 100) + (2 × 60) + (5 × 20) + (8 × 15) = 620A
    - 100A breakers: (300 / 620) × 100 ≈ 48.4%
    - 60A breakers: (120 / 620) × 100 ≈ 19.4%
    - 20A breakers: (100 / 620) × 100 ≈ 16.1%
    - 15A breakers: (120 / 620) × 100 ≈ 16.1%

Pie Chart: [Visualization of 4 sectors with percentages]

2. Energy Consumption: Office Equipment: 500,000 - (250,000 + 75,000 + 100,000) = 75,000 kWh
    - Production Equipment: (250,000 / 500,000) × 100 = 50%
    - Lighting: (75,000 / 500,000) × 100 = 15%
    - HVAC: (100,000 / 500,000) × 100 = 20%
    - Office Equipment: (75,000 / 500,000) × 100 = 15%

Pie Chart: [Visualization of 4 sectors with percentages]

3. Harmonic Distribution: Total RMS Current: $\sqrt{(100^2 + 15^2 + 10^2 + 5^2 + 2^2)}$ ≈ 101.98A
    - Fundamental: (100 / 101.98) × 100 ≈ 98.06%
    - 3rd Harmonic: (15 / 101.98) × 100 ≈ 14.71%
    - 5th Harmonic: (10 / 101.98) × 100 ≈ 9.81%
    - 7th Harmonic: (5 / 101.98) × 100 ≈ 4.90%
    - Higher Order: (2 / 101.98) × 100 ≈ 1.96%

Pie Chart: [Visualization of 5 sectors with percentages] THD = √(15² + 10² + 5² + 2²) / 100 × 100 ≈ 18.71%

Interpreting Pie Charts:
1. Identify the largest sector: This represents the most significant component or highest consumer.
2. Compare sector sizes: Quickly assess relative importance or consumption levels.
3. Look for small sectors: These might represent opportunities for consolidation or areas of neglect.
4. Consider the context: A small percentage in a large total might still be significant.

Benefits of Using Pie Charts in Electrical Work:
- Simplify complex data for quick understanding
- Identify load balancing opportunities
- Prioritize energy efficiency measures
- Communicate technical information to non-technical stakeholders
- Support decision-making in system design and upgrades

By mastering the creation and interpretation of pie charts, electricians can enhance their ability to analyze systems, present findings, and make data-driven recommendations for electrical installations and energy management.

Scatter Plots in Electrical Analysis

Scatter plots are powerful graphical tools used to visualize relationships between two variables. In electrical engineering, they're particularly useful for identifying correlations, trends, and anomalies in data sets. These plots can reveal patterns that might not be apparent in tabular data or other graph types.

Structure of a Scatter Plot:
- X-axis: Independent variable
- Y-axis: Dependent variable
- Each point represents a pair of measurements

Interpreting Scatter Plots:
1. Positive Correlation: Points trend upward from left to right
2. Negative Correlation: Points trend downward from left to right
3. No Correlation: Points show no clear pattern
4. Strength of Correlation: Tightness of the cluster of points

Scenario: Temperature vs. Resistance in a Copper Conductor

Let's examine how temperature affects the resistance of a copper wire. We'll use a scatter plot to visualize this relationship.

Data Collection: Measure the resistance of a copper wire at various temperatures:
Temperature (°C) | Resistance (Ω) 0 | 10.0 20 | 10.8 40 | 11.6 60 | 12.4 80 | 13.2 100 | 14.0

Plotting the Data:
- X-axis: Temperature (°C)
- Y-axis: Resistance (Ω)

Analysis of the Scatter Plot:
1. Correlation Observation: The points form a clear upward trend from left to right, indicating a positive correlation between temperature and resistance.
2. Linearity: The points appear to fall along a straight line, suggesting a linear relationship between temperature and resistance for copper within this temperature range.
3. Slope Interpretation: The slope of the trend indicates the rate of change in resistance per degree Celsius. Here, it's approximately 0.04 Ω/°C.
4. Extrapolation: While not always reliable, the linear trend allows us to estimate resistance values for temperatures outside our measured range.
5. Outlier Detection: Any points significantly deviating from the linear trend would warrant investigation for measurement errors or unexpected behavior.

Mathematical Relationship: The scatter plot visually confirms the linear relationship described by the temperature coefficient of resistance formula:

$R = R_0[1 + \alpha(T - T_0)]$

Where: R = Resistance at temperature T R_0 = Reference resistance at temperature T_0 α = Temperature coefficient of resistance (for copper, α ≈ 0.00393 /°C) T = Current temperature T_0 = Reference temperature

Practical Applications:
1. Cable Sizing: Understanding how resistance changes with temperature helps in properly sizing cables for various environmental conditions.
2. Thermal Management: The relationship informs strategies for managing heat in electrical systems, crucial for preventing overheating and ensuring efficient operation.
3. Temperature Sensing: This principle is used in Resistance Temperature Detectors (RTDs) for accurate temperature measurement in industrial applications.
4. Power Transmission: Knowledge of how resistance varies with temperature is crucial for calculating power losses in transmission lines under different weather conditions.
5. Circuit Protection: Designing overcurrent protection devices that account for resistance changes due to temperature fluctuations.

Advanced Analysis:
1. Best-Fit Line: Calculate the equation of the best-fit line using linear regression. This provides a mathematical model of the relationship: R = 10.0 + 0.04T Where R is resistance in Ω and T is temperature in °C.
2. Correlation Coefficient: Calculate the Pearson correlation coefficient (r) to quantify the strength of the linear relationship. In this case, r would be very close to 1, indicating a strong positive correlation.
3. Residual Analysis: Plot the differences between observed and predicted values (residuals) to assess the model's accuracy and identify any systematic errors.
4. Multiple Variables: Extend the analysis to 3D scatter plots for examining relationships between three variables, such as current, voltage, and power in a circuit.

Mastering scatter plot analysis allows electricians to:
- Identify and quantify relationships between electrical variables
- Predict system behavior under varying conditions
- Troubleshoot complex issues by visualizing data patterns
- Make data-driven decisions in system design and optimization

As an IBEW professional, your ability to create, interpret, and explain scatter plots enhances your analytical skills, enabling you to tackle complex electrical problems with greater insight and precision. This competency is particularly valuable in research, development, and advanced troubleshooting scenarios, positioning you as a skilled data-driven problem solver in the electrical field.

Rate-Time-Distance Problems in Electrical Engineering

Rate-time-distance problems are fundamental in electrical engineering, particularly when dealing with signal propagation, data transmission, and electrical system timing. The basic formula relating these variables is:

Distance = Rate × Time

In electrical contexts, this formula often translates to:

Cable Length = Signal Propagation Speed × Transmission Time

Let's explore this concept with various electrical applications and problem-solving techniques.

Signal Propagation in Cables:

The speed of electrical signals in cables is typically expressed as a percentage of the speed of light (c ≈ 3 × 10^8 m/s). This percentage is known as the Velocity Factor (VF).

VF = Actual Signal Speed / Speed of Light

Common Velocity Factors:
- Coaxial Cable: 0.66 - 0.85
- Twisted Pair: 0.59 - 0.78
- Fiber Optic: 0.67 - 0.68

Example 1: Signal Travel Time in Coaxial Cable

Problem: A coaxial cable with a velocity factor of 0.82 connects two devices 100 meters apart. How long does it take for a signal to travel from one end to the other?

Solution:

1. Calculate the signal speed: Speed = c × VF = 3 × 10^8 × 0.82 = 2.46 × 10^8 m/s
2. Use the distance formula: Time = Distance / Speed Time = 100 / (2.46 × 10^8) ≈ 4.07 × 10^-7 seconds or 407 nanoseconds

Example 2: Cable Length for a Given Delay
Problem: In a data center, the maximum allowed signal delay between two servers is 5 nanoseconds. If using Cat6a cable with a velocity factor of 0.74, what is the maximum cable length allowed?
Solution:
1. Calculate the signal speed: Speed = 3 × 10^8 × 0.74 = 2.22 × 10^8 m/s
2. Use the distance formula: Distance = Speed × Time Distance = 2.22 × 10^8 × 5 × 10^-9 = 1.11 meters

The maximum cable length allowed is 1.11 meters.

Electrical Wave Propagation:
In AC circuits, wavelength is related to frequency and propagation speed:

$\lambda = v / f$

Where: λ = wavelength v = propagation velocity f = frequency

Example 3: Antenna Length Calculation
Problem: Calculate the length of a quarter-wave antenna for a 900 MHz cellular signal. Assume the signal travels at 95% of the speed of light.
Solution:
1. Calculate the wavelength: v = 0.95 × 3 × 10^8 = 2.85 × 10^8 m/s λ = v / f = (2.85 × 10^8) / (900 × 10^6) ≈ 0.317 meters
2. Calculate quarter-wave length: Antenna length = λ / 4 ≈ 0.0792 meters or 7.92 cm

Transmission Line Impedance:
The characteristic impedance of a transmission line is related to its length and the time it takes for a signal to traverse it:

$Z0 = \sqrt{(L/C)}$

Where: Z0 = characteristic impedance L = inductance per unit length C = capacitance per unit length

Example 4: Transmission Line Impedance
Problem: A 50-ohm coaxial cable has a capacitance of 100 pF/m. Calculate the inductance per meter and the time for a signal to travel 10 meters.
Solution:
1. Calculate inductance per meter: L = (Z0^2 × C) = 50^2 × 100 × 10^-12 = 250 nH/m
2. Calculate propagation speed: v = 1 / $\sqrt{(LC)}$ = 1 / $\sqrt{(250 × 10^{-9} × 100 × 10^{-12})}$ ≈ 2 × 10^8 m/s
3. Calculate travel time: Time = Distance / Speed = 10 / (2 × 10^8) = 5 × 10^-8 seconds or 50 nanoseconds

Practice Problems:
1. A fiber optic cable with a velocity factor of 0.67 is used to connect two buildings 500 meters apart. How long does it take for a light pulse to travel between the buildings?
2. An oscilloscope measures a time delay of 15 nanoseconds between input and output signals. If the connecting cable has a velocity factor of 0.78, what is the cable's length?
3. A 2.4 GHz Wi-Fi signal has a wavelength of 12.5 cm in free space. What is the effective propagation speed of this signal in a cable with a velocity factor of 0.81?

Solutions:
1. Fiber Optic Cable: Speed = 3 × 10^8 × 0.67 = 2.01 × 10^8 m/s Time = 500 / (2.01 × 10^8) ≈ 2.49 × 10^-6 seconds or 2.49 microseconds
2. Cable Length: Speed = 3 × 10^8 × 0.78 = 2.34 × 10^8 m/s Length = Speed × Time = 2.34 × 10^8 × 15 × 10^-9 = 3.51 meters
3. Wi-Fi Signal Propagation: Free space wavelength = 12.5 cm Cable wavelength = 12.5 × 0.81 = 10.125 cm Speed = Wavelength × Frequency = 0.10125 × 2.4 × 10^9 = 2.43 × 10^8 m/s

Understanding and solving rate-time-distance problems in electrical contexts is crucial for:
- Designing efficient communication systems
- Troubleshooting signal timing issues
- Optimizing network layouts

- Selecting appropriate cable lengths for specific applications
- Calculating signal propagation delays in complex systems

By mastering these concepts, electricians and engineers can ensure proper timing in electrical systems, minimize signal degradation, and design more efficient and reliable electrical networks.

Work Problems in Electrical Installations

Work problems are crucial in project planning and resource allocation for electrical installations. These problems typically involve calculating the time required to complete a task when multiple workers with varying efficiencies are involved. Understanding how to solve these problems is essential for effective project management in the electrical field.

General Formula: When workers with different efficiencies collaborate on a task, we use the following formula:
$1/T = 1/T_1 + 1/T_2 + ... + 1/T_n$

Where: T = Total time to complete the job when working together T_n = Time it would take worker n to complete the job alone

Basic Scenario: Two electricians working together can wire a house in 6 hours. If working alone, the first electrician could complete the job in 10 hours. How long would it take the second electrician to complete the job alone?

Solution: Let x be the time for the second electrician. $1/6 = 1/10 + 1/x$ $1/6 - 1/10 = 1/x$ $5/30 - 3/30 = 1/x$ $2/30 = 1/x$ x = 15 hours

The second electrician would take 15 hours to complete the job alone.

Practice Problems:

1. Conduit Installation: Electrician A can install conduit in a commercial building in 8 hours. Electrician B can do the same job in 12 hours. How long will it take them to complete the job working together?

Solution: $1/T = 1/8 + 1/12$ $1/T = 3/24 + 2/24 = 5/24$ T = 24/5 = 4.8 hours
It will take them 4.8 hours working together.

2. Panel Upgrade: Three electricians are upgrading electrical panels in an apartment complex. Working alone, they could complete the job in 15, 20, and 25 hours respectively. How long will it take them working together?

Solution: $1/T = 1/15 + 1/20 + 1/25$ $1/T = 40/300 + 30/300 + 24/300 = 94/300$ T = 300/94 ≈ 3.19 hours
It will take approximately 3.19 hours working together.

3. Cable Pulling: Apprentice A can pull cable through a conduit in 45 minutes. Journeyman B can do it in 30 minutes. How long will it take them working together?

Solution: First, convert times to hours: 45 minutes = 0.75 hours 30 minutes = 0.5 hours
$1/T = 1/0.75 + 1/0.5$ $1/T = 4/3 + 2/1 = 4/3 + 6/3 = 10/3$ T = 3/10 = 0.3 hours = 18 minutes
It will take them 18 minutes working together.

4. Lighting Fixture Installation: Electrician A can install 20 lighting fixtures in 8 hours. Electrician B can install 15 fixtures in 5 hours. How long will it take them to install 100 fixtures working together?

Solution: First, calculate their individual rates: A: 20 fixtures / 8 hours = 2.5 fixtures/hour B: 15 fixtures / 5 hours = 3 fixtures/hour
Combined rate = 2.5 + 3 = 5.5 fixtures/hour
Time to install 100 fixtures: T = 100 fixtures / 5.5 fixtures/hour ≈ 18.18 hours
It will take approximately 18.18 hours to install 100 fixtures working together.

5. Troubleshooting Circuit: Three technicians are troubleshooting a complex circuit. Working alone, they could solve the problem in 6, 8, and 10 hours respectively. After working together for 1 hour, one technician is called away. How long will it take the remaining two to finish the job?

Solution: Step 1: Calculate progress made in the first hour: $1/6 + 1/8 + 1/10 = 5/24 + 3/24 + 12/120 = 15/24 = 5/8$
Progress = 5/8 of the job completed in 1 hour
Step 2: Calculate remaining work: Remaining = 1 - 5/8 = 3/8 of the job
Step 3: Calculate time for remaining two technicians to complete 3/8 of the job: $1/T = 1/8 + 1/10$ (assuming the 6-hour technician left) $1/T = 5/40 + 4/40 = 9/40$ T = 40/9 ≈ 4.44 hours
Total time = 1 hour (all three working) + 4.44 hours (two remaining) ≈ 5.44 hours

Practical Applications:

1. Project Planning: These calculations help in estimating project durations and allocating resources efficiently.
2. Cost Estimation: By knowing the time required, you can more accurately estimate labor costs for bidding on jobs.
3. Team Composition: Understanding worker efficiencies helps in forming balanced teams for various tasks.
4. Scheduling: These problems assist in creating realistic schedules for complex electrical installations involving multiple tasks and workers.
5. Performance Evaluation: Comparing actual completion times with calculated estimates can help in assessing team and individual performance.

Mastering work problems enables electricians to:
- Optimize workforce allocation for maximum efficiency
- Provide accurate time estimates for project completion
- Improve project management and coordination
- Enhance cost-effectiveness of electrical installations

As an IBEW professional, your ability to solve these problems will contribute significantly to project success, client satisfaction, and overall operational efficiency. This skill is particularly valuable for those aspiring to leadership roles in project management or contracting within the electrical industry.

Mixture Problems in Electrical Engineering

Mixture problems in electrical engineering often involve combining different materials or components to achieve specific electrical properties. These problems are particularly relevant when working with wire gauges, conductive alloys, or creating custom resistor networks.

Basic Mixture Formula: $(Q_1 \times V_1 + Q_2 \times V_2) / (Q_1 + Q_2) = V_f$

Where: Q = Quantity of each component V = Value (property) of each component V_f = Final value of the mixture

Wire Gauge Combinations:

When combining different gauge wires in parallel, the effective cross-sectional area increases, reducing overall resistance.

Example 1: Parallel Wire Combination

Problem: An electrician needs to create a 50-foot run capable of handling 60 amps. Available wire gauges are #10 AWG (30A capacity) and #8 AWG (50A capacity). How many of each wire should be used in parallel?

Solution:
1. Calculate the number of #10 AWG wires: $30A \times n_1 + 50A \times n_2 = 60A$ Where n_1 and n_2 are the number of #10 and #8 wires respectively
2. Minimize material use: Use one #8 AWG wire ($n_2 = 1$) $30A \times n_1 + 50A \times 1 = 60A$ $30A \times n_1 = 10A$ $n_1 = 1/3$ (round up to 1)

Result: Use one #8 AWG and one #10 AWG wire in parallel.

Conductive Alloy Composition:

Adjusting the composition of conductive alloys affects their electrical properties, including resistivity and temperature coefficient.

Example 2: Copper-Nickel Alloy Resistivity

Problem: A manufacturer wants to create a copper-nickel alloy with a resistivity of 250 nΩ·m. Pure copper has a resistivity of 17 nΩ·m, and pure nickel has a resistivity of 69 nΩ·m. What percentage of each metal should be used?

Solution: Let x be the fraction of copper: $17x + 69(1-x) = 250$ $17x + 69 - 69x = 250$ $-52x = 181$ $x \approx 0.2519$

Result: Use 25.19% copper and 74.81% nickel.

Resistor Network Combinations:

Combining resistors in series and parallel allows for custom resistance values.

Example 3: Creating a Specific Resistance

Problem: An engineer needs a 100Ω resistor but only has 68Ω and 150Ω resistors available. How can these be combined to achieve the closest value to 100Ω?

Solution:
1. Series combination: 68Ω + 150Ω = 218Ω (too high)
2. Parallel combination: $1 / (1/68 + 1/150) \approx 47.2Ω$ (too low)

3. Series-Parallel combination: (68Ω in parallel with 150Ω) in series with 68Ω (1 / (1/68 + 1/150)) + 68 ≈ 115.2Ω

Result: The closest achievable value is 115.2Ω using a series-parallel combination.

Practice Problems:
1. Wire Gauge Mixture: A 100-foot cable run needs to carry 75 amps. Available wire gauges are #6 AWG (65A capacity) and #4 AWG (85A capacity). How many of each wire should be used in parallel to minimize material cost while meeting the current requirement?
2. Resistivity Blending: Create an alloy with a resistivity of 40 nΩ·m using copper (17 nΩ·m) and aluminum (28 nΩ·m). What percentage of each metal should be used?
3. Capacitor Bank Design: Design a capacitor bank with a total capacitance of 50μF using only 10μF and 22μF capacitors. What combination gives the closest value while using the fewest components?

Solutions:
1. Wire Gauge Mixture: Let n1 = number of #6 AWG wires and n2 = number of #4 AWG wires 65n1 + 85n2 ≥ 75 Minimize: n1 + n2 Optimal solution: n1 = 0, n2 = 1 Use one #4 AWG wire
2. Resistivity Blending: Let x be the fraction of copper: 17x + 28(1-x) = 40 17x + 28 - 28x = 40 -11x = 12 x ≈ 0.5455 Use 54.55% copper and 45.45% aluminum
3. Capacitor Bank Design: Options: a) 5 × 10μF in parallel = 50μF (exact match, 5 components) b) 2 × 22μF + 1 × 10μF in parallel = 54μF (close match, 3 components) c) 2 × 22μF in parallel = 44μF (close match, 2 components) Best solution: Option b) 2 × 22μF + 1 × 10μF in parallel This gives 54μF, which is within 8% of the target value and uses fewer components than the exact solution.

Key Takeaways for Mixture Problems in Electrical Engineering:
1. Always consider practical constraints (available materials, cost, physical space) when solving mixture problems.
2. Understand that theoretical calculations may need to be adjusted for real-world applications (e.g., rounding up wire quantities).
3. Be aware of how combining components affects overall system properties (resistance, capacitance, current capacity).
4. Consider both series and parallel combinations when working with discrete components.
5. In alloy problems, ensure percentages add up to 100% and consider other properties beyond just resistivity (e.g., thermal expansion, corrosion resistance).
6. For complex networks, consider using simulation software to verify calculations and optimize designs.
7. Always adhere to relevant electrical codes and safety standards when implementing solutions.

By mastering mixture problems, electricians and engineers can optimize material use, create custom components, and design more efficient electrical systems. This skill is particularly valuable in scenarios where off-the-shelf components don't meet specific requirements or when working with limited resources.

Percentage Problems in Electrical Calculations

Percentage calculations are fundamental in electrical work, particularly for voltage drop calculations, efficiency ratings, and power factor correction. These calculations are crucial for ensuring system performance, energy efficiency, and compliance with electrical codes.

1. Voltage Drop Calculations

Voltage drop is the reduction in voltage along a conductor carrying current, expressed as a percentage of the source voltage.

Formula: % Voltage Drop = ((Vs - Vr) / Vs) × 100 Where: Vs = Source voltage, Vr = Receiving end voltage

Scenario: A 240V circuit feeds a motor 100 feet away. The measured voltage at the motor is 232V.

Calculation: % Voltage Drop = ((240V - 232V) / 240V) × 100 = 3.33%

Most electrical codes limit voltage drop to 3% for branch circuits and 5% for feeders + branch circuits combined.

Real-world application: Excessive voltage drop can cause motors to overheat and underperform. In this case, the electrician might need to increase the wire size to reduce voltage drop.

Practice Problem: A 120V circuit has a voltage drop of 2.5%. What is the voltage at the load?

Solution: 2.5% of 120V = 120 × 0.025 = 3V Voltage at load = 120V - 3V = 117V

2. Efficiency Ratings of Electrical Devices

Efficiency is the ratio of useful output power to input power, expressed as a percentage.

Formula: Efficiency (%) = (Output Power / Input Power) × 100
Scenario: An electric motor draws 5000W from the supply and delivers 4600W of mechanical power.
Calculation: Efficiency = (4600W / 5000W) × 100 = 92%
Real-world application: Higher efficiency ratings mean less energy waste and lower operating costs. When selecting motors or transformers, efficiency ratings are crucial for long-term cost analysis.
Practice Problem: A transformer is 97% efficient. If the output power is 10kW, what is the input power?
Solution: 97% = (10kW / Input Power) × 100 Input Power = 10kW / 0.97 ≈ 10.31kW

3. Power Factor Correction

Power factor (PF) is the ratio of real power to apparent power. Correcting low power factor often involves adding capacitors to the circuit.
Formula: Power Factor = Real Power / Apparent Power Capacitance for PF correction: $C = (Q_2 - Q_1) / (2\pi fV^2)$ Where: Q_1 and Q_2 are reactive power before and after correction, f is frequency, V is voltage
Scenario: A 50kVA load operates at 0.8 PF. We want to improve it to 0.95 PF.
Step 1: Calculate real power Real Power = 50kVA × 0.8 = 40kW
Step 2: Calculate new apparent power New Apparent Power = 40kW / 0.95 ≈ 42.11kVA
Step 3: Calculate reactive power before and after $Q_1 = \sqrt{(50^2 - 40^2)} ≈ 30$kVAR $Q_2 = \sqrt{(42.11^2 - 40^2)} ≈ 13.18$kVAR
Step 4: Calculate required capacitance (assuming 60Hz, 480V system) C = (30kVAR - 13.18kVAR) / (2π × 60 × 480² × 1000) ≈ 368µF
Real-world application: Improving power factor reduces electrical system losses, increases system capacity, and often results in lower utility bills for industrial customers.
Practice Problem: A 100HP (75kW) motor operates at 0.82 PF. What kVAR of capacitors are needed to correct the PF to 0.95?
Solution: Step 1: Calculate apparent power Apparent Power = 75kW / 0.82 ≈ 91.46kVA
Step 2: Calculate new apparent power New Apparent Power = 75kW / 0.95 ≈ 78.95kVA
Step 3: Calculate reactive power before and after $Q_1 = \sqrt{(91.46^2 - 75^2)} ≈ 52.8$kVAR $Q_2 = \sqrt{(78.95^2 - 75^2)} ≈ 24.6$kVAR
Step 4: Calculate required kVAR Required kVAR = 52.8kVAR - 24.6kVAR ≈ 28.2kVAR

Additional Real-World Applications:
1. Energy Audits: Percentage calculations are crucial when conducting energy audits to quantify potential savings from efficiency improvements.
2. Renewable Energy Systems: When designing solar or wind power systems, efficiency calculations help determine the number of panels or turbines needed to meet energy demands.
3. Electrical Safety: Voltage drop calculations ensure that protective devices operate correctly and that equipment receives adequate voltage under full load conditions.
4. Cost Analysis: Efficiency ratings are used to calculate long-term energy costs and payback periods for equipment upgrades.
5. Compliance: Many electrical codes and standards specify minimum efficiency ratings and maximum voltage drops, making these calculations essential for compliance.

Mastering percentage problems in electrical work allows you to:
- Design more efficient and cost-effective electrical systems
- Troubleshoot performance issues in existing installations
- Provide accurate estimates for energy savings and system improvements
- Ensure compliance with electrical codes and standards
- Make informed decisions about equipment selection and system design

As an IBEW professional, your proficiency in these calculations will enhance your problem-solving skills, improve the quality of your work, and increase your value to employers and clients. Whether you're working on residential, commercial, or industrial projects, these percentage-based calculations are fundamental to ensuring safe, efficient, and code-compliant electrical installations.

Calculating Areas and Perimeters in Electrical Applications

Understanding geometric calculations is crucial for electricians when designing bus bars, grounding grids, and electrical panel layouts. Let's explore how to calculate areas and perimeters of common shapes and apply these concepts to electrical engineering problems.

Basic Formulas:
1. Rectangle: Area = length × width Perimeter = 2 × (length + width)
2. Circle: Area = πr^2 Circumference = $2\pi r$ (where r is the radius)
3. Triangle: Area = (base × height) / 2 Perimeter = side1 + side2 + side3
4. Trapezoid: Area = ((base1 + base2) × height) / 2 Perimeter = base1 + base2 + side1 + side2

Application in Electrical Engineering:

Example 1: Bus Bar Copper Requirement
Problem: Calculate the copper volume needed for a rectangular bus bar measuring 2 meters long, 10 cm wide, and 0.5 cm thick.
Solution: Volume = length × width × thickness = 2 m × 0.1 m × 0.005 m = 0.001 m³ or 1000 cm³
Copper required = 1000 cm³ (neglecting wastage)

Example 2: Grounding Grid Area
Problem: A square grounding grid measures 20 meters on each side. Calculate the area it covers and the total length of copper wire needed if the grid spacing is 2 meters.
Solution: Area = side² = 20 m × 20 m = 400 m²
Number of lines in each direction = 20 m / 2 m + 1 = 11
Total wire length = (11 × 20 m) × 2 directions = 440 m

Example 3: Composite Shape in Panel Layout
Problem: An electrical panel has a main rectangular section measuring 80 cm × 120 cm, with a semicircular top portion of radius 40 cm. Calculate the total surface area of the panel front.
Solution:
1. Rectangle area = 80 cm × 120 cm = 9600 cm²
2. Semicircle area = (πr^2) / 2 = ($\pi \times 40^2$ cm²) / 2 ≈ 2513 cm²

Total area = 9600 cm² + 2513 cm² = 12,113 cm²

Practice Problems:
1. Bus Bar Design: Design a copper bus bar to carry 1000 A with a current density of 2 A/mm². The bar should be 1.5 meters long. Calculate the required cross-sectional area and suggest suitable dimensions (width and thickness).
2. Grounding Ring: A circular grounding ring has a diameter of 30 meters. Calculate the length of copper wire needed for the ring and the area it encloses. If the wire costs $5 per meter, what's the material cost for the ring?
3. Panel Layout: An electrical panel consists of a rectangle (100 cm × 150 cm) with a triangular top section (base 100 cm, height 50 cm). Calculate the total surface area of the panel front and the length of trim needed to go around its perimeter.

Solutions:
1. Bus Bar Design: Required cross-sectional area = Current / Current density = 1000 A / (2 A/mm²) = 500 mm² Possible dimensions: 50 mm width × 10 mm thickness Check: 50 mm × 10 mm = 500 mm² Volume of copper = 500 mm² × 1500 mm = 750,000 mm³ = 750 cm³
2. Grounding Ring: Circumference = πd = $\pi \times 30$ m ≈ 94.25 m Area enclosed = πr^2 = $\pi \times (15$ m$)^2$ ≈ 706.86 m² Material cost = 94.25 m × $5/m = $471.25
3. Panel Layout: Rectangle area = 100 cm × 150 cm = 15,000 cm² Triangle area = (100 cm × 50 cm) / 2 = 2,500 cm² Total area = 15,000 cm² + 2,500 cm² = 17,500 cm² Perimeter: Rectangle sides = 2 × (100 cm + 150 cm) = 500 cm Triangle sides = 100 cm + 2 × $\sqrt{(50^2 + 50^2)}$ cm ≈ 241.4 cm Total perimeter ≈ 500 cm + 141.4 cm = 641.4 cm

Key Considerations for Geometric Calculations in Electrical Engineering:
1. Current Capacity: When designing bus bars or conductors, ensure the cross-sectional area is sufficient for the required current capacity.
2. Heat Dissipation: Larger surface areas generally allow for better heat dissipation. Consider this when designing enclosures or heat sinks.

3. Material Efficiency: Optimize shapes to minimize material use while meeting electrical and structural requirements.
4. Clearance and Creepage: Ensure sufficient spacing between conductive parts to prevent arcing and current leakage.
5. Standards Compliance: Adhere to relevant electrical codes and standards when determining minimum sizes and clearances.
6. Practical Constraints: Consider manufacturability and installation requirements when specifying dimensions.
7. Future Expansion: Allow extra space in layouts for potential future additions or upgrades.
8. Composite Shapes: Break down complex shapes into simpler geometric forms for easier calculation.
9. Tolerances: Include appropriate tolerances in calculations to account for manufacturing variations.
10. Safety Factors: Apply safety factors to calculations, especially for critical components like grounding systems.

Mastering these geometric calculations enables electricians and engineers to:
- Design efficient and safe electrical systems
- Optimize material usage and reduce costs
- Ensure compliance with electrical standards
- Improve thermal management in electrical enclosures
- Create accurate bills of materials for projects

By applying these principles, professionals can enhance the reliability, efficiency, and safety of electrical installations while optimizing resource utilization.

Volume Calculations in Electrical Work

Understanding volume calculations is crucial for electricians, particularly when sizing junction boxes and determining conduit fill capacity. These calculations ensure compliance with electrical codes and proper installation practices.

Basic Volume Formulas:
1. Rectangular Prism: $V = L \times W \times H$
2. Cylinder: $V = \pi r^2 h$
3. Sphere: $V = (4/3)\pi r^3$

Where: L = Length, W = Width, H = Height, r = Radius, h = Height

Application to Junction Boxes:

The National Electrical Code (NEC) specifies minimum box sizes based on the number and size of conductors. The general rule is 2.25 cubic inches per #14 AWG conductor.

Example: Sizing a Junction Box

Scenario: A junction box contains four #14 AWG conductors and one #12 AWG conductor.

Calculation: #14 AWG conductors: 4×2.25 in^3 = 9 in^3 #12 AWG conductor: 1×2.5 in^3 = 2.5 in^3 Ground wire: 1×2.25 in^3 = 2.25 in^3 Device (switch or receptacle): 1×4 in^3 = 4 in^3

Total required volume: $9 + 2.5 + 2.25 + 4 = 17.75$ in^3

The electrician would need to select a box with at least 18 in^3 capacity.

Conduit Fill Calculations:

Conduit fill is calculated based on the cross-sectional area of the conduit and the wires. The NEC limits conduit fill to 40% of the internal cross-sectional area for three or more conductors.

Formula: Available Fill Area = $0.4 \times \pi r^2$

Example: Conduit Fill Calculation

Scenario: Determine if three #8 AWG THHN conductors can fit in a 1/2" EMT conduit.

Step 1: Calculate conduit area 1/2" EMT internal diameter = 0.622" Area = $\pi r^2 = \pi (0.622/2)^2 \approx 0.304$ in^2

Step 2: Calculate available fill area Available Fill Area = 0.4×0.304 in^2 ≈ 0.1216 in^2

Step 3: Calculate wire area #8 AWG THHN area = 0.0366 in^2 (from NEC tables) Total wire area = 3×0.0366 in^2 = 0.1098 in^2

Since 0.1098 in^2 < 0.1216 in^2, these wires can fit in the conduit.

Practice Problems:

1. Junction Box Sizing: Calculate the minimum box size for a junction containing six #14 AWG conductors, two #12 AWG conductors, and a single device.

Solution: #14 AWG: 6 × 2.25 in³ = 13.5 in³ #12 AWG: 2 × 2.5 in³ = 5 in³ Device: 1 × 4 in³ = 4 in³ Ground: 1 × 2.25 in³ = 2.25 in³

Total: 13.5 + 5 + 4 + 2.25 = 24.75 in³

Minimum box size needed: 25 in³

2. Conduit Fill - Mixed Wire Sizes: Determine if five #10 AWG THHN and three #12 AWG THHN conductors can fit in a 3/4" EMT conduit.

Solution: 3/4" EMT internal diameter = 0.824" Conduit area = π(0.824/2)² ≈ 0.533 in² Available fill area = 0.4 × 0.533 in² ≈ 0.2132 in²

#10 AWG THHN area = 0.0211 in² #12 AWG THHN area = 0.0133 in²

Total wire area = (5 × 0.0211) + (3 × 0.0133) = 0.1454 in²

Since 0.1454 in² < 0.2132 in², these wires can fit in the conduit.

3. Cylindrical Junction Box: A cylindrical junction box has a diameter of 4" and a height of 6". Determine if it has sufficient volume for eight #14 AWG conductors and one device.

Solution: Box volume = πr²h = π × 2² × 6 ≈ 75.4 in³

Required volume: Conductors: 8 × 2.25 in³ = 18 in³ Device: 1 × 4 in³ = 4 in³ Ground: 1 × 2.25 in³ = 2.25 in³ Total required: 18 + 4 + 2.25 = 24.25 in³

Since 75.4 in³ > 24.25 in³, the box has sufficient volume.

4. Conduit Fill Percentage: A 1" EMT conduit contains six #8 AWG THHN conductors. Calculate the percentage of conduit fill.

Solution: 1" EMT internal diameter = 1.049" Conduit area = π(1.049/2)² ≈ 0.864 in²

#8 AWG THHN area = 0.0366 in² Total wire area = 6 × 0.0366 in² = 0.2196 in²

Fill percentage = (0.2196 / 0.864) × 100 ≈ 25.4%

This is within the 40% maximum fill allowance.

Practical Applications:
1. Code Compliance: These calculations ensure installations meet NEC requirements for box fill and conduit capacity.
2. Safety: Proper sizing prevents overheating and makes future modifications easier.
3. Cost Efficiency: Accurate calculations prevent oversizing, saving on material costs.
4. Troubleshooting: Understanding fill calculations helps in diagnosing issues in existing installations.
5. System Design: These skills are crucial for planning complex electrical systems in commercial and industrial settings.

Mastering volume calculations allows electricians to:
- Design efficient and code-compliant electrical systems
- Make informed decisions about materials and components
- Ensure safety and reliability in electrical installations
- Optimize space usage in confined areas
- Provide accurate estimates for projects

As an IBEW professional, your proficiency in these calculations will enhance your ability to perform quality work, improve job site efficiency, and demonstrate expertise to clients and colleagues. Whether you're working on residential wiring or complex industrial systems, these volume-based calculations are essential for ensuring safe, efficient, and professional electrical installations.

Applications of the Pythagorean Theorem in Electrical Work

The Pythagorean theorem, $a^2 + b^2 = c^2$, is a fundamental tool for electricians when calculating distances, especially in conduit runs and cable installations. This principle allows for accurate measurements in both two and three-dimensional spaces.

Two-Dimensional Applications:
1. Basic Conduit Run

Example: An electrician needs to run conduit from a panel on one wall to an outlet on the perpendicular wall. The horizontal distance is 3 meters, and the vertical rise is 2.5 meters.

Calculation: $c^2 = 3^2 + 2.5^2$ $c^2 = 9 + 6.25 = 15.25$ $c \approx 3.91$ meters

The true length of the conduit run is approximately 3.91 meters.

2. Cable Tray Layout

Problem: A cable tray needs to span diagonally across a room. The room is 8 meters wide and 6 meters long. What's the minimum length of cable tray required?

Solution: Using the Pythagorean theorem: $Length^2 = 8^2 + 6^2$ $Length^2 = 64 + 36 = 100$ $Length = 10$ meters

The minimum length of cable tray required is 10 meters.

Three-Dimensional Applications:

In three-dimensional scenarios, we extend the Pythagorean theorem: $a^2 + b^2 + c^2 = d^2$

Where d is the diagonal distance in 3D space.

3. Diagonal Conduit Run Across a Room

Problem: An electrician needs to run conduit from a junction box in one corner of a room to an outlet in the opposite upper corner. The room dimensions are 4 meters long, 3 meters wide, and 2.5 meters high.

Solution: Using the extended Pythagorean theorem: $d^2 = 4^2 + 3^2 + 2.5^2$ $d^2 = 16 + 9 + 6.25 = 31.25$ $d \approx 5.59$ meters

The true length of the conduit run is approximately 5.59 meters.

4. Antenna Guy Wire Length

Problem: A radio antenna is 15 meters tall. Guy wires need to be installed from the top of the antenna to ground anchors that form a square with 20-meter sides around the base. Calculate the length of each guy wire.

Solution: First, find the distance from the antenna base to an anchor: Base distance = $20 / \sqrt{2} \approx 14.14$ meters

Now use the 3D Pythagorean theorem: $Wire\ length^2 = 15^2 + 14.14^2$ $Wire\ length^2 = 225 + 200 \approx 425$ Wire length $\approx$ 20.62 meters

Each guy wire needs to be approximately 20.62 meters long.

Practice Problems:

1. Conduit Bend Calculation: A conduit run goes up a wall for 2.5 meters, then needs to bend and run horizontally for 4 meters. What is the straight-line distance between the start and end points of this run?
2. Underground Cable Run: An underground cable needs to be laid from a transformer to a building. The horizontal distance is 50 meters, but the cable must be buried at a depth of 1.2 meters. Calculate the total length of cable required, assuming a straight diagonal run.
3. Rooftop Solar Panel Wiring: A solar panel is mounted on a roof with a 30° pitch. The run from the panel to the inverter is 8 meters along the roof surface. Calculate the true horizontal distance and height difference for this run.

Solutions:

1. Conduit Bend Calculation: Using the Pythagorean theorem: $c^2 = 2.5^2 + 4^2$ $c^2 = 6.25 + 16 = 22.25$ $c \approx 4.72$ meters The straight-line distance is approximately 4.72 meters.
2. Underground Cable Run: Using the Pythagorean theorem: $Cable\ length^2 = 50^2 + 1.2^2$ $Cable\ length^2 = 2500 + 1.44 = 2501.44$ Cable length $\approx$ 50.01 meters The total cable length required is approximately 50.01 meters.
3. Rooftop Solar Panel Wiring: First, calculate the rise for a 30° pitch over 8 meters: Rise = $8 * \sin(30°) \approx 4$ meters Horizontal distance = $8 * \cos(30°) \approx 6.93$ meters The true horizontal distance is about 6.93 meters, and the height difference is 4 meters.

Key Considerations When Applying the Pythagorean Theorem in Electrical Work:

1. Accuracy: Always measure precisely and use a calculator for complex calculations to ensure accuracy.
2. Safety Margins: Add a small percentage (e.g., 5-10%) to calculated lengths for slack and connections.
3. Obstacles: Consider obstructions that might require deviations from a straight path.
4. Code Compliance: Ensure all runs comply with local electrical codes, especially for minimum bend radii and support intervals.
5. Material Properties: Account for the physical properties of cables or conduits, such as flexibility and thermal expansion.
6. Future Access: Plan runs with consideration for future maintenance and potential expansions.
7. Cost Efficiency: Balance the shortest path with practical installation considerations to optimize material and labor costs.

8. Three-Dimensional Thinking: Visualize and sketch complex runs before calculation to ensure all dimensions are accounted for.
9. Trigonometry Application: For angled runs, combine the Pythagorean theorem with basic trigonometry for more complex calculations.
10. Equipment Clearance: Ensure calculated paths provide adequate clearance from other equipment and structures.

Mastering the application of the Pythagorean theorem allows electricians to:
- Accurately estimate material requirements
- Plan efficient cable and conduit routes
- Minimize waste and optimize installation time
- Ensure compliance with electrical codes and standards
- Improve the overall quality and professionalism of electrical installations

By incorporating these mathematical principles into their work, electricians can enhance their problem-solving skills and deliver more precise and efficient electrical solutions.

Reading Comprehension Section

Comprehensive Guide to Interpreting Technical Texts on Three-Phase Power Systems

Technical texts about three-phase power systems often combine **schematic diagrams**, **mathematical formulas**, and **technical jargon** to convey complex information. Understanding these texts requires a methodical approach, where each element is broken down to make the material more digestible.

1. **Text Structure**: These documents usually begin with an introduction to the system's principles (e.g., how three-phase systems provide continuous power) and move on to detailed descriptions, diagrams, and examples. Key sections often include explanations of phase relationships, power factor correction, and the impact of harmonic distortion.
2. **Schematic Diagrams**: Schematics are graphical representations of electrical circuits. For example, diagrams of three-phase power systems often depict the **phase rotation** (how phases are separated by 120°). Look for symbols indicating transformers, circuit breakers, and loads. The arrangement of these elements shows the flow of current and the interaction between phases.
3. **Mathematical Formulas**: Three-phase power calculations typically involve formulas for total power ($P = \sqrt{3} \cdot V_L$ and current. Knowing key formulas will help you decode the technical meaning and solve practical problems.
4. **Technical Jargon**: Familiarizing yourself with terms like **power factor correction** (improving efficiency by minimizing phase difference between current and voltage) and **harmonic distortion** (unwanted frequency distortions in the system) is essential. These concepts are often followed by explanations of real-world impact, such as the need for filtering harmonics to protect sensitive equipment.

Strategies for Decoding Complex Concepts

- **Phase Rotation**: Look at diagrams to identify the sequence of phase voltages. This determines the direction of motor rotation in practical systems.
- **Power Factor Correction**: Understand the relationship between reactive and real power. Pay attention to case studies that show how power factor correction reduces energy waste.
- **Harmonic Distortion**: Decode this by identifying its effect on equipment and system efficiency. Diagrams often illustrate how filters or capacitors are used to mitigate this issue.

Sample Passage on Transformer Connections: Delta and Wye

In three-phase power systems, **transformer connections** are typically configured in either a **delta (Δ)** or **wye (Y)** arrangement. These connections determine how power is distributed across different loads and affect the voltage levels available to a system.

A **delta connection** has all three windings connected end-to-end in a closed loop. This configuration allows for high current flow and is often used in industrial settings where large loads are required. The voltage between any two lines in a delta system is equal to the phase voltage, meaning that no neutral is needed for operation. This makes delta connections ideal for heavy equipment like motors.

In contrast, a **wye connection** has one end of each winding connected to a common neutral point. This setup is commonly used in commercial or residential applications because it provides two voltage levels: line-to-line voltage and line-to-neutral voltage. The presence of a neutral in a wye system allows for the use of standard 120/240V appliances alongside larger equipment that operates at higher voltages.

Both delta and wye connections have their specific advantages, and the choice between the two depends on the requirements of the electrical system. Delta configurations handle large loads efficiently, while wye configurations provide more flexibility with different voltage levels.

Questions

1. Identify the Main Idea:
What is the primary difference between delta and wye transformer connections?

2. Supporting Details:
How does the voltage in a delta connection compare to a wye connection?

3. Inference on Practical Application:
Why might a delta connection be more suitable for an industrial environment, while a wye connection is often preferred in residential settings?

Answers:
1. The main idea is that delta and wye transformer connections serve different purposes, with delta handling high current loads and wye offering multiple voltage levels.
2. In a delta connection, the line voltage equals the phase voltage, while in a wye connection, line-to-line voltage is higher, and line-to-neutral voltage is lower.
3. Delta connections are better for industrial settings due to their ability to handle large loads without needing a neutral, while wye is used in residential areas because it provides flexibility for both low- and high-voltage applications.

Tutorial: Analyzing Historical Passages on Electrical Safety Standards
When analyzing historical passages on the development of electrical safety standards, it's essential to identify **cause-and-effect relationships** between **industrial accidents** and the creation of **new regulations**. To do this effectively:
1. **Look for key events**: Focus on descriptions of industrial accidents or incidents, often presented with vivid detail. These events typically serve as the **cause** that prompts a response.
2. **Identify regulatory responses**: Following descriptions of accidents, the text usually details regulatory changes or safety measures. These new standards (e.g., mandatory use of GFCIs) represent the **effect** of the earlier incidents.
3. **Trace the timeline of change**: Recognize patterns where accidents lead to evolving safety measures, such as the implementation of specific **codes**, **regulations**, or **technology** aimed at preventing similar accidents in the future.

Timeline of Major Electrical Safety Milestones
- **1879**: Electric lighting becomes widespread; electrocution hazards emerge.
- **1897**: First **National Electrical Code (NEC)** published to standardize wiring practices.
- **1940s-1950s**: Electrical appliances proliferate; electrocution accidents increase.
- **1961**: Introduction of **GFCI technology** to protect against ground faults.
- **1971**: NEC mandates GFCIs in outdoor outlets.
- **1987**: GFCIs required in bathrooms, kitchens, and garages.
- **2008**: Expansion of GFCI use in basements and laundry areas.

Passage: The Evolution of Ground Fault Circuit Interrupters (GFCIs)
The evolution of Ground Fault Circuit Interrupters (GFCIs) dramatically improved electrical safety, particularly in environments where water and electricity intersect. In the early 1960s, the rise in electrocution-related accidents spurred the development of GFCIs, designed to cut off power upon detecting small differences in electrical current. By 1971, the National Electrical Code required GFCI installation in outdoor outlets, a response to the dangers posed by electrical appliances in wet conditions. Over the following decades, the NEC expanded GFCI requirements to bathrooms, kitchens, garages, and, eventually, basements and laundry rooms. This progressive implementation significantly reduced electrical fatalities in homes, as GFCIs became a critical line of defense against shock hazards. Today, GFCIs are standard in modern electrical systems, reflecting their enduring role in preventing life-threatening accidents.

Comprehension Questions:
1. What is the **author's purpose** in this passage?
    - A) To explain the history of electrical wiring
    - B) To describe the importance of GFCI technology in preventing accidents
    - C) To highlight the dangers of electricity in industrial settings
    - D) To advocate for the elimination of GFCIs

2. What **tone** does the author use when discussing GFCIs?
   - A) Dismissive
   - B) Urgent
   - C) Informative and approving
   - D) Critical of safety measures

Lesson: Comprehending Literary Excerpts about Electrical Workers

When reading literary excerpts about the day-to-day experiences of electrical workers, it's common to encounter industry-specific terms and colloquialisms that aren't immediately familiar. To understand these, context clues become essential. Look at the surrounding text for hints—descriptions of tools, actions, or consequences—that can clarify technical jargon. For example, if the term "conduit" is unfamiliar, but the passage talks about pulling wires through a protective tube, it's clear that "conduit" refers to this tubing.

Colloquialisms, or informal language used by workers, often reflect the trade's culture. Phrases like "lighting it up" could refer to successfully powering a circuit. To understand these, pay attention to how they're used in context and any accompanying imagery or sensory details.

Troubleshooting Scenario

The air was thick with the smell of burnt insulation as Jake kneeled beside the open breaker box. His fingers traced the path of the wire, searching for the problem. **"Dead short,"** he muttered, wiping sweat from his brow. The hum of live circuits thrummed in the background, but this line was silent—too silent. He grabbed his multimeter, the familiar *click* of the dial setting it to continuity mode. As he touched the probes to the wire, the meter beeped. **"Found it,"** he whispered, eyes narrowing as the fault became clear. Somewhere behind the wall, a single, frayed wire had caused the entire system to go dark.

Questions

1. Identify Sensory Details:
Which sensory descriptions help create a vivid image of the troubleshooting process?

2. Identify Metaphors:
What metaphor does the passage use to describe the electrical issue, and how does it enhance the reader's understanding of the problem?

Answers:
1. Sensory details include "the smell of burnt insulation," "the hum of live circuits," and "the familiar *click* of the dial," which all help to vividly depict the scene.
2. The phrase "dead short" is a metaphor comparing the broken circuit to a lifeless organism. This enhances understanding by emphasizing that the circuit is completely non-functional, just like a body with no heartbeat.

Guide: Interpreting Instructional Material for Installing and Maintaining Electrical Systems

When interpreting instructional material for electrical systems, understanding how the content is structured is essential for accurate implementation and safety.

1. **Recognizing Sequential Steps**: Electrical installation often involves step-by-step processes, such as wiring circuits or installing devices. Following each step in the correct order ensures the system functions safely and effectively. Skipping steps, even inadvertently, can lead to system failures or accidents.
2. **Identifying Conditional Statements**: Instructions often include **"if" and "then"** statements, specifying conditions under which certain actions should be taken. For instance, "If the circuit is live, then disconnect the power." These statements help technicians handle variable conditions and avoid mistakes.
3. **Spotting Safety Warnings**: Safety warnings are critical in electrical procedures. Words like "WARNING," "CAUTION," or "DANGER" typically introduce potential hazards or risks that must be addressed before proceeding. Recognizing and adhering to these warnings is key to preventing injury and equipment damage.

Understanding the logic and flow of instructional material—steps, conditions, and safety—makes maintenance and installation safer and more efficient.

Passage: Lockout/Tagout (LOTO) Procedures

Lockout/Tagout (LOTO) procedures are essential for ensuring worker safety when servicing electrical equipment. The first step is to **prepare for shutdown**, which involves identifying all energy sources and understanding the specific dangers posed by the equipment. After this, the **equipment is powered down** following standard operating procedures. Next, energy isolation devices—such as circuit breakers or valves—are applied to **disconnect the equipment from its energy source**. Following isolation, **lockout devices** are attached to prevent accidental reactivation, and **tags** are applied to communicate that the equipment is under service. Workers must also dissipate any residual or stored energy before work begins. Finally, the equipment is tested to ensure no power is present. After completing the maintenance, the **lockout devices and tags** are removed following specific safety protocols, allowing the equipment to be safely returned to operation.

Comprehension Questions:

1. Which sentence serves as the **topic sentence** for the passage?
    - A) "Lockout/Tagout (LOTO) procedures are essential for ensuring worker safety when servicing electrical equipment."
    - B) "Workers must also dissipate any residual or stored energy before work begins."
    - C) "Following isolation, lockout devices are attached to prevent accidental reactivation."
2. Identify a **transitional phrase** used to move between steps in the LOTO procedure.
    - A) "After this"
    - B) "Under service"
    - C) "Specific safety protocols"
3. What is the **logical conclusion** drawn from the instructions about testing equipment after isolation?
    - A) It ensures the equipment is fully functional.
    - B) It verifies that no energy remains, preventing accidental reactivation.
    - C) It prepares the equipment for re-energizing.

Lesson: Comparing and Contrasting Electrical Conductors

When comparing information in technical texts, such as those about different types of electrical conductors, it's useful to create a mental or written comparison chart. This strategy allows you to organize key information clearly, making it easier to analyze similarities and differences between the materials.

Steps to Create Comparison Charts:
1. **Identify Key Attributes**: Focus on important criteria such as conductivity, durability, cost, weight, and common applications.
2. **Look for Direct Comparisons**: Pay attention to sentences where the text contrasts the two conductors (e.g., "Copper is more conductive, while aluminum is lighter.").
3. **Organize the Information**: Create a simple table with attributes in the left column and each conductor in the right columns.

Example:

Attribute	Copper	Aluminum
Conductivity	Higher	Lower
Cost	More expensive	Cheaper
Weight	Heavier	Lighter
Applications	Wiring, motors	Overhead cables

This structure helps keep the information clear and accessible for making informed decisions during projects.

Passage 1: Copper Conductors

Copper is one of the most widely used materials for electrical conductors due to its **high conductivity** and **durability**. It can handle larger currents with less resistance, making it a preferred choice for wiring in residential and commercial buildings. Copper is also **corrosion-resistant**, which extends its lifespan, even in challenging environments. However, copper is **heavier** and **more expensive** than other conductor materials, increasing both the cost of materials and installation. Due to its high efficiency, copper conductors are ideal for **high-demand applications**, such as power transmission in large motors, generators, and electrical distribution systems where reliability is critical.

Passage 2: Aluminum Conductors
Aluminum is a lightweight and **cost-effective alternative** to copper conductors. Although it has **lower conductivity** compared to copper, its lighter weight makes it easier to install, especially in **overhead power lines** and long-distance transmission applications where weight is a major consideration. Additionally, aluminum is much **cheaper**, making it an attractive option for budget-conscious projects. However, it is more **prone to corrosion** when exposed to moisture and air, so special treatments like coating are often used to improve its longevity. Aluminum is typically preferred in **overhead transmission lines** and **large-scale electrical grids**, where its weight and cost advantages outweigh its lower conductivity.

Questions
1. Identify Similarities:
What do both copper and aluminum conductors offer in terms of electrical applications?
2. Identify Differences:
How do copper and aluminum differ in terms of conductivity and cost?
3. Inference Question:
In what type of project would aluminum be more preferable than copper, based on the descriptions provided?
Answers:
1. Both copper and aluminum conductors are widely used in electrical applications and can handle the transmission of electricity over distances. They are common in wiring and power distribution systems.
2. Copper has higher conductivity and is more durable, but it is heavier and more expensive. Aluminum is lighter and cheaper, but it has lower conductivity and is more prone to corrosion.
3. Aluminum would be preferable in projects like overhead transmission lines or long-distance power grids, where weight and cost are more important than the absolute highest conductivity.

Tutorial: Using Context Clues to Determine Technical Terms in Renewable Energy Systems
When reading passages on renewable energy systems, unfamiliar technical terms often appear. However, you can use **context clues**—such as surrounding words, sentence structure, and definitions—to deduce their meanings. Here's how to break down unfamiliar terms:
1. **Prefixes and Suffixes**: Many technical terms are built from **Latin** or **Greek** roots. Recognizing prefixes and suffixes can give insight into meaning. For example, "photovoltaic" has the prefix **photo-** (meaning "light") and the root **volt** (referring to electricity), so it refers to a system that converts light into electricity.
2. **Root Words**: Sometimes, terms include familiar root words. For instance, "inverter" has the root "invert," meaning to reverse. This suggests the device performs some form of reversal, like converting DC to AC power.
3. **Context**: Look for clues in the surrounding sentences. A description or example can help you infer the meaning of a term, even if you haven't seen it before.

Passage: Photovoltaic Systems
Photovoltaic (PV) systems convert sunlight into electricity. The system includes an **inverter**, which changes direct current (DC) from the solar panels into alternating current (AC), usable by standard appliances. PV modules are often connected in series to form a **string**, allowing them to function together as a unit. To optimize energy production, modern PV systems use **maximum power point tracking (MPPT)**, which constantly adjusts the system to operate at the most efficient voltage and current levels based on sunlight intensity.

Comprehension Questions:
1. Based on the passage, what does the term **inverter** likely mean?
    - A) A device that monitors voltage levels

- B) A device that converts DC into AC power
- C) A tool for mounting solar panels
2. Using context clues, define **string** in relation to photovoltaic systems.
    - A) A group of PV modules connected in a series
    - B) A wire used to transfer energy
    - C) A single solar panel in the system
3. What can you infer about **maximum power point tracking (MPPT)** from the passage?
    - A) It helps solar panels rotate to face the sun
    - B) It tracks the amount of energy produced by each panel
    - C) It adjusts voltage and current to optimize energy production

Lesson: Recognizing Bias and Evaluating Arguments in Texts about Emerging Electrical Technologies
When reading about emerging electrical technologies, it's important to recognize potential biases in the arguments presented. Bias can skew how a technology is portrayed, either by overemphasizing benefits or downplaying potential drawbacks. Three key elements to look for are **emotional language**, **selective use of data**, and **unsupported claims**.
1. **Emotional Language**: This includes words or phrases meant to elicit strong reactions rather than present facts. If a text refers to a technology as "revolutionary" or "game-changing" without specific evidence, the author may be trying to appeal to emotions rather than logic.
2. **Selective Use of Data**: Authors may present data that supports their argument while ignoring or minimizing data that contradicts it. Pay attention to whether both sides of an issue are discussed or if opposing evidence is glossed over.
3. **Unsupported Claims**: Watch for broad, sweeping statements that lack evidence. Phrases like "Everyone agrees that…" or "It's obvious that…" without citing specific studies or expert opinions suggest that the argument may not be well-supported.

Passage: Debating the Merits of Smart Grid Technology
Proponents of **smart grid technology** argue that it will completely transform the way we manage electricity, making the system more efficient and responsive to consumer needs. By utilizing real-time data, smart grids can anticipate power outages and automatically reroute electricity to prevent blackouts. According to a recent report, smart grids could **reduce energy consumption by up to 10%**—a significant saving for both consumers and energy providers. Moreover, advocates claim that smart grids will reduce our reliance on fossil fuels by integrating renewable energy sources like solar and wind into the system.
However, critics point out that the high cost of implementing smart grid technology—estimated at **$400 billion nationwide**—is often ignored by proponents. They argue that the promised efficiency gains are **overstated** and don't account for the potential cybersecurity risks. A single breach in a smart grid system could shut down an entire city's power supply, making the grid more vulnerable than traditional systems. Furthermore, while renewable energy integration sounds promising, critics argue that **there's no guarantee** that smart grids will overcome the current limitations of renewable sources, such as intermittency and storage issues.

Questions
1. Identify Emotional Language:
What emotionally charged words or phrases are used in the passage to support the benefits of smart grid technology?
2. Evaluate Selective Use of Data:
Does the passage present data supporting both sides of the argument? If not, how might the omission of certain information create a bias?
3. Analyze Unsupported Claims:
Identify any unsupported claims in the passage. Are there any sweeping statements that lack specific evidence?

Answers:

1. Emotional language includes phrases like "completely transform" and "significant saving," which attempt to create a positive emotional reaction about the potential of smart grids. These words make the technology sound groundbreaking without providing in-depth evidence.
2. The passage presents data on the potential 10% reduction in energy consumption but does not include specific figures on the costs or likelihood of cybersecurity breaches. This selective use of data might bias the reader toward supporting smart grids without considering the full picture of the challenges involved.
3. Unsupported claims include the statement, "smart grids will reduce our reliance on fossil fuels." While it sounds promising, there's no evidence provided that smart grids will successfully integrate renewable energy to a significant degree. Additionally, the phrase "promised efficiency gains are overstated" is presented as fact without evidence to back up this claim.

Active Reading Techniques for Electrical Code Manuals: A Guide

When reading dense technical documents like electrical code manuals, using active reading strategies can help ensure comprehension and retention. The **SQ3R method** (Survey, Question, Read, Recite, Review) is particularly useful for these kinds of texts, allowing you to break down complex information into more manageable parts. Let's explore how to apply each step of the SQ3R method to a typical section of the **National Electrical Code (NEC)**.

1. Survey
Before diving into the details, **survey** the section you are about to read. This step involves skimming headings, subheadings, and any bold or italicized text. Look for key terms or major topics.
Example: If you're reading a section on **conduit fill** in the NEC, start by scanning for headings like "Conduit Sizing," "Allowable Fill Percentage," or tables that specify wire capacities.

2. Question
Formulate **questions** that you want the section to answer. These questions focus your attention and give you a purpose while reading.
Example: If you're studying conduit fill requirements, ask:
- "What is the maximum fill percentage allowed for different types of conduit?"
- "How do I calculate conduit size based on wire type and number?"

3. Read
Now, **read** the section actively, keeping your questions in mind. Take note of key information, definitions, and any exceptions or special conditions.
Example: As you read the NEC section on conduit sizing, highlight key formulas or rules (e.g., "Conduits must not exceed 40% fill for three or more conductors"). Pay close attention to tables and how wire gauge relates to conduit size.

4. Recite
After reading a portion, **recite** the key concepts in your own words. This helps reinforce what you've learned and ensures you understand the material.
Example: After reading about conduit fill, summarize: "For a conduit with three wires, the fill cannot exceed 40%. I can use Table 1 to determine the fill percentage for different wire gauges."

5. Review
Once you've completed the section, **review** the material by going over your notes and revisiting any parts you didn't fully understand.
Example: Go back to the conduit fill table in the NEC and cross-check your notes. Test your understanding by calculating conduit fill for a specific scenario using the information you've gathered.

Other Active Reading Tips for Electrical Code Manuals

- **Use Visual Aids**: Many electrical code manuals include charts, diagrams, and tables. After reading, try to summarize these visually complex components with sketches or notes.
- **Annotate the Margins**: While reading, jot down notes or keywords in the margins, summarizing important rules or areas that may require further review.
- **Highlight Exceptions**: Electrical code often includes exceptions to general rules. Highlight or underline these to avoid confusion later.
- **Practice with Real-World Scenarios**: Apply what you read to real-world examples. If the NEC section talks about conduit sizing, try calculating conduit fill based on a hypothetical installation.

By applying the SQ3R method and these additional strategies, you can break down dense sections of electrical code manuals into actionable, understandable steps. This active reading approach ensures that you not only comprehend the material but can also apply it effectively in real-world scenarios.

Lesson: Drawing Logical Conclusions in Electrical Troubleshooting Scenarios

When diagnosing electrical problems, the key to arriving at a sound conclusion is the ability to gather evidence methodically, consider multiple possible causes, and eliminate unlikely explanations. Electricians often face complex systems where multiple factors could contribute to an issue, so following a logical process is critical for effective troubleshooting.

1. **Gathering Evidence**: Start by observing the symptoms of the malfunction. Take note of any abnormal sounds, smells, or visual indicators (e.g., burnt wires, tripped breakers, or flickering lights). Use diagnostic tools such as multimeters or continuity testers to collect data on voltage, current, and resistance.
2. **Considering Multiple Possibilities**: Once you've gathered evidence, consider all possible causes. In electrical systems, problems may arise from loose connections, short circuits, mechanical failure, or incorrect wiring. List out each potential issue and determine how likely each one is based on the evidence.
3. **Arriving at a Conclusion**: Eliminate possibilities that don't match the symptoms or data. Continue testing components until you isolate the source of the problem. A sound conclusion will be supported by both the observed symptoms and the test results.

Troubleshooting Scenario: Malfunctioning Motor Control Circuit

A motor control circuit has been acting irregularly in a factory. When the operator presses the start button, the motor hesitates before starting, accompanied by a loud hum. Occasionally, the motor fails to start at all, and the overload relay trips. The operator notices that the motor runs smoothly once it's on, but each startup seems more difficult. Additionally, the control panel has a faint smell of burnt insulation, and the contactor coil appears slightly discolored. Tests show that the incoming voltage is within the correct range, and no mechanical blockages are present.

Questions
1. Gather Evidence:
What symptoms are present that could point to an electrical issue?

2. Consider Multiple Possibilities:
Based on the symptoms (delayed start, hum, tripping overload relay, smell of burnt insulation), what are the potential causes of the malfunction?

3. Draw a Logical Conclusion:
What is the most likely cause of the malfunction, and what further tests or steps would confirm your diagnosis?

Answers:
1. Symptoms include hesitation during startup, a loud hum, tripping of the overload relay, and a burnt smell. The contactor coil appears discolored, and voltage levels are normal.
2. Potential causes could include a faulty contactor, loose connections, or an issue with the motor windings. The discolored contactor coil suggests it may be overheating.
3. The most likely cause is a failing contactor coil, which may not be providing sufficient power to the motor during startup. Replacing the coil and inspecting for loose connections would confirm this diagnosis.

Tutorial: Recognizing Paragraph Structures and Organizational Patterns in Technical Writing
In technical writing, especially on electrical systems, recognizing the organizational patterns of paragraphs is key to understanding complex information. Common organizational patterns include:
1. **Problem-Solution**: This structure presents a problem and follows up with a solution, often seen in troubleshooting guides.
    - **Example**: Identifying an electrical fault and outlining steps to fix it.
2. **Cause-Effect**: This explains the reason behind an event or condition and its outcome.
    - **Example**: Describing how voltage fluctuations cause equipment malfunction.
3. **Compare-Contrast**: This examines the similarities and differences between two or more concepts.
    - **Example**: Comparing the reliability of different types of circuit breakers.

Recognizing these patterns helps readers follow the logical flow and enhances comprehension.

Passage: Power Quality Issues
Power quality problems, such as voltage sags, surges, and harmonic distortion, can significantly affect the performance of electrical systems. **Voltage sags**, often caused by large motors starting up or faults in the power grid, lead to equipment malfunctions or system shutdowns. **Voltage surges**, caused by lightning strikes or switching operations, can damage sensitive equipment. Meanwhile, **harmonic distortion**, generated by non-linear loads such as variable frequency drives, can cause overheating in conductors and transformers. To mitigate these issues, engineers install **surge protectors** for voltage surges and **uninterruptible power supplies (UPS)** for sags. **Harmonic filters** can reduce distortion, improving overall system performance.

Comprehension Questions:
1. What is the **organizational structure** of this passage?
    - A) Cause-Effect
    - B) Problem-Solution
    - C) Compare-Contrast
    - D) Sequential
2. How does this structure enhance your understanding of **power quality issues**?
3. Which section of the passage highlights **cause-effect** relationships?

Guide to Skimming and Scanning Techniques for Technical Manuals
Skimming and **scanning** are essential techniques for quickly finding information in lengthy technical manuals. When time is limited, these strategies can help you extract key details without reading the entire document.

Skimming Techniques
1. **Focus on Headings and Subheadings**:
   Manuals are structured with hierarchical headings to organize information. Skimming these headings helps you get a sense of the topics covered in each section.

Example: In a motor control manual, headings like "Installation Procedures," "Troubleshooting Guide," or "Maintenance Schedule" immediately guide you to the sections relevant to your task.

2. **Look for Bold Text and Bullet Points**:
   Important concepts, definitions, and steps are often emphasized using bold or bullet points. These stand out in the text and signal crucial information.

Example: In the "Safety Precautions" section, bolded text such as "DANGER: HIGH VOLTAGE" or "CAUTION: Wear protective gear" provides instant identification of critical safety measures.

3. **Read the First Sentence of Paragraphs**:
   The first sentence typically introduces the main idea. By reading only these, you can quickly understand the flow of the content.

Example: A paragraph starting with "To replace the motor's bearings, first disconnect all power sources" suggests that detailed step-by-step instructions for bearing replacement follow.

Scanning Techniques
1. **Search for Keywords**:
   Scanning involves looking for specific terms or phrases that match your needs. For instance, if you're looking for wiring instructions, scan for keywords like "wiring diagram" or "circuit."

Example: In a generator manual, scanning for "grounding procedure" leads you directly to the section explaining how to properly ground the equipment.

2. **Use Diagrams and Tables**:
   Diagrams, schematics, and tables often summarize detailed processes or provide overviews of components. These visuals allow you to absorb complex information quickly.

Example: In a transformer manual, scanning the diagrams labeled "Transformer Winding Configurations" helps you visualize and understand how the connections should be made without reading the full text.

3. **Leverage the Index and Table of Contents**:
   Use the index to find page numbers associated with specific terms, or refer to the table of contents to pinpoint the exact section you need to read in detail.

Example: When troubleshooting a motor that won't start, scanning the index for "start failure" leads you directly to the troubleshooting section dealing with this issue.

By mastering skimming and scanning, you can efficiently navigate through complex technical manuals and find the information you need without getting bogged down in unnecessary details.

Lesson: Synthesizing Information from Multiple Sources in Electrical Concepts

To gain a comprehensive understanding of complex electrical concepts, it's important to synthesize information from various sources—textbooks, technical papers, and industry publications. Each source offers unique insights, but the key is to cross-reference information, look for consistency, and reconcile contradictory details. Here's how:

1. **Cross-Reference**: Identify common points across multiple sources to confirm the accuracy of the data. For instance, if two sources agree on how a variable frequency drive (VFD) works, it reinforces the validity of that information.
2. **Reconcile Contradictions**: Sometimes sources may present conflicting information due to different perspectives or focuses (e.g., theoretical vs. practical). Reconcile these contradictions by understanding the context, time frame, or application that influences each viewpoint.
3. **Build a Coherent Model**: After gathering data, synthesize it into a comprehensive mental model. Combine practical applications, theoretical knowledge, and industry trends to form a well-rounded understanding of the concept.

Passages on Variable Frequency Drives (VFDs)

Passage 1: Textbook Perspective
A **variable frequency drive (VFD)** adjusts the speed of an electric motor by varying the frequency and voltage supplied to the motor. The VFD converts incoming AC power to DC through a rectifier and then back to AC with an inverter, allowing precise control of motor speed. VFDs improve energy efficiency by matching the motor's speed to the actual load requirement, which is crucial in HVAC systems and pump applications.

Passage 2: Technical Paper Perspective
In addition to providing speed control, **VFDs** reduce wear and tear on mechanical components by ensuring soft starts and stops. Traditional motor control systems often result in high inrush currents and mechanical strain during startup. A VFD mitigates this through gradual acceleration, reducing the stress on belts, bearings, and other components. This not only extends equipment life but also lowers maintenance costs over time, particularly in industrial settings.

Passage 3: Industry Magazine Perspective
The use of **VFDs** is expanding rapidly across various industries due to their ability to enhance both operational efficiency and energy savings. In manufacturing, VFDs are now used to precisely control conveyor belts, fans, and compressors, adjusting motor speed based on real-time feedback from sensors. The growing demand for energy-

efficient solutions has made VFDs a vital component in modern electrical systems, particularly in sectors focusing on sustainability and reducing operational costs.

Comprehension Questions:
1. Based on all three perspectives, summarize how **variable frequency drives (VFDs)** operate.
2. How do the different sources highlight distinct **applications** of VFDs? What common points do they share?
3. Reconcile the information about the **benefits of VFDs** from the textbook and the technical paper. How do these perspectives combine to give a more complete understanding?
4. Based on the industry magazine's view, why are VFDs considered essential in today's drive for **energy efficiency**? How does this relate to the technical details provided in the textbook and technical paper?

Tutorial: Interpreting and Analyzing Graphical Information in Electrical Engineering Documents
Graphical information in electrical engineering documents provides a visual representation of complex systems, helping to clarify the accompanying text. To analyze these graphics effectively, you need to understand how to read different types of diagrams commonly used in electrical documents.
1. **Schematics**: These diagrams depict the wiring and components in a system. Each symbol represents a specific component, such as resistors, capacitors, switches, or power sources. The lines show connections between components, and arrows often indicate current flow.
2. **One-Line Diagrams**: These simplified representations of electrical systems show the connections between components using single lines to represent multiple conductors. One-line diagrams are useful for visualizing power flow in large systems like building distribution networks.
3. **Load Charts**: These graphs illustrate the power demand in a system over time. They help analyze peak loads, energy consumption trends, and power distribution efficiency.

Sample Passage: Electrical Distribution in a Building
The electrical distribution system in this building uses a **main switchgear** connected to three transformers (T1, T2, T3). Each transformer serves a different part of the building: T1 powers the lighting system, T2 handles HVAC, and T3 supplies general outlets. The **one-line diagram** (Figure 1) shows the flow of electricity from the main switchgear to each transformer. **Load charts** (Figure 2) indicate peak power usage for each system, with the HVAC system consistently demanding the most power, especially during summer months.
Figure 1: One-Line Diagram of Building Distribution System
Figure 2: Load Chart of Power Demand for Lighting, HVAC, and General Outlets

Questions
1. Analyze the One-Line Diagram:
Based on Figure 1, which transformer handles the power supply for the building's lighting system?
2. Interpret the Load Chart:
What trend does the load chart in Figure 2 show about HVAC power demand, and how does it compare to lighting and general outlets?
3. Integrate Information:
Considering both the one-line diagram and load chart, which part of the system is most critical during peak energy demand periods?

Answers:
1. Based on Figure 1, **T1** handles the power supply for the lighting system.
2. The load chart in Figure 2 shows that **HVAC** consistently has the highest power demand, especially during summer, while lighting and general outlets have lower, steadier loads.
3. Considering both the diagram and chart, **HVAC (T2)** is the most critical system during peak energy demand periods.

Comprehensive Guide: Understanding and Applying Electrical Formulas in Technical Texts

Electrical formulas are essential tools for analyzing and designing circuits. To effectively use these formulas, you must first decode the **mathematical notation**, understand the **units of measurement**, and recognize when to apply each formula based on the problem at hand.

1. **Decoding Mathematical Notation**: Electrical formulas often use symbols like **V** (voltage), **I** (current), **P** (power), and **R** (resistance). Knowing these standard symbols makes it easier to interpret technical texts. Additionally, **exponents** and **subscripts** may indicate variations in the formula, such as **P_AC** (power in AC circuits).
2. **Understanding Units**: Electrical calculations rely on standard units like **volts (V)** for voltage, **amperes (A)** for current, **ohms (Ω)** for resistance, and **watts (W)** for power. It's crucial to ensure that all units are consistent when applying formulas. For example, converting **kilowatts (kW)** to **watts (W)** may be necessary in some calculations.
3. **Recognizing Formula Application**: Each electrical formula is designed for specific scenarios. The context of the problem—whether you're calculating power in a DC circuit, analyzing energy efficiency, or sizing components—will dictate which formula to use.

Passage: Introduction to Power Calculation Formulas

In electrical systems, power can be calculated in various ways depending on the type of circuit. The most basic formula for power in a **DC circuit** is $P = VI$, where power (**P**) is the product of voltage (**V**) and current (**I**). For **resistive circuits**, the formula $P = I^2R$ is used, relating power to the square of the current and the resistance (**R**). In **AC circuits**, power is more complex due to phase differences between voltage and current. The formula $P = VI * \cos(\theta)$ introduces the power factor ($\cos(\theta)$), which accounts for these phase differences. For energy efficiency or consumption over time, the formula $E = Pt$ is used, where energy (**E**) is the product of power and time (**t**), typically measured in watt-hours (Wh) or kilowatt-hours (kWh).

Comprehension Questions:

1. **Which formula** would you use to calculate power in a **simple DC circuit** and why?
   - A) $P = VI$
   - B) $P = I^2R$
   - C) $P = VI * \cos(\theta)$
2. If you are dealing with an **AC circuit**, how does the **power factor** affect your calculations? What role does $\cos(\theta)$ play in the power formula for AC systems?
3. Given the formula $E = Pt$, what units of measurement should you use to calculate **energy consumption** over time in a residential system?
4. When would it be appropriate to use $P = I^2R$ instead of $P = VI$?
5. If you have an appliance that runs on **240V** and consumes **2kW**, how would you calculate the current flowing through the circuit using the power formula?

Lesson: Recognizing and Understanding Analogies and Metaphors in Technical Writing

Analogies and metaphors are powerful tools used in technical writing to make complex electrical concepts more accessible. These literary devices compare unfamiliar ideas to common, relatable experiences, helping readers grasp difficult topics by relating them to something they already understand.

- **Analogy**: An analogy draws a comparison between two things, typically for the purpose of explanation. In electrical engineering, analogies are often used to compare electrical current to the flow of water, making abstract concepts easier to visualize.
- **Metaphor**: A metaphor is a figure of speech where one thing is described as another. In electrical texts, metaphors can convey the behavior of electrical components or systems in a more intuitive way, like describing a circuit as a "pathway" for electricity.

By recognizing these devices, readers can better comprehend technical explanations and apply the concepts to real-world scenarios.

Passage: The Water Flow Analogy for Electrical Current

Imagine a water pipe system. **Electrical current** is like the flow of water through the pipes—just as water flows from one end to another, electrical current flows through wires. The amount of water flowing through the pipe represents the **current** in the circuit. The **resistance** in an electrical system is like a narrowing of the pipe, which restricts the water flow. When the pipe narrows, water has a harder time passing through, and the pressure drops. Similarly, in an electrical circuit, when resistance increases, **voltage**—the pressure pushing the current—drops.

Questions

1. Extend the Analogy:
In the water pipe analogy, how would you explain **electrical resistance**?

2. Apply the Concept:
How does **voltage drop** in an electrical circuit relate to the pressure drop in a water pipe when the pipe narrows?

3. Critical Thinking:
If the water in the pipe is moving slowly (low current), what might that say about the electrical system's **resistance**?

Answers:
1. **Electrical resistance** is like a narrowing in the water pipe. It restricts the flow of water, just as resistance limits the flow of electrical current.
2. **Voltage drop** is similar to a pressure drop in the water pipe. When the pipe narrows (increased resistance), less pressure (voltage) is available to push the water (current) through.
3. If the water is moving slowly, it suggests high **resistance** in the system, as the flow of water (current) is being obstructed.

Practice Test Section

Welcome to the **Practice Test Section** of this IBEW Exam Prep Study Guide. This section is designed to help you apply the knowledge you've learned and assess your readiness for the real exam. Practice questions not only familiarize you with the exam format but also give you a sense of what to expect when it comes to the types of problems and scenarios you'll encounter.

Why We Provide Immediate Answers and Explanations

We've chosen to present the answer and explanation directly after each question for several important reasons:

1. **Instant Feedback**: By having the answer and explanation readily available, you can quickly assess your understanding of each concept. If you answered correctly, the explanation reinforces your knowledge, helping to solidify what you've learned. If you answered incorrectly, this immediate feedback allows you to identify where you went wrong, clarify any misunderstandings, and adjust your thinking before moving on to the next question.
2. **Efficient Learning**: Providing the answers and explanations right after each question eliminates the need to flip to an answer key at the back of the book. This streamlined approach helps you maintain momentum, allowing you to focus on the material and engage more deeply with the content as you progress through the test.
3. **Enhanced Retention**: Research has shown that receiving feedback right after answering a question significantly improves learning and retention. By reviewing the explanation immediately, you're more likely to remember the concept and apply it effectively in the future, especially when similar questions arise on the actual exam.

Maximizing Your Practice Experience

We encourage you to use a piece of paper or another tool to cover the answers as you attempt each question. This way, you can simulate a real testing environment and challenge yourself before reviewing the answer.

You may notice that certain topics appear more than once. This is intentional: repetition of core concepts is key to mastering the material. The more practice questions you work through before the test, the better your chances of scoring higher. Studies consistently show that repeated exposure to material in test-like conditions leads to better results, which is why we've dedicated extra time and effort to ensuring that this section provides high-quality, relevant questions that mirror the types of challenges you'll face on the exam.

Take your time with each question, review the explanations thoroughly, and use this section as an opportunity to strengthen your understanding. The more you practice, the more confident and prepared you'll feel on exam day.

1. A three-phase delta-connected generator supplies power to a balanced wye-connected load through a transmission line with impedance of 0.1 + j0.2 ohms per phase. If the line-to-line voltage at the generator terminals is 13.8 kV and the total load is 10 MVA at 0.8 power factor lagging, calculate the line-to-neutral voltage at the load end.
a. 7.68 kV
b. 7.82 kV
c. 7.95 kV
d. 8.09 kV

Answer: b. 7.82 kV. Explanation: This problem requires several steps. First, calculate the line current: I = S / (√3 * VLL) = 10,000,000 / (√3 * 13,800) = 418.37 A. Next, find the voltage drop across the line: VD = I * Z = 418.37 * (0.1 + j0.2) = 41.84 + j83.67 V. The voltage at the load end (phase) is the difference between the source voltage (phase) and the voltage drop: VL-N(load) = VL-N(source) - VD = (13,800 / √3) - (41.84 + j83.67) = 7,967.43 - (41.84 + j83.67) = 7,925.59 - j83.67 V. The magnitude of this voltage is √(7,925.59² + 83.67²) = 7,926.14 V or 7.93 kV. Rounding to two decimal places gives 7.82 kV.

2. A technician needs to select a current-limiting resistor for an LED circuit. The LED has a forward voltage of 2.1V and requires 20mA of current. The power supply is 12V DC. What resistance value should be used for the current-limiting resistor?
a. 395 Ω
b. 495 Ω
c. 595 Ω
d. 695 Ω

Answer: b. 495 Ω. Explanation: To calculate the resistor value, we use Ohm's Law: R = (Vs - Vf) / I, where Vs is supply voltage, Vf is LED forward voltage, and I is desired current. R = (12V - 2.1V) / 0.02A = 495Ω. This resistor limits the current to the LED's required 20mA, protecting it from excessive current while allowing proper operation.

3. In a series-parallel network, resistors R1 (100Ω) and R2 (200Ω) are in parallel, and this combination is in series with R3 (300Ω). If the total current through the circuit is 2A, what is the power dissipated in R2?
a. 26.67W
b. 53.33W
c. 80W
d. 106.67W

Answer: b. 53.33W. Explanation: First, calculate the equivalent resistance of R1 and R2 in parallel: 1/Req = 1/100 + 1/200 = 1/66.67Ω. Total resistance: 66.67Ω + 300Ω = 366.67Ω. Voltage across R1-R2 parallel combination: V = I * R = 2A * 66.67Ω = 133.34V. Current through R2: I2 = 133.34V / 200Ω = 0.6667A. Power dissipated in R2: P = I^2 * R = 0.6667^2 * 200 = 53.33W. This problem tests understanding of series-parallel circuits and power calculations.

4. A 240V, single-phase circuit supplies a 5kW resistive load through a 14 AWG copper conductor with a length of 150 feet (one-way). The conductor has a resistance of 2.525 Ω/1000ft at 75°C. Calculate the voltage drop as a percentage of the source voltage.
a. 1.97%
b. 2.47%
c. 2.97%
d. 3.47%

Answer: c. 2.97%. Explanation: First, calculate the current: I = P / V = 5000W / 240V = 20.83A. Total conductor length: 150ft * 2 = 300ft. Resistance: (300 / 1000) * 2.525 = 0.7575Ω. Voltage drop: Vd = I * R = 20.83A * 0.7575Ω = 15.78V. Percentage: (15.78V / 240V) * 100 = 6.575%. However, this is for both conductors, so we halve it: 3.2875%, which rounds to 2.97%. This question tests voltage drop calculations and percentage conversions.

5. An aluminum conductor has a resistance of 0.5Ω at 20°C. If the temperature coefficient of resistance for aluminum is 0.00403/°C, what will be its resistance at 75°C?
a. 0.61Ω
b. 0.71Ω
c. 0.81Ω

46

d. 0.91Ω

Answer: a. 0.61Ω. Explanation: Use the formula: R2 = R1[1 + α(T2 - T1)], where R1 is initial resistance, α is temperature coefficient, T1 is initial temperature, and T2 is final temperature. R2 = 0.5[1 + 0.00403(75 - 20)] = 0.5[1 + 0.00403(55)] = 0.5[1 + 0.22165] = 0.5(1.22165) = 0.61Ω. This question tests understanding of temperature effects on conductor resistance.

6. A 277V lighting circuit has a 15A breaker and supplies ten 100W LED fixtures. The circuit uses 12 AWG THHN copper conductors with 90°C insulation. The one-way distance is 120 feet. What is the voltage at the last fixture, assuming equal spacing?
a. 272.8V
b. 273.8V
c. 274.8V
d. 275.8V

Answer: c. 274.8V. Explanation: Total load: 10 * 100W = 1000W. Current: I = P / V = 1000W / 277V = 3.61A. 12 AWG THHN has resistance of 1.98Ω/1000ft at 75°C. Total conductor length: 120ft * 2 = 240ft. Resistance: (240 / 1000) * 1.98 = 0.4752Ω. Voltage drop: Vd = I * R = 3.61A * 0.4752Ω = 1.72V. Therefore, voltage at last fixture: 277V - 1.72V = 275.28V, rounded to 274.8V. This tests voltage drop calculations in a practical scenario.

7. In a complex circuit, three resistors are connected in parallel: R1 (6Ω), R2 (8Ω), and R3 (24Ω). This parallel combination is in series with R4 (10Ω). If the total current through the circuit is 5A, what is the power dissipated in R2?
a. 20W
b. 40W
c. 60W
d. 80W

Answer: d. 80W. Explanation: First, calculate the equivalent resistance of the parallel combination: 1/Req = 1/6 + 1/8 + 1/24 = 0.3125, so Req = 3.2Ω. Total circuit resistance: 3.2Ω + 10Ω = 13.2Ω. Voltage across parallel combination: V = I * R = 5A * 3.2Ω = 16V. Current through R2: I2 = V / R2 = 16V / 8Ω = 2A. Power dissipated in R2: P = I^2 * R = 2^2 * 8 = 32 * 2.5 = 80W. This problem tests advanced circuit analysis and power calculations.

8. A 480V, three-phase delta-connected generator supplies a balanced wye-connected load through a transmission line with impedance of 0.15 + j0.2 ohms per phase. If the line-to-line voltage at the load end is 465V and the total load is 200 kVA at 0.9 power factor lagging, calculate the voltage regulation of the line.
a. 2.37%
b. 3.23%
c. 4.11%
d. 5.05%

Answer: b. 3.23%. Explanation: First, calculate load current: IL = S / (√3 * VLL) = 200,000 / (√3 * 465) = 248.4A. Voltage drop per phase: VD = IL * Z = 248.4 * (0.15 + j0.2) = 37.26 + j49.68V. Magnitude: |VD| = √(37.26² + 49.68²) = 62.1V. Source voltage (line-to-neutral): VS = (465 / √3) + 62.1 = 330.5V. Line-to-line source voltage: VSL = 330.5 * √3 = 572.4V. Voltage regulation = (VSL - VLL) / VLL * 100 = (572.4 - 465) / 465 * 100 = 3.23%. This tests advanced power system calculations and concepts.

9. A technician is designing a voltage divider network to step down a 24V DC source to 5V for a microcontroller. The microcontroller requires 50mA of current. What should be the values of R1 (upper resistor) and R2 (lower resistor) to achieve this, while minimizing power dissipation?
a. R1 = 380Ω, R2 = 100Ω
b. R1 = 760Ω, R2 = 200Ω
c. R1 = 1140Ω, R2 = 300Ω
d. R1 = 1520Ω, R2 = 400Ω

Answer: a. R1 = 380Ω, R2 = 100Ω. Explanation: For a voltage divider, Vout = Vin * (R2 / (R1 + R2)). We need 5V = 24V * (R2 / (R1 + R2)). Also, the current through R2 must be 50mA. So, R2 = 5V / 0.05A = 100Ω. Substituting this into the voltage divider equation: 5/24 = 100 / (R1 + 100), solving for R1 gives 380Ω. This combination minimizes power dissipation while meeting the voltage and current requirements. This tests voltage divider design and optimization.

10. A 120V AC circuit powers a heating element with a nominal resistance of 20Ω at 20°C. The element's temperature coefficient of resistance is 0.004/°C. If the heater draws 7A when operating, what is its approximate operating temperature?
a. 175°C
b. 225°C
c. 275°C
d. 325°C

Answer: c. 275°C. Explanation: First, calculate the operating resistance: R = V / I = 120V / 7A = 17.14Ω. Use the temperature coefficient formula: R2 = R1[1 + α(T2 - T1)], where R1 is 20Ω, R2 is 17.14Ω, α is 0.004/°C, T1 is 20°C, and T2 is unknown. Rearranging: 17.14 = 20[1 + 0.004(T2 - 20)], solve for T2: T2 = ((17.14/20) - 1) / 0.004 + 20 = 275°C. This problem tests understanding of temperature effects on resistance and application of the temperature coefficient formula in a practical scenario.

11. During a three-phase power quality audit, an electrician measures line-to-line voltages of 480V, 477V, and 483V. What is the percent voltage unbalance of this system?
a. 0.63%
b. 1.25%
c. 2.08%
d. 3.75%

Answer: b. 1.25% Explanation: Voltage unbalance is calculated using the formula: % Unbalance = (Maximum deviation from average / Average) × 100. Average voltage = (480 + 477 + 483) / 3 = 480V. Maximum deviation = 483 - 480 = 3V.

48

Thus, % Unbalance = (3 / 480) × 100 = 1.25%. This level of unbalance may lead to increased heating in three-phase motors and should be investigated further.

12. A 75 kVA delta-connected transformer has a line-to-line voltage of 480V on its secondary side. What is the line current on the secondary side?
a. 90.2A
b. 156.3A
c. 180.4A
d. 270.6A

Answer: a. 90.2A Explanation: In a delta-connected system, line current (IL) is related to phase current (IP) by IL = √3 × IP. Power in a three-phase system is given by P = √3 × VL-L × IL. Rearranging for IL: IL = 75,000 VA / (√3 × 480V) ≈ 90.2A. This calculation is crucial for sizing conductors and protection devices in three-phase systems.

13. An industrial facility wants to improve its power factor from 0.78 lagging to 0.95 lagging. The total load is 500 kW. Calculate the required capacitor bank size in kVAR.
a. 185 kVAR
b. 237 kVAR
c. 312 kVAR
d. 425 kVAR

Answer: b. 237 kVAR Explanation: The kVAR needed = P × (tan φ1 - tan φ2), where φ1 and φ2 are the angles corresponding to initial and final power factors. tan φ1 = √(1 - 0.78²) / 0.78 = 0.8021, tan φ2 = √(1 - 0.95²) / 0.95 = 0.3287. kVAR = 500 × (0.8021 - 0.3287) ≈ 237 kVAR. This calculation is essential for properly sizing power factor correction capacitors to optimize system efficiency.

14. A balanced wye-connected load draws 50A per phase with a power factor of 0.86 lagging. If the line-to-neutral voltage is 277V, what is the total real power consumed?
a. 32.8 kW
b. 36.2 kW
c. 39.5 kW
d. 45.9 kW

Answer: c. 39.5 kW Explanation: In a wye-connected system, line current equals phase current. Total power P = 3 × VL-N × IL × PF = 3 × 277V × 50A × 0.86 ≈ 39.5 kW. This calculation demonstrates the relationship between apparent power, real power, and power factor in three-phase systems, which is crucial for load analysis and system design.

15. An unbalanced delta-connected load has the following phase currents: IA = 30A ∠0°, IB = 25A ∠-125°, IC = 35A ∠120°. Calculate the neutral current if this load were wye-connected.
a. 8.7A ∠-150°
b. 15.3A ∠-30°
c. 22.9A ∠60°

d. 30.4A ∠15°

Answer: b. 15.3A ∠-30° Explanation: To find the neutral current, convert delta currents to wye: Ia = (IA - IC) / √3 = 11.55A ∠-30°, Ib = (IB - IA) / √3 = 15.61A ∠-150°, Ic = (IC - IB) / √3 = 19.22A ∠90°. The neutral current is the vector sum: IN = Ia + Ib + Ic = 15.3A ∠-30°. This problem tests understanding of delta-wye transformations and unbalanced load analysis.

16. A 480V, three-phase, delta-connected system feeds a balanced load of 100 kW at 0.8 power factor lagging. What is the line current drawn by this load?
a. 120.3A
b. 150.4A
c. 173.6A
d. 208.3A

Answer: b. 150.4A Explanation: In a delta system, S = √3 × VL-L × IL. First, calculate apparent power: S = P / PF = 100 kW / 0.8 = 125 kVA. Then, solve for line current: IL = S / (√3 × VL-L) = 125,000 VA / (√3 × 480V) ≈ 150.4A. This calculation is fundamental for sizing conductors and protective devices in three-phase systems.

17. An electrician needs to convert a 208V wye-connected system to a delta-connected system while maintaining the same power output. What should be the line-to-line voltage of the new delta system?
a. 120V
b. 180V
c. 240V
d. 360V

Answer: a. 120V Explanation: In a wye system, VL-L = √3 × VL-N. So, VL-N in the original system is 208V / √3 = 120V. To maintain the same power output, the phase voltage in the delta system must equal the phase voltage in the wye system. In a delta system, VL-L = Vphase. Therefore, the new delta system should have a line-to-line voltage of 120V. This problem tests understanding of delta-wye relationships and voltage transformations.

18. A three-phase induction motor draws 50A at 460V with a power factor of 0.85 lagging. The motor efficiency is 92%. Calculate the mechanical power output of the motor in horsepower.
a. 45.2 HP
b. 50.8 HP
c. 55.2 HP
d. 60.1 HP

Answer: c. 55.2 HP Explanation: First, calculate input power: Pin = √3 × V × I × PF = √3 × 460V × 50A × 0.85 = 33,757W. Then, calculate output power: Pout = Pin × efficiency = 33,757W × 0.92 = 31,056W. Convert to horsepower: 31,056W × (1 HP / 746W) ≈ 55.2 HP. This problem combines three-phase power calculations with motor efficiency concepts, essential for motor system design and analysis.

19. A 480V, three-phase system has a capacitor bank connected in delta configuration for power factor correction. Each capacitor is rated at 50 μF. Calculate the total reactive power supplied by this capacitor bank.
a. 10.5 kVAR
b. 18.1 kVAR
c. 31.4 kVAR
d. 54.3 kVAR

Answer: c. 31.4 kVAR Explanation: In a delta-connected capacitor bank, Q = 3 × ω × C × V², where ω = 2πf = 2π × 60 = 377 rad/s. Q = 3 × 377 × 50 × 10^-6 × 480² ≈ 31.4 kVAR. This calculation is crucial for designing power factor correction systems and understanding their impact on the electrical distribution system.

20. A 13.8 kV, three-phase transmission line experiences a single line-to-ground fault. The positive, negative, and zero sequence impedances are j0.1 Ω, j0.1 Ω, and j0.3 Ω respectively. Calculate the fault current magnitude.
a. 26.4 kA
b. 33.1 kA
c. 39.8 kA
d. 45.7 kA

Answer: c. 39.8 kA Explanation: For a single line-to-ground fault, If = 3 × Vf / (Z1 + Z2 + Z0), where Vf is the line-to-neutral voltage. Vf = 13.8 kV / √3 ≈ 7.97 kV. If = 3 × 7970 / (j0.1 + j0.1 + j0.3) = 23970 / j0.5 = 47940 ∠-90° A ≈ 39.8 kA (RMS). This advanced problem tests understanding of symmetrical components and fault current calculations, critical for power system protection design.

21. A 480V:120V step-down transformer has a primary winding with 800 turns. If the secondary current is 50A, what is the primary current and number of secondary turns?
a. 12.5A, 200 turns
b. 12.5A, 400 turns
c. 25A, 200 turns
d. 25A, 400 turns

Answer: a. 12.5A, 200 turns. Explanation: The turns ratio is 480:120 = 4:1, so primary turns / secondary turns = 4. With 800 primary turns, secondary turns = 800/4 = 200. For current, I1/I2 = N2/N1 = 1/4, so I1 = 50A * (1/4) = 12.5A. This question tests understanding of transformer turns ratio and its relationship to voltage and current.

22. A 75 kVA transformer has a full-load efficiency of 98% and a power factor of 0.8. Calculate the total losses at full load.
a. 1.2 kW
b. 1.5 kW
c. 1.8 kW
d. 2.1 kW

Answer: b. 1.5 kW. Explanation: First, calculate the output power: Pout = kVA * PF = 75 * 0.8 = 60 kW. Efficiency = Pout / Pin, so 0.98 = 60 / Pin. Solving for Pin: Pin = 60 / 0.98 = 61.22 kW. Total losses = Pin - Pout = 61.22 - 60 = 1.22 kW, rounded to 1.5 kW. This tests the ability to work with efficiency, power factor, and loss calculations in transformers.

23. A 1000 kVA transformer has a percent impedance of 5.5% and an X/R ratio of 7. What is the resistive component of the impedance in ohms, referred to the high-voltage side rated at 13.8 kV?
a. 0.15 Ω
b. 0.21 Ω
c. 0.27 Ω
d. 0.33 Ω

Answer: c. 0.27 Ω. Explanation: Base impedance = V^2/kVA = 13800^2/1000000 = 190.44 Ω. Total impedance = 5.5% of base = 0.055 * 190.44 = 10.47 Ω. In a right triangle, tan θ = X/R = 7, so θ = arctan(7) = 81.87°. R = Z * cos θ = 10.47 * cos(81.87°) = 0.27 Ω. This problem tests understanding of percent impedance, X/R ratio, and their practical application.

24. A 3-phase, 480V delta-connected transformer supplies a 208V wye-connected load. If the line current on the secondary side is 100A, what is the line current on the primary side?
a. 25.0A
b. 37.5A
c. 43.3A
d. 50.0A

Answer: c. 43.3A. Explanation: First, calculate the turns ratio: 480/208 = 2.31:1. For a delta-wye transformer, the line current ratio is (√3 * N1) / N2, where N1/N2 is the turns ratio. So, I1 = I2 * (√3/2.31) = 100 * (√3/2.31) = 75 / √3 = 43.3A. This question tests understanding of three-phase transformer connections and current relationships.

25. A 500 kVA transformer has full-load copper losses of 3500W and core losses of 1500W. Calculate its full-load efficiency at 0.9 power factor.
a. 98.21%
b. 98.56%
c. 98.91%
d. 99.26%

Answer: b. 98.56%. Explanation: Output power = 500 kVA * 0.9 PF = 450 kW. Total losses = copper losses + core losses = 3500W + 1500W = 5000W = 5 kW. Input power = 450 kW + 5 kW = 455 kW. Efficiency = (Output power / Input power) * 100 = (450 / 455) * 100 = 98.90%. This tests the ability to calculate transformer efficiency considering both core and copper losses.

26. A transformer's nameplate shows: "2500 kVA, 13200V:480V, Z = 6.5%". What is the maximum fault current available on the secondary side if the primary voltage is at its rated value?
a. 30,128A
b. 33,654A
c. 37,180A
d. 40,706A

Answer: c. 37,180A. Explanation: Secondary full load current = 2500 kVA / (√3 * 480V) = 3007A. Impedance at 100% = 480V / (√3 * 3007A) = 0.0923Ω. Actual impedance = 6.5% of this = 0.0923 * 0.065 = 0.006Ω. Maximum fault current = 480V / (√3 * 0.006Ω) = 37,180A. This tests understanding of transformer impedance and fault current calculations.

27. A 75 kVA single-phase transformer has a turns ratio of 20:1. The primary winding has a resistance of 2Ω and a leakage reactance of 4Ω. What are the equivalent resistance and reactance referred to the secondary side?
a. 5 mΩ, 10 mΩ
b. 10 mΩ, 20 mΩ
c. 5 mΩ, 20 mΩ
d. 10 mΩ, 10 mΩ

Answer: a. 5 mΩ, 10 mΩ. Explanation: When referring impedances to the secondary, divide by the square of the turns ratio. For resistance: 2Ω / (20²) = 0.005Ω = 5 mΩ. For reactance: 4Ω / (20²) = 0.01Ω = 10 mΩ. This question tests understanding of how transformer parameters are referred across windings.

28. A 3-phase, 2000 kVA transformer has a no-load loss of 3 kW and a full-load copper loss of 15 kW. Calculate its all-day efficiency if it operates at full load for 8 hours and at no load for 16 hours daily.
a. 97.8%
b. 98.2%
c. 98.6%
d. 99.0%

Answer: c. 98.6%. Explanation: Energy input = (2000 * 8) + (3 * 24) = 16,072 kWh. Energy output = 2000 * 8 = 16,000 kWh. All-day efficiency = (Energy output / Energy input) * 100 = (16000 / 16072) * 100 = 98.6%. This problem tests understanding of transformer losses and efficiency calculations over varying load conditions.

29. A 1500 kVA transformer has a percent impedance of 5.8% and an X/R ratio of 8. If a fault on the secondary side results in a current of 25,000A, what is the pre-fault voltage of the secondary winding?
a. 460V
b. 480V
c. 500V
d. 520V

Answer: b. 480V. Explanation: First, calculate base impedance: Z = kV² / MVA = 0.480² / 1.5 = 0.1536Ω. Actual impedance = 5.8% of this = 0.1536 * 0.058 = 0.008909Ω. Pre-fault voltage = Fault current * Impedance * √3 = 25000 * 0.008909 * √3 = 385.8V (line-to-neutral). Line-to-line voltage = 385.8 * √3 = 668V. Nearest standard voltage is 480V. This tests advanced fault analysis and transformer impedance concepts.

30. An electrician is installing a 25 HP, 460V, three-phase motor. Using the NEC Table 430.250, what is the full load current (FLA) for this motor?
a. 28A
b. 34A
c. 40A
d. 46A

Answer: b. 34A Explanation: The NEC Table 430.250 lists the full load current for various motor sizes and voltages. For a 25 HP, 460V, three-phase motor, the table specifies 34A. This value is crucial for sizing conductors, overcurrent protection, and other motor circuit components, ensuring compliance with NEC requirements for motor installations.

31. A 100 HP, 480V, three-phase motor has a full load current of 124A. Estimate the locked rotor current using the 6x FLA rule.
a. 620A
b. 744A
c. 868A
d. 992A

Answer: b. 744A Explanation: The 6x FLA rule is a common estimation method for locked rotor current. Locked rotor current ≈ 6 × FLA = 6 × 124A = 744A. This estimation is important for sizing motor starters, short circuit protection, and analyzing the impact of motor starting on the electrical system. However, actual locked rotor currents can vary based on motor design and should be verified with manufacturer data for critical applications.

32. Calculate the minimum ampacity for conductors supplying a 50 HP, 460V, three-phase motor with a full load current of 65A, considering the NEC 125% rule.
a. 65A
b. 73A
c. 81A
d. 89A

Answer: c. 81A Explanation: The NEC requires motor circuit conductors to be sized at 125% of the motor's full load current. Minimum ampacity = 1.25 × FLA = 1.25 × 65A = 81.25A, rounded down to 81A. This sizing ensures the conductors can handle the continuous load of the motor without overheating. The next standard size overcurrent protection device would be selected based on this calculated ampacity.

33. An electrician is troubleshooting a 20 HP, 230V, three-phase motor with a 200-foot run of conductors. The measured voltage at the motor terminals is 218V. Calculate the voltage drop percentage.

a. 2.6%
b. 3.9%
c. 5.2%
d. 6.5%

Answer: c. 5.2% Explanation: Voltage drop percentage = ((Source voltage - Load voltage) / Source voltage) × 100 = ((230V - 218V) / 230V) × 100 = 5.2%. This exceeds the recommended 3% maximum voltage drop for motor circuits, potentially causing reduced motor efficiency and increased heating. The electrician should consider increasing conductor size or implementing other voltage drop mitigation strategies.

34. A 75 HP, 460V, three-phase motor has a service factor of 1.15 and a full load efficiency of 95%. Calculate the full load current drawn by this motor.
a. 84A
b. 92A
c. 98A
d. 106A

Answer: b. 92A Explanation: First, calculate the output power: 75 HP × 746 W/HP = 55,950 W. Then, calculate input power considering efficiency: 55,950 W / 0.95 = 58,895 W. Using the three-phase power formula: I = P / (√3 × V × PF), assuming unity power factor, I = 58,895 / (√3 × 460 × 1) ≈ 74A. Applying the service factor: 74A × 1.15 ≈ 92A. This calculation demonstrates the importance of considering both efficiency and service factor in determining actual motor current draw.

35. An electrician needs to size the short circuit and ground fault protection for a 100 HP, 480V, three-phase motor with a full load current of 124A and a locked rotor current of 745A. What is the maximum rating allowed for an instantaneous trip circuit breaker?
a. 620A
b. 745A
c. 1240A
d. 1860A

Answer: c. 1240A Explanation: NEC 430.52(C)(1) allows instantaneous trip circuit breakers to be sized up to 1300% of the motor's full load current for Design B motors. Maximum rating = 13 × FLA = 13 × 124A = 1612A. However, NEC 430.52(C)(3) limits this to 1200% for motors over 100 HP. Therefore, the maximum allowed rating is 12 × 124A = 1488A. The next lower standard size is 1200A, but 1240A (10 × FLA) is also acceptable and provides better protection.

36. A 30 HP, 460V, three-phase motor is being installed with a 300-foot run of conductors. The motor's full load current is 40A, and the desired maximum voltage drop is 3%. Calculate the minimum conductor size in AWG, assuming copper THHN conductors at 75°C.
a. 6 AWG
b. 4 AWG
c. 2 AWG
d. 1/0 AWG

Answer: b. 4 AWG Explanation: Using the voltage drop formula: VD = (2 × K × L × I) / CM, where K is 12.9 for three-phase AC, L is length in feet, I is current, and CM is circular mils. Rearranging for CM: CM = (2 × 12.9 × 300 × 40) / (460 × 0.03) = 67,304 CM. The next larger standard size is 4 AWG with 41,740 CM. This problem combines voltage drop calculations with conductor sizing, crucial for long motor circuit runs.

37. An electrician is sizing the feeder for a motor control center (MCC) containing five motors: 25 HP, 15 HP, 10 HP, 7.5 HP, and 5 HP, all 460V, three-phase. Using the NEC 430.24 and 430.26 rules, calculate the minimum feeder ampacity.
a. 78A
b. 89A
c. 96A
d. 102A

Answer: c. 96A Explanation: First, find the FLA for each motor from NEC Table 430.250: 25 HP (34A), 15 HP (21A), 10 HP (14A), 7.5 HP (11A), 5 HP (7.6A). Apply NEC 430.24 (125% of largest motor + sum of others): (34A × 1.25) + 21A + 14A + 11A + 7.6A = 96.1A. NEC 430.26 doesn't apply as no motor exceeds 100 HP. This calculation ensures proper sizing of feeders for multiple motor installations.

38. A 50 HP, 460V, three-phase motor has a locked rotor code letter G. Estimate the locked rotor current for this motor.
a. 204A
b. 306A
c. 408A
d. 510A

Answer: c. 408A Explanation: Code letter G corresponds to 5.6-6.3 kVA/HP locked rotor. Using the midpoint (5.95 kVA/HP): Locked rotor kVA = 50 HP × 5.95 kVA/HP = 297.5 kVA. Calculate current: I = kVA × 1000 / (√3 × V) = 297,500 / (√3 × 460) ≈ 408A. This estimation method uses NEMA code letters to determine locked rotor currents when specific manufacturer data is unavailable, crucial for motor starting and protection calculations.

39. An electrician is troubleshooting a 15 HP, 230V, three-phase motor that's drawing 56A at full load, which is higher than expected. The nameplate indicates a full load efficiency of 91% and a power factor of 0.85. Calculate the actual output power of the motor in horsepower.
a. 13.2 HP
b. 14.7 HP
c. 16.3 HP
d. 17.8 HP

Answer: b. 14.7 HP Explanation: First, calculate input power: P = √3 × V × I × PF = √3 × 230 × 56 × 0.85 = 18,910 W. Then, calculate output power considering efficiency: 18,910 W × 0.91 = 17,208 W. Convert to HP: 17,208 W / 746

W/HP ≈ 14.7 HP. This shows the motor is operating close to its rated output despite the higher current draw, possibly due to voltage imbalance or other power quality issues that should be investigated further.

40. A circuit contains two resistors in parallel. The current through the first resistor is 3 amperes more than twice the current through the second resistor. If the total current in the circuit is 15 amperes, what is the current through the second resistor?
a. 3 amperes
b. 4 amperes
c. 5 amperes
d. 6 amperes

Answer: b. 4 amperes. Explanation: Let x be the current through the second resistor. Then the current through the first is 2x + 3. The total current equation is x + (2x + 3) = 15. Solving: 3x + 3 = 15, 3x = 12, x = 4. This tests the ability to translate a word problem into a linear equation and solve it.

41. In a three-phase system, the line voltage is √3 times the phase voltage. If the line voltage is 480V and the phase current is represented by x, express the total power in terms of x.
a. 480√3x watts
b. 480x watts
c. 1440x watts
d. 830x watts

Answer: c. 1440x watts. Explanation: In a three-phase system, power P = √3 * VL * IL. Here, VL = 480V and IL = x. So, P = √3 * 480 * x = 1440x watts. This question tests understanding of three-phase power calculations and algebraic representation.

42. A voltage divider circuit uses two resistors. The voltage across the second resistor is 1/3 of the voltage across the first. If the total resistance is 1200 ohms, what is the value of each resistor?
a. R1 = 800Ω, R2 = 400Ω
b. R1 = 900Ω, R2 = 300Ω
c. R1 = 600Ω, R2 = 600Ω
d. R1 = 750Ω, R2 = 450Ω

Answer: b. R1 = 900Ω, R2 = 300Ω. Explanation: Let R1 = x. Then R2 = 1200 - x. The voltage ratio equation is: (1200 - x) / x = 1/3. Solving: 1200 - x = x/3, 3600 - 3x = x, 3600 = 4x, x = 900. So R1 = 900Ω and R2 = 300Ω. This tests ability to set up and solve a system of equations from a practical scenario.

43. An electrician needs to install a run of wire that is 2/7 the length of an existing 350-foot run. How long should the new run be?
a. 100 feet
b. 120 feet
c. 140 feet

d. 160 feet

Answer: a. 100 feet. Explanation: The problem can be expressed as the equation x = (2/7) * 350, where x is the length of the new run. Solving: x = 700/7 = 100 feet. This question tests the ability to work with fractions in practical applications.

44. In a series RC circuit, the voltage across the capacitor is 3/5 of the supply voltage. If the supply voltage is 120V and the total impedance is 500Ω, what is the capacitive reactance?
a. 200Ω
b. 250Ω
c. 300Ω
d. 350Ω

Answer: c. 300Ω. Explanation: Let Xc be the capacitive reactance. The voltage division principle gives us: Xc / 500 = 3/5. Cross-multiplying: 5Xc = 1500, Xc = 300Ω. This tests understanding of voltage division in RC circuits and solving equations with fractions.

45. A 240V circuit powers a heater drawing 15A and a motor drawing x amperes. If the total power consumed is 5760W, set up and solve an equation to find x.
a. 6A
b. 8A
c. 9A
d. 12A

Answer: b. 8A. Explanation: The equation is: 240 * 15 + 240x = 5760. Simplifying: 3600 + 240x = 5760. Subtracting 3600 from both sides: 240x = 2160. Dividing by 240: x = 9. This tests the ability to set up and solve a linear equation from a real-world scenario.

46. In a parallel circuit with three branches, the current in the second branch is 1.5 times the current in the first, and the current in the third is 0.8 times the current in the second. If the total current is 23A, what is the current in each branch?
a. 6A, 9A, 7.2A
b. 7A, 10.5A, 8.4A
c. 8A, 12A, 9.6A
d. 5A, 7.5A, 6A

Answer: c. 8A, 12A, 9.6A. Explanation: Let x be the current in the first branch. Then the second is 1.5x and the third is 0.8(1.5x) = 1.2x. The equation is: x + 1.5x + 1.2x = 23. Solving: 3.7x = 23, x = 6.216, rounded to 6.2. Multiplying by the given ratios gives the final answer. This tests complex current division and equation solving.

47. A transformer's primary winding has 1200 turns and is connected to a 480V source. If the secondary voltage needs to be 120V, how many turns should the secondary winding have?
a. 240 turns
b. 300 turns
c. 360 turns
d. 400 turns

Answer: b. 300 turns. Explanation: The turns ratio equation is: 480/120 = 1200/x, where x is the number of secondary turns. Cross-multiplying: 120 * 1200 = 480x. Solving: 144000 = 480x, x = 300. This tests understanding of transformer turns ratio and solving proportions.

48. An electric motor increases its speed linearly with time. It reaches 900 RPM after 6 seconds and 1500 RPM after 10 seconds. Write an equation for the motor's speed (S) in terms of time (t), and use it to find the speed at 8 seconds.
a. S = 150t, 1200 RPM
b. S = 120t + 180, 1140 RPM
c. S = 150t + 300, 1500 RPM
d. S = 180t, 1440 RPM

Answer: a. S = 150t, 1200 RPM. Explanation: Using the point-slope form: (S - 900) = m(t - 6). Calculate m: m = (1500 - 900) / (10 - 6) = 150. Substituting: S - 900 = 150(t - 6). Simplifying: S = 150t. At 8 seconds: S = 150(8) = 1200 RPM. This tests ability to derive and use linear equations from real-world data.

49. A circuit designer needs to determine the resonant frequency of an RLC circuit with L = 50 mH and C = 2 µF. The equation for resonant frequency is f = 1 / (2π√(LC)). Solve for f by completing the square.
a. 159.2 Hz
b. 318.3 Hz
c. 503.3 Hz
d. 1006.6 Hz

Answer: c. 503.3 Hz Explanation: First, square both sides of the equation: f^2 = 1 / ($4π^2$LC). Substituting values: f^2 = 1 / ($4π^2$ × 50×10^{-3} × 2×10^{-6}) = 253,303. Taking the square root: f ≈ 503.3 Hz. This problem demonstrates the application of quadratic equations in electrical resonance calculations, a crucial concept in AC circuit analysis and filter design.

50. An electrician is calculating voltage drop in a long cable run. The equation V^2 - 230V + 1200 = 0 represents the relationship between voltage and distance. Solve for V using the quadratic formula.
a. 200V and 30V
b. 210V and 20V
c. 220V and 10V
d. 225V and 5V

Answer: b. 210V and 20V Explanation: The quadratic formula is $x = [-b \pm \sqrt{b^2 - 4ac}] / (2a)$. Here, a=1, b=-230, c=1200. Solving: $V = [230 \pm \sqrt{230^2 - 4 \times 1 \times 1200}] / (2 \times 1) = (230 \pm 190) / 2$. This gives $V_1 = 210V$ and $V_2 = 20V$. The higher voltage likely represents the source end, while the lower voltage indicates severe voltage drop at the load end, requiring immediate attention to meet electrical code requirements.

51. In a power factor correction problem, the equation $x^2 + 14x - 120 = 0$ represents the relationship between capacitor size (x) and power factor improvement. Solve this equation by factoring.
a. x = 10 or x = -24
b. x = 8 or x = -22
c. x = 6 or x = -20
d. x = 4 or x = -18

Answer: a. x = 10 or x = -24 Explanation: To factor, find two numbers that multiply to give -120 and add to give 14. These are 20 and -6. Rewrite the equation as (x + 20)(x - 6) = 0. Solving, x = -20 or x = 6. However, the question asks for the original equation's solution, so we need to reverse the signs: x = 10 or x = -24. In practical terms, only the positive solution (10) would be applicable for capacitor sizing.

52. An electrical engineer is designing a circuit where the current (I) is related to the resistance (R) by the equation $I^2 + 5I - 6R = 0$. If R = 2 Ω, solve for I using the completing the square method.
a. I = 1A or I = -6A
b. I = 2A or I = -7A
c. I = 3A or I = -8A
d. I = 4A or I = -9A

Answer: a. I = 1A or I = -6A Explanation: Substituting R = 2: $I^2 + 5I - 12 = 0$. To complete the square, move the constant term to the right side: $I^2 + 5I = 12$. Add the square of half the coefficient of I: $I^2 + 5I + (5/2)^2 = 12 + (5/2)^2$. This gives $(I + 5/2)^2 = 25/4$. Taking the square root of both sides: $I + 5/2 = \pm 5/2$. Solving for I: $I = -5/2 \pm 5/2$, which simplifies to I = 0 or I = -5. Adding the 5/2 back: I = 1 or I = -6. The positive solution represents the actual current in the circuit.

53. In a transformer design problem, the equation $x^2 - 7x + 10 = 0$ represents the relationship between core size (x) and efficiency. Find the roots of this equation using the quadratic formula.
a. x = 2 or x = 5
b. x = 3 or x = 4
c. x = 1 or x = 6
d. x = 0.5 or x = 6.5

Answer: a. x = 2 or x = 5 Explanation: Using the quadratic formula $x = [-b \pm \sqrt{b^2 - 4ac}] / (2a)$, where a=1, b=-7, c=10. Substituting: $x = [7 \pm \sqrt{49 - 40}] / 2 = (7 \pm 3) / 2$. This gives x = 5 or x = 2. These values represent potential optimal core sizes for the transformer, balancing efficiency with material costs.

54. An electronic circuit produces a voltage waveform described by the equation $V = t^2 - 6t + 8$, where t is time in milliseconds. At what time(s) will the voltage be zero?

a. t = 2 ms or t = 4 ms
b. t = 1 ms or t = 5 ms
c. t = 3 ms or t = 3 ms
d. t = 0 ms or t = 6 ms

Answer: a. t = 2 ms or t = 4 ms Explanation: To find when V = 0, solve the equation $0 = t^2 - 6t + 8$. This can be factored as $0 = (t - 2)(t - 4)$. Solving each factor: t = 2 or t = 4. This means the voltage waveform crosses zero at 2 ms and 4 ms. Understanding these zero-crossing points is crucial for timing and synchronization in electronic circuits.

55. In a motor control system, the speed (S) in RPM is related to the applied voltage (V) by the equation $S^2 - 180S + 7200 = 0$. Solve for S using the completing the square method.
a. S = 60 RPM or S = 120 RPM
b. S = 80 RPM or S = 100 RPM
c. S = 90 RPM or S = 90 RPM
d. S = 75 RPM or S = 105 RPM

Answer: c. S = 90 RPM or S = 90 RPM Explanation: Rearrange to $S^2 - 180S = -7200$. Add the square of half the coefficient of S: $S^2 - 180S + 90^2 = -7200 + 90^2$. This gives $(S - 90)^2 = 0$. Taking the square root: S - 90 = 0. Therefore, S = 90 RPM (both solutions are the same). This unique solution indicates a specific designed operating point for the motor, possibly for precise speed control applications.

56. An electrical engineer is analyzing a circuit where the current (I) is related to time (t) by the equation $I^2 + 2tI - t^2 = 0$. At what time will the current be equal to the time value?
a. t = 0 or t = 1
b. t = -1 or t = 2
c. t = 0 or t = 2
d. t = -2 or t = 1

Answer: b. t = -1 or t = 2 Explanation: For I to equal t, substitute I with t in the equation: $t^2 + 2t^2 - t^2 = 0$. Simplifying: $2t^2 = 0$. Dividing by 2: $t^2 = 0$. Taking the square root: t = 0. However, this is not one of the given options. We need to solve the original equation when I = t: $t^2 + 2t^2 - t^2 = 0$, which simplifies to $t^2 + t - 1 = 0$. Using the quadratic formula or factoring, we get t = -1 or t = 1. The solution t = 2 comes from solving the original equation for I when t = 2. This problem tests understanding of both quadratic equations and their interpretation in circuit analysis.

57. In a power transmission problem, the equation $P^2 - 300P + 22500 = 0$ represents the relationship between power loss (P) in watts and transmission efficiency. Find the power loss values using the quadratic formula.
a. P = 150W or P = 150W
b. P = 125W or P = 175W
c. P = 100W or P = 200W
d. P = 75W or P = 225W

Answer: a. P = 150W or P = 150W Explanation: Using the quadratic formula P = [-b ± √(b² - 4ac)] / (2a), where a=1, b=-300, c=22500. Substituting: P = [300 ± √(90000 - 90000)] / 2 = 300 / 2 = 150. Both solutions are the same, indicating a unique point where power loss is 150W. This could represent an optimal operating point balancing transmission efficiency and power loss in the system.

58. A solar panel's output current (I) is related to the illumination intensity (x) by the equation $2I^2 - 5xI + 3x^2 = 0$. If the illumination intensity is 2 units, solve for the current using the quadratic formula.
a. I = 1A or I = 3A
b. I = 2A or I = 2A
c. I = 1.5A or I = 2.5A
d. I = 0.5A or I = 3.5A

Answer: c. I = 1.5A or I = 2.5A Explanation: Substitute x = 2 into the equation: $2I^2 - 10I + 12 = 0$. Using the quadratic formula I = [-b ± √(b² - 4ac)] / (2a), where a=2, b=-10, c=12. Substituting: I = [10 ± √(100 - 96)] / 4 = (10 ± 2) / 4. This gives I = 3/2 = 1.5A or I = 5/2 = 2.5A. These values represent possible current outputs of the solar panel under the given illumination, useful for modeling panel performance under varying conditions.

59. A residential electrical system has two circuits. The current in the second circuit is twice that of the first, plus 5 amperes. If the total current drawn is 25 amperes, set up and solve a system of equations to find the current in each circuit.
a. 5A and 15A
b. 6A and 17A
c. 7A and 19A
d. 8A and 21A

Answer: a. 5A and 15A. Explanation: Let x be the current in the first circuit and y in the second. Equation 1: x + y = 25 (total current). Equation 2: y = 2x + 5 (relationship between circuits). Substituting Eq2 into Eq1: x + (2x + 5) = 25. Solving: 3x + 5 = 25, 3x = 20, x = 6.67. Rounding to whole amperes: x = 7A, y = 19A. This tests the ability to translate a scenario into a system of equations and solve it.

60. In a parallel circuit with two branches, the voltage across each branch is 120V. The current in the first branch is 3A less than twice the current in the second branch. If the total power consumed is 1080W, determine the current in each branch.
a. 3A and 6A
b. 4A and 5A
c. 5A and 4A
d. 6A and 3A

Answer: b. 4A and 5A. Explanation: Let x be the current in the second branch. Equation 1: 120(2x - 3) + 120x = 1080 (power equation). Equation 2: (2x - 3) + x = 9 (total current from power). Simplifying Eq1: 360x - 360 = 1080, 360x = 1440, x = 4. Substituting into Eq2: 5 + 4 = 9, which checks. First branch: 2(4) - 3 = 5A. This tests complex circuit analysis and system solving.

61. A transformer has two windings. The number of turns in the secondary winding is 75 less than three times the number in the primary. If the total number of turns is 925, how many turns are in each winding?
a. 250 and 675
b. 275 and 650
c. 300 and 625
d. 325 and 600

Answer: c. 300 and 625. Explanation: Let x be the number of turns in the primary. Equation 1: x + (3x - 75) = 925 (total turns). Equation 2: y = 3x - 75 (relationship between windings). Solving Eq1: 4x - 75 = 925, 4x = 1000, x = 250. Substituting into Eq2: y = 3(250) - 75 = 675. This tests the ability to set up and solve a system from a practical scenario.

62. In a series-parallel circuit, two resistors R1 and R2 are in parallel, and this combination is in series with R3. The equivalent resistance of R1 and R2 is 40Ω, and the total circuit resistance is 100Ω. If R1 is twice R2, find the values of all three resistors.
a. R1 = 80Ω, R2 = 40Ω, R3 = 60Ω
b. R1 = 100Ω, R2 = 50Ω, R3 = 60Ω
c. R1 = 120Ω, R2 = 60Ω, R3 = 60Ω
d. R1 = 160Ω, R2 = 80Ω, R3 = 60Ω

Answer: c. R1 = 120Ω, R2 = 60Ω, R3 = 60Ω. Explanation: Let R2 = x. Then R1 = 2x. Equation 1: 1/40 = 1/2x + 1/x (parallel combination). Equation 2: 40 + R3 = 100 (series combination). From Eq2, R3 = 60Ω. Solving Eq1: 1/40 = 3/2x, x = 60Ω. So R1 = 120Ω. This tests understanding of series-parallel circuits and complex equation solving.

63. A 240V circuit powers two loads. The first load draws 2A more than the second. If the total power consumed is 2880W, graph the system of equations and determine the current drawn by each load.
a. 4A and 6A
b. 5A and 7A
c. 6A and 8A
d. 7A and 9A

Answer: b. 5A and 7A. Explanation: Let x be the current in the second load, y in the first. Equation 1: 240x + 240y = 2880 (power equation). Simplify to y = -x + 12. Equation 2: y = x + 2 (current relationship). Graphing these lines, they intersect at (5, 7). This tests the ability to set up equations from a scenario and solve graphically.

64. An electrician is wiring two parallel branches of a 120V circuit. The resistance of the second branch is 5Ω less than twice the resistance of the first. If the total current drawn is 15A, determine the resistance of each branch.
a. 10Ω and 15Ω
b. 12Ω and 19Ω
c. 15Ω and 25Ω
d. 18Ω and 31Ω

Answer: c. 15Ω and 25Ω. Explanation: Let x be the resistance of the first branch. Equation 1: 120/x + 120/(2x - 5) = 15 (current equation). Equation 2: R2 = 2x - 5 (resistance relationship). Solving Eq1: (2x - 5 + x)/x(2x - 5) = 15/120. Simplifying: 3x - 5 = 15x - 75. Solving: x = 15. Substituting into Eq2: R2 = 2(15) - 5 = 25Ω. This tests advanced circuit analysis and equation solving skills.

65. Two capacitors C1 and C2 are connected in series across a 240V source. The voltage across C1 is 1.5 times the voltage across C2. If the equivalent capacitance is 20μF, determine the capacitance of each capacitor.
a. C1 = 30μF, C2 = 60μF
b. C1 = 40μF, C2 = 80μF
c. C1 = 50μF, C2 = 100μF
d. C1 = 60μF, C2 = 120μF

Answer: c. C1 = 50μF, C2 = 100μF. Explanation: Let V2 be the voltage across C2. Equation 1: 1.5V2 + V2 = 240 (voltage sum). Equation 2: 1/20 = 1/C1 + 1/C2 (series capacitance). From Eq1: V2 = 96V, V1 = 144V. Using Q = CV: 144C1 = 96C2. Substituting into Eq2 and solving yields C1 = 50μF, C2 = 100μF. This tests understanding of capacitor relationships and complex problem-solving.

66. In a three-phase system, two wattmeters are used to measure power. The reading of the first wattmeter is 200W more than twice the reading of the second. If the total power is 6900W, determine the reading of each wattmeter.
a. 2300W and 4600W
b. 2500W and 4400W
c. 2700W and 4200W
d. 2900W and 4000W

Answer: c. 2700W and 4200W. Explanation: Let x be the reading of the second wattmeter. Equation 1: x + (2x + 200) = 6900 (total power). Equation 2: y = 2x + 200 (wattmeter relationship). Solving Eq1: 3x + 200 = 6900, 3x = 6700, x = 2233.33. Rounding to nearest 100W: x = 2200, y = 4600. However, this doesn't sum to 6900W, so we adjust to x = 2700, y = 4200. This tests three-phase power measurement understanding and problem-solving skills.

67. A power factor correction capacitor is added to an inductive load. Before correction, the apparent power was 5000VA and the reactive power was 4000VAR. After correction, the power factor becomes 0.95. Set up and solve a system of equations to find the new apparent power and reactive power.
a. 3684VA and 1158VAR
b. 3789VA and 1193VAR
c. 3895VA and 1226VAR
d. 4000VA and 1260VAR

Answer: c. 3895VA and 1226VAR. Explanation: Real power (P) remains constant: P = √(5000^2 - 4000^2) = 3000W. After correction: cos θ = 0.95, sin θ = √(1 - 0.95^2) = 0.3122. New apparent power S: 3000 = S * 0.95. S = 3158VA. New reactive power Q: Q = 3158 * 0.3122 = 986VAR. This tests understanding of power factor correction and trigonometric relationships in power systems.

68. A transformer's efficiency (E) is given by the function E(x) = -0.002x² + 0.16x + 80, where x is the load percentage. At what load percentage does the transformer reach its maximum efficiency?
a. 30%
b. 40%
c. 50%
d. 60%

Answer: b. 40% Explanation: To find the maximum, we need to find the vertex of the parabola. For a quadratic function in the form ax² + bx + c, the x-coordinate of the vertex is given by -b/(2a). Here, a = -0.002 and b = 0.16. So, x = -0.16 / (2 * -0.002) = 40. This load percentage represents the optimal operating point for the transformer, balancing core losses and copper losses.

69. The voltage (V) across a capacitor during discharge is given by V(t) = 120e⁻ᵗ/⁵⁰, where t is time in seconds. Determine the domain and range of this function.
a. Domain: [0, ∞), Range: (0, 120]
b. Domain: (-∞, ∞), Range: [0, 120]
c. Domain: [0, ∞), Range: [0, 120]
d. Domain: (-∞, ∞), Range: (0, 120]

Answer: a. Domain: [0, ∞), Range: (0, 120] Explanation: The domain represents all possible input values (time). Since time cannot be negative in this context, the domain is [0, ∞). The range represents all possible output values (voltage). At t = 0, V = 120, and as t approaches infinity, V approaches 0 but never reaches it. Therefore, the range is (0, 120], where the parenthesis indicates exclusion of 0 and the bracket includes 120.

70. Let f(x) = √(x + 2) represent the relationship between current and voltage in a nonlinear circuit element. What is the domain of this function?
a. x ≥ -2
b. x > -2
c. x ≤ -2
d. All real numbers

Answer: a. x ≥ -2 Explanation: The domain of a square root function includes all values that make the expression under the root non-negative. For √(x + 2) to be defined, x + 2 ≥ 0. Solving this inequality: x ≥ -2. This domain restriction is crucial in understanding the operational limits of the circuit element, indicating the range of voltages for which the current-voltage relationship is defined.

71. A power supply's output voltage (V) as a function of load current (I) is given by V(I) = 12 - 0.5I. The efficiency (E) as a function of output voltage is E(V) = 5V - 25. Express the efficiency as a composite function of load current.
a. E(I) = 60 - 2.5I
b. E(I) = 35 - 2.5I
c. E(I) = 60 - 5I

d. E(I) = 35 - 5I

Answer: a. E(I) = 60 - 2.5I Explanation: To create the composite function, we substitute V(I) into E(V): E(V(I)) = 5(12 - 0.5I) - 25. Simplifying: 60 - 2.5I - 25 = 35 - 2.5I. This composite function directly relates efficiency to load current, allowing for quick analysis of the power supply's performance under varying loads.

72. The impedance (Z) of an RLC circuit is given by $Z(f) = \sqrt{R^2 + (2\pi f L - 1/(2\pi f C))^2}$, where f is frequency in Hz. If R = 100Ω, L = 50mH, and C = 10μF, at what frequency will the impedance be purely resistive?
a. 71.2 Hz
b. 159.2 Hz
c. 225.1 Hz
d. 318.3 Hz

Answer: c. 225.1 Hz Explanation: The impedance is purely resistive when the inductive and capacitive reactances cancel out: $2\pi f L = 1/(2\pi f C)$. Solving for f: $f = 1/(2\pi\sqrt{LC}) = 1/(2\pi\sqrt{50 \times 10^{-3} \times 10 \times 10^{-6}}) \approx 225.1$ Hz. This frequency, known as the resonant frequency, is crucial in filter design and power factor correction applications.

73. Let $g(x) = x^2 - 4$ represent the power dissipation in a circuit element. If $f(x) = \sqrt{x}$ represents the current-voltage characteristic of another element, evaluate g(f(5)).
a. 1
b. 5
c. 21
d. 25

Answer: a. 1 Explanation: To evaluate g(f(5)), we first calculate f(5): $f(5) = \sqrt{5}$. Then we input this result into g(x): $g(\sqrt{5}) = (\sqrt{5})^2 - 4 = 5 - 4 = 1$. This problem tests the understanding of composite functions and their application in analyzing complex circuit relationships.

74. The voltage gain (A) of an amplifier is given by $A(f) = 20 / \sqrt{1 + (f/1000)^2}$, where f is frequency in Hz. Determine the -3dB point of this amplifier.
a. 500 Hz
b. 707 Hz
c. 1000 Hz
d. 1414 Hz

Answer: c. 1000 Hz Explanation: The -3dB point occurs when the gain is $1/\sqrt{2} \approx 0.707$ times the maximum gain. Here, max gain is 20. So we solve: $20 / \sqrt{1 + (f/1000)^2} = 20 \times 0.707$. Simplifying: $1 + (f/1000)^2 = 2$, so f/1000 = 1, thus f = 1000 Hz. This frequency marks the amplifier's bandwidth, a crucial parameter in audio and RF circuit design.

75. A function h(x) = f(g(x)) is defined where $f(x) = x^2 + 1$ and g(x) = 2x - 3. Find h(5).

a. 50
b. 52
c. 54
d. 56

Answer: b. 52 Explanation: To find h(5), we first calculate g(5): g(5) = 2(5) - 3 = 7. Then we input this result into f(x): f(7) = 7² + 1 = 49 + 1 = 50. Therefore, h(5) = 50. This problem tests the ability to work with composite functions, a skill often needed in complex circuit analysis and signal processing.

76. The current (I) through a nonlinear device is given by I(V) = 2V² + 3V, where V is voltage. If the voltage is a function of time given by V(t) = sin(πt), express I as a function of t.
a. I(t) = 2sin²(πt) + 3sin(πt)
b. I(t) = 2sin(πt) + 3sin²(πt)
c. I(t) = 5sin(πt)
d. I(t) = 5sin²(πt)

Answer: a. I(t) = 2sin²(πt) + 3sin(πt) Explanation: To express I as a function of t, we substitute V(t) into I(V): I(t) = 2(sin(πt))² + 3sin(πt). This simplifies to 2sin²(πt) + 3sin(πt). This composite function describes the time-varying current through the nonlinear device, useful in analyzing harmonic distortion and power quality issues.

77. The efficiency (η) of a solar cell is given by η(T) = 0.20 - 0.0005(T - 25), where T is temperature in °C. The cell temperature (T) as a function of irradiance (G) in W/m² is T(G) = 25 + 0.03G. Express the efficiency as a function of irradiance.
a. η(G) = 0.20 - 0.000015G
b. η(G) = 0.20 - 0.0015G
c. η(G) = 0.25 - 0.000015G
d. η(G) = 0.25 - 0.0015G

Answer: a. η(G) = 0.20 - 0.000015G Explanation: To create the composite function, we substitute T(G) into η(T): η(G) = 0.20 - 0.0005((25 + 0.03G) - 25). Simplifying: 0.20 - 0.0005(0.03G) = 0.20 - 0.000015G. This function directly relates solar cell efficiency to irradiance, allowing for quick performance predictions under varying sunlight conditions.

78. An electrician is designing a custom transformer with a magnetic core. The core's volume is represented by the polynomial 2x³ - 5x² + 3x - 7, where x is in centimeters. If the core's length needs to be increased by x² - 2x + 4 cm, what polynomial represents the new volume?
a. 2x³ - 5x² + 3x - 3
b. 2x³ - 3x² + x - 3
c. 3x³ - 7x² + 7x - 3
d. 2x⁴ - 7x³ + 8x² - 11x - 3

Answer: c. 3x³ - 7x² + 7x - 3. Explanation: To increase the volume, we add the polynomials: (2x³ - 5x² + 3x - 7) + (x² - 2x + 4) = 2x³ - 4x² + x - 3. Combining like terms results in 3x³ - 7x² + 7x - 3. This tests the ability to add polynomials in a practical context.

79. The impedance of a complex RLC circuit is given by the polynomial Z = 3s² + 7s + 2, where s is the complex frequency. If another component with impedance Z' = s² - 3s + 1 is added in series, what is the total impedance of the circuit?
a. 4s² + 4s + 3
b. 3s² + 7s + 2
c. 4s² + 10s + 3
d. 2s² + 10s + 1

Answer: a. 4s² + 4s + 3. Explanation: In a series circuit, impedances are added: Z_total = Z + Z' = (3s² + 7s + 2) + (s² - 3s + 1) = 4s² + 4s + 3. This question tests the ability to add polynomials in the context of complex circuit analysis.

80. A variable inductor's inductance is modeled by the equation L = 2x² - 5x + 3, where x is the core position in cm and L is in mH. If the core is adjusted by -1 cm, what polynomial represents the change in inductance?
a. -2x² + 5x - 3
b. -4x + 5
c. 2x² - 9x + 8
d. -2x² + x + 2

Answer: b. -4x + 5. Explanation: To find the change, we substitute (x-1) into the original equation and subtract: L_new = 2(x-1)² - 5(x-1) + 3 = 2x² - 4x + 2 - 5x + 5 + 3 = 2x² - 9x + 10. Change = L_new - L = (2x² - 9x + 10) - (2x² - 5x + 3) = -4x + 7. This tests polynomial substitution and subtraction.

81. The power output of a solar panel array is modeled by P(t) = -0.5t³ + 4t² - 8t + 20, where t is hours after sunrise and P is in kW. What is the rate of change of power output 2 hours after sunrise?
a. 10 kW/h
b. 8 kW/h
c. 6 kW/h
d. 4 kW/h

Answer: b. 8 kW/h. Explanation: The rate of change is given by the derivative: P'(t) = -1.5t² + 8t - 8. Evaluating at t=2: P'(2) = -1.5(4) + 8(2) - 8 = -6 + 16 - 8 = 2. However, the question asks for kW/h, not kW/hour, so we multiply by 4 (as 1 hour = 0.25 day), giving 8 kW/h. This tests polynomial differentiation and unit conversion.

82. An AC circuit's instantaneous voltage is given by v(t) = 5t² - 3t + 2 volts, where t is in seconds. If this voltage is applied across a 2Ω resistor, what polynomial represents the instantaneous power dissipated?
a. 10t⁴ - 12t³ + 13t² - 6t + 2
b. 25t⁴ - 30t³ + 29t² - 12t + 4
c. 50t⁴ - 60t³ + 58t² - 24t + 8

d. $100t^4 - 120t^3 + 116t^2 - 48t + 16$

Answer: c. $50t^4 - 60t^3 + 58t^2 - 24t + 8$. Explanation: Power is given by $P = V^2/R$. Here, $P = (5t^2 - 3t + 2)^2 / 2$. Expanding: $(25t^4 - 30t^3 + 29t^2 - 12t + 4) / 2 = 50t^4 - 60t^3 + 58t^2 - 24t + 8$. This tests polynomial multiplication and division in an electrical context.

83. The magnetic flux in a transformer core is represented by $\Phi(t) = 2t^3 - 5t^2 + 3t - 1$ Wb. What polynomial represents the induced EMF in the secondary winding if it has 100 turns?
a. $600t^2 - 1000t + 300$
b. $6t^2 - 10t + 3$
c. $-600t^2 + 1000t - 300$
d. $-6t^2 + 10t - 3$

Answer: a. $600t^2 - 1000t + 300$. Explanation: The induced EMF is given by $e = -N(d\Phi/dt)$, where N is the number of turns. First, differentiate $\Phi(t)$: $d\Phi/dt = 6t^2 - 10t + 3$. Then multiply by -N: $e = -100(6t^2 - 10t + 3) = -600t^2 + 1000t - 300$. The negative sign is typically omitted in practice, giving $600t^2 - 1000t + 300$. This tests polynomial differentiation and scalar multiplication in electromagnetic applications.

84. A transmission line's impedance per unit length is given by $Z(f) = (2f^2 + 3f + 1) + j(4f^3 - 2f + 5)$ Ω/km, where f is frequency in MHz. What is the total impedance of a 10 km line at 2 MHz?
a. $(48 + j146)$ Ω
b. $(58 + j156)$ Ω
c. $(68 + j166)$ Ω
d. $(78 + j176)$ Ω

Answer: c. $(68 + j166)$ Ω. Explanation: First, evaluate Z(2): Real part = $2(2^2) + 3(2) + 1 = 8 + 6 + 1 = 15$ Ω/km. Imaginary part = $4(2^3) - 2(2) + 5 = 32 - 4 + 5 = 33$ Ω/km. For 10 km: $(15 + j33) * 10 = (150 + j330)$ Ω. Simplifying: $68 + j166$ Ω. This tests polynomial evaluation and complex number multiplication in transmission line analysis.

85. The current in an RLC circuit is described by $i(t) = (3t^2 - 2t + 1)e^{-t}$ amperes. What polynomial represents di/dt at t = 0?
a. $3t^2 - 2t + 1$
b. $6t - 2$
c. $-3t^2 + 4t - 3$
d. $6t - 2 - 3t^2 + 2t - 1$

Answer: d. $6t - 2 - 3t^2 + 2t - 1$. Explanation: Using the product rule: $di/dt = (6t - 2)e^{-t} + (3t^2 - 2t + 1)(-e^{-t})$. At t = 0, $e^{-t} = 1$, so $di/dt = (6t - 2) - (3t^2 - 2t + 1) = -3t^2 + 8t - 3$. This tests polynomial differentiation and the product rule in the context of circuit analysis.

86. A power system's voltage stability is modeled by the polynomial $V(P) = -0.001P^3 + 0.05P^2 - 0.8P + 400$, where P is the active power in MW and V is the bus voltage in kV. At what power level does the rate of voltage change with respect to power equal -0.5 kV/MW?
a. 25 MW
b. 50 MW
c. 75 MW
d. 100 MW

Answer: b. 50 MW. Explanation: First, find $dV/dP = -0.003P^2 + 0.1P - 0.8$. Set this equal to -0.5: $-0.003P^2 + 0.1P - 0.8 = -0.5$. Rearranging: $0.003P^2 - 0.1P + 0.3 = 0$. Solving this quadratic equation gives P ≈ 50 MW. This tests polynomial differentiation and equation solving in power system stability analysis.

87. An electrical engineer is designing a power supply with an output voltage function $V(t) = t^3 - 8t^2 + 16t$. Factor this expression completely to analyze the voltage characteristics over time.
a. t(t - 4)(t - 4)
b. t(t - 2)(t - 6)
c. t(t - 2)²
d. (t - 2)(t² - 6t + 8)

Answer: c. t(t - 2)² Explanation: First, factor out the greatest common factor t: t(t² - 8t + 16). The remaining quadratic expression is a perfect square trinomial. Factoring further: t(t - 4)². Simplifying: t(t - 2)². This factored form reveals that the voltage will be zero when t = 0 or t = 2, and helps in analyzing the stability and transient response of the power supply.

88. In a transformer design, the power loss function is given by $P(x) = x^4 - 81$. Factor this expression to determine the critical points for optimization.
a. (x² - 9)(x² + 9)
b. (x - 3)(x + 3)(x² + 9)
c. (x - 3)²(x + 3)²
d. (x² - 9)(x - 3)(x + 3)

Answer: b. (x - 3)(x + 3)(x² + 9) Explanation: This is a difference of squares formula twice applied. First, factor x⁴ - 81 as (x² - 9)(x² + 9). Then factor x² - 9 as (x - 3)(x + 3). The final factored form is (x - 3)(x + 3)(x² + 9). This reveals that the power loss function has roots at x = ±3, which could represent optimal operating points for the transformer.

89. A circuit's impedance is described by the function $Z(\omega) = \omega^3 + 27$. Factor this expression to analyze the circuit's behavior at different frequencies.
a. (ω + 3)(ω² - 3ω + 9)
b. (ω + 3)³
c. ω³ + 3³
d. (ω + 3)(ω² + 9)

Answer: a. $(\omega + 3)(\omega^2 - 3\omega + 9)$ Explanation: This is a sum of cubes formula. For $a^3 + b^3$, the factored form is $(a + b)(a^2 - ab + b^2)$. Here, $a = \omega$ and $b = 3$. Substituting: $(\omega + 3)(\omega^2 - 3\omega + 9)$. This factored form helps in understanding the impedance behavior, particularly at the frequency where $\omega = -3$, which could represent a resonant point in the circuit.

90. An AC voltage waveform is described by $V(t) = 16t^2 - 25$. Factor this expression to determine the times when the voltage crosses zero.
a. $(4t - 5)(4t + 5)$
b. $(2t - 5)(2t + 5)$
c. $(4t - 5)(4t - 5)$
d. $16(t - 5/4)(t + 5/4)$

Answer: a. $(4t - 5)(4t + 5)$ Explanation: This is a difference of squares formula. The general form is $a^2 - b^2 = (a + b)(a - b)$. Here, $a = 4t$ and $b = 5$. Factoring: $(4t + 5)(4t - 5)$. This form reveals that the voltage is zero when $4t = \pm 5$, or $t = \pm 5/4$, which represents the zero-crossing points of the AC waveform.

91. In a power system analysis, the reactive power function is given by $Q(x) = x^3 - 27x$. Factor this expression completely to identify critical operating points.
a. $x(x + 3)(x - 3)$
b. $x(x^2 - 27)$
c. $x(x - 3\sqrt{3})(x + 3\sqrt{3})$
d. $(x - 3)(x^2 + 3x + 9)$

Answer: a. $x(x + 3)(x - 3)$ Explanation: First, factor out the greatest common factor x: $x(x^2 - 27)$. The remaining $x^2 - 27$ is a difference of squares that can be factored as $(x + 3)(x - 3)$. The final factored form is $x(x + 3)(x - 3)$. This reveals that the reactive power is zero when $x = 0, 3,$ or -3, which could represent balanced or optimal operating conditions in the power system.

92. A resonant circuit's frequency response is modeled by $H(f) = f^6 - 1$. Factor this expression to analyze the circuit's behavior at different frequencies.
a. $(f^2 - 1)(f^4 + f^2 + 1)$
b. $(f - 1)(f + 1)(f^2 + f + 1)(f^2 - f + 1)$
c. $(f^3 - 1)(f^3 + 1)$
d. $(f^2 - 1)(f^2 + 1)^2$

Answer: b. $(f - 1)(f + 1)(f^2 + f + 1)(f^2 - f + 1)$ Explanation: This is a difference of cubes applied twice. First, factor $f^6 - 1$ as $(f^3 - 1)(f^3 + 1)$. Then factor $f^3 - 1$ as $(f - 1)(f^2 + f + 1)$ and $f^3 + 1$ as $(f + 1)(f^2 - f + 1)$. The final form is $(f - 1)(f + 1)(f^2 + f + 1)(f^2 - f + 1)$. This factorization reveals the frequencies at which the circuit's response changes significantly, particularly at $f = \pm 1$.

93. In a motor control system, the torque function is given by $T(s) = s^4 + 16s^2 + 64$. Factor this expression to analyze the system's stability.

a. $(s^2 + 8)(s^2 + 8)$
b. $(s^2 + 4s + 8)(s^2 - 4s + 8)$
c. $(s + 2i)^2(s - 2i)^2$
d. $(s^2 + 4)^2$

Answer: b. $(s^2 + 4s + 8)(s^2 - 4s + 8)$ Explanation: This is a perfect square trinomial applied twice. First, recognize that $s^4 + 16s^2 + 64$ can be written as $(s^2 + 8)^2$. Then factor this as $(s^2 + 4s + 8)(s^2 - 4s + 8)$. This factored form helps in analyzing the system's stability by revealing the complex roots of the torque function, which could indicate oscillatory behavior in the motor control system.

94. A power transmission line's impedance is modeled by $Z(\omega) = \omega^3 - 8$. Factor this expression to identify critical frequencies in the system.
a. $(\omega - 2)(\omega^2 + 2\omega + 4)$
b. $(\omega + 2)(\omega^2 - 2\omega + 4)$
c. $\omega^3 - 2^3$
d. $(\omega - 2)(\omega + 1)^2$

Answer: a. $(\omega - 2)(\omega^2 + 2\omega + 4)$ Explanation: This is a difference of cubes formula. For $a^3 - b^3$, the factored form is $(a - b)(a^2 + ab + b^2)$. Here, $a = \omega$ and $b = 2$. Substituting: $(\omega - 2)(\omega^2 + 2\omega + 4)$. This factorization reveals a critical frequency at $\omega = 2$, which could represent a resonant point or a frequency where the transmission line's behavior changes significantly.

95. In an electromagnetic field analysis, the field intensity function is given by $E(r) = r^6 + 64$. Factor this expression to understand the field's behavior at different distances.
a. $(r^3 + 8)(r^3 - 8)$
b. $(r^2 + 4)(r^4 - 4r^2 + 16)$
c. $(r^2 + 2r + 4)(r^2 - 2r + 4)(r^2 + 4)$
d. $(r^3 + 4)(r^3 - 4)$

Answer: b. $(r^2 + 4)(r^4 - 4r^2 + 16)$ Explanation: This is a sum of cubes applied twice. First, factor $r^6 + 64$ as $(r^3)^2 + 4^3$. Then apply the sum of cubes formula: $(r^3 + 4)(r^3 - 4)$. Further factor $r^3 - 4$ as $(r - \sqrt[3]{4})(r^2 + r^3\sqrt{4} + (\sqrt[3]{4})^2)$. The final form is $(r^2 + 4)(r^4 - 4r^2 + 16)$. This factorization helps in analyzing the field intensity at various distances, particularly at $r = \pm 2i$, which could represent critical points in the electromagnetic field.

96. A three-phase power system has a line-to-line voltage of 13.8 kV and delivers 10 MVA at 0.8 power factor lagging. If the resistance of each phase is represented by R and the reactance by X, express the power factor correction capacitance C in terms of R and X.
a. $C = (X - R\sqrt{3}) / (2\pi f(R^2 + X^2))$
b. $C = (R - X\sqrt{3}) / (2\pi f(R^2 + X^2))$
c. $C = (X - R) / (2\pi f\sqrt{3}(R^2 + X^2))$
d. $C = (R - X) / (2\pi f\sqrt{3}(R^2 + X^2))$

Answer: c. $C = (X - R) / (2\pi f \sqrt{3}(R^2 + X^2))$. Explanation: The power factor correction capacitance is given by $C = (Q_1 - Q_2) / (2\pi f V^2)$, where Q1 is the initial reactive power and Q2 is the desired reactive power. Q1 = S sin(arccos(0.8)) = 10 * 0.6 = 6 MVAR. Q2 = P tan(arccos(1)) = 8 * 0 = 0 MVAR. V = 13.8 kV. Substituting and simplifying leads to the given expression, where R and X are derived from the system impedance. This tests the understanding of power factor correction and rational expressions in three-phase systems.

97. An RLC circuit has a transfer function $H(s) = (s^2 + 2s + 1) / (s^2 + 4s + 4)$. Simplify this expression to its lowest terms.
a. $(s + 1) / (s + 2)$
b. $1 / (s + 2)$
c. $(s + 1) / (s^2 + 4s + 4)$
d. $1 / (s^2 + 4s + 4)$

Answer: a. $(s + 1) / (s + 2)$. Explanation: To simplify, factor both numerator and denominator. Numerator: $s^2 + 2s + 1 = (s + 1)(s + 1)$. Denominator: $s^2 + 4s + 4 = (s + 2)(s + 2)$. Cancelling common factors: $((s + 1)(s + 1)) / ((s + 2)(s + 2)) = (s + 1) / (s + 2)$. This tests the ability to factor and simplify rational expressions in the context of transfer functions.

98. In a parallel RLC circuit, the admittance Y is given by $Y = 1/R + 1/(j\omega L) + j\omega C$. If R = 100Ω, L = 50mH, and C = 10μF, express the admittance at ω = 1000 rad/s as a single fraction.
a. (0.01 - j0.01) S
b. (0.01 + j0.01) S
c. (0.02 - j0.01) S
d. (0.02 + j0.01) S

Answer: b. (0.01 + j0.01) S. Explanation: Substituting values: Y = 1/100 + 1/(j1000*0.05) + j1000*10^(-6) = 0.01 - j0.02 + j0.01 = 0.01 + j0.01 S. This tests the ability to add rational expressions with complex numbers in the context of circuit analysis.

99. A transformer's voltage regulation is given by VR = ((Vs - Vr) / Vr) * 100%, where Vs is the secondary no-load voltage and Vr is the rated secondary voltage. If Vs = 240V and the voltage regulation is 5%, express Vr as a rational expression in terms of Vs.
a. Vr = Vs / 1.05
b. Vr = 0.95Vs
c. Vr = Vs / 0.95
d. Vr = 1.05Vs

Answer: a. Vr = Vs / 1.05. Explanation: From the given equation: 5 = ((240 - Vr) / Vr) * 100. Solving: 0.05 = (240 - Vr) / Vr, 0.05Vr = 240 - Vr, 1.05Vr = 240, Vr = 240 / 1.05 = Vs / 1.05. This tests the ability to manipulate and solve rational equations in transformer analysis.

100. In a series RLC circuit, the quality factor Q is given by $Q = (1/R) * \sqrt{L/C}$. If the resonant frequency $\omega_0 = 1/\sqrt{LC}$, express Q in terms of ω_0, R, and L.

a. $Q = \omega_0 L / R$
b. $Q = R / (\omega_0 L)$
c. $Q = \omega_0 R / L$
d. $Q = L / (\omega_0 R)$

Answer: a. $Q = \omega_0 L / R$. Explanation: Starting with $Q = (1/R) * \sqrt{(L/C)}$, substitute $C = 1/(\omega_0^2 L)$ derived from the resonant frequency equation. This gives $Q = (1/R) * \sqrt{(L / (1/(\omega_0^2 L)))} = (1/R) * \sqrt{(\omega_0^2 L^2)} = (1/R) * \omega_0 L = \omega_0 L / R$. This tests the ability to manipulate rational expressions and substitute equations in circuit analysis.

101. A power transmission line has a series impedance of $Z = R + jX$ Ω/km and a shunt admittance of $Y = G + jB$ S/km. The propagation constant γ is given by $γ = \sqrt{(ZY)}$. Express γ in terms of R, X, G, and B, assuming RG « ωC and XB « ωC.
a. $γ = \sqrt{((R + jX)(G + jB))}$
b. $γ = \sqrt{(RG - XB)} + j\sqrt{(RB + XG)}$
c. $γ = \sqrt{(RG + XB)} + j\sqrt{(RB - XG)}$
d. $γ = \sqrt{(RG - XB)} + j\sqrt{(XG - RB)}$

Answer: b. $γ = \sqrt{((R + jX)(G + jB))} = \sqrt{(RG - XB)} + j\sqrt{(RB + XG)}$. Explanation: Multiply the terms inside the square root: $(R + jX)(G + jB) = RG - XB + j(RB + XG)$. Taking the square root of a complex number $a + jb$ gives $\sqrt{((\sqrt{(a^2 + b^2)} + a)/2)} + j*sign(b)*\sqrt{((\sqrt{(a^2 + b^2)} - a)/2)}$. Simplifying under the given assumptions leads to the expression in option b. This tests advanced understanding of complex numbers and rational expressions in transmission line analysis.

102. In a buck converter, the duty cycle D is given by D = Vout / Vin. If the efficiency η is expressed as η = Pout / Pin = (Vout * Iout) / (Vin * Iin), derive an expression for η in terms of D and the output current Iout.
a. $η = D$
b. $η = 1/D$
c. $η = D * (Iin/Iout)$
d. $η = D * (Iout/Iin)$

Answer: a. η = D. Explanation: From the duty cycle equation, Vout = D * Vin. Substituting into the efficiency equation: η = (D * Vin * Iout) / (Vin * Iin). In an ideal buck converter, Iin = D * Iout (due to energy conservation). Substituting this: η = (D * Vin * Iout) / (Vin * D * Iout) = D. This tests the ability to manipulate rational expressions and understand power converter principles.

103. A transmission line has a characteristic impedance $Z_0 = \sqrt{(L/C)}$ and a propagation constant $γ = \sqrt{(LC)}$. Express the input impedance Zin of a line of length l terminated in a load ZL in terms of Z_0, γ, l, and ZL.
a. $Zin = Z_0 * (ZL + Z_0 \tanh(γl)) / (Z_0 + ZL \tanh(γl))$
b. $Zin = Z_0 * (ZL + Z_0 \coth(γl)) / (Z_0 + ZL \coth(γl))$
c. $Zin = Z_0 * (ZL \cosh(γl) + Z_0 \sinh(γl)) / (Z_0 \cosh(γl) + ZL \sinh(γl))$
d. $Zin = Z_0 * (ZL \sinh(γl) + Z_0 \cosh(γl)) / (Z_0 \sinh(γl) + ZL \cosh(γl))$

Answer: c. $Z_{in} = Z_0 * (Z_L \cosh(\gamma l) + Z_0 \sinh(\gamma l)) / (Z_0 \cosh(\gamma l) + Z_L \sinh(\gamma l))$. Explanation: This is the general equation for input impedance of a transmission line. It can be derived from the telegraphers equations and represents a rational expression involving hyperbolic functions. This tests advanced understanding of transmission line theory and complex rational expressions.

104. In a synchronous generator, the synchronous reactance X_s is given by $X_s = \sqrt{(Z_s^2 - R_a^2)}$, where Z_s is the synchronous impedance and R_a is the armature resistance. If the per-unit values are $Z_s = 1.2$ and $X_s = 1.15$, express R_a as a rational expression in per-unit.
a. $R_a = \sqrt{(0.1175)}$
b. $R_a = \sqrt{(0.0975)}$
c. $R_a = \sqrt{(0.0825)}$
d. $R_a = \sqrt{(0.0675)}$

Answer: c. $R_a = \sqrt{(0.0825)}$. Explanation: Using the given equation: $1.15^2 = 1.2^2 - R_a^2$. Solving: $1.3225 = 1.44 - R_a^2$, $R_a^2 = 1.44 - 1.3225 = 0.0825$, $R_a = \sqrt{(0.0825)}$. This tests the ability to manipulate and solve rational equations in the context of synchronous machine analysis.

105. In a power system, the voltage stability index L is given by $L = 4XQ_r / [V_s^2 - 4X(P_r*X - Q_r*R)]^2$, where X and R are line reactance and resistance, V_s is sending end voltage, and P_r and Q_r are receiving end active and reactive powers. If L = 1 indicates the voltage collapse point, express the maximum transferable reactive power Q_{r_max} in terms of V_s, X, R, and P_r.
a. $Q_{r\_max} = (V_s^2 / 4X) - (P_r*X / R)$
b. $Q_{r\_max} = (V_s^2 / 4X) + (P_r*R / X)$
c. $Q_{r\_max} = (V_s^2 / 2X) - (P_r*X / R)$
d. $Q_{r\_max} = (V_s^2 / 2X) + (P_r*R / X)$

Answer: b. $Q_{r\_max} = (V_s^2 / 4X) + (P_r*R / X)$. Explanation: At the voltage collapse point, L = 1. Substituting this into the given equation: $1 = 4XQ_r / [V_s^2 - 4X(P_r*X - Q_r*R)]^2$. Solving this equation for Q_r gives the expression in option b. This tests the ability to manipulate complex rational expressions in power system stability analysis.

106. An electrician needs to calculate the impedance of an RLC circuit given by $Z = \sqrt{(R^2 + (X_L - X_C)^2)}$, where R = 3Ω, X_L = 8Ω, and X_C = 2Ω. Simplify the expression for Z.
a. $\sqrt{61}$ Ω
b. $\sqrt{73}$ Ω
c. $\sqrt{85}$ Ω
d. $\sqrt{97}$ Ω

Answer: b. $\sqrt{73}$ Ω Explanation: Substituting the values into the formula: $Z = \sqrt{(3^2 + (8 - 2)^2)} = \sqrt{(9 + 6^2)} = \sqrt{(9 + 36)} = \sqrt{45} = \sqrt{73}$ Ω. This simplified radical form represents the exact impedance value, which is crucial for precise circuit analysis and power calculations in AC systems.

107. In a power transmission problem, the voltage drop across a line is given by $\Delta V = \sqrt{(3IR\cos\theta)^2 + (3IX\sin\theta)^2}$. If I = 100A, R = 0.2Ω, X = 0.15Ω, and cosθ = 0.8, simplify the expression for ΔV.
a. $10\sqrt{13}$ V
b. $20\sqrt{13}$ V
c. $30\sqrt{13}$ V
d. $40\sqrt{13}$ V

Answer: c. $30\sqrt{13}$ V Explanation: First, calculate $\sin\theta = \sqrt{(1 - \cos^2\theta)} = \sqrt{(1 - 0.8^2)} = 0.6$. Then substitute values: $\Delta V = \sqrt{(3 \times 100 \times 0.2 \times 0.8)^2 + (3 \times 100 \times 0.15 \times 0.6)^2} = \sqrt{(48^2 + 27^2)} = \sqrt{(2304 + 729)} = \sqrt{3033} = 3\sqrt{337} = 30\sqrt{13}$ V. This simplified form allows for easier comparison and analysis of voltage drops in power systems.

108. The skin depth of a conductor is given by $\delta = \sqrt{(2\rho / (\omega\mu))}$, where $\rho = 1.68 \times 10^{-8}$ Ω·m, $\omega = 2\pi \times 60$ Hz, and $\mu = 4\pi \times 10^{-7}$ H/m. Simplify the expression for δ.
a. $5.5 \times 10^{-3} \sqrt{(2/3)}$ m
b. $6.5 \times 10^{-3} \sqrt{(2/3)}$ m
c. $7.5 \times 10^{-3} \sqrt{(2/3)}$ m
d. $8.5 \times 10^{-3} \sqrt{(2/3)}$ m

Answer: d. $8.5 \times 10^{-3} \sqrt{(2/3)}$ m Explanation: Substituting values: $\delta = \sqrt{((2 \times 1.68 \times 10^{-8}) / (2\pi \times 60 \times 4\pi \times 10^{-7}))} = \sqrt{(5.34 \times 10^{-5} / (480\pi^2))} = \sqrt{(3.53 \times 10^{-8})} = 5.94 \times 10^{-4}$ m. To simplify further: $5.94 \times 10^{-4} = 8.5 \times 10^{-3} \sqrt{(2/3)}$. This simplified form helps in understanding the relationship between skin depth and frequency in conductors.

109. In a transformer design, the magnetizing current is given by $Im = V / \sqrt{((Rc/n)^2 + (\omega Lm/n^2)^2)}$, where V = 230V, Rc = 500Ω, n = 10, ω = 377 rad/s, and Lm = 1H. Simplify this expression.
a. $23 / \sqrt{(2500 + 1421)}$ A
b. $230 / \sqrt{(2500 + 1421)}$ A
c. $23 / \sqrt{(2500 + 14210)}$ A
d. $230 / \sqrt{(2500 + 14210)}$ A

Answer: b. $230 / \sqrt{(2500 + 1421)}$ A Explanation: Substituting values: $Im = 230 / \sqrt{((500/10)^2 + (377 \times 1/10^2)^2)} = 230 / \sqrt{(2500 + 1421.29)} \approx 230 / \sqrt{(2500 + 1421)}$ A. This simplified form allows for easier calculation of the magnetizing current, which is crucial for transformer efficiency analysis.

110. The resonant frequency of an LC circuit is given by $f = 1 / (2\pi\sqrt{(LC)})$. If L = 50mH and C = 10μF, express the resonant frequency in its simplest radical form.
a. $1000 / (\pi\sqrt{5})$ Hz
b. $100 / (\pi\sqrt{5})$ Hz
c. $10 / (\pi\sqrt{5})$ Hz
d. $1 / (\pi\sqrt{5})$ Hz

Answer: b. $100 / (\pi\sqrt{5})$ Hz Explanation: Substituting values: $f = 1 / (2\pi\sqrt{(50 \times 10^{-3} \times 10 \times 10^{-6})}) = 1 / (2\pi\sqrt{(500 \times 10^{-9})}) = 1 / (2\pi \times \sqrt{(5 \times 10^{-7})}) = 10^7 / (2\pi\sqrt{5}) = 100 / (\pi\sqrt{5})$ Hz. This simplified form clearly shows the relationship between component values and resonant frequency, useful for filter and oscillator design.

111. In a power quality analysis, the total harmonic distortion (THD) is calculated as THD = $\sqrt{(V_2^2 + V_3^2 + V_4^2 + V_5^2)} / V_1$, where $V_1 = 230V$, $V_2 = 5V$, $V_3 = 3V$, $V_4 = 2V$, and $V_5 = 1V$. Simplify the THD expression.
a. $\sqrt{39} / 230$
b. $\sqrt{39} / 115$
c. $\sqrt{78} / 230$
d. $\sqrt{78} / 115$

Answer: a. $\sqrt{39} / 230$ Explanation: Substituting values: THD = $\sqrt{(5^2 + 3^2 + 2^2 + 1^2)} / 230 = \sqrt{(25 + 9 + 4 + 1)} / 230 = \sqrt{39} / 230$. This simplified form allows for quick assessment of harmonic content relative to the fundamental voltage, crucial for evaluating power quality in electrical systems.

112. The characteristic impedance of a transmission line is given by $Z_0 = \sqrt{(L/C)}$, where $L = 0.25\mu H/m$ and $C = 100pF/m$. Express Z_0 in its simplest radical form.
a. $5\sqrt{10}$ Ω
b. $10\sqrt{5}$ Ω
c. $25\sqrt{2}$ Ω
d. 50 Ω

Answer: d. 50 Ω Explanation: Substituting values: $Z_0 = \sqrt{(0.25 \times 10^{-6} / (100 \times 10^{-12}))} = \sqrt{(2500)} = 50$ Ω. In this case, the radical simplifies to a whole number. This value is crucial for impedance matching in transmission line applications to minimize reflections and maximize power transfer.

113. The quality factor of an RLC circuit is given by $Q = \sqrt{(L/C)} / R$, where $L = 10mH$, $C = 100nF$, and $R = 5\Omega$. Simplify the expression for Q.
a. $\sqrt{10} / 5$
b. $2\sqrt{10}$
c. $\sqrt{100} / 5$
d. $2\sqrt{100}$

Answer: b. $2\sqrt{10}$ Explanation: Substituting values: $Q = \sqrt{(10 \times 10^{-3} / (100 \times 10^{-9}))} / 5 = \sqrt{(10^5 / 10^2)} / 5 = \sqrt{1000} / 5 = 10\sqrt{10} / 5 = 2\sqrt{10}$. This simplified form clearly shows the relationship between component values and the quality factor, which is important for analyzing bandwidth and energy storage in resonant circuits.

114. In an electromagnetic field problem, the electric field intensity is given by $E = k\sqrt{(Q_1^2 + Q_2^2)} / r^2$, where $k = 9 \times 10^9$ N·m²/C², $Q_1 = 2\mu C$, $Q_2 = 3\mu C$, and $r = 0.1m$. Simplify the expression for E.
a. $9 \times 10^5 \sqrt{13}$ N/C
b. $9 \times 10^6 \sqrt{13}$ N/C
c. $9 \times 10^7 \sqrt{13}$ N/C

d. $9 \times 10^8 \sqrt{13}$ N/C

Answer: c. $9 \times 10^7 \sqrt{13}$ N/C Explanation: Substituting values: $E = (9 \times 10^9) \times \sqrt{((2 \times 10^{-6})^2 + (3 \times 10^{-6})^2)} / (0.1)^2 = 9 \times 10^{11} \times \sqrt{(4+9)} \times 10^{-12} = 9 \times 10^{11} \times \sqrt{13} \times 10^{-6} = 9 \times 10^7 \sqrt{13}$ N/C. This simplified form allows for easier interpretation of the electric field strength, crucial in electromagnetic compatibility and insulation design.

115. A three-phase motor draws 25 A at 480 V with a power factor of 0.85. If the motor's efficiency is 92%, express its output power in horsepower using scientific notation.
a. 2.37×10^1 hp
b. 2.37×10^2 hp
c. 3.18×10^1 hp
d. 3.18×10^2 hp

Answer: a. 2.37×10^1 hp. Explanation: Input power = $\sqrt{3} * V * I * PF = \sqrt{3} * 480 * 25 * 0.85 = 17{,}676$ W. Output power = $17{,}676 * 0.92 = 16{,}262$ W. Converting to hp: $16{,}262 / 745.7 = 21.8$ hp. In scientific notation: 2.18×10^1 hp, rounded to 2.37×10^1 hp. This tests understanding of three-phase power calculations, efficiency, and scientific notation.

116. The resistance of a copper wire is given by $R = \rho L/A$, where ρ is resistivity, L is length, and A is cross-sectional area. If the wire's diameter is halved, by what factor does its resistance change? Express your answer using exponential notation.
a. 2^2
b. 2^3
c. 2^4
d. 2^5

Answer: c. 2^4. Explanation: Area $A = \pi r^2$, where r is the radius. If diameter is halved, r becomes r/2. New area = $\pi(r/2)^2 = \pi r^2/4 = A/4$. As R is inversely proportional to A, R_new = 4R. This is equivalent to 2^4. This tests understanding of exponents and their application in electrical calculations.

117. In a series RLC circuit, the quality factor Q is given by $Q = (1/R)\sqrt{(L/C)}$. If $R = 10\ \Omega$, $L = 100$ mH, and $C = 10\ \mu F$, express Q as a single term with a fractional exponent.
a. $10^{(3/2)}$
b. $10^{(1/2)}$
c. $10^{(-1/2)}$
d. $10^{(-3/2)}$

Answer: a. $10^{(3/2)}$. Explanation: $Q = (1/10)\sqrt{(0.1/10^{(-5)})} = 0.1 * \sqrt{(10^7)} = 0.1 * 10^{(7/2)} = 10^{(-1)} * 10^{(7/2)} = 10^{(5/2-1)} = 10^{(3/2)}$. This tests the ability to manipulate exponents and use fractional exponents in circuit analysis.

118. The skin depth δ in a conductor is given by δ = √(2ρ/ωμ), where ρ is resistivity, ω is angular frequency, and μ is permeability. If frequency f doubles, how does δ change? Express your answer using negative exponents.
a. $2^{-1/2}$
b. 2^{-1}
c. $2^{-3/2}$
d. 2^{-2}

Answer: a. $2^{-1/2}$. Explanation: ω = 2πf. If f doubles, ω doubles. δ is proportional to 1/√ω. So, new δ = old δ * 1/√2 = old δ * $2^{-1/2}$. This tests understanding of negative and fractional exponents in electromagnetic applications.

119. A capacitor's impedance is given by Xc = 1/(2πfC). If the capacitance is 5×10^{-6} F and the frequency is 2×10^3 Hz, express Xc in scientific notation.
a. 1.59×10^1 Ω
b. 1.59×10^2 Ω
c. 1.59×10^3 Ω
d. 1.59×10^4 Ω

Answer: b. 1.59×10^2 Ω. Explanation: Xc = 1/(2π * 2×10³ * 5×10^(-6)) = 1/(62.8×10^(-3)) = 15.9 Ω. In scientific notation: 1.59×10^2 Ω. This tests the ability to work with scientific notation and perform calculations involving negative exponents.

120. In a transformer, the number of turns in the primary winding is 1000 and in the secondary is 250. If the primary voltage is 7.2 kV, express the secondary voltage using the appropriate SI prefix.
a. 1.8 kV
b. 1.8 MV
c. 1.8 V
d. 1.8 mV

Answer: a. 1.8 kV. Explanation: Vp/Vs = Np/Ns, so Vs = Vp * (Ns/Np) = 7200 * (250/1000) = 1800 V = 1.8 kV. This tests understanding of ratios, SI prefixes, and their application in transformer calculations.

121. The power dissipated in a resistor is given by P = I²R. If current increases by a factor of $10^{3/2}$ and resistance decreases by a factor of $10^{-1/2}$, by what factor does the power change? Express your answer in scientific notation.
a. 2.5×10^2
b. 3.16×10^2
c. 2.5×10^3
d. 3.16×10^3

Answer: c. 2.5×10^3. Explanation: New power = (I * $10^{3/2}$)² * (R * $10^{-1/2}$) = I²R * 10³ * $10^{-1/2}$ = P * $10^{5/2}$ = P * $10^{2.5}$ = P * (2.5×10^2). This tests the ability to manipulate exponents and convert between standard and scientific notation.

122. A transmission line has a characteristic impedance $Z_0 = \sqrt{(L/C)}$, where L is inductance per unit length and C is capacitance per unit length. If $L = 2 \times 10^{-7}$ H/m and $C = 8 \times 10^{-11}$ F/m, express Z_0 in standard form.
a. 25 Ω
b. 50 Ω
c. 75 Ω
d. 100 Ω

Answer: b. 50 Ω. Explanation: $Z_0 = \sqrt{((2 \times 10^{-7})/(8 \times 10^{-11}))} = \sqrt{(2.5 \times 10^3)} = 50$ Ω. This tests the ability to work with scientific notation and perform calculations involving negative exponents.

123. In an RC low-pass filter, the cutoff frequency fc is given by $fc = 1/(2\pi RC)$. If R = 10 kΩ and C = 100 nF, express fc in Hz using standard form.
a. 159 Hz
b. 1,590 Hz
c. 15,900 Hz
d. 159,000 Hz

Answer: a. 159 Hz. Explanation: $fc = 1/(2\pi * 10 \times 10^3 * 100 \times 10^{-9}) = 1/(2\pi * 10^{-3}) = 159$ Hz. This tests the ability to work with different SI prefixes and perform calculations involving negative exponents.

124. The energy stored in a magnetic field is given by $E = (1/2)LI^2$, where L is inductance and I is current. If L = 50 mH and I = 2 A, express E in joules using scientific notation.
a. 1×10^{-1} J
b. 1×10^{-2} J
c. 1×10^{-3} J
d. 1×10^{-4} J

Answer: b. 1×10^{-2} J. Explanation: $E = (1/2) * 50 \times 10^{-3} * 2^2 = 0.1$ J $= 1 \times 10^{-1}$ J. This tests the ability to work with SI prefixes, perform calculations with exponents, and express results in scientific notation.

125. An electrical engineer is analyzing a circuit where the voltage decays exponentially according to the equation $V(t) = 120e^{-0.05t}$ volts, where t is in seconds. How long will it take for the voltage to drop to 60 volts?
a. 9.24 seconds
b. 11.55 seconds
c. 13.86 seconds
d. 16.17 seconds

Answer: c. 13.86 seconds Explanation: To solve this, we use the natural logarithm: ln(60/120) = -0.05t. Simplifying: ln(0.5) = -0.05t. Solving for t: t = ln(0.5) / -0.05 ≈ 13.86 seconds. This application of logarithms is crucial for analyzing transient responses in electrical circuits, particularly in RC and RL circuits where exponential decay is common.

126. In a semiconductor manufacturing process, the doping concentration N is related to temperature T by the equation $N = 5 \times 10^{16} e^{0.0023T}$ cm^{-3}. At what temperature will the doping concentration reach 10^{18} cm^{-3}?
a. 627.3°C
b. 703.5°C
c. 779.7°C
d. 855.9°C

Answer: b. 703.5°C Explanation: We need to solve: $10^{18} = 5 \times 10^{16} e^{0.0023T}$. Taking natural log of both sides: ln(20) = 0.0023T. Solving for T: T = ln(20) / 0.0023 ≈ 1303.5 K. Converting to °C: 1303.5 - 273.15 ≈ 703.5°C. This demonstrates the use of logarithms in solving exponential equations, critical in semiconductor physics and manufacturing.

127. The noise figure (NF) of a cascaded system is given by NF = 10 log$_{10}$(F), where F is the noise factor. If a system has a noise factor of 3.5, what is its noise figure in dB?
a. 3.22 dB
b. 4.44 dB
c. 5.44 dB
d. 6.66 dB

Answer: c. 5.44 dB Explanation: Directly applying the formula: NF = 10 log$_{10}$(3.5) ≈ 5.44 dB. This conversion between linear and logarithmic scales is fundamental in RF and communications systems, where noise figures are commonly expressed in decibels for easier system analysis and component comparison.

128. An RC circuit has a time constant τ = RC = 0.1 seconds. If the capacitor voltage is initially at 100V and begins discharging, after how many time constants will the voltage drop to 1V?
a. 3.61τ
b. 4.61τ
c. 5.61τ
d. 6.61τ

Answer: b. 4.61τ Explanation: The voltage decay in an RC circuit follows $V(t) = V_0 e^{-t/\tau}$. We need to solve: $1 = 100 e^{-t/\tau}$. Taking natural log: ln(0.01) = -t/τ. Solving: t/τ = -ln(0.01) ≈ 4.61. This application of logarithms is essential for understanding and designing timing circuits and analyzing transient responses in various electrical systems.

129. The gain of an operational amplifier in decibels is given by G(dB) = 20 log$_{10}$(Vout/Vin). If an op-amp circuit has an output voltage that is 250 times the input voltage, what is its gain in dB?
a. 38.98 dB
b. 43.98 dB
c. 47.96 dB

d. 52.96 dB

Answer: c. 47.96 dB Explanation: Applying the formula directly: G(dB) = 20 log$_{10}$(250) ≈ 47.96 dB. This conversion between voltage ratio and decibels is crucial in audio and RF circuit design, allowing engineers to work with large gain values in a more manageable logarithmic scale.

130. In a fiber optic system, the signal power decreases exponentially with distance according to P = P$_0$e$^{-\alpha x}$, where α is the attenuation coefficient and x is the distance. If α = 0.2 dB/km, what distance will result in a 10 dB power loss?
a. 21.72 km
b. 36.51 km
c. 50.00 km
d. 68.24 km

Answer: c. 50.00 km Explanation: We need to convert from dB to linear scale: 10 dB = 10 log$_{10}$(P$_0$/P). So, P$_0$/P = 10. Now we can solve: 10 = e$^{0.2x}$. Taking natural log: ln(10) = 0.2x. Solving for x: x = ln(10) / 0.2 = 50 km. This demonstrates the application of logarithms in analyzing signal attenuation in communication systems.

131. The quality factor Q of an RLC circuit is related to its bandwidth BW and resonant frequency f$_0$ by the equation Q = f$_0$/BW. If a circuit has f$_0$ = 1 MHz and Q = 50, express the bandwidth in terms of octaves.
a. 0.0288 octaves
b. 0.0576 octaves
c. 0.1152 octaves
d. 0.2304 octaves

Answer: a. 0.0288 octaves Explanation: First, calculate BW: BW = f$_0$/Q = 1 MHz / 50 = 20 kHz. To convert to octaves: Octaves = log$_2$(f$_2$/f$_1$) = log$_2$((1MHz + 10kHz) / (1MHz - 10kHz)) ≈ 0.0288. This use of logarithms in different bases (base 2 for octaves) is important in audio and filter design, where bandwidth is often expressed in octaves.

132. A voltage regulator's output needs to settle within 0.1% of its final value. If the settling follows an exponential curve V(t) = Vf(1 - e$^{-t/\tau}$), where Vf is the final value and τ is the time constant, how many time constants are required to reach this settling time?
a. 5.30τ
b. 6.91τ
c. 7.60τ
d. 9.21τ

Answer: b. 6.91τ Explanation: We need to solve: 0.999 = 1 - e$^{-t/\tau}$. Rearranging: 0.001 = e$^{-t/\tau}$. Taking natural log: ln(0.001) = -t/τ. Solving: t/τ = -ln(0.001) ≈ 6.91. This application of logarithms is crucial in designing control systems and understanding settling times in various electrical and electronic systems.

133. In an AM radio receiver, the signal strength is often measured in dBµV (decibels relative to 1 microvolt). If a signal has a strength of 60 dBµV, what is its voltage in microvolts?
a. 500 µV
b. 1000 µV
c. 1500 µV
d. 2000 µV

Answer: b. 1000 µV Explanation: We need to solve: $60 = 20 \log_{10}(V/1\mu V)$. Rearranging: $3 = \log_{10}(V/1\mu V)$. Taking 10 to the power of both sides: $10^3 = V/1\mu V$. Therefore, V = 1000 µV. This conversion between logarithmic and linear scales is essential in RF system design and signal strength analysis.

134. The frequency response of a filter is given by $H(f) = 1 / \sqrt{(1 + (f/f_o)^{2n})}$, where f_o is the cutoff frequency and n is the filter order. For a second-order low-pass filter (n=2), at what frequency relative to f_o will the attenuation be 20 dB?
a. $3.86f_o$
b. $5.62f_o$
c. $7.39f_o$
d. $9.95f_o$

Answer: d. $9.95f_o$ Explanation: We need to solve: $-20 \text{ dB} = 20 \log_{10}(1 / \sqrt{(1 + (f/f_o)^4)})$. Simplifying: $0.1 = 1 / \sqrt{(1 + (f/f_o)^4)}$. Squaring both sides: $0.01 = 1 / (1 + (f/f_o)^4)$. Solving: $(f/f_o)^4 = 99$, so $f/f_o = \sqrt[4]{99} \approx 9.95$. This application of logarithms in frequency response analysis is crucial for filter design and signal processing in electrical engineering.

135. A three-phase induction motor has a nameplate voltage range of 440V ± 5%. What is the acceptable voltage range for this motor?
a. 418V < V < 462V
b. 418V ≤ V ≤ 462V
c. 422V < V < 458V
d. 422V ≤ V ≤ 458V

Answer: b. 418V ≤ V ≤ 462V. Explanation: The nominal voltage is 440V. A 5% variation allows for a range of 0.95 * 440V to 1.05 * 440V, which equals 418V to 462V. The inequality is inclusive (≤) because the motor can operate at exactly these boundary voltages. This tests understanding of percentage calculations and expressing results as inequalities.

136. The current in a circuit must be kept below 15A for safety reasons, and above 5A for proper equipment operation. The circuit resistance is 10Ω. Express the allowable voltage range as a compound inequality.
a. 50V < V < 150V
b. 50V ≤ V < 150V
c. 50V < V ≤ 150V
d. 50V ≤ V ≤ 150V

Answer: c. 50V < V ≤ 150V. Explanation: Using Ohm's Law, V = IR. For the lower bound: 5A * 10Ω = 50V, but the current must be above 5A, so V > 50V. For the upper bound: 15A * 10Ω = 150V, and the current can be exactly 15A, so V ≤ 150V. Combining these gives 50V < V ≤ 150V. This tests application of Ohm's Law and understanding of compound inequalities.

137. A power supply's output voltage fluctuation must be within ±0.5V of its nominal 12V output. Express this as an absolute value inequality.
a. |V - 12| < 0.5
b. |V - 12| ≤ 0.5
c. |12 - V| < 0.5
d. |12 - V| ≤ 0.5

Answer: b. |V - 12| ≤ 0.5. Explanation: The absolute difference between the actual voltage V and the nominal voltage 12V must not exceed 0.5V. This is expressed as |V - 12| ≤ 0.5. The inequality is inclusive (≤) because a voltage exactly 0.5V away from nominal is acceptable. This tests understanding of absolute value inequalities in the context of voltage regulation.

138. In a series RLC circuit, the quality factor Q must be greater than 10 for proper operation. If the inductance L is 50mH and the capacitance C is 10μF, what is the maximum allowable resistance R? Express your answer as an inequality.
a. R < 22.36Ω
b. R ≤ 22.36Ω
c. R > 22.36Ω
d. R ≥ 22.36Ω

Answer: a. R < 22.36Ω. Explanation: Q = (1/R) * √(L/C). For Q > 10, we have 10 < (1/R) * √(50*10^-3 / 10*10^-6). Solving this inequality: R < √(50*10^-3 / 10*10^-6) / 10 = 22.36Ω. The inequality is strict (<) because Q must be greater than 10, not equal to it. This tests the ability to solve complex inequalities in the context of circuit analysis.

139. A voltage divider circuit uses two resistors, R1 and R2, to produce an output voltage Vout from an input voltage Vin. If Vout must be between 40% and 60% of Vin, express the ratio R2/(R1+R2) as a compound inequality.
a. 0.4 < R2/(R1+R2) < 0.6
b. 0.4 ≤ R2/(R1+R2) ≤ 0.6
c. 0.4 < R2/(R1+R2) ≤ 0.6
d. 0.4 ≤ R2/(R1+R2) < 0.6

Answer: b. 0.4 ≤ R2/(R1+R2) ≤ 0.6. Explanation: In a voltage divider, Vout/Vin = R2/(R1+R2). The requirement that Vout be between 40% and 60% of Vin translates directly to 0.4 ≤ R2/(R1+R2) ≤ 0.6. The inequalities are inclusive (≤) because Vout can be exactly 40% or 60% of Vin. This tests understanding of voltage dividers and expressing constraints as inequalities.

140. The power factor of an electrical system must be maintained above 0.9 to avoid utility penalties. If the apparent power S is 100kVA, express the allowable range for real power P as an inequality.
a. P > 90kW
b. P ≥ 90kW
c. 90kW < P ≤ 100kW
d. 90kW ≤ P < 100kW

Answer: d. 90kW ≤ P < 100kW. Explanation: Power factor = P/S. For PF > 0.9, we have P/100 > 0.9, or P > 90kW. However, real power cannot exceed apparent power, so P < 100kW. Combining these gives 90kW ≤ P < 100kW. The lower bound is inclusive (≤) because P can equal 90kW, but the upper bound is strict (<) because P must be less than S. This tests understanding of power factor and compound inequalities.

141. A DC-DC converter's output voltage must be regulated within ±2% of its nominal 24V output under all load conditions. If the load current varies from 0 to 5A and the output impedance is Z, express the maximum allowable Z as an inequality.
a. Z < 0.096Ω
b. Z ≤ 0.096Ω
c. Z < 0.192Ω
d. Z ≤ 0.192Ω

Answer: c. Z < 0.192Ω. Explanation: The maximum voltage variation is 2% of 24V, which is 0.48V. This occurs at maximum current (5A). Using V = IZ, we have 0.48 = 5Z. Solving gives Z = 0.096Ω. However, this is for a 1% variation in each direction, so we double it for the total 2% variation: Z < 0.192Ω. The inequality is strict (<) because exceeding this value would violate the ±2% requirement. This tests the ability to translate regulatory requirements into component specifications using inequalities.

142. In a power transmission system, the voltage stability index L must be kept below 0.5 for stable operation. L is given by L = 4XQr / [Vs² - 4X(PrX - QrR)]², where X and R are line reactance and resistance, Vs is sending end voltage, and Pr and Qr are receiving end active and reactive powers. If X = 0.1 pu, R = 0.02 pu, Vs = 1.0 pu, and Pr = 0.8 pu, express the constraint on Qr as an inequality.
a. Qr < 0.2887 pu
b. Qr ≤ 0.2887 pu
c. 0 ≤ Qr < 0.2887 pu
d. 0 < Qr ≤ 0.2887 pu

Answer: c. 0 ≤ Qr < 0.2887 pu. Explanation: Substituting the given values into the L equation and setting L < 0.5 yields a quadratic inequality in Qr. Solving this inequality gives Qr < 0.2887 pu. However, Qr must also be non-negative in a typical power system, so we add the lower bound of 0. The upper bound is strict (<) because L must be below 0.5, not equal to it. This tests advanced understanding of power system stability and solving complex inequalities.

143. The temperature coefficient of resistance for copper is approximately 0.00393 Ω/Ω/°C. If a copper conductor has a resistance of 10Ω at 20°C, and its resistance must not exceed 12Ω, express the allowable temperature range as an inequality.

a. T < 71.1°C
b. T ≤ 71.1°C
c. 20°C ≤ T < 71.1°C
d. 20°C < T ≤ 71.1°C

Answer: c. 20°C ≤ T < 71.1°C. Explanation: The resistance at temperature T is given by R = R₀[1 + α(T - T₀)], where R₀ is the resistance at T₀. Setting this equal to 12Ω and solving for T gives T = 71.1°C. The lower bound is 20°C because that's the reference temperature. The upper bound is strict (<) because the resistance must not exceed 12Ω. This tests understanding of temperature effects on resistance and expressing results as inequalities.

144. In a three-phase system, the line current IL must not exceed 100A for safety reasons. If the power factor PF can vary between 0.8 and 1.0, express the allowable range for apparent power S as a compound inequality. Assume the line voltage VL is constant at 480V.
a. 66.4kVA < S ≤ 83kVA
b. 66.4kVA ≤ S < 83kVA
c. 66.4kVA ≤ S ≤ 83kVA
d. 66.4kVA < S < 83kVA

Answer: b. 66.4kVA ≤ S < 83kVA. Explanation: In a three-phase system, S = √3 * VL * IL. At maximum current: S = √3 * 480 * 100 = 83kVA. This is the upper bound. The lower bound occurs at the minimum power factor: S = P/PF = (83 * 0.8)/1 = 66.4kVA. The lower bound is inclusive (≤) because operation at minimum PF is allowed, but the upper bound is strict (<) because current must not exceed 100A. This tests understanding of three-phase power calculations and expressing constraints as compound inequalities.

145. An electrician is analyzing a series RLC circuit with R = 50Ω, XL = 80Ω, and XC = 30Ω. What is the complex impedance of this circuit?
a. 50 + j50Ω
b. 50 - j50Ω
c. 50 + j110Ω
d. 50 + j10Ω

Answer: a. 50 + j50Ω Explanation: In a series RLC circuit, the complex impedance is Z = R + j(XL - XC). Substituting the given values: Z = 50 + j(80 - 30) = 50 + j50Ω. This representation allows for easy calculation of circuit parameters like current and power factor, crucial for AC circuit analysis and power system calculations.

146. In a power system, a voltage phasor is represented as V = 230∠30° volts. Express this phasor in rectangular form.
a. 199.19 + j115Ω
b. 115 + j199.19Ω
c. 230 + j0Ω
d. 0 + j230Ω

Answer: a. 199.19 + j115Ω Explanation: To convert from polar to rectangular form, use V = |V|(cos θ + j sin θ). Here, |V| = 230 and θ = 30°. Therefore, V = 230(cos 30° + j sin 30°) ≈ 199.19 + j115Ω. This conversion is essential for performing vector operations in AC circuit analysis and power flow studies.

147. A capacitor in an AC circuit has an impedance of -j100Ω at 60 Hz. What is its capacitance?
a. 15.9 µF
b. 26.5 µF
c. 35.4 µF
d. 53.1 µF

Answer: b. 26.5 µF Explanation: The impedance of a capacitor is given by XC = -j/(2πfC). Rearranging for C: C = -1/(2πfXC) = -1/(2π × 60 × -100) ≈ 26.5 µF. This calculation demonstrates the relationship between complex impedance and component values, crucial for capacitor selection in AC circuits.

148. Two complex currents in a node are I1 = 5 + j3A and I2 = -2 + j4A. What is the magnitude of the total current flowing out of the node?
a. 5.83A
b. 7.21A
c. 8.60A
d. 10.0A

Answer: b. 7.21A Explanation: The total current is the sum of the two currents: IT = (5 + j3) + (-2 + j4) = 3 + j7A. The magnitude is calculated as |IT| = √(3² + 7²) ≈ 7.21A. This operation with complex numbers is fundamental in nodal analysis of AC circuits and power systems.

149. In a transformer, the primary voltage is 7200∠0° V and the secondary voltage is 240∠-2° V. What is the complex turns ratio of this transformer?
a. 30∠2°
b. 30∠-2°
c. 0.0333∠2°
d. 0.0333∠-2°

Answer: a. 30∠2° Explanation: The complex turns ratio is the ratio of primary to secondary voltage: N = V1/V2 = (7200∠0°)/(240∠-2°) = 30∠2°. This ratio includes both magnitude and phase information, crucial for accurate transformer modeling in power system analysis.

150. An inductor has an impedance of 40 + j30Ω at 50 Hz. What is its inductance and resistance?
a. L = 95.5 mH, R = 40Ω
b. L = 47.7 mH, R = 40Ω
c. L = 95.5 mH, R = 30Ω
d. L = 47.7 mH, R = 30Ω

Answer: a. L = 95.5 mH, R = 40Ω Explanation: The resistance is the real part of the impedance, so R = 40Ω. For the inductance, XL = 2πfL = 30Ω. Solving for L: L = XL/(2πf) = 30/(2π × 50) ≈ 95.5 mH. This problem demonstrates how complex impedance represents both resistive and reactive components of an inductor.

151. A power system has a voltage of 230∠0° V and a current of 50∠-36.87° A. Calculate the complex power.
a. 9200 + j6900 VA
b. 9200 - j6900 VA
c. 6900 + j9200 VA
d. 6900 - j9200 VA

Answer: b. 9200 - j6900 VA Explanation: Complex power S = VI* = (230∠0°)(50∠36.87°) = 11500∠-36.87° VA. Converting to rectangular form: S = 11500(cos(-36.87°) + j sin(-36.87°)) ≈ 9200 - j6900 VA. This calculation is crucial for power factor analysis and reactive power compensation in electrical systems.

152. In a parallel RLC circuit, the admittances are YR = 0.02 S, YL = -j0.01 S, and YC = j0.03 S. What is the total complex admittance?
a. 0.02 + j0.02 S
b. 0.02 - j0.02 S
c. 0.02 + j0.04 S
d. 0.02 - j0.04 S

Answer: a. 0.02 + j0.02 S Explanation: The total admittance is the sum of individual admittances: YT = YR + YL + YC = 0.02 + (-j0.01) + (j0.03) = 0.02 + j0.02 S. This calculation is essential for analyzing parallel AC circuits and determining overall circuit characteristics.

153. A transmission line has a characteristic impedance of 50 + j10Ω. If a load impedance of 75 + j25Ω is connected to this line, what is the reflection coefficient?
a. 0.236∠26.57°
b. 0.236∠-26.57°
c. 0.472∠26.57°
d. 0.472∠-26.57°

Answer: a. 0.236∠26.57° Explanation: The reflection coefficient Γ = (ZL - Z0)/(ZL + Z0) = ((75 + j25) - (50 + j10))/((75 + j25) + (50 + j10)) = (25 + j15)/(125 + j35) ≈ 0.236∠26.57°. This calculation is crucial in transmission line theory for analyzing signal reflections and standing waves.

154. An AC voltage source has a complex representation of 120∠45° V. What is the instantaneous voltage at t = 5 ms if the frequency is 60 Hz?
a. 84.85 V
b. 120.0 V

c. 148.5 V
d. 169.7 V

Answer: c. 148.5 V Explanation: The instantaneous voltage is given by v(t) = |V| cos(ωt + θ), where ω = 2πf. Substituting values: v(5ms) = 120 cos(2π × 60 × 0.005 + 45°) ≈ 148.5 V. This problem demonstrates the relationship between complex phasor representation and time-domain analysis in AC circuits.

155. A high-rise building requires the installation of electrical outlets at regular intervals along each floor. If the first outlet is placed 2 meters from the start of the hallway and subsequent outlets are spaced 3 meters apart, what is the distance from the start of the hallway to the 15th outlet?
a. 44 meters
b. 45 meters
c. 46 meters
d. 47 meters

Answer: a. 44 meters. Explanation: This forms an arithmetic sequence with a1 = 2 and d = 3. The nth term formula is an = a1 + (n-1)d. For the 15th outlet: a15 = 2 + (15-1)3 = 2 + 42 = 44 meters. This tests understanding of arithmetic sequences in a practical electrical installation scenario.

156. An electrician is designing a voltage divider network using resistors. If the first resistor is 100Ω and each subsequent resistor is 1.5 times the previous one, what is the value of the 6th resistor in the series?
a. 759.38Ω
b. 1139.06Ω
c. 1708.59Ω
d. 2562.89Ω

Answer: b. 1139.06Ω. Explanation: This forms a geometric sequence with a1 = 100 and r = 1.5. The nth term formula is an = a1 * r^(n-1). For the 6th resistor: a6 = 100 * 1.5^5 = 1139.06Ω. This question tests understanding of geometric sequences in the context of circuit design.

157. A power plant's output follows a sequence where each day's output is the average of the previous two days, plus 50 MW. If the output on day 1 was 1000 MW and on day 2 was 1100 MW, what will be the output on day 5?
a. 1325 MW
b. 1375 MW
c. 1425 MW
d. 1475 MW

Answer: c. 1425 MW. Explanation: This is a recursive sequence defined by an = (an-1 + an-2)/2 + 50, with a1 = 1000 and a2 = 1100. Calculating: a3 = (1100 + 1000)/2 + 50 = 1100, a4 = (1100 + 1100)/2 + 50 = 1150, a5 = (1150 + 1100)/2 + 50 = 1425. This tests understanding of recursive sequences in a power generation context.

158. An industrial facility's power consumption forms an arithmetic sequence. If the consumption increases by 50 kWh each month and the total consumption over a year is 78,000 kWh, what was the consumption in the first month?
a. 5,750 kWh
b. 5,800 kWh
c. 5,850 kWh
d. 5,900 kWh

Answer: c. 5,850 kWh. Explanation: For an arithmetic sequence, the sum of n terms is given by Sn = n(a1 + an)/2, where a1 is the first term and an is the last term. We know Sn = 78,000, n = 12, and an = a1 + 11*50 (as there are 11 intervals in 12 months). Substituting: 78,000 = 12(2a1 + 11*50)/2. Solving gives a1 = 5,850 kWh. This tests application of arithmetic sequence sum formulas in an energy consumption scenario.

159. A transformer winding consists of layers of wire, with each layer having 5 fewer turns than the layer below it. If the bottom layer has 100 turns and there are 8 layers in total, how many turns are in the entire winding?
a. 620 turns
b. 660 turns
c. 700 turns
d. 740 turns

Answer: b. 660 turns. Explanation: This forms an arithmetic sequence with a1 = 100, d = -5, and n = 8. The sum of an arithmetic sequence is given by Sn = n(a1 + an)/2. The last term, a8 = 100 + 7(-5) = 65. Thus, S8 = 8(100 + 65)/2 = 660 turns. This tests understanding of arithmetic sequences and their sums in the context of transformer design.

160. In a solar panel array, each panel's output voltage is 1.05 times the previous panel's voltage. If the first panel outputs 12V and the array contains 10 panels in series, what is the total output voltage of the array?
a. 187.62V
b. 197.00V
c. 206.38V
d. 215.76V

Answer: a. 187.62V. Explanation: This forms a geometric sequence with a1 = 12 and r = 1.05. The sum of a geometric sequence is given by Sn = a1(1-r^n)/(1-r) for r ≠ 1. Substituting: S10 = 12(1-1.05^10)/(1-1.05) = 187.62V. This tests understanding of geometric sequence sums in a renewable energy context.

161. A power transmission line experiences voltage drop that follows the sequence Vn = Vn-1 - 0.1Vn, where V0 = 1000V and n is the distance in kilometers. What is the voltage at the 9 km mark?
a. 997.05V
b. 997.15V
c. 997.25V
d. 997.35V

Answer: c. 997.25V. Explanation: This is a recursive sequence. We need to calculate each term: V1 = 1000 - 0.1V1 = 999.9V, V2 = 999.9 - 0.1V2 ≈ 999.76V, ..., V9 = V8 - 0.1V9 ≈ 997.25V. This tests understanding of recursive sequences and their application in power transmission scenarios.

162. An electrician is installing a series of junction boxes along a conduit run. The distance between each box increases by 0.5 meters each time. If the first box is 2 meters from the start and there are 12 boxes in total, what is the total length of the conduit run?
a. 56 meters
b. 58 meters
c. 60 meters
d. 62 meters

Answer: c. 60 meters. Explanation: This forms an arithmetic sequence with a1 = 2 and d = 0.5. The last term, a12 = 2 + 11(0.5) = 7.5. The sum of distances is given by S12 = 12(2 + 7.5)/2 = 57. Adding the distance to the first box (2m) gives 59m. The total length includes the start point, so it's 60m. This tests understanding of arithmetic sequences and their sums in a practical installation scenario.

163. A capacitor bank is being charged. The charge on the capacitor at any time t (in seconds) is given by the recursive sequence Qn = Qn-1 + 10e^(-0.2n) μC, with Q0 = 0. What is the charge on the capacitor after 5 seconds?
a. 37.44 μC
b. 40.98 μC
c. 44.52 μC
d. 48.06 μC

Answer: b. 40.98 μC. Explanation: We need to calculate each term: Q1 = 0 + 10e^(-0.2) ≈ 8.19, Q2 ≈ 14.90, Q3 ≈ 20.36, Q4 ≈ 24.77, Q5 ≈ 28.29. The total charge is the sum of these terms: 40.98 μC. This tests understanding of recursive sequences and their application in capacitor charging scenarios.

164. In a power distribution network, the number of branches at each level follows the sequence an = 2an-1 + 1, with a1 = 3. How many branches are there at the 5th level of distribution?
a. 63 branches
b. 95 branches
c. 127 branches
d. 191 branches

Answer: c. 127 branches. Explanation: This is a recursive sequence. We calculate each term: a2 = 2(3) + 1 = 7, a3 = 2(7) + 1 = 15, a4 = 2(15) + 1 = 31, a5 = 2(31) + 1 = 63. However, this represents the number of new branches added at each level. The total at the 5th level is the sum of all previous levels: 3 + 7 + 15 + 31 + 63 = 127. This tests understanding of recursive sequences and their cumulative effects in network design.

165. An electrician needs to install a conduit run from the top of a 15-foot pole to a junction box on the ground 20 feet away from the base of the pole. What angle should the conduit make with the ground to reach the top of the pole?
a. 36.9°
b. 41.8°
c. 48.2°
d. 53.1°

Answer: a. 36.9° Explanation: This problem can be solved using the tangent function. tan θ = opposite / adjacent = 15 / 20 = 0.75. Taking the inverse tangent: θ = tan⁻¹(0.75) ≈ 36.9°. This application of trigonometry is crucial for planning conduit runs and cable installations in various electrical settings.

166. A 3-phase motor draws 25 A at 480 V with a power factor of 0.85 lagging. Calculate the reactive power consumed by the motor.
a. 8.64 kVAR
b. 10.37 kVAR
c. 12.45 kVAR
d. 14.88 kVAR

Answer: c. 12.45 kVAR Explanation: First, calculate apparent power: S = √3 × V × I = √3 × 480 × 25 = 20,784 VA. The power factor angle is θ = cos⁻¹(0.85) ≈ 31.79°. Reactive power Q = S × sin θ = 20,784 × sin(31.79°) ≈ 12,450 VAR or 12.45 kVAR. This calculation demonstrates the use of trigonometric functions in power factor and reactive power analysis.

167. In a power transmission system, the voltage and current phasors are represented as V = 230∠0° kV and I = 500∠-30° A. Calculate the real power transmitted.
a. 86.25 MW
b. 99.64 MW
c. 115.00 MW
d. 132.79 MW

Answer: b. 99.64 MW Explanation: Real power P = |V| × |I| × cos θ, where θ is the angle between voltage and current. Here, θ = 0° - (-30°) = 30°. Thus, P = 230,000 × 500 × cos(30°) = 99.64 MW. This problem illustrates the application of trigonometry in phasor calculations for power system analysis.

168. A ladder needs to reach a window 24 feet above the ground. Due to an obstruction, the base of the ladder must be placed 10 feet away from the building. What is the minimum length of ladder required?
a. 25.3 feet
b. 26.0 feet
c. 27.2 feet
d. 28.5 feet

Answer: b. 26.0 feet Explanation: This forms a right triangle. Using the Pythagorean theorem: ladder² = 24² + 10² = 676. Taking the square root: ladder = √676 = 26.0 feet. While not directly electrical, this problem tests spatial reasoning and trigonometric principles often needed in electrical installation planning.

169. In an AC circuit, the voltage is given by v(t) = 170 sin(377t + 30°) volts. What is the RMS value of this voltage, and what is the phase angle in radians?
a. 120 V, π/6 rad
b. 120 V, π/3 rad
c. 170 V, π/6 rad
d. 170 V, π/3 rad

Answer: a. 120 V, π/6 rad Explanation: The RMS value of a sinusoidal voltage is the peak value divided by √2. So, VRMS = 170 / √2 ≈ 120 V. The phase angle 30° in radians is 30° × (π/180°) = π/6 rad. This problem tests understanding of RMS values and angle conversions in AC circuit analysis.

170. A transmission tower guy wire is anchored 15 meters from the base of the tower and makes an angle of 60° with the ground. How tall is the tower?
a. 12.99 meters
b. 17.32 meters
c. 25.98 meters
d. 30.00 meters

Answer: c. 25.98 meters Explanation: Using the sine function: sin(60°) = tower height / 15. Solving for tower height: height = 15 × sin(60°) = 15 × (√3/2) ≈ 25.98 meters. This application of trigonometry is essential for structural calculations in power transmission systems.

171. An impedance triangle shows a resistance of 40Ω and a reactance of 30Ω. What is the power factor of this circuit?
a. 0.75
b. 0.80
c. 0.85
d. 0.90

Answer: b. 0.80 Explanation: The power factor is the cosine of the angle in the impedance triangle. Using the Pythagorean theorem: |Z| = √(40² + 30²) = 50Ω. The power factor is then cos θ = 40 / 50 = 0.80. This calculation demonstrates the relationship between impedance components and power factor in AC circuits.

172. A 3-phase system has line voltages VAB = 480∠0° V, VBC = 480∠-120° V, and VCA = 480∠120° V. What is the magnitude of the line-to-neutral voltage?
a. 277.1 V
b. 320.0 V

c. 415.7 V
d. 480.0 V

Answer: a. 277.1 V Explanation: In a balanced 3-phase system, the line-to-neutral voltage magnitude is the line voltage divided by √3. So, VLN = 480 / √3 ≈ 277.1 V. This problem tests understanding of 3-phase systems and the relationship between line and phase quantities.

173. An electrical panel is mounted at a 15° angle from vertical on a sloped ceiling. If the panel is 36 inches tall, what is the vertical height it occupies on the ceiling?
a. 34.31 inches
b. 34.76 inches
c. 35.21 inches
d. 35.66 inches

Answer: b. 34.76 inches Explanation: The vertical component is found using the cosine function: vertical height = 36 × cos(15°) ≈ 34.76 inches. This application of trigonometry is useful in electrical installation planning, especially in non-standard mounting situations.

174. In a power triangle, the apparent power is 50 kVA and the reactive power is 30 kVAR. Calculate the real power and the power factor.
a. 40 kW, 0.80
b. 40 kW, 0.60
c. 30 kW, 0.80
d. 30 kW, 0.60

Answer: a. 40 kW, 0.80 Explanation: Using the Pythagorean theorem in the power triangle: $P^2 = S^2 - Q^2 = 50^2 - 30^2 = 1600$, so P = 40 kW. The power factor is cos θ = P / S = 40 / 50 = 0.80. This problem demonstrates the use of trigonometry in power calculations and power factor analysis.

175. A power system's load curve is represented by the piecewise function P(t) = {2t + 10, 0 ≤ t < 6; -t + 22, 6 ≤ t < 12; 10, 12 ≤ t < 24}, where P is power in MW and t is time in hours. What is the total energy consumption in MWh over a 24-hour period?
a. 288 MWh
b. 312 MWh
c. 336 MWh
d. 360 MWh

Answer: c. 336 MWh. Explanation: To find total energy, we integrate P(t) over 24 hours. For 0 ≤ t < 6: ∫(2t+10)dt = t^2+10t = 66 MWh. For 6 ≤ t < 12: ∫(-t+22)dt = -0.5t^2+22t = 90 MWh. For 12 ≤ t < 24: ∫10dt = 10t = 120 MWh. Total: 66 + 90 + 120 = 336 MWh. This tests understanding of piecewise functions and their application in power system analysis.

176. The voltage across a capacitor during discharge is given by V(t) = 100e^(-t/RC), where R = 10kΩ and C = 100μF. If this function is transformed by a horizontal stretch of factor 2 and a vertical compression of factor 0.5, what is the new function V'(t)?
a. V'(t) = 50e^(-t/2RC)
b. V'(t) = 50e^(-2t/RC)
c. V'(t) = 50e^(-t/RC)
d. V'(t) = 100e^(-t/2RC)

Answer: a. V'(t) = 50e^(-t/2RC). Explanation: A horizontal stretch by factor 2 replaces t with t/2. A vertical compression by factor 0.5 multiplies the function by 0.5. Thus, V'(t) = 0.5 * 100e^(-(t/2)/RC) = 50e^(-t/2RC). This tests understanding of function transformations in the context of capacitor discharge.

177. An industrial motor's torque-speed characteristic is represented by the function T(ω) = -0.05ω² + 10ω + 50, where T is torque in Nm and ω is angular speed in rad/s. At what speed does the motor produce maximum torque?
a. 50 rad/s
b. 100 rad/s
c. 150 rad/s
d. 200 rad/s

Answer: b. 100 rad/s. Explanation: To find the maximum, we differentiate T(ω) and set it to zero: dT/dω = -0.1ω + 10 = 0. Solving gives ω = 100 rad/s. We can verify this is a maximum by checking the second derivative is negative. This tests ability to interpret quadratic functions and apply calculus in motor characteristics analysis.

178. The current in an RLC circuit is given by i(t) = 5sin(ωt + π/6) A. If this function is transformed by a phase shift of -π/3 and an amplitude increase of 20%, what is the new function i'(t)?
a. i'(t) = 6sin(ωt - π/6) A
b. i'(t) = 6sin(ωt + π/2) A
c. i'(t) = 5sin(ωt - π/6) A
d. i'(t) = 6sin(ωt - π/2) A

Answer: a. i'(t) = 6sin(ωt - π/6) A. Explanation: A phase shift of -π/3 is applied to the argument: (ωt + π/6) - π/3 = ωt - π/6. An amplitude increase of 20% changes 5 to 5 * 1.2 = 6. Thus, i'(t) = 6sin(ωt - π/6) A. This tests understanding of trigonometric function transformations in AC circuit analysis.

179. A transformer's efficiency η as a function of load factor x is given by η(x) = -0.2x² + 0.3x + 0.85. At what load factor does the transformer achieve maximum efficiency?
a. 0.65
b. 0.70
c. 0.75
d. 0.80

Answer: c. 0.75. Explanation: To find the maximum, we differentiate η(x) and set it to zero: dη/dx = -0.4x + 0.3 = 0. Solving gives x = 0.75. We can verify this is a maximum by checking the second derivative is negative (-0.4). This tests ability to interpret quadratic functions and apply calculus in transformer efficiency analysis.

180. The voltage regulation of a transmission line is given by VR = (|Vs| - |Vr|) / |Vr| * 100%, where Vs is sending end voltage and Vr is receiving end voltage. If |Vs| = 230kV and VR is represented by the function VR(P) = 0.0002P² + 0.05P, where P is transmitted power in MW, at what power level does |Vr| equal 220kV?
a. 235.7 MW
b. 250.0 MW
c. 264.3 MW
d. 278.6 MW

Answer: c. 264.3 MW. Explanation: We need to solve: (230 - 220) / 220 * 100 = 0.0002P² + 0.05P. Simplifying: 4.545 = 0.0002P² + 0.05P. This quadratic equation solves to P ≈ 264.3 MW. This tests ability to interpret and solve equations derived from practical power system scenarios.

181. A phasor diagram shows the relationship between voltage and current in an AC circuit. If the voltage phasor is represented by V = 100∠30° V and the current phasor by I = 5∠-15° A, what is the complex power S delivered to the circuit?
a. 500 + j134.7 VA
b. 433 + j250 VA
c. 250 + j433 VA
d. 134.7 + j500 VA

Answer: b. 433 + j250 VA. Explanation: Complex power S = VI* = 100∠30° * 5∠15° = 500∠45° VA. In rectangular form, this is 500(cos45° + jsin45°) = 353.6 + j353.6 VA. Rounding to the nearest whole number gives 433 + j250 VA. This tests understanding of phasor diagrams and complex power calculations.

182. The magnetization curve of a transformer core is approximated by the piecewise function B(H) = {0.5H, 0 ≤ H < 100; 50 + 0.1(H-100), 100 ≤ H < 1000; 140 + 0.01(H-1000), H ≥ 1000}, where B is flux density in Tesla and H is magnetic field intensity in A/m. What is the incremental permeability µi at H = 500 A/m?
a. 0.1 H/m
b. 0.5 H/m
c. 1.26 * 10^-4 H/m
d. 6.28 * 10^-4 H/m

Answer: c. 1.26 * 10^-4 H/m. Explanation: Incremental permeability µi = dB/dH. At H = 500, we're in the second piece of the function where dB/dH = 0.1. To convert to H/m, we multiply by µ0 = 4π * 10^-7 H/m. Thus, µi = 0.1 * 4π * 10^-7 = 1.26 * 10^-4 H/m. This tests understanding of piecewise functions and magnetic material properties.

183. The harmonic content of a non-linear load current is represented by the Fourier series i(t) = 10sin(ωt) + 3sin(3ωt) + 1.5sin(5ωt) A. What is the Total Harmonic Distortion (THD) of this current?
a. 18.37%
b. 25.00%
c. 33.54%
d. 37.50%

Answer: c. 33.54%. Explanation: THD = √(∑I_h^2) / I_1, where I_h are the harmonic amplitudes and I_1 is the fundamental. Here, THD = √(3² + 1.5²) / 10 = 0.3354 = 33.54%. This tests understanding of Fourier series representation of non-sinusoidal waveforms and power quality metrics.

184. A power electronic converter's output voltage as a function of control angle α is given by V(α) = Vm(1 + cosα) / 2, where Vm is the peak input voltage. If this function is transformed by a vertical stretch of factor 1.5 and a horizontal compression of factor 2, what is the new function V'(α)?
a. V'(α) = 1.5Vm(1 + cos(2α)) / 2
b. V'(α) = 0.75Vm(1 + cos(2α))
c. V'(α) = 1.5Vm(1 + cos(α/2)) / 2
d. V'(α) = 0.75Vm(1 + cos(α/2))

Answer: b. V'(α) = 0.75Vm(1 + cos(2α)). Explanation: A vertical stretch by factor 1.5 multiplies the function by 1.5. A horizontal compression by factor 2 replaces α with 2α. Thus, V'(α) = 1.5 * Vm(1 + cos(2α)) / 2 = 0.75Vm(1 + cos(2α)). This tests understanding of function transformations in power electronics applications.

185. A parabolic antenna dish has a focal length of 3 meters and a diameter of 8 meters. What is the depth of the dish at its center?
a. 0.67 meters
b. 1.33 meters
c. 2.00 meters
d. 2.67 meters

Answer: b. 1.33 meters Explanation: For a parabolic dish, the depth (d) is related to the diameter (D) and focal length (f) by the equation: d = D²/(16f). Substituting values: d = 8²/(16 × 3) = 1.33 meters. This calculation is crucial for designing parabolic antennas used in satellite communications and radio astronomy, where precise focusing of electromagnetic waves is essential.

186. An elliptical cooling pond for a power plant has a major axis of 200 meters and a minor axis of 120 meters. What is the eccentricity of this ellipse?
a. 0.60
b. 0.73
c. 0.80
d. 0.87

Answer: b. 0.73 Explanation: The eccentricity (e) of an ellipse is given by $e = \sqrt{1 - b^2/a^2}$, where a is half the major axis and b is half the minor axis. Here, a = 100 and b = 60. Calculating: $e = \sqrt{1 - 60^2/100^2} \approx 0.73$. This parameter is important in designing cooling ponds to optimize heat dissipation and water circulation for power plant cooling systems.

187. A hyperbolic cooling tower has an asymptote angle of 15° from the vertical. What is the eccentricity of this hyperbola?
a. 1.04
b. 1.15
c. 1.26
d. 1.37

Answer: a. 1.04 Explanation: For a hyperbola, the eccentricity (e) is related to the asymptote angle (θ) by the equation: $e = 1/\cos(\theta)$. Here, $\theta = 15°$. Calculating: $e = 1/\cos(15°) \approx 1.04$. Understanding hyperbolic geometries is crucial for designing efficient cooling towers in power plants, where the shape affects air flow and cooling efficiency.

188. An electrician needs to design a parabolic reflector for a streetlight. The light source will be placed 0.5 meters from the vertex of the parabola, and the reflector needs to be 1.2 meters wide. What is the equation of this parabola in vertex form?
a. $y = 0.3x^2$
b. $y = 0.4x^2$
c. $y = 0.5x^2$
d. $y = 0.6x^2$

Answer: c. $y = 0.5x^2$ Explanation: The general form of a parabola with vertex at the origin is $y = ax^2$, where $a = 1/(4f)$ and f is the focal length. Here, f = 0.5 meters, so $a = 1/(4 \times 0.5) = 0.5$. The equation is $y = 0.5x^2$. This calculation is essential for designing efficient lighting systems with optimal light distribution.

189. A satellite in elliptical orbit around Earth has a perigee (closest approach) of 6,700 km and an apogee (farthest point) of 42,300 km from Earth's center. What is the semi-major axis of this orbit?
a. 17,500 km
b. 24,500 km
c. 31,500 km
d. 38,500 km

Answer: b. 24,500 km Explanation: The semi-major axis (a) of an elliptical orbit is the average of the perigee and apogee distances: $a = (r_p + r_a)/2$, where r_p is perigee and r_a is apogee. Calculating: $a = (6,700 + 42,300)/2 = 24,500$ km. This parameter is crucial in satellite communications and space mission planning, affecting orbital period and energy requirements.

190. A hyperbolic antenna reflector has a vertex-to-focus distance of 2 meters and an eccentricity of 1.2. What is the equation of this hyperbola in standard form, assuming the transverse axis is along the x-axis?
a. $(x^2/9) - (y^2/5) = 1$
b. $(x^2/16) - (y^2/12) = 1$
c. $(x^2/25) - (y^2/21) = 1$
d. $(x^2/36) - (y^2/32) = 1$

Answer: b. $(x^2/16) - (y^2/12) = 1$ Explanation: For a hyperbola with eccentricity e and vertex-to-focus distance a, the standard form is $(x^2/a^2) - (y^2/b^2) = 1$, where $b^2 = a^2(e^2 - 1)$. Here, a = 2 and e = 1.2. Calculate b^2: $b^2 = 2^2(1.2^2 - 1) = 3$. The equation is $(x^2/4) - (y^2/3) = 1$, which simplifies to $(x^2/16) - (y^2/12) = 1$. This equation is used in designing specialized antennas for directional communication systems.

191. A parabolic trough solar collector is 6 meters long and 1.5 meters wide. If the focal length is 0.45 meters, what is the rim angle of this collector?
a. 45.0°
b. 52.5°
c. 60.0°
d. 67.5°

Answer: c. 60.0° Explanation: The rim angle (ψ) of a parabolic trough is given by $ψ = \tan^{-1}(W/(4f))$, where W is the aperture width and f is the focal length. Here, W = 1.5 m and f = 0.45 m. Calculating: $ψ = \tan^{-1}(1.5/(4 \times 0.45)) ≈ 60.0°$. The rim angle is crucial in optimizing the collection efficiency of solar energy in concentrating solar power systems.

192. An elliptical gear in a specialized motor has a major axis of 10 cm and a minor axis of 8 cm. What is the distance between the foci of this elliptical gear?
a. 3 cm
b. 4 cm
c. 5 cm
d. 6 cm

Answer: d. 6 cm Explanation: In an ellipse, the distance between foci (2c) is related to the major (2a) and minor (2b) axes by the equation: $c^2 = a^2 - b^2$. Here, a = 5 cm and b = 4 cm. Calculating: $c^2 = 5^2 - 4^2 = 9$, so c = 3 cm. The distance between foci is 2c = 6 cm. Understanding elliptical gear geometry is important in designing specialized mechanical systems with variable torque transmission.

193. A hyperbolic cooling tower has a throat diameter of 50 meters and a height of 120 meters. If the asymptotes of the hyperbola intersect at a point 30 meters below ground level, what is the equation of this hyperbola in standard form, assuming the origin is at ground level?
a. $((x/25)^2 - ((y+30)/150)^2 = 1$
b. $((x/25)^2 - ((y+30)/90)^2 = 1$
c. $((x/50)^2 - ((y+30)/150)^2 = 1$
d. $((x/50)^2 - ((y+30)/90)^2 = 1$

Answer: b. $((x/25)^2 - ((y+30)/90)^2 = 1$ Explanation: For a hyperbolic cooling tower, the standard form is $(x/a)^2 - ((y-k)/b)^2 = 1$, where a is half the throat diameter, b is the distance from the throat to the asymptote intersection, and k is the y-coordinate of the center. Here, a = 25 m, b = 120 + 30 = 150 m, and k = -30 m. The equation is $((x/25)^2 - ((y+30)/150)^2 = 1$. This equation is crucial in designing cooling towers for optimal air flow and cooling efficiency.

194. A parabolic microphone reflector needs to focus sound waves from a distance of 50 meters onto a receiver 10 cm behind the vertex. What is the diameter of this parabolic reflector?
a. 1.79 meters
b. 2.24 meters
c. 2.83 meters
d. 3.16 meters

Answer: c. 2.83 meters Explanation: For a parabolic reflector, the relationship between focal length (f), diameter (D), and depth (d) is: $f = D^2/(16d)$. Here, f = 50 m and d = 0.1 m. Rearranging: $D^2 = 16fd = 16 \times 50 \times 0.1 = 80$. Taking the square root: D ≈ 2.83 meters. This calculation is essential in designing directional microphones for long-distance sound recording or surveillance applications.

195. A three-phase balanced system has line voltages VAB = 480∠0°V, VBC = 480∠-120°V, and VCA = 480∠120°V. Express these voltages as a 3x1 matrix in rectangular form.
a. [480+j0; -240-j415.7; -240+j415.7]
b. [480+j0; -240+j415.7; -240-j415.7]
c. [277.1+j0; -138.6-j240; -138.6+j240]
d. [277.1+j0; -138.6+j240; -138.6-j240]

Answer: b. [480+j0; -240+j415.7; -240-j415.7]. Explanation: Line voltages are given, so we don't need to convert to phase voltages. We convert each phasor to rectangular form: 480∠0° = 480+j0, 480∠-120° = -240+j415.7, 480∠120° = -240-j415.7. This tests understanding of phasor representation and matrix notation in three-phase systems.

196. An electrical network is represented by the nodal admittance matrix Y = [4-j2, -2+j1; -2+j1, 3-j1.5] S. If the node voltages are V = [120∠0°; 100∠-30°] V, calculate the injected currents at each node.
a. [381.6-j290.0; -138.4+j359.8] A
b. [381.6+j290.0; -138.4-j359.8] A
c. [290.0-j381.6; 359.8+j138.4] A
d. [290.0+j381.6; 359.8-j138.4] A

Answer: b. [381.6+j290.0; -138.4-j359.8] A. Explanation: Injected currents I = YV. First, convert V to rectangular form: [120+j0; 86.6-j50]. Perform matrix multiplication: [4-j2, -2+j1; -2+j1, 3-j1.5] * [120+j0; 86.6-j50] = [381.6+j290.0; -138.4-j359.8] A. This tests application of matrix operations in network analysis.

197. A power system has three buses with the following bus admittance matrix Y (in per unit): [5-j15, -2+j6, -3+j9; -2+j6, 4-j12, -2+j6; -3+j9, -2+j6, 5-j15]. Calculate the Thévenin equivalent impedance seen from bus 1 with buses 2 and 3 short-circuited.
a. 0.1+j0.3 pu
b. 0.2+j0.6 pu
c. 0.3+j0.9 pu
d. 0.4+j1.2 pu

Answer: a. 0.1+j0.3 pu. Explanation: The Thévenin impedance is the inverse of the Thévenin admittance, which is the sum of all elements in row 1 and column 1 of Y. Zth = 1 / (5-j15 + (-2+j6) + (-3+j9)) = 1 / (0-j0) = 0.1+j0.3 pu. This tests understanding of bus admittance matrices and Thévenin equivalent circuits.

198. A 3x3 impedance matrix Z represents a three-winding transformer. If Z = [0.02+j0.08, 0.01+j0.05, 0.01+j0.04; 0.01+j0.05, 0.03+j0.1, 0.02+j0.06; 0.01+j0.04, 0.02+j0.06, 0.025+j0.09] Ω, determine the mutual impedance between windings 1 and 3.
a. 0.01+j0.04 Ω
b. 0.02+j0.06 Ω
c. 0.025+j0.09 Ω
d. 0.03+j0.1 Ω

Answer: a. 0.01+j0.04 Ω. Explanation: In an impedance matrix, the mutual impedance between windings i and j is given by the element Zij. The mutual impedance between windings 1 and 3 is Z13 = 0.01+j0.04 Ω. This tests understanding of impedance matrices in transformer analysis.

199. A power flow study uses the Newton-Raphson method, which requires the Jacobian matrix. If the Jacobian J = [∂P/∂δ, ∂P/∂|V|; ∂Q/∂δ, ∂Q/∂|V|] and the mismatch vector [ΔP; ΔQ] = [0.05; -0.03], calculate the required changes in voltage angle δ and magnitude |V| for the next iteration.
a. [0.0375; -0.0225]
b. [0.0225; -0.0375]
c. [-0.0375; 0.0225]
d. [-0.0225; 0.0375]

Answer: a. [0.0375; -0.0225]. Explanation: The Newton-Raphson method solves J[Δδ; Δ|V|] = [ΔP; ΔQ]. Assuming J is the identity matrix for simplicity (in reality, it would be calculated based on system parameters), [Δδ; Δ|V|] = [0.05; -0.03] * 0.75 = [0.0375; -0.0225]. This tests understanding of power flow analysis and iterative methods.

200. An unbalanced three-phase system has the following sequence components: V0 = 5∠0°V, V1 = 100∠30°V, V2 = 10∠-45°V. Using the sequence-to-phase transformation matrix A = [1, 1, 1; 1, a, a²; 1, a², a], where a = 1∠120°, calculate the phase voltages Va, Vb, and Vc.
a. [112.9∠27.1°; 86.6∠-113.8°; 94.7∠137.9°] V
b. [115.0∠26.3°; 88.5∠-114.6°; 96.5∠138.7°] V
c. [117.1∠25.5°; 90.4∠-115.4°; 98.3∠139.5°] V
d. [119.2∠24.7°; 92.3∠-116.2°; 100.1∠140.3°] V

101

Answer: b. [115.0∠26.3°; 88.5∠-114.6°; 96.5∠138.7°] V. Explanation: Phase voltages are calculated using [Va; Vb; Vc] = A[V0; V1; V2]. Performing this matrix multiplication and converting to polar form gives the result. This tests understanding of symmetrical components and matrix operations in unbalanced system analysis.

201. A transmission line is represented by its ABCD parameters: A = 0.98∠2°, B = 60∠80°Ω, C = 0.0005∠88°S, D = 0.98∠2°. If the receiving end voltage is 220∠0°kV and current is 500∠-30°A, calculate the sending end voltage and current.
a. Vs = 228.8∠4.2°kV, Is = 514.3∠-27.8°A
b. Vs = 230.6∠4.5°kV, Is = 518.6∠-27.5°A
c. Vs = 232.4∠4.8°kV, Is = 522.9∠-27.2°A
d. Vs = 234.2∠5.1°kV, Is = 527.2∠-26.9°A

Answer: c. Vs = 232.4∠4.8°kV, Is = 522.9∠-27.2°A. Explanation: Using the ABCD equations: Vs = AVr + BIr, Is = CVr + DIr. Substituting the given values and performing the calculations yields the result. This tests understanding of transmission line modeling and phasor calculations.

202. A power system stability study requires the calculation of the inertia constant H for a group of generators. Given the following data: Generator 1: 100 MVA, H1 = 5 s; Generator 2: 150 MVA, H2 = 6 s; Generator 3: 200 MVA, H3 = 4 s. Calculate the equivalent inertia constant Heq for the group.
a. 4.89 s
b. 5.00 s
c. 5.11 s
d. 5.22 s

Answer: a. 4.89 s. Explanation: The equivalent inertia constant is calculated as Heq = (H1S1 + H2S2 + H3S3) / (S1 + S2 + S3), where S is the MVA rating. Substituting the values: Heq = (5*100 + 6*150 + 4*200) / (100 + 150 + 200) = 4.89 s. This tests understanding of generator parameters and their aggregation in stability studies.

203. A 3-phase, 480V, 60Hz induction motor has the following equivalent circuit parameters referred to the stator: R1 = 0.2Ω, X1 = 0.8Ω, R2 = 0.3Ω, X2 = 0.9Ω, Xm = 30Ω. Using the exact equivalent circuit, calculate the starting current and power factor.
a. 567.8 A, 0.316 lagging
b. 585.6 A, 0.324 lagging
c. 603.4 A, 0.332 lagging
d. 621.2 A, 0.340 lagging

Answer: b. 585.6 A, 0.324 lagging. Explanation: At start, slip s = 1. Total impedance Z = (R1 + jX1) + ((R2/s + jX2) || jXm) = 0.5 + j1.69Ω. Starting current I = V / (√3 * Z) = 480 / (√3 * √(0.5² + 1.69²)) = 585.6 A. Power factor = cos(tan^(-1)(1.69/0.5)) = 0.324 lagging. This tests understanding of induction motor equivalent circuits and starting characteristics.

204. A digital protective relay uses the following trip characteristic: operate if I > 5 + 0.5t, where I is the current in per unit and t is the time in seconds. Express this characteristic as a matrix equation in the form Ax ≤ b, where x = [I; t].
a. [1, -0.5][I; t] ≤ 5
b. [1, 0.5][I; t] ≤ 5
c. [-1, 0.5][I; t] ≤ -5
d. [-1, -0.5][I; t] ≤ -5

Answer: c. [-1, 0.5][I; t] ≤ -5. Explanation: The original inequality I > 5 + 0.5t can be rewritten as -I + 0.5t < -5. In matrix form, this becomes [-1, 0.5][I; t] ≤ -5. This tests the ability to express protection characteristics in matrix form, which is useful for relay coordination studies.

205. An electrician needs to hang a 100 lb light fixture from a ceiling using two cables. One cable makes a 30° angle with the ceiling, and the other makes a 45° angle. What is the tension in the cable at 30°?
a. 50.0 lb
b. 57.7 lb
c. 66.8 lb
d. 86.6 lb

Answer: b. 57.7 lb Explanation: This problem requires vector decomposition. Let T_1 and T_2 be the tensions in the 30° and 45° cables respectively. Resolving forces vertically: $T_1 \sin 30° + T_2 \sin 45° = 100$ lb. Horizontally: $T_1 \cos 30° = T_2 \cos 45°$. Solving these equations simultaneously yields $T_1 \approx 57.7$ lb. This calculation is crucial for safe installation of suspended electrical equipment.

206. Two vectors represent currents in a circuit: $I_1 = 3i + 4j$ amperes and $I_2 = -2i + 5j$ amperes. What is the magnitude of the resultant current?
a. 5.0 A
b. 7.1 A
c. 8.6 A
d. 10.0 A

Answer: c. 8.6 A Explanation: The resultant current is $I = I_1 + I_2 = (3-2)i + (4+5)j = i + 9j$ amperes. The magnitude is $|I| = \sqrt{1^2 + 9^2} \approx 8.6$ A. This vector addition is essential in analyzing complex circuits with multiple current sources or branches.

207. A magnetic field B = 2i - 3j + 4k tesla acts on a current-carrying conductor with a length vector L = 5i + 2j - 1k meters. Calculate the magnitude of the force on the conductor if it carries a current of 10 amperes.
a. 110 N
b. 150 N
c. 190 N
d. 230 N

Answer: b. 150 N Explanation: The force is given by F = I(L × B), where × denotes cross product. F = 10[(5i + 2j - 1k) × (2i - 3j + 4k)] = 10(11i + 23j + 19k) N. The magnitude is |F| = 10√(11² + 23² + 19²) ≈ 150 N. This calculation is crucial in electromechanical systems and motor design.

208. An overhead power line experiences two forces due to wind: F_1 = 200N at 30° above horizontal and F_2 = 150N at 45° above horizontal. What is the magnitude of the resultant force?
a. 305.3 N
b. 328.6 N
c. 342.9 N
d. 367.4 N

Answer: c. 342.9 N Explanation: Convert forces to vector components: F_1 = 173.2i + 100j N, F_2 = 106.1i + 106.1j N. The resultant R = (173.2 + 106.1)i + (100 + 106.1)j = 279.3i + 206.1j N. Magnitude |R| = √(279.3² + 206.1²) ≈ 342.9 N. This vector analysis is essential for structural calculations in power line installations.

209. A coil with 500 turns and area 0.02 m² is placed in a magnetic field B = 0.5i + 0.3j + 0.4k tesla. What is the magnitude of the magnetic flux through the coil if its normal vector is n = 0.6i + 0.8j?
a. 3.70 mWb
b. 4.80 mWb
c. 5.90 mWb
d. 7.00 mWb

Answer: b. 4.80 mWb Explanation: The magnetic flux Φ = NBA·n, where N is number of turns, B is magnetic field, A is area, and n is unit normal vector. First, normalize n: n = (0.6i + 0.8j) / √(0.6² + 0.8²). Then, Φ = 500 × 0.02 × (0.5 × 0.6 + 0.3 × 0.8) / √(0.6² + 0.8²) ≈ 4.80 mWb. This calculation is crucial in transformer and generator design.

210. An electric field E = 200i + 300j - 100k V/m acts on a charge q = 2 × 10⁻⁶ C. What is the angle between the force on the charge and the positive x-axis?
a. 33.7°
b. 45.0°
c. 56.3°
d. 71.6°

Answer: c. 56.3° Explanation: The force F = qE = (400i + 600j - 200k) × 10⁻⁶ N. The angle θ with the x-axis is given by cos θ = F·i / |F| = 400 / √(400² + 600² + 200²) ≈ cos(56.3°). This vector analysis is important in understanding particle motion in electromagnetic fields.

211. A transmission tower experiences three forces: F_1 = 5000N at 30° north of east, F_2 = 4000N at 45° south of west, and F_3 = 3000N vertically upward. What is the magnitude of the resultant force?
a. 2.94 kN

b. 3.87 kN
c. 4.56 kN
d. 5.32 kN

Answer: c. 4.56 kN Explanation: Convert to vector components: F_1 = 4330i + 2500j N, F_2 = -2828i - 2828j N, F_3 = 3000k N. Resultant R = 1502i - 328j + 3000k N. Magnitude |R| = √(1502² + 328² + 3000²) ≈ 4560 N = 4.56 kN. This calculation is essential for structural analysis of transmission towers.

212. Two vectors A = 3i - 4j + 2k and B = -1i + 5j + 3k represent complex impedances in a circuit. Calculate |A × B|.
a. 17
b. 23
c. 29
d. 35

Answer: b. 23 Explanation: A × B = (3 × 5 - (-4) × (-1))i + (2 × (-1) - 3 × 3)j + (3 × (-4) - (-1) × 2)k = 19i - 11j - 14k. |A × B| = √(19² + 11² + 14²) = √529 = 23. While cross product is less common in circuit analysis, this calculation demonstrates vector operations that may be useful in advanced electromagnetic field problems.

213. A solenoid has 1000 turns and a length of 0.5 meters. If it carries a current of 2 amperes, what is the magnitude of the magnetic field inside the solenoid?
a. 2.51 mT
b. 3.14 mT
c. 4.02 mT
d. 5.03 mT

Answer: c. 4.02 mT Explanation: The magnetic field in a solenoid is given by B = μ_0nI, where μ_0 = 4π × 10⁻⁷ H/m, n is turns per unit length, and I is current. Here, n = 1000 / 0.5 = 2000 turns/m. B = 4π × 10⁻⁷ × 2000 × 2 = 5.03 × 10⁻³ T = 5.03 mT. This calculation is crucial in designing electromagnets and understanding magnetic field generation.

214. An electrician needs to move a 500 kg transformer across a floor with a coefficient of friction μ = 0.3. What is the minimum angle above the horizontal at which a force should be applied to start moving the transformer?
a. 11.3°
b. 16.7°
c. 22.6°
d. 28.4°

Answer: b. 16.7° Explanation: The minimum angle occurs when the applied force is just enough to overcome friction. If F is the applied force, then F cos θ = μmg and F sin θ = μF cos θ. Solving for θ: tan θ = μ = 0.3. Therefore, θ = tan⁻¹(0.3) ≈ 16.7°. This vector analysis is important for safe and efficient handling of heavy electrical equipment.

215. A manufacturing plant produces circuit breakers with a 2% defect rate. If 100 circuit breakers are randomly selected for quality control, what is the probability that exactly 3 are defective?
a. 0.1803
b. 0.2240
c. 0.2702
d. 0.3156

Answer: c. 0.2702. Explanation: This scenario follows a binomial distribution with n=100, p=0.02, and k=3. The probability is calculated using the formula: $P(X=k) = C(n,k) * p^k * (1-p)^{(n-k)}$, where $C(n,k)$ is the binomial coefficient. Plugging in the values gives 0.2702. This tests understanding of probability distributions in quality control applications.

216. An electrical substation has three main transformers. The probability of failure for each transformer in a given year is 0.05, independent of the others. What is the probability that at least one transformer will fail within the next year?
a. 0.1426
b. 0.1539
c. 0.1653
d. 0.1768

Answer: a. 0.1426. Explanation: The probability of at least one failure is the complement of all transformers not failing. Probability of no failures = $(1-0.05)^3$ = 0.8574. Therefore, probability of at least one failure = 1 - 0.8574 = 0.1426. This tests application of probability concepts in reliability analysis of power systems.

217. A power distribution company finds that during summer, the probability of a transformer overload is 0.3, and given an overload, the probability of failure is 0.4. What is the probability of a transformer failing due to overload during summer?
a. 0.12
b. 0.18
c. 0.24
d. 0.30

Answer: a. 0.12. Explanation: This is a conditional probability problem. P(Failure due to overload) = P(Overload) * P(Failure | Overload) = 0.3 * 0.4 = 0.12. This tests understanding of conditional probability in the context of power system reliability.

218. An electrician is troubleshooting a faulty circuit. Based on experience, there's a 40% chance the problem is in the wiring, 35% in the components, and 25% in the power source. If the problem is in the wiring, there's a 70% chance of fixing it in under an hour. For components, it's 60%, and for the power source, it's 80%. What's the probability of fixing the problem in under an hour?
a. 0.685
b. 0.700
c. 0.715

106

d. 0.730

Answer: a. 0.685. Explanation: This problem uses the law of total probability. P(Fix < 1hr) = 0.4*0.7 + 0.35*0.6 + 0.25*0.8 = 0.28 + 0.21 + 0.20 = 0.69, or 0.685 when rounded to three decimal places. This tests application of probability in practical troubleshooting scenarios.

219. A power plant has two generators. Generator A has a 95% reliability, and Generator B has a 90% reliability. What is the probability that at least one generator will be operational at any given time?
a. 0.9925
b. 0.9950
c. 0.9975
d. 0.9990

Answer: b. 0.9950. Explanation: The probability of at least one generator being operational is the complement of both failing. P(At least one operational) = 1 - P(Both fail) = 1 - (0.05 * 0.10) = 0.9950. This tests understanding of reliability calculations in power generation systems.

220. An electrical contractor is bidding on three projects. The probability of winning each bid is 0.6, 0.5, and 0.4 respectively. Assuming the bids are independent, what is the probability of winning at least two of the three projects?
a. 0.568
b. 0.608
c. 0.648
d. 0.688

Answer: c. 0.648. Explanation: We can calculate this using the complement of winning 0 or 1 project. P(2 or 3) = 1 - [P(0) + P(1)]. P(0) = 0.4 * 0.5 * 0.6 = 0.12. P(1) = 0.6 * 0.5 * 0.6 + 0.6 * 0.5 * 0.4 + 0.4 * 0.5 * 0.4 = 0.232. So, P(2 or 3) = 1 - (0.12 + 0.232) = 0.648. This tests application of probability in business decision-making for electrical contractors.

221. A factory uses three-phase motors. The probability of a single-phase failure is 0.02. Given a single-phase failure, the probability of the motor continuing to run is 0.7. What is the probability that a randomly selected motor is running with a single-phase failure?
a. 0.014
b. 0.028
c. 0.042
d. 0.056

Answer: a. 0.014. Explanation: This is a joint probability problem. P(Running with single-phase failure) = P(Single-phase failure) * P(Running | Single-phase failure) = 0.02 * 0.7 = 0.014. This tests understanding of conditional probability in industrial motor applications.

222. An electrical supply company stocks 1000 LED bulbs, of which 2% are expected to be defective. What is the expected number of defective bulbs, and what is the standard deviation of this expectation?
a. $\mu = 20$, $\sigma = 4.43$
b. $\mu = 20$, $\sigma = 4.47$
c. $\mu = 20$, $\sigma = 4.51$
d. $\mu = 20$, $\sigma = 4.55$

Answer: b. $\mu = 20$, $\sigma = 4.47$. Explanation: This follows a binomial distribution. The expected value (mean) $\mu = np = 1000 * 0.02 = 20$. The standard deviation $\sigma = \sqrt{np(1-p)} = \sqrt{1000 * 0.02 * 0.98} \approx 4.47$. This tests understanding of expected value and standard deviation in inventory management.

223. A power utility is considering installing a new transmission line. The cost of installation is $10 million. If installed, there's a 70% chance of increased revenue of $15 million, and a 30% chance of $5 million. Should the utility install the line based on expected value?
a. Yes, expected value is $1.5 million
b. Yes, expected value is $2.0 million
c. No, expected value is -$1.5 million
d. No, expected value is -$2.0 million

Answer: b. Yes, expected value is $2.0 million. Explanation: Expected value = 0.7 * ($15M - $10M) + 0.3 * ($5M - $10M) = $3.5M - $1.5M = $2.0M. Since the expected value is positive, the utility should install the line. This tests application of expected value in decision-making for power utilities.

224. An electrician is troubleshooting a complex circuit. Based on experience, the probability of identifying the fault in the first hour is 0.4, in the second hour is 0.3 (given it wasn't found in the first hour), and in the third hour is 0.5 (given it wasn't found in the first two hours). What is the probability of identifying the fault within three hours?
a. 0.750
b. 0.790
c. 0.830
d. 0.870

Answer: c. 0.830. Explanation: This is a sequential probability problem. P(Within 3 hours) = P(1st hour) + P(Not 1st) * P(2nd hour) + P(Not 1st or 2nd) * P(3rd hour) = 0.4 + 0.6 * 0.3 + 0.6 * 0.7 * 0.5 = 0.4 + 0.18 + 0.25 = 0.83. This tests understanding of conditional probability in troubleshooting scenarios.

225. An electrical contractor is analyzing the lifespans of LED streetlights. A sample of 100 streetlights shows a mean lifespan of 50,000 hours with a standard deviation of 5,000 hours. Assuming a normal distribution, what percentage of streetlights are expected to last between 45,000 and 55,000 hours?
a. 34.1%
b. 68.2%
c. 95.4%
d. 99.7%

Answer: b. 68.2% Explanation: In a normal distribution, approximately 68.2% of data falls within one standard deviation of the mean. The range 45,000 to 55,000 hours represents ±1 standard deviation from the mean of 50,000 hours. This statistical knowledge is crucial for predicting maintenance schedules and warranty terms in large-scale lighting projects.

226. A power company is monitoring voltage fluctuations at a substation. Over a 24-hour period, the following RMS voltage readings (in volts) were recorded: 118, 122, 119, 121, 120, 117, 123. What is the median voltage?
a. 119 V
b. 120 V
c. 121 V
d. 122 V

Answer: b. 120 V Explanation: To find the median, first arrange the data in ascending order: 117, 118, 119, 120, 121, 122, 123. With an odd number of values, the median is the middle value, which is 120 V. Understanding measures of central tendency is important for assessing power quality and identifying potential issues in electrical distribution systems.

227. An electrician is testing the resistance of a batch of 500 resistors rated at 100Ω ±5%. The measured resistances follow a normal distribution with a mean of 101Ω and a standard deviation of 2Ω. How many resistors are expected to fall outside the specified tolerance?
a. 12
b. 25
c. 38
d. 51

Answer: c. 38 Explanation: The tolerance range is 95Ω to 105Ω. We need to find how many resistors fall below 95Ω or above 105Ω. Using z-scores: z = (x - μ) / σ, we get z_1 = (95 - 101) / 2 = -3 and z_2 = (105 - 101) / 2 = 2. From a standard normal table, the area beyond these z-scores is approximately 0.0013 + 0.0228 = 0.0241. Therefore, about 0.0241 × 500 ≈ 12 resistors are expected to be out of tolerance. This statistical analysis is crucial for quality control in manufacturing and inventory management.

228. A study of electrical accidents in industrial settings over the past year revealed the following data: Mean number of accidents per month = 3.5, Variance = 2.25. What is the standard deviation of accidents per month?
a. 1.15
b. 1.32
c. 1.50
d. 1.68

Answer: c. 1.50 Explanation: The standard deviation is the square root of the variance. √2.25 = 1.50. Understanding these statistical measures is essential for risk assessment and safety planning in industrial electrical work.

229. An energy company is analyzing the daily power consumption (in MWh) of a small town. The data for a week is: 240, 235, 255, 245, 250, 230, 260. Calculate the range and the coefficient of variation (CV) for this data set.
a. Range: 30 MWh, CV: 4.2%
b. Range: 30 MWh, CV: 5.3%
c. Range: 35 MWh, CV: 4.2%
d. Range: 35 MWh, CV: 5.3%

Answer: a. Range: 30 MWh, CV: 4.2% Explanation: Range = Max - Min = 260 - 230 = 30 MWh. To calculate CV, first find mean (245 MWh) and standard deviation (10.31 MWh). CV = (Standard Deviation / Mean) × 100 = (10.31 / 245) × 100 ≈ 4.2%. These statistics help in understanding the variability of power consumption, which is crucial for load balancing and capacity planning.

230. A manufacturing plant produces circuit breakers. Quality control data shows that the probability of a breaker being defective is 0.02. In a batch of 1000 breakers, what is the expected number of defective units, and what is the standard deviation of this expectation?
a. Mean: 20, SD: 4.43
b. Mean: 20, SD: 4.90
c. Mean: 50, SD: 4.43
d. Mean: 50, SD: 4.90

Answer: a. Mean: 20, SD: 4.43 Explanation: This follows a binomial distribution. Expected number (mean) = np = 1000 × 0.02 = 20. Standard deviation = √(np(1-p)) = √(1000 × 0.02 × 0.98) ≈ 4.43. Understanding these statistical concepts is crucial for implementing effective quality control measures in manufacturing processes.

231. An electrical engineer is analyzing the time-to-failure data (in years) for a specific type of transformer: 12, 15, 18, 20, 22, 25, 28. Calculate the first quartile (Q1) and the interquartile range (IQR) for this data set.
a. Q1: 15, IQR: 10
b. Q1: 15, IQR: 13
c. Q1: 18, IQR: 10
d. Q1: 18, IQR: 13

Answer: a. Q1: 15, IQR: 10 Explanation: For the ordered data set, Q1 is the (n+1)/4 = 2nd value, which is 15. Q3 is the 3(n+1)/4 = 6th value, which is 25. IQR = Q3 - Q1 = 25 - 15 = 10. These quartile statistics are valuable for understanding the distribution of failure times and planning maintenance schedules.

232. A power distribution company is studying the correlation between outdoor temperature (X) and power consumption (Y). They calculated ΣX = 750, ΣY = 12000, ΣX² = 47500, ΣY² = 1200000, ΣXY = 750000 for 30 data points. Calculate the Pearson correlation coefficient (r).
a. 0.65
b. 0.78
c. 0.86
d. 0.92

Answer: c. 0.86 Explanation: Using the formula r = (nΣXY - ΣXΣY) / √[(nΣX² - (ΣX)²)(nΣY² - (ΣY)²)], we get r ≈ 0.86. This strong positive correlation indicates that power consumption tends to increase with temperature. Understanding such correlations is crucial for load forecasting and capacity planning in power distribution systems.

233. An electrician is testing the breaking capacity of circuit breakers. Out of 200 tests, 190 were successful. Calculate the 95% confidence interval for the true proportion of successful breaks.
a. (0.92, 0.98)
b. (0.93, 0.97)
c. (0.94, 0.96)
d. (0.95, 0.97)

Answer: b. (0.93, 0.97) Explanation: The sample proportion p̂ = 190/200 = 0.95. For a 95% confidence interval, z = 1.96. The standard error SE = √(p̂(1-p̂)/n) = √(0.95 × 0.05 / 200) ≈ 0.0154. The confidence interval is p̂ ± z×SE = 0.95 ± 1.96 × 0.0154 ≈ (0.93, 0.97). This statistical inference is crucial for quality assurance and reliability assessment in electrical equipment manufacturing.

234. A utility company is analyzing the monthly electricity bills (in dollars) for residential customers. A random sample of 50 bills yields a mean of $120 and a standard deviation of $30. Construct a 90% confidence interval for the population mean.
a. ($112.93, $127.07)
b. ($113.85, $126.15)
c. ($114.77, $125.23)
d. ($115.69, $124.31)

Answer: b. ($113.85, $126.15) Explanation: For a 90% confidence interval with 49 degrees of freedom, t ≈ 1.677. The standard error of the mean SE = s / √n = 30 / √50 ≈ 4.24. The confidence interval is x̄ ± t×SE = 120 ± 1.677 × 4.24 ≈ ($113.85, $126.15). This type of analysis is essential for pricing strategies and understanding customer consumption patterns in utility services.

235. An electrician can wire a standard residential room in 3 hours, while an apprentice takes 5 hours for the same job. If they work together, how long will it take them to wire 6 identical rooms?
a. 5.45 hours
b. 6.32 hours
c. 7.50 hours
d. 8.18 hours

Answer: c. 7.50 hours. Explanation: The combined work rate is 1/3 + 1/5 = 8/15 rooms per hour. For 6 rooms, time = 6 / (8/15) = 11.25 hours. Dividing by 1.5 (as they're working together) gives 7.50 hours. This tests understanding of work rate problems in a practical electrical context.

236. A three-phase motor draws 50A at 480V with a power factor of 0.85 lagging. How long will it take this motor to consume 100 kWh of energy?
a. 2.89 hours
b. 3.27 hours
c. 3.65 hours
d. 4.03 hours

Answer: b. 3.27 hours. Explanation: Power = √3 * V * I * PF = √3 * 480 * 50 * 0.85 = 35.23 kW. Time = Energy / Power = 100 kWh / 35.23 kW = 2.84 hours. This tests application of three-phase power calculations and energy consumption rates.

237. An electrical contractor needs to install 5000 feet of conduit. Crew A can install 100 feet per hour, Crew B can install 150 feet per hour, and Crew C can install 200 feet per hour. If all crews work together, how long will the job take?
a. 9.09 hours
b. 10.00 hours
c. 11.11 hours
d. 12.50 hours

Answer: c. 11.11 hours. Explanation: Combined rate = 100 + 150 + 200 = 450 feet/hour. Time = 5000 feet / 450 feet/hour = 11.11 hours. This tests understanding of combined work rates in large-scale electrical installations.

238. A 200-amp service panel is being upgraded to a 400-amp service. The old panel is 60% loaded. If the new load is expected to increase by 25%, what percentage of the new panel's capacity will be utilized?
a. 37.5%
b. 45.0%
c. 52.5%
d. 60.0%

Answer: a. 37.5%. Explanation: Current load = 200 * 0.60 = 120 amps. New load = 120 * 1.25 = 150 amps. Percentage of new panel = 150 / 400 = 0.375 or 37.5%. This tests the ability to calculate load percentages in service upgrades.

239. A 100 kVA transformer is filled with 80 gallons of mineral oil with a dielectric strength of 30 kV/mm. If 20 gallons of this oil is replaced with new oil having a dielectric strength of 40 kV/mm, what is the new average dielectric strength of the mixture?
a. 31.5 kV/mm
b. 32.0 kV/mm
c. 32.5 kV/mm
d. 33.0 kV/mm

Answer: b. 32.0 kV/mm. Explanation: Original strength = 30 kV/mm * 60 gallons = 1800 kV·gal/mm. New oil strength = 40 kV/mm * 20 gallons = 800 kV·gal/mm. Total = 2600 kV·gal/mm. New average = 2600 / 80 = 32.5 kV/mm. This tests understanding of mixture problems in transformer maintenance.

240. An electric vehicle charging station can charge a car's battery from 20% to 80% in 30 minutes. Assuming a linear charging rate, how long would it take to charge the battery from 10% to 90%?
a. 35 minutes
b. 40 minutes
c. 45 minutes
d. 50 minutes

Answer: b. 40 minutes. Explanation: In 30 minutes, the battery charges 60% (80% - 20%). Rate = 60% / 30 minutes = 2% per minute. To charge from 10% to 90% is 80%, so time = 80% / (2% per minute) = 40 minutes. This tests rate calculations in modern electrical applications.

241. A power plant has three generators with capacities of 100 MW, 150 MW, and 200 MW. If the 100 MW generator can reach full capacity in 30 minutes, the 150 MW in 45 minutes, and the 200 MW in 60 minutes, how long will it take for the plant to reach 300 MW output if all generators start simultaneously?
a. 48 minutes
b. 52 minutes
c. 56 minutes
d. 60 minutes

Answer: c. 56 minutes. Explanation: Generator rates: 100/30 = 3.33 MW/min, 150/45 = 3.33 MW/min, 200/60 = 3.33 MW/min. Combined rate = 10 MW/min. Time to reach 300 MW = 300 / 10 = 30 minutes. This tests understanding of combined rates in power generation scenarios.

242. An electrician is pulling wire through conduit at a rate of 50 feet per minute. If the conduit run is 1000 feet long and has pull boxes every 200 feet that take 2 minutes each to pass through, how long will it take to complete the pull?
a. 24 minutes
b. 28 minutes
c. 32 minutes
d. 36 minutes

Answer: b. 28 minutes. Explanation: Time for wire pull = 1000 / 50 = 20 minutes. Number of pull boxes = 1000 / 200 = 5. Time for pull boxes = 5 * 2 = 10 minutes. Total time = 20 + 8 = 28 minutes. This tests application of rate problems with interruptions, common in electrical installations.

243. A 3-phase, 480V motor draws 50A at startup and accelerates uniformly to full speed in 5 seconds, at which point it draws 30A. Assuming a power factor of 0.85, calculate the energy consumed during startup in watt-seconds.
a. 173,665 W·s

b. 189,618 W·s
c. 205,571 W·s
d. 221,524 W·s

Answer: c. 205,571 W·s. Explanation: Average current = (50 + 30) / 2 = 40A. Power = √3 * 480 * 40 * 0.85 = 28,108 W. Energy = 28,108 W * 5 s = 140,540 W·s. However, as current decreases linearly, we need to add 1/3 of the difference between max and min energy: (28,108 - 16,865) * 5 / 3 = 18,743 W·s. Total = 140,540 + 18,743 = 159,283 W·s. This tests advanced understanding of energy calculations during motor startup.

244. A factory has two electrical systems: System A operates at 240V and System B at 480V. If a 5 kW load is transferred from System A to System B, by what percentage will the current in the receiving system increase, assuming both systems have the same power factor?
a. 1.04%
b. 2.08%
c. 3.12%
d. 4.16%

Answer: a. 1.04%. Explanation: Current in System B before transfer: I = 5000 / (√3 * 480) = 6.01A. Current after transfer: I = 10000 / (√3 * 480) = 12.02A. Percentage increase = (12.02 - 6.01) / 576.4 * 100 = 1.04%. This tests understanding of power transfer between systems and its effect on current.

245. An electrician upgrades a motor from 85% efficiency to 92% efficiency. What is the percentage reduction in power loss?
a. 7%
b. 35.3%
c. 46.7%
d. 52.9%

Answer: c. 46.7% Explanation: Initial loss = 15%, new loss = 8%. Percentage reduction = (15% - 8%) / 15% × 100 = 46.7%. This calculation is crucial for evaluating the cost-effectiveness of motor upgrades and energy-saving initiatives in industrial settings.

246. A power plant increases its output by 20% in the first year and another 15% in the second year. What is the total percentage increase in output over the two years?
a. 35%
b. 38%
c. 41%
d. 44%

Answer: b. 38% Explanation: Let initial output be 100 units. After first year: 100 × 1.20 = 120 units. After second year: 120 × 1.15 = 138 units. Total increase: (138 - 100) / 100 × 100 = 38%. Understanding compound percentage changes is essential for long-term planning and forecasting in power generation.

247. An electrical contractor estimates a job will take 160 hours. If the actual time is 12% less than estimated, how many hours did the job take?
a. 134.4 hours
b. 140.8 hours
c. 147.2 hours
d. 153.6 hours

Answer: b. 140.8 hours Explanation: 12% less than 160 hours is calculated as: 160 - (160 × 0.12) = 160 × 0.88 = 140.8 hours. Accurate time estimation and analysis are critical for project management and bidding in electrical contracting.

248. A transformer's efficiency drops by 0.5% for every 10°C increase in temperature. If the efficiency is 98% at 20°C, what will be the efficiency at 70°C?
a. 95.0%
b. 95.5%
c. 96.0%
d. 96.5%

Answer: b. 95.5% Explanation: Temperature increase = 70°C - 20°C = 50°C. Number of 10°C intervals = 50 / 10 = 5. Total efficiency drop = 5 × 0.5% = 2.5%. New efficiency = 98% - 2.5% = 95.5%. This calculation is important for assessing transformer performance under varying environmental conditions.

249. An electric utility plans to reduce its carbon emissions by 15% per year for the next three years. What percentage of its original emissions will remain after three years?
a. 55.0%
b. 61.4%
c. 67.8%
d. 74.2%

Answer: b. 61.4% Explanation: After each year, emissions are reduced to 85% of the previous year. After three years: 0.85 × 0.85 × 0.85 = 0.614 or 61.4% of original emissions remain. This type of calculation is crucial for long-term environmental planning and regulatory compliance in the energy sector.

250. A factory's electricity consumption increases by 5% each month for 6 months, then decreases by 3% each month for the next 4 months. What is the net percentage change in electricity consumption?
a. 22.5% increase
b. 27.6% increase
c. 30.8% increase
d. 34.2% increase

Answer: c. 30.8% increase Explanation: After 6 months of 5% increase: 1.05^6 = 1.3401. After 4 months of 3% decrease: 1.3401 × 0.97^4 = 1.3082. Net change: (1.3082 - 1) × 100 = 30.8% increase. This complex percentage calculation is important for energy management and cost forecasting in industrial settings.

251. An electrical equipment manufacturer improves its production efficiency, reducing defects from 5% to 3%. By what percentage has the defect rate been reduced?
a. 20%
b. 30%
c. 40%
d. 50%

Answer: c. 40% Explanation: Percentage reduction = (5% - 3%) / 5% × 100 = 40%. This calculation is crucial for quality control and process improvement in manufacturing, demonstrating the impact of efficiency measures.

252. A power line has losses of 4% per 100 km. If power transmitted at the source is 1000 MW, what percentage of this power will reach a substation 350 km away?
a. 84.6%
b. 86.7%
c. 88.8%
d. 90.9%

Answer: b. 86.7% Explanation: Loss over 350 km = 4% × (350/100) = 14%. Power reaching substation = 100% - 14% = 86%. Using the compound effect: $(1 - 0.04)^{3.5}$ = 0.867 or 86.7%. This calculation is essential for planning power transmission and distribution systems.

253. An electric car's battery capacity degrades by 2% per year. After how many years will the battery retain 90% of its original capacity?
a. 3.8 years
b. 4.7 years
c. 5.2 years
d. 6.1 years

Answer: c. 5.2 years Explanation: We need to solve: $(1 - 0.02)^n$ = 0.90, where n is the number of years. Taking natural log of both sides: n × ln(0.98) = ln(0.90). Solving: n ≈ 5.2 years. This type of calculation is crucial for predicting battery life and planning maintenance schedules in electric vehicle fleets.

254. A solar panel's efficiency decreases by 0.8% of its current value each year. If the initial efficiency is 22%, what will be its efficiency after 10 years?
a. 19.8%

116

b. 20.2%
c. 20.6%
d. 21.0%

Answer: b. 20.2% Explanation: After 10 years, the efficiency will be: 22% × (1 - 0.008)¹⁰ ≈ 20.2%. This compound percentage decrease calculation is essential for long-term performance prediction and economic analysis of solar installations.

255. A three-phase transformer has a turns ratio of 10:1. If the primary voltage is 13.8 kV line-to-line, what is the secondary line-to-line voltage, and how does the current ratio compare to the voltage ratio?
a. 1.38 kV, current ratio is inverse of voltage ratio
b. 1.38 kV, current ratio is same as voltage ratio
c. 0.798 kV, current ratio is inverse of voltage ratio
d. 0.798 kV, current ratio is same as voltage ratio

Answer: a. 1.38 kV, current ratio is inverse of voltage ratio. Explanation: Secondary voltage = 13.8 kV / 10 = 1.38 kV. In transformers, the current ratio is inverse to the voltage ratio to maintain power balance (P = VI). This tests understanding of transformer ratios and their implications on voltage and current.

256. An electrician needs to create a scale model of an electrical room for a presentation. The actual room dimensions are 20 ft x 30 ft x 10 ft (L x W x H). If the model's length is 10 inches, what are its width and height to maintain proper proportions?

a. 15 inches x 5 inches
b. 12 inches x 4 inches
c. 18 inches x 6 inches
d. 20 inches x 8 inches

Answer: a. 15 inches x 5 inches. Explanation: The scale is 10 inches : 20 feet, or 1:24. Applying this scale: Width = 30 ft / 24 = 15 inches, Height = 10 ft / 24 = 5 inches. This tests the ability to work with scale ratios in practical applications.

257. In a series RLC circuit, the voltage across the resistor, inductor, and capacitor are in the ratio of 3:4:2 respectively. If the total applied voltage is 270V, what is the voltage across the inductor?
a. 90V
b. 120V
c. 135V
d. 150V

Answer: b. 120V. Explanation: Let x be the unit of ratio. Then 3x + 4x + 2x = 270V, or 9x = 270V. Thus, x = 30V. Voltage across inductor = 4x = 4(30) = 120V. This tests understanding of voltage division in series circuits and ratio applications.

258. A 75 hp motor operates at 90% efficiency with a power factor of 0.85 lagging. If the motor's current draw is directly proportional to its horsepower and inversely proportional to its efficiency and power factor, how would the current change if the efficiency improved to 95% and the power factor to 0.92, assuming constant horsepower?
a. Decrease by 10.5%
b. Decrease by 12.7%
c. Increase by 10.5%
d. Increase by 12.7%

Answer: b. Decrease by 12.7%. Explanation: Current is proportional to 1 / (efficiency * power factor). Ratio of new to old current = (0.90 * 0.85) / (0.95 * 0.92) = 0.873. This represents a 12.7% decrease. This tests understanding of proportional relationships in motor characteristics.

259. A 100W incandescent bulb produces 1600 lumens of light. Assuming light output is directly proportional to power consumption, how many watts would an LED bulb consume to produce the same amount of light if it has an efficacy of 100 lumens per watt?
a. 12W
b. 14W
c. 16W
d. 18W

Answer: c. 16W. Explanation: LED power = Lumens / Efficacy = 1600 / 100 = 16W. This tests understanding of direct proportion in the context of lighting efficiency.

260. In a balanced Wye-connected load, the line current is √3 times the phase current. If a particular load draws 20A line current at 208V line-to-line voltage, what would be the phase current and phase voltage?
a. 11.55A, 120V
b. 11.55A, 208V
c. 20A, 120V
d. 20A, 208V

Answer: a. 11.55A, 120V. Explanation: Phase current = Line current / √3 = 20 / √3 ≈ 11.55A. Phase voltage = Line voltage / √3 = 208 / √3 = 120V. This tests understanding of three-phase Wye connections and the relationships between line and phase quantities.

261. A 1000 MCM copper conductor has a resistance of 0.01 ohms per 100 feet at 75°C. What would be the approximate resistance of a 500 MCM copper conductor of the same length and temperature?
a. 0.005 ohms
b. 0.01 ohms
c. 0.02 ohms
d. 0.04 ohms

Answer: c. 0.02 ohms. Explanation: Resistance is inversely proportional to cross-sectional area. 500 MCM has half the area of 1000 MCM, so its resistance will be twice as much: 0.01 * 2 = 0.02 ohms. This tests understanding of the relationship between conductor size and resistance.

262. An electrical contractor is bidding on a job that requires 500 feet of 4/0 AWG copper wire. If the price of copper increases by 20%, by what percentage must the contractor increase the bid price for wire to maintain the same profit margin, assuming wire cost is 40% of the total bid?
a. 6%
b. 8%
c. 10%
d. 12%

Answer: b. 8%. Explanation: Wire cost increase = 20% * 40% = 8% of total bid. To maintain the same profit margin, the entire bid must increase by 8%. This tests the ability to apply percentage changes and proportions in practical bidding scenarios.

263. A 5 kVA single-phase transformer has a primary voltage of 7200V and a secondary voltage of 240V. If the primary winding has 1800 turns, how many turns does the secondary winding have?
a. 30 turns
b. 60 turns
c. 90 turns
d. 120 turns

Answer: b. 60 turns. Explanation: Turns ratio = Voltage ratio = 7200:240 = 30:1. If primary has 1800 turns, secondary has 1800/30 = 60 turns. This tests understanding of transformer turn ratios and their relationship to voltage ratios.

264. In a parallel RC circuit, the total current is the vector sum of the resistive and capacitive currents. If the resistive current is 3A and the capacitive current is 4A, what is the total current drawn by the circuit?
a. 5A
b. 7A
c. 3.5A
d. 2.5A

Answer: a. 5A. Explanation: The currents form a right triangle, with total current as the hypotenuse. Using the Pythagorean theorem: I_total = √(3² + 4²) = 5A. This tests understanding of vector addition in AC circuits and the application of the Pythagorean theorem to electrical quantities.

265. An electrician needs to convert a wire's resistance from 0.015 Ω/ft to Ω/km. What is the equivalent resistance in Ω/km?
a. 0.0492 Ω/km

b. 4.92 Ω/km
c. 49.2 Ω/km
d. 492 Ω/km

Answer: c. 49.2 Ω/km Explanation: To convert, multiply by the conversion factor: 0.015 Ω/ft × (3280.84 ft / 1 km) = 49.2 Ω/km. This conversion is crucial for comparing wire specifications across different standards and ensuring proper cable selection for long-distance installations.

266. The magnetic flux density B is related to magnetic field strength H by the equation B = μH, where μ is the permeability. If B is measured in teslas (T), H in ampere-turns per meter (At/m), what are the units of μ?
a. H/m
b. Wb/A·m
c. T·m/A
d. N/A²

Answer: a. H/m Explanation: Rearranging the units in the equation: [T] = [μ] × [At/m]. Therefore, [μ] = [T] / [At/m] = [N/A·m] / [At/m] = [N/A²] = [H/m] (henry per meter). Understanding derived units is essential for analyzing electromagnetic systems and ensuring dimensional consistency in calculations.

267. A 3-phase motor draws 25 A at 480 V with a power factor of 0.85. Calculate the power consumption in horsepower (hp).
a. 21.3 hp
b. 28.5 hp
c. 35.7 hp
d. 42.9 hp

Answer: c. 35.7 hp Explanation: First, calculate power in watts: P = √3 × V × I × PF = √3 × 480 × 25 × 0.85 = 17,658 W. Convert to horsepower: 17,658 W × (1 hp / 746 W) ≈ 23.7 hp. This calculation demonstrates the importance of unit conversions in assessing motor performance and energy consumption.

268. The capacitance of a parallel plate capacitor is given by C = εA/d, where ε is permittivity, A is plate area, and d is plate separation. If C is in farads (F), A in square meters (m²), and d in meters (m), what are the units of ε?
a. F/m
b. C/V·m
c. N·m²/C²
d. kg·m/s²·A²

Answer: a. F/m Explanation: Rearranging the units in the equation: [F] = [ε] × [m²] / [m]. Therefore, [ε] = [F] × [m] / [m²] = [F/m] (farad per meter). This dimensional analysis is crucial for understanding the physical meaning of permittivity and its role in electrostatic calculations.

269. An electric field E of 5000 V/m acts on a charge q of 2×10^{-6} C. What is the force F on the charge in newtons?
a. 0.01 N
b. 0.1 N
c. 1 N
d. 10 N

Answer: a. 0.01 N Explanation: Using the equation F = qE, we get F = (2×10^{-6} C) × (5000 V/m) = 0.01 N. This calculation demonstrates the relationship between electric field strength and force on a charge, essential for understanding electrostatic phenomena and particle accelerator physics.

270. A transformer's primary winding has 1000 turns and carries a current of 10 A. The secondary winding has 100 turns. Assuming 100% efficiency, what is the secondary current?
a. 1 A
b. 10 A
c. 100 A
d. 1000 A

Answer: c. 100 A Explanation: Using the transformer turns ratio equation: $N_1/N_2 = I_2/I_1$, where N is number of turns and I is current. Rearranging: $I_2 = I_1 \times (N_1/N_2)$ = 10 A × (1000/100) = 100 A. This calculation is fundamental in transformer design and power distribution systems.

271. The energy stored in a magnetic field is given by E = (1/2)LI², where L is inductance and I is current. If E is in joules (J), I in amperes (A), what are the units of L?
a. H (henry)
b. Wb (weber)
c. T (tesla)
d. V·s (volt-second)

Answer: a. H (henry) Explanation: Rearranging the units in the equation: [J] = [L] × [A]². Therefore, [L] = [J] / [A]² = [kg·m²/s²·A²] = [H] (henry). This dimensional analysis reinforces the understanding of inductance and its role in energy storage in magnetic fields.

272. A 100 W incandescent bulb is replaced with an LED bulb that produces the same lumens but consumes only 15 W. If electricity costs $0.12 per kWh, how much money is saved over 1000 hours of operation?
a. $6.80
b. $10.20
c. $13.60
d. $17.00

Answer: b. $10.20 Explanation: Energy saved = (100 W - 15 W) × 1000 h = 85 kWh. Cost saved = 85 kWh × $0.12/kWh = $10.20. This calculation combines unit conversion (W to kW) with cost analysis, essential for evaluating energy efficiency upgrades.

273. The skin depth δ in a conductor is given by δ = √(ρ/πfμ), where ρ is resistivity, f is frequency, and μ is permeability. If δ is in meters (m), ρ in ohm-meters (Ω·m), f in hertz (Hz), what are the units of μ?
a. H/m
b. Wb/A·m
c. T·m/A
d. N/A²

Answer: a. H/m Explanation: Rearranging the units in the equation: [m] = √([Ω·m] / ([Hz] × [μ])). For this to be dimensionally consistent, [μ] must be [H/m] (henry per meter). This analysis is crucial for understanding skin effect in conductors at high frequencies.

274. A 3-phase, 480 V motor draws 50 A with a power factor of 0.8 lagging. What is the reactive power consumed by the motor in kVAR?
a. 16.6 kVAR
b. 24.9 kVAR
c. 33.2 kVAR
d. 41.5 kVAR

Answer: c. 33.2 kVAR Explanation: First, calculate apparent power: S = √3 × V × I = √3 × 480 × 50 = 41.57 kVA. Reactive power Q = S × sin(cos⁻¹(PF)) = 41.57 × sin(cos⁻¹(0.8)) ≈ 33.2 kVAR. This calculation demonstrates the relationship between various power components in AC systems and is crucial for power factor correction and system design.

275. A three-phase power system operates at 60 Hz. In a digital protection relay, the sampling rate must be a multiple of the fundamental frequency and prime for optimal performance. What is the smallest suitable sampling rate above 1000 Hz?
a. 1009 Hz
b. 1013 Hz
c. 1019 Hz
d. 1021 Hz

Answer: c. 1019 Hz. Explanation: The sampling rate must be a multiple of 60 Hz and prime. The first multiple of 60 above 1000 is 1020, but it's not prime. The next prime multiple is 1019 Hz (1019 = 17 * 60 - 1). This tests understanding of prime numbers and their application in digital sampling for power systems.

276. An industrial control system uses a 12-bit analog-to-digital converter (ADC) to measure voltage. If the full-scale voltage is 10V, what is the smallest voltage change that can be detected?
a. 2.44 mV
b. 4.88 mV

c. 9.77 mV
d. 19.53 mV

Answer: a. 2.44 mV. Explanation: A 12-bit ADC has 2^12 = 4096 discrete levels. The resolution is 10V / 4096 = 2.44 mV. This tests understanding of binary number systems and their application in measurement systems.

277. In a digital circuit, two signals with periods of 18 and 24 clock cycles respectively are combined. What is the number of clock cycles after which both signals will align again?
a. 36 cycles
b. 54 cycles
c. 72 cycles
d. 108 cycles

Answer: c. 72 cycles. Explanation: This problem requires finding the least common multiple (LCM) of 18 and 24. LCM(18, 24) = 72. This tests understanding of LCM and its application in digital timing analysis.

278. A power line carrier (PLC) communication system uses a cyclic redundancy check (CRC) with the generator polynomial $x^4 + x + 1$. If the message to be transmitted is 1101 and the initial CRC register state is 0000, what is the final CRC value?
a. 0110
b. 1001
c. 1100
d. 0011

Answer: b. 1001. Explanation: Perform polynomial division of 11010000 (message shifted left by 4 bits) by 10011 ($x^4 + x + 1$ in binary). The remainder 1001 is the CRC value. This tests understanding of CRC calculation in communication systems.

279. An electrician needs to cut several pieces of conduit from a 20-foot length. The required pieces are 3 feet, 4 feet, and 5 feet long. What is the maximum number of complete sets (one of each size) that can be cut, and how much conduit will be left over?
a. 2 sets, 2 feet left
b. 2 sets, 1 foot left
c. 3 sets, 0 feet left
d. 3 sets, 2 feet left

Answer: b. 2 sets, 1 foot left. Explanation: Each set requires 3 + 4 + 5 = 12 feet. Two sets require 24 feet, which exceeds 20 feet. One set leaves 8 feet, enough for one more 3-foot and one 4-foot piece, with 1 foot left over. This tests application of arithmetic and optimization in practical scenarios.

280. A programmable logic controller (PLC) uses 16-bit registers. If a temperature sensor outputs a value between 0°C and 100°C with 0.1°C resolution, what is the maximum value that can be stored in the register, and how many bits are actually needed for this application?
a. 65535, 10 bits
b. 32767, 10 bits
c. 65535, 11 bits
d. 32767, 11 bits

Answer: a. 65535, 10 bits. Explanation: A 16-bit register can store values from 0 to 2^16 - 1 = 65535. For the temperature range, we need to represent 1000 values (0 to 100 in 0.1 increments). This requires ceil(log2(1000)) = 10 bits. This tests understanding of binary representation and data storage optimization.

281. In a digital control system, three periodic tasks have execution times of 2 ms, 3 ms, and 5 ms respectively. What is the minimum time interval at which all three tasks will complete simultaneously?
a. 15 ms
b. 30 ms
c. 60 ms
d. 90 ms

Answer: b. 30 ms. Explanation: This requires finding the least common multiple (LCM) of 2, 3, and 5. LCM(2, 3, 5) = 30 ms. This tests understanding of LCM in the context of task scheduling in control systems.

282. A power quality analyzer uses the Fast Fourier Transform (FFT) to analyze harmonic content. If the sampling rate is 10 kHz and the FFT size is 1024 points, what is the frequency resolution of the FFT?
a. 4.88 Hz
b. 9.77 Hz
c. 19.53 Hz
d. 39.06 Hz

Answer: b. 9.77 Hz. Explanation: Frequency resolution = Sampling rate / FFT size = 10000 / 1024 ≈ 9.77 Hz. This tests understanding of FFT principles and their application in power quality analysis.

283. An encryption system for secure communication in a SCADA network uses modular exponentiation. If the base is 7, the exponent is 23, and the modulus is 26, what is the result of the operation?
a. 17
b. 19
c. 21
d. 23

Answer: a. 17. Explanation: We need to calculate 7^23 mod 26. Using the properties of modular arithmetic: 7^2 ≡ 23 (mod 26), 7^4 ≡ 9 (mod 26), 7^8 ≡ 3 (mod 26), 7^16 ≡ 9 (mod 26). Therefore, 7^23 ≡ 7^16 * 7^4 * 7^2 * 7 ≡ 9 * 9 * 23 * 7 ≡ 17 (mod 26). This tests understanding of modular arithmetic in cryptography applications.

284. A fault current calculation requires finding the greatest common divisor (GCD) of 180 A and 252 A to simplify the expression. What is the GCD of these currents?
a. 36 A
b. 48 A
c. 60 A
d. 72 A

Answer: a. 36 A. Explanation: Using the Euclidean algorithm: 252 = 1 * 180 + 72, 180 = 2 * 72 + 36, 72 = 2 * 36 + 0. Therefore, GCD(180, 252) = 36. This tests understanding of GCD calculation and its application in electrical engineering calculations.

285. In a factory with 100 employees, 60 are trained in electrical work, 45 in mechanical work, and 30 in both. How many employees are trained in neither electrical nor mechanical work?
a. 15
b. 20
c. 25
d. 30

Answer: c. 25 Explanation: Using the set theory formula: Total = (Electrical + Mechanical) - (Both) + (Neither). 100 = (60 + 45) - 30 + x, where x is the number trained in neither. Solving for x gives 25. This application of set theory is crucial for workforce planning and skill gap analysis in industrial settings.

286. A logic circuit has three inputs: A, B, and C. The output is true if at least two inputs are true. Which Boolean expression represents this circuit?
a. A·B + B·C + A·C
b. A + B + C
c. (A + B)·(B + C)·(A + C)
d. A·B·C

Answer: a. A·B + B·C + A·C Explanation: This is a majority function. The expression A·B + B·C + A·C represents all combinations where at least two inputs are true. Understanding Boolean algebra and set operations is essential for designing and troubleshooting complex control systems and digital circuits.

287. In a power distribution system, Circuit A supplies 80 homes, Circuit B supplies 65 homes, and 20 homes are connected to both circuits for redundancy. How many unique homes are supplied by these two circuits?
a. 105
b. 115
c. 125

d. 135

Answer: c. 125 Explanation: Using the set union formula: |A ∪ B| = |A| + |B| - |A ∩ B|, where |A ∩ B| represents homes connected to both circuits. Thus, 80 + 65 - 20 = 125 unique homes. This set theory application is important for load balancing and redundancy planning in power distribution networks.

288. A PLC system monitors four sensors: A, B, C, and D. An alarm triggers if sensor A is active AND either B or C is active, regardless of D's state. Which Boolean expression represents this alarm condition?
a. A + (B·C) + D
b. A·(B + C)
c. (A·B) + (A·C)
d. A·B·C + A·B·D + A·C·D

Answer: c. (A·B) + (A·C) Explanation: This expression represents A AND (B OR C), which satisfies the given condition. The state of D is irrelevant, so it's not included in the expression. Applying set theory and Boolean logic in this manner is crucial for programming PLCs and designing industrial control systems.

289. In a building's electrical system, 50 circuits are protected by circuit breakers, 40 by fuses, and 15 by both. How many circuits are protected by either circuit breakers or fuses?
a. 65
b. 75
c. 85
d. 90

Answer: b. 75 Explanation: Using the set union formula: |A ∪ B| = |A| + |B| - |A ∩ B|. Here, 50 + 40 - 15 = 75 circuits. This application of set theory is important for system design, safety analysis, and maintenance planning in electrical installations.

290. A digital system has inputs P, Q, and R. The output is true when P is true, Q is false, and R can be either. Which Boolean expression represents this system?
a. P·Q·R + P·Q·R'
b. P·Q' + P·Q'·R
c. P·Q'
d. P + Q' + R

Answer: c. P·Q' Explanation: The condition is met when P is true (P) AND Q is false (Q', the complement of Q). R's state doesn't affect the output, so it's not included. This type of Boolean expression simplification is essential in digital circuit design and optimization.

291. In an industrial automation system, 120 devices use Ethernet/IP, 95 use Modbus TCP, and 35 use both protocols. How many devices use at least one of these protocols?
a. 145
b. 180
c. 185
d. 215

Answer: b. 180 Explanation: Using the set union formula: |A ∪ B| = |A| + |B| - |A ∩ B|. Here, 120 + 95 - 35 = 180 devices. Understanding set operations in this context is crucial for network design, bandwidth allocation, and protocol management in industrial communication systems.

292. A safety interlock system has three switches: X, Y, and Z. The machine operates only when X is closed, and either Y or Z (but not both) is closed. Which Boolean expression represents this condition?
a. X·(Y + Z)
b. X·Y·Z' + X·Y'·Z
c. X + (Y·Z')
d. (X·Y) + (X·Z)

Answer: b. X·Y·Z' + X·Y'·Z Explanation: This expression represents X AND (Y AND NOT Z) OR (NOT Y AND Z), satisfying the exclusive OR condition for Y and Z. Applying set theory and Boolean logic in safety systems is critical for ensuring proper operation and preventing accidents in industrial environments.

293. In a power quality survey of 200 industrial clients, 120 reported harmonic issues, 150 reported voltage fluctuations, and 90 reported both. How many clients reported neither issue?
a. 10
b. 20
c. 30
d. 40

Answer: b. 20 Explanation: Let x be the number reporting neither issue. Using the formula: Total = (Harmonic + Voltage) - (Both) + (Neither), we get 200 = 120 + 150 - 90 + x. Solving for x gives 20. This application of set theory is valuable in analyzing power quality problems and prioritizing mitigation strategies.

294. A programmable logic controller (PLC) has inputs A, B, C, and D. The output activates when either (A AND B) OR (C AND D) is true. Which of the following is the simplest equivalent Boolean expression?
a. (A + C)·(B + D)
b. A·B + C·D
c. (A·B) + (C·D) + (A·C) + (B·D)
d. (A + B)·(C + D)

Answer: b. A·B + C·D Explanation: This expression directly represents the given condition without any redundant terms. Understanding Boolean algebra and set operations at this level is crucial for efficient PLC programming and optimizing control logic in industrial automation systems.

295. A panel board has 20 circuit breaker slots. If 12 single-pole breakers and 4 double-pole breakers need to be installed, in how many ways can they be arranged?
a. 3,108,105
b. 4,586,340
c. 5,200,300
d. 6,375,600

Answer: d. 6,375,600. Explanation: This is a permutation problem with distinguishable objects. We have 16 objects (12 single-pole and 4 double-pole breakers) to arrange in 20 slots. The number of arrangements is 20! / (20-16)! = 20! / 4! = 6,375,600. This tests understanding of permutations in practical electrical installation scenarios.

296. An electrician has a set of 10 different colored wire markers. How many ways can they select 4 markers to identify the conductors in a 4-wire circuit?
a. 210
b. 5,040
c. 10,000
d. 40,320

Answer: a. 210. Explanation: This is a combination problem. We need to calculate C(10,4) = 10! / (4! * 6!) = 210. This tests understanding of combinations in wire identification applications.

297. In a three-phase system, line-to-line faults can occur between any two phases. If there are 5 transmission lines, how many different line-to-line faults are possible across the entire system?
a. 15
b. 30
c. 45
d. 60

Answer: b. 30. Explanation: For each line, there are C(3,2) = 3 possible line-to-line faults. With 5 lines, the total number of possible faults is 5 * 3 = 15. However, each fault affects two lines, so the total number of unique faults is 15 * 2 = 30. This tests application of combinations in fault analysis.

298. A power distribution system uses binary-coded decimal (BCD) for device addressing. Each device requires a 4-digit BCD address. How many unique device addresses are possible in this system?
a. 9,999
b. 10,000
c. 65,535
d. 65,536

Answer: b. 10,000. Explanation: In BCD, each digit can have 10 values (0-9). With 4 digits, we have 10 * 10 * 10 * 10 = 10,000 possible combinations. This tests understanding of number systems and their application in addressing schemes.

299. An industrial control system has 8 input sensors and 6 output actuators. Each component can be either functioning or faulty. How many different system states are possible considering all combinations of functioning and faulty components?
a. 2^14
b. 14^2
c. 8! * 6!
d. C(14,8)

Answer: a. 2^14. Explanation: Each component has 2 possible states (functioning or faulty). With 14 total components (8 inputs + 6 outputs), the total number of possible states is 2^14 = 16,384. This tests understanding of the multiplication principle in system state analysis.

300. In a power quality study, harmonic distortion up to the 7th order is being analyzed. Using the binomial theorem, expand (1 + x)^7 to determine the coefficient of the 5th order term (x^5).
a. 21
b. 35
c. 42
d. 56

Answer: a. 21. Explanation: The binomial expansion of (1 + x)^7 is 1 + 7x + 21x^2 + 35x^3 + 35x^4 + 21x^5 + 7x^6 + x^7. The coefficient of x^5 is 21, which can be calculated using the combination C(7,5). This tests application of the binomial theorem in harmonic analysis.

301. A substation has 5 incoming feeders and 8 outgoing feeders. How many different ways can 3 incoming feeders be connected to 3 outgoing feeders?
a. 1,680
b. 3,360
c. 6,720
d. 13,440

Answer: c. 6,720. Explanation: First, choose 3 incoming feeders: C(5,3) = 10. Then choose 3 outgoing feeders: C(8,3) = 56. Finally, arrange these 3 pairs: 3! = 6. Total arrangements: 10 * 56 * 6 = 3,360. However, each arrangement can be made in 2 ways (by swapping the ends of each connection), so the final answer is 3,360 * 2 = 6,720. This tests complex application of combinations and permutations in substation configuration.

302. An electrician needs to select wire colors for a complex control panel. If there are 8 available colors and each wire must be a single color, how many color combinations are possible for a 12-wire harness if repetition is allowed?
a. 8^12
b. 12^8
c. P(8,12)
d. C(8,12)

Answer: a. 8^12. Explanation: This is a case of repetition allowed. For each of the 12 wires, all 8 colors are available choices. Therefore, the total number of possibilities is 8^12. This tests understanding of the multiplication principle with repetition.

303. A digital logic circuit has 6 inputs. How many different input combinations must be tested to fully verify its truth table?
a. 32
b. 64
c. 128
d. 256

Answer: b. 64. Explanation: With 6 binary inputs, there are 2^6 = 64 possible input combinations. This tests understanding of binary systems and exhaustive testing requirements in digital logic.

304. In a three-phase system, a line-to-line fault can evolve into a three-phase fault. If the probability of a line-to-line fault evolving to a three-phase fault is 0.2, what is the probability of exactly 2 out of 5 line-to-line faults evolving to three-phase faults?
a. 0.0512
b. 0.2048
c. 0.3072
d. 0.4096

Answer: b. 0.2048. Explanation: This is a binomial probability problem. P(X=2) = C(5,2) * 0.2^2 * 0.8^3 = 10 * 0.04 * 0.512 = 0.2048. This tests application of the binomial theorem in probability calculations for fault analysis.

305. An electrician needs to install a new power line between two utility poles. Pole A is located at coordinates (2, 3) and Pole B is at (10, 15) on a grid where each unit represents 10 meters. What is the straight-line distance between the poles?
a. 120 meters
b. 130 meters
c. 140 meters
d. 150 meters

Answer: c. 140 meters Explanation: Using the distance formula: $d = \sqrt{(x_2-x_1)^2 + (y_2-y_1)^2} = \sqrt{(10-2)^2 + (15-3)^2} = \sqrt{64 + 144} = \sqrt{208} = 14.42$ units. Since each unit is 10 meters, the actual distance is 144.2 meters, rounded to 140 meters. This calculation is crucial for determining cable length and tension in overhead line installations.

306. A substation is planned at the midpoint between two existing substations. If Substation A is at (5, 10) and Substation B is at (15, 30), where should the new substation be located?
a. (10, 15)
b. (10, 20)
c. (12, 18)
d. (15, 25)

Answer: b. (10, 20) Explanation: Using the midpoint formula: $x = (x_1 + x_2)/2 = (5 + 15)/2 = 10$, $y = (y_1 + y_2)/2 = (10 + 30)/2 = 20$. Therefore, the midpoint is (10, 20). This application of analytical geometry is essential for optimizing power distribution networks and minimizing transmission losses.

307. Two parallel power lines are represented by the equations $y = 2x + 5$ and $y = 2x + 12$. What is the perpendicular distance between these lines?
a. 3.5 units
b. 5.0 units
c. 7.0 units
d. 8.5 units

Answer: a. 3.5 units Explanation: For parallel lines with equations $y = mx + b_1$ and $y = mx + b_2$, the perpendicular distance is $|b_2 - b_1| / \sqrt{1 + m^2}$. Here, $|12 - 5| / \sqrt{1 + 2^2} = 7 / 2 = 3.5$ units. Understanding parallel line properties is crucial for maintaining safe clearances between power lines and planning transmission corridors.

308. An underground cable needs to be laid perpendicular to an existing line represented by $3x - 4y + 10 = 0$. What is the equation of the line representing the new cable's path if it passes through the point (2, 5)?
a. 4x + 3y - 23 = 0
b. 4x + 3y - 26 = 0
c. 3x + 4y - 23 = 0
d. 3x + 4y - 26 = 0

Answer: b. 4x + 3y - 26 = 0 Explanation: The slope of the existing line is 3/4. For perpendicular lines, $m_1 \times m_2 = -1$, so the new line's slope is -4/3. Using point-slope form: $y - 5 = (-4/3)(x - 2)$. Simplifying to standard form: $4x + 3y - 26 = 0$. This application of perpendicular lines is essential for planning utility layouts and avoiding interference between services.

309. A triangular grounding grid has vertices at A(0, 0), B(6, 0), and C(3, 4). What is the area of this grounding grid?
a. 10 square units
b. 12 square units
c. 14 square units

d. 16 square units

Answer: b. 12 square units Explanation: Using the formula Area = $|(x_1(y_2 - y_3) + x_2(y_3 - y_1) + x_3(y_1 - y_2))| / 2$, we get: $|(0(0 - 4) + 6(4 - 0) + 3(0 - 0))| / 2 = |24| / 2 = 12$ square units. This calculation is important for designing effective grounding systems and ensuring adequate surface area for dissipating fault currents.

310. An electrician needs to install a junction box at a point that is twice as close to power source A(2, 3) as it is to power source B(14, 15). What are the coordinates of this junction box?
a. (5, 6)
b. (6, 7)
c. (7, 8)
d. (8, 9)

Answer: b. (6, 7) Explanation: This is an application of the section formula. For a point P(x, y) that divides AB in the ratio 2:1, $x = (2x_1 + x_2)/3$ and $y = (2y_1 + y_2)/3$. Thus, $x = (2(2) + 14)/3 = 6$, $y = (2(3) + 15)/3 = 7$. This concept is useful in optimizing cable runs and minimizing voltage drop in complex electrical installations.

311. Two utility poles are located at A(1, 2) and B(5, 6). A third pole C needs to be installed so that angle ABC is a right angle. If the x-coordinate of C is 3, what is its y-coordinate?
a. 0
b. 2
c. 4
d. 6

Answer: c. 4 Explanation: For ABC to be a right angle, AC must be perpendicular to AB. The slope of AB is (6-2)/(5-1) = 1. The perpendicular slope is -1. Using point-slope form with A(1, 2): y - 2 = -1(x - 1). When x = 3, y = 4. This application of perpendicular lines and slopes is crucial in maintaining proper angles and tensions in overhead line installations.

312. A circular substation has a radius of 50 meters. If the center is at (100, 100), what is the equation of the substation's perimeter?
a. $(x - 100)^2 + (y - 100)^2 = 2500$
b. $(x - 100)^2 + (y - 100)^2 = 5000$
c. $(x + 100)^2 + (y + 100)^2 = 2500$
d. $(x + 100)^2 + (y + 100)^2 = 5000$

Answer: a. $(x - 100)^2 + (y - 100)^2 = 2500$ Explanation: The general equation of a circle is $(x - h)^2 + (y - k)^2 = r^2$, where (h, k) is the center and r is the radius. Here, (h, k) = (100, 100) and r = 50, so $r^2 = 2500$. This equation is essential for planning substation layouts, clearance zones, and equipment placement.

313. An electrical conduit runs along the line 2x + 3y = 12. A perpendicular branch needs to be installed from the point (3, 2). What is the equation of the line representing this branch?
a. 2x - 3y = 0
b. 3x - 2y = 5
c. 3x + 2y = 13
d. 2x + 3y = 18

Answer: c. 3x + 2y = 13 Explanation: The slope of the original line is -2/3. For perpendicular lines, $m_1 \times m_2 = -1$, so the new line's slope is 3/2. Using point-slope form: y - 2 = (3/2)(x - 3). Simplifying to standard form: 3x + 2y = 13. This application of perpendicular lines is crucial for planning conduit layouts and ensuring proper angles in electrical installations.

314. A power line is represented by the parametric equations x = 2t + 1 and y = 3t - 2, where t is a parameter. What is the slope of this power line?
a. 2/3
b. 3/2
c. 3/4
d. 4/3

Answer: b. 3/2 Explanation: To find the slope, we need dy/dx. From the parametric equations, dx/dt = 2 and dy/dt = 3. Therefore, dy/dx = (dy/dt) / (dx/dt) = 3/2. Understanding parametric equations and their relation to slope is important for analyzing complex power line paths and trajectories in transmission line design.

315. A voltage regulator's output characteristic is given by V(t) = 12 + 2sin(πt/6), where t is in seconds. If the regulator is modified to produce a 25% larger voltage swing and a 90-degree phase shift, what is the new output function?
a. V(t) = 12 + 2.5sin(πt/6 + π/2)
b. V(t) = 15 + 2.5sin(πt/6 + π/2)
c. V(t) = 12 + 2.5sin(πt/6 - π/2)
d. V(t) = 15 + 2.5sin(πt/6 - π/2)

Answer: a. V(t) = 12 + 2.5sin(πt/6 + π/2). Explanation: The 25% larger swing changes 2 to 2.5. The 90-degree phase shift adds π/2 inside the sine function. The DC offset (12) remains unchanged. This tests understanding of function transformations in the context of voltage regulation.

316. The current through an inductor during a transient is modeled by i(t) = 10(1 - e^(-t/0.5)), where t is in milliseconds. If the time constant is doubled and the steady-state current is halved, what is the new function?
a. i(t) = 5(1 - e^(-t/0.25))
b. i(t) = 5(1 - e^(-t))
c. i(t) = 5(1 - e^(-t/0.5))
d. i(t) = 5(1 - e^(-t/1))

Answer: d. i(t) = 5(1 - e^(-t/1)). Explanation: Doubling the time constant changes 0.5 to 1 in the exponent. Halving the steady-state current changes 10 to 5. This tests understanding of exponential functions and their parameters in electrical transients.

317. A power factor correction capacitor's reactive power is given by Q(V) = 0.1V², where V is the RMS voltage. If the capacitor is reconfigured to provide 20% more reactive power at 1.1 times the original voltage, what is the new function?
a. Q(V) = 0.11(V/1.1)²
b. Q(V) = 0.12(V/1.1)²
c. Q(V) = 0.11V²
d. Q(V) = 0.12V²

Answer: b. Q(V) = 0.12(V/1.1)². Explanation: 20% more power means multiplying by 1.2, so 0.1 * 1.2 = 0.12. Operating at 1.1 times the voltage requires dividing V by 1.1 inside the function. This tests understanding of quadratic function transformations in power factor correction applications.

318. The torque-speed characteristic of an induction motor is approximated by T(ω) = 100 - 0.5ω², where ω is in rad/s. If the motor is rewound to produce 25% more torque at 80% of the original speed, what is the new characteristic function?
a. T(ω) = 125 - 0.78125(ω/0.8)²
b. T(ω) = 125 - 0.625(ω/0.8)²
c. T(ω) = 125 - 0.78125ω²
d. T(ω) = 125 - 0.625ω²

Answer: a. T(ω) = 125 - 0.78125(ω/0.8)². Explanation: 25% more torque changes 100 to 125. 80% of original speed means dividing ω by 0.8. The coefficient 0.5 changes to 0.5/(0.8²) = 0.78125 to maintain the shape. This tests understanding of quadratic function transformations in motor characteristics.

319. The voltage across a capacitor during discharge is given by V(t) = 100e^(-t/RC), where R = 10kΩ and C = 100μF. If the capacitor is replaced with one that has 50% more capacitance and the resistor with one that has 25% less resistance, what is the new discharge function?
a. V(t) = 100e^(-t/1.125RC)
b. V(t) = 100e^(-t/0.875RC)
c. V(t) = 150e^(-t/1.125RC)
d. V(t) = 150e^(-t/0.875RC)

Answer: a. V(t) = 100e^(-t/1.125RC). Explanation: The new RC time constant is (0.75R)(1.5C) = 1.125RC. The initial voltage (100) remains unchanged. This tests understanding of exponential function transformations in RC circuits.

320. A transformer's magnetization curve is approximated by B(H) = 2tanh(H/1000), where B is in Tesla and H in A/m. If the core material is changed to one with 20% higher saturation flux density and requiring 10% less magnetizing force, what is the new function?
a. B(H) = 2.4tanh(H/900)
b. B(H) = 2.4tanh(1.1H/1000)
c. B(H) = 2tanh(1.1H/1000)
d. B(H) = 2tanh(H/900)

Answer: a. B(H) = 2.4tanh(H/900). Explanation: 20% higher saturation changes 2 to 2.4. 10% less magnetizing force changes 1000 to 900 in the denominator. This tests understanding of hyperbolic function transformations in magnetic materials.

321. The efficiency of a solar panel as a function of temperature is given by η(T) = 20 - 0.05(T - 25)², where T is in °C. If a new coating increases efficiency by 2 percentage points and shifts the optimal temperature by 5°C, what is the new function?
a. η(T) = 22 - 0.05(T - 30)²
b. η(T) = 22 - 0.05(T - 20)²
c. η(T) = 20 - 0.05(T - 30)²
d. η(T) = 20 - 0.05(T - 20)²

Answer: a. η(T) = 22 - 0.05(T - 30)². Explanation: Increasing efficiency by 2 percentage points changes 20 to 22. Shifting optimal temperature by 5°C changes 25 to 30. This tests understanding of quadratic function transformations in solar panel efficiency modeling.

322. The frequency response of a low-pass RC filter is given by |H(f)| = 1/√(1 + (f/fc)²), where fc is the cutoff frequency. If the filter is modified to have a cutoff frequency 1.5 times higher and a passband gain of 0.9, what is the new function?
a. |H(f)| = 0.9/√(1 + (f/1.5fc)²)
b. |H(f)| = 0.9/√(1 + (1.5f/fc)²)
c. |H(f)| = 1/√(1 + (f/1.5fc)²)
d. |H(f)| = 1/√(1 + (1.5f/fc)²)

Answer: a. |H(f)| = 0.9/√(1 + (f/1.5fc)²). Explanation: 1.5 times higher cutoff frequency means replacing fc with 1.5fc. Passband gain of 0.9 multiplies the entire function by 0.9. This tests understanding of rational function transformations in filter design.

323. The power output of a wind turbine as a function of wind speed is modeled by P(v) = 0.5ρAv³Cp(λ,β), where ρ is air density, A is swept area, v is wind speed, and Cp is the power coefficient. If the turbine blades are lengthened to increase A by 20% and a new control system increases the maximum Cp by 10%, how does the maximum power output change?
a. Increases by 30%
b. Increases by 32%
c. Increases by 33%

135

d. Increases by 35%

Answer: b. Increases by 32%. Explanation: Increasing A by 20% multiplies the function by 1.2. Increasing Cp by 10% multiplies by 1.1. The total effect is 1.2 * 1.1 = 1.32, or a 32% increase. This tests understanding of composite function transformations in wind power generation.

324. The voltage-current characteristic of a nonlinear device is given by $I(V) = 0.1V^2 + 0.2V$. If the device is modified to operate with twice the voltage and half the current, what is the new characteristic function?
a. $I(V) = 0.025(V/2)^2 + 0.05(V/2)$
b. $I(V) = 0.025V^2 + 0.1V$
c. $I(V) = 0.05(V/2)^2 + 0.1(V/2)$
d. $I(V) = 0.05V^2 + 0.2V$

Answer: c. $I(V) = 0.05(V/2)^2 + 0.1(V/2)$. Explanation: Operating at twice the voltage means replacing V with V/2. Halving the current multiplies the entire function by 0.5. This changes 0.1 to 0.05 and 0.2 to 0.1. This tests understanding of polynomial function transformations in device characteristics.

325. A voltage regulator's output is described by the following piecewise function: V(I) = {5V, if 0 ≤ I < 1A   5 - 0.5(I - 1)V, if 1A ≤ I < 3A   4V, if I ≥ 3A. What is the output voltage when the current draw is 2.5A?
a. 4.25V
b. 4.50V
c. 4.75V
d. 5.00V

Answer: a. 4.25V Explanation: For I = 2.5A, we use the second piece of the function: 5 - 0.5(2.5 - 1) = 5 - 0.75 = 4.25V. This piecewise function models the voltage drop characteristics of a regulator under different load conditions, crucial for understanding power supply behavior in varying current demand scenarios.

326. An overcurrent protection device has a time-current characteristic defined by: t(I) = {∞, if I < 1.5In $10/((I/In)^2$ - 1))s, if 1.5In ≤ I < 10In   0.1s, if I ≥ 10In where In is the nominal current. If In = 100A, how long will it take for the device to trip at 500A?
a. 0.1s
b. 0.4s
c. 0.8s
d. 1.2s

Answer: b. 0.4s Explanation: At 500A, I/In = 5, which falls in the second range. Applying the formula: $t = 10/((5)^2 - 1) = 10/24 ≈ 0.4s$. This piecewise function models the inverse-time characteristic of the protection device, balancing rapid response to severe faults with tolerance for brief overloads.

327. A power factor correction system's capacitor bank switches according to the function: C(P) = {0 µF, if P < 10 kW   100P µF, if 10 kW ≤ P < 50 kW   5000 µF, if P ≥ 50 kW where P is the active power. What capacitance is switched in at 30 kW?
a. 1000 µF
b. 2000 µF
c. 3000 µF
d. 4000 µF

Answer: c. 3000 µF Explanation: For P = 30 kW, we use the second piece: C = 100P = 100 × 30 = 3000 µF. This piecewise function models a stepped capacitor bank, adjusting power factor correction based on load demand, essential for optimizing power quality in industrial settings.

328. An LED driver's current-voltage characteristic is given by: I(V) = {0 mA, if V < 2.7V   100(V - 2.7) mA, if 2.7V ≤ V < 3.2V   50 mA, if V ≥ 3.2V What is the current when the voltage is 3.0V?
a. 20 mA
b. 25 mA
c. 30 mA
d. 35 mA

Answer: c. 30 mA Explanation: At 3.0V, we use the second piece: I = 100(3.0 - 2.7) = 30 mA. This piecewise function accurately models the non-linear behavior of LEDs, crucial for designing efficient and stable LED driving circuits.

329. A generator's output power is controlled by a governor system described by: P(f) = {0 MW, if f < 59.5 Hz   20(f - 59.5) MW, if 59.5 Hz ≤ f < 60.5 Hz   20 MW, if f ≥ 60.5 Hz where f is the grid frequency. What is the output power at 60.2 Hz?
a. 10 MW
b. 12 MW
c. 14 MW
d. 16 MW

Answer: c. 14 MW Explanation: At 60.2 Hz, we use the second piece: P = 20(60.2 - 59.5) = 14 MW. This piecewise function models the frequency-dependent power output of a generator, essential for maintaining grid stability and load-following capabilities.

330. An induction motor's torque-speed characteristic is approximated by: T(s) = {2Tn, if s > 0.8   2.5Tn(1 - s), if 0 < s ≤ 0.8   0, if s ≤ 0 where Tn is the nominal torque and s is the slip. If Tn = 100 N·m, what is the torque at a slip of 0.4?
a. 125 N·m
b. 150 N·m
c. 175 N·m
d. 200 N·m

Answer: b. 150 N·m Explanation: For s = 0.4, we use the second piece: T = 2.5 × 100 × (1 - 0.4) = 150 N·m. This piecewise function approximates the non-linear torque-speed relationship of induction motors, crucial for analyzing motor performance under various load conditions.

331. A solar inverter's efficiency is modeled by: η(P) = {0%, if P < 50W   85 + 0.05P%, if 50W ≤ P < 300W   100%, if P ≥ 300W where P is the input power in watts. What is the efficiency at 200W input?
a. 90%
b. 92%
c. 94%
c. 95%

Answer: d. 95% Explanation: At 200W, we use the second piece: η = 85 + 0.05 × 200 = 95%. This piecewise function models the varying efficiency of a solar inverter across its operating range, essential for predicting system performance and optimizing energy harvest.

332. A battery management system uses the following piecewise function to estimate State of Charge (SoC): SoC(V) = {0%, if V < 3.2V   25(V - 3.2)%, if 3.2V ≤ V < 4.0V   100%, if V ≥ 4.0V where V is the cell voltage. What is the estimated SoC when V = 3.6V?
a. 40%
b. 50%
c. 60%
d. 70%

Answer: b. 50% Explanation: At 3.6V, we use the second piece: SoC = 25(3.6 - 3.2) = 50%. This piecewise function provides a simplified model of the non-linear relationship between cell voltage and state of charge, crucial for battery management and energy storage systems.

333. A power line's sag is approximated by the piecewise function: S(T) = {0.1 + 0.001T m, if -20°C ≤ T < 0°C   0.1 + 0.002T m, if 0°C ≤ T < 20°C   0.1 + 0.003T m, if T ≥ 20°C where T is the temperature in °C. What is the sag at 15°C?
a. 0.10 m
b. 0.13 m
c. 0.16 m
d. 0.19 m

Answer: b. 0.13 m Explanation: At 15°C, we use the second piece: S = 0.1 + 0.002 × 15 = 0.13 m. This piecewise function models the temperature-dependent sag of power lines, crucial for maintaining proper clearances and avoiding safety hazards in transmission line design.

334. An electric vehicle's regenerative braking force is described by: F(v) = {0 N, if v < 5 km/.   200v N, if 5 km/h ≤ v < 50 km/h   10000 N, if v ≥ 50 km/h. where v is the vehicle speed. What is the braking force at 30 km/h?
a. 4000 N
b. 5000 N
c. 6000 N

d. 7000 N

Answer: c. 6000 N Explanation: At 30 km/h, we use the second piece: F = 200 × 30 = 6000 N. This piecewise function models the speed-dependent regenerative braking force, essential for optimizing energy recovery and designing efficient electric vehicle drivetrains.

335. A power supply's output voltage as a function of control input is given by V(x) = 5x² + 10, where x is in volts and 0 ≤ x ≤ 5. What is the inverse function that gives the required control input for a desired output voltage?
a. x(V) = √((V - 10)/5)
b. x(V) = √((V + 10)/5)
c. x(V) = √((V - 10)/2)
d. x(V) = √((V + 10)/2)

Answer: a. x(V) = √((V - 10)/5). Explanation: To find the inverse, swap x and V, then solve for x. V = 5x² + 10 becomes x = 5V² + 10. Subtracting 10 and dividing by 5 gives x² = (V - 10)/5. Taking the square root of both sides yields the answer. This tests understanding of inverse function derivation in power supply control.

336. The current through a nonlinear device is given by I(V) = 2ln(V/5), where V > 5 volts. If this device is used in a feedback circuit, what is the transfer function that gives voltage as a function of current?
a. V(I) = 5e^(I/2)
b. V(I) = 5e^I/2
c. V(I) = 5e^(2I)
d. V(I) = 5e^I/2

Answer: a. V(I) = 5e^(I/2). Explanation: To find the inverse, swap I and V, then solve for V. I = 2ln(V/5) becomes V = 2ln(I/5). Dividing both sides by 2 gives V/2 = ln(I/5). Taking e to the power of both sides and simplifying yields the answer. This tests ability to find inverse functions involving logarithms in device characteristics.

337. A temperature control system has a transfer function G(s) = K/(s + 1), where K is the gain. If the inverse Laplace transform of the system's step response is given by T(t) = K(1 - e^(-t)), what is the expression for the time constant τ in terms of K?

a. τ = K
b. τ = 1/K
c. τ = 1
d. τ = K^2

Answer: c. τ = 1. Explanation: The general form of a first-order step response is T(t) = A(1 - e^(-t/τ)), where A is the steady-state value. Comparing this to the given expression, we see that τ = 1, regardless of K. This tests understanding of inverse Laplace transforms and time constants in control systems.

338. An analog-to-digital converter (ADC) has a transfer function V = 5(1 - e^(-D/256)), where V is the analog input voltage and D is the 8-bit digital output. What is the inverse function that gives the digital output for a given analog input?
a. D = -256ln(1 - V/5)
b. D = 256ln(1 - V/5)
c. D = -256ln(V/5)
d. D = 256ln(V/5)

Answer: a. D = -256ln(1 - V/5). Explanation: To find the inverse, swap V and D, then solve for D. 5(1 - e^(-D/256)) = V becomes 1 - e^(-D/256) = V/5. Subtracting both sides from 1 and taking the natural log gives -D/256 = ln(1 - V/5). Multiplying by -256 yields the answer. This tests ability to find inverse functions with exponentials in ADC applications.

339. A DC motor's angular velocity ω as a function of applied voltage V is given by ω(V) = K(V - IR), where K is the motor constant, I is the current, and R is the armature resistance. If ω = 1000 rad/s when V = 100V, and ω = 500 rad/s when V = 60V, what is the equation for V in terms of ω?
a. V(ω) = ω/20 + 50
b. V(ω) = ω/10 + 40
c. V(ω) = ω/15 + 45
d. V(ω) = ω/25 + 55

Answer: a. V(ω) = ω/20 + 50. Explanation: Using the two given points, we can create a system of equations: 1000 = K(100 - IR) and 500 = K(60 - IR). Subtracting these equations eliminates IR: 500 = 40K, so K = 12.5. Substituting back, we find IR = 20. The inverse function is thus V = ω/12.5 + 20, which simplifies to V = ω/20 + 50. This tests ability to derive inverse functions from experimental data in motor control.

340. The gain of an operational amplifier in inverting configuration is given by G = -Rf/Ri, where Rf is the feedback resistance and Ri is the input resistance. If the desired gain is -10, what is the relationship between Rf and Ri?
a. Rf = 10Ri
b. Ri = 10Rf
c. Rf = -10Ri
d. Ri = -10Rf

Answer: a. Rf = 10Ri. Explanation: From the given equation, -10 = -Rf/Ri. Solving for Rf yields Rf = 10Ri. This tests understanding of inverse proportionality in amplifier design.

341. A PID controller has a transfer function C(s) = Kp + Ki/s + Kds. If the inverse Laplace transform of the controller's impulse response is c(t) = Kpδ(t) + Ki + Kdδ'(t), where δ(t) is the Dirac delta function, what is the expression for the derivative term in the time domain?
a. Kd(de(t)/dt)
b. Kde(t)
c. Kd∫e(t)dt

140

d. Kd/e(t)

Answer: a. Kd(de(t)/dt). Explanation: The Laplace transform of δ'(t) is s, which corresponds to differentiation in the time domain. Therefore, the Kds term in the transfer function translates to Kd(de(t)/dt) in the time domain. This tests understanding of inverse Laplace transforms and PID control.

342. The impedance of a series RLC circuit is given by Z(s) = R + sL + 1/(sC). If the admittance Y(s) is the inverse of Z(s), what is the expression for Y(s)?
a. Y(s) = 1/(R + sL + 1/(sC))
b. Y(s) = (R + sL + 1/(sC))^(-1)
c. Y(s) = sC/(1 + sRC + s²LC)
d. Y(s) = 1/R + 1/(sL) + sC

Answer: c. Y(s) = sC/(1 + sRC + s²LC). Explanation: Y(s) is indeed 1/Z(s), but this needs to be rationalized. Multiplying numerator and denominator by sC gives Y(s) = sC/(R(sC) + s²LC + 1) = sC/(1 + sRC + s²LC). This tests ability to find and simplify inverse functions in circuit analysis.

343. A thermistor's resistance as a function of temperature is given by R(T) = R0e^(B(1/T - 1/T0)), where R0 is the resistance at reference temperature T0, and B is the thermistor constant. What is the inverse function that gives temperature as a function of resistance?
a. T(R) = B / (ln(R/R0) + B/T0)
b. T(R) = B / (ln(R/R0) - B/T0)
c. T(R) = 1 / (ln(R/R0)/B + 1/T0)
d. T(R) = 1 / (ln(R0/R)/B + 1/T0)

Answer: c. T(R) = 1 / (ln(R/R0)/B + 1/T0). Explanation: To find the inverse, swap R and T, then solve for T. Taking the natural log of both sides gives ln(R/R0) = B(1/T - 1/T0). Solving for 1/T and then T yields the answer. This tests ability to find inverse functions with exponentials in temperature sensing applications.

344. The charge Q stored on a nonlinear capacitor is given by Q(V) = CV^(3/2), where C is a constant and V is the voltage. What is the expression for the capacitance as a function of voltage?
a. C(V) = 3CV^(1/2)/2
b. C(V) = CV^(1/2)
c. C(V) = 3CV^(-1/2)/2
d. C(V) = CV^(-1/2)

Answer: a. C(V) = 3CV^(1/2)/2. Explanation: Capacitance is defined as dQ/dV. Differentiating Q(V) with respect to V gives C(V) = d(CV^(3/2))/dV = 3CV^(1/2)/2. This tests understanding of derivative-based inverse relationships in nonlinear circuit elements.

345. An RC circuit has a time constant τ = 0.5 seconds. If the initial voltage across the capacitor is 100V, what will be the voltage after 1.5 seconds during discharge?
a. 36.8V
b. 25.9V
c. 18.1V
d. 13.5V

Answer: b. 25.9V Explanation: The voltage during discharge follows $V(t) = V_0 e^{-t/\tau}$. Substituting values: $V(1.5) = 100e^{-1.5/0.5} = 100e^{-3} \approx 25.9V$. This exponential decay model is crucial for understanding capacitor discharge behavior in various electrical systems, including timing circuits and power supplies.

346. A lithium-ion battery's capacity degrades exponentially over time, modeled by $C(t) = C_0 e^{-kt}$, where C_0 is the initial capacity, k is the decay constant, and t is time in years. If a battery retains 80% of its capacity after 5 years, what is the decay constant k?
a. 0.0446 year^{-1}
b. 0.0365 year^{-1}
c. 0.0223 year^{-1}
d. 0.0149 year^{-1}

Answer: a. 0.0446 year^{-1} Explanation: Using the equation: $0.8 C_0 = C_0 e^{-5k}$. Simplifying: $0.8 = e^{-5k}$. Taking natural log of both sides: $\ln(0.8) = -5k$. Solving for k: $k = -\ln(0.8)/5 \approx 0.0446$ year^{-1}. This calculation is essential for predicting battery life and planning replacement schedules in various electrical systems.

347. An electrical load's power consumption grows exponentially, modeled by $P(t) = 1000e^{0.03t}$ watts, where t is time in hours. How long will it take for the power consumption to double?
a. 16.7 hours
b. 23.1 hours
c. 28.5 hours
d. 33.2 hours

Answer: b. 23.1 hours Explanation: To find the doubling time, solve: $2000 = 1000e^{0.03t}$. Simplifying: $2 = e^{0.03t}$. Taking natural log: $\ln(2) = 0.03t$. Solving for t: $t = \ln(2)/0.03 \approx 23.1$ hours. Understanding exponential growth is crucial for load forecasting and capacity planning in power systems.

348. A voltage signal decays according to the function $V(t) = 10e^{-0.2t} \sin(\pi t)$ volts, where t is in seconds. At what time does the envelope of this signal reach 5V?
a. 1.73 seconds
b. 2.31 seconds
c. 3.47 seconds
d. 4.62 seconds

Answer: c. 3.47 seconds Explanation: The envelope is given by $10e^{-0.2t}$. To find when this equals 5V, solve: $5 = 10e^{-0.2t}$. Taking natural log: $\ln(0.5) = -0.2t$. Solving for t: $t = -\ln(0.5)/0.2 \approx 3.47$ seconds. This type of exponential decay with sinusoidal oscillation is common in damped electrical systems and signal processing.

349. A transformer's insulation resistance decreases exponentially with temperature, following the model $R(T) = R_0 e^{-\alpha T}$, where R_0 is the resistance at 0°C, α is a constant, and T is temperature in °C. If the resistance halves every 10°C increase, what is the value of α?
a. 0.0462 °C^{-1}
b. 0.0693 °C^{-1}
c. 0.0924 °C^{-1}
d. 0.1155 °C^{-1}

Answer: b. 0.0693 °C^{-1} Explanation: For resistance to halve every 10°C, $0.5 = e^{-10\alpha}$. Taking natural log: $\ln(0.5) = -10\alpha$. Solving for α: $\alpha = -\ln(0.5)/10 \approx 0.0693$ °C^{-1}. This exponential relationship is crucial for assessing insulation degradation and planning maintenance in high-voltage equipment.

350. An electric vehicle's battery charging follows the exponential model $Q(t) = Q_{max}(1 - e^{-t/\tau})$, where Q_{max} is the maximum charge and τ is the charging time constant. If the battery reaches 63.2% of its maximum charge in 30 minutes, what is the charging time constant τ?
a. 15 minutes
b. 30 minutes
c. 45 minutes
d. 60 minutes

Answer: b. 30 minutes Explanation: At 63.2% charge, $Q(t) = 0.632 Q_{max}$. Substituting into the model: $0.632 = 1 - e^{-30/\tau}$. Solving: $e^{-30/\tau} = 0.368$. Taking natural log: $-30/\tau = \ln(0.368)$. Solving for τ: $\tau = -30/\ln(0.368) \approx 30$ minutes. Understanding this charging behavior is essential for designing efficient EV charging systems.

351. The number of defects in a batch of electrical components follows a Poisson distribution with a mean of λ defects per batch. The probability of exactly k defects is given by $P(k) = (\lambda^k e^{-\lambda})/k!$. If $\lambda = 2$, what is the probability of finding exactly 3 defects in a batch?
a. 0.135
b. 0.180
c. 0.225
d. 0.270

Answer: b. 0.180 Explanation: Substituting into the formula: $P(3) = (2^3 e^{-2})/3! = 8e^{-2}/6 \approx 0.180$. This application of exponential functions in probability distributions is crucial for quality control and reliability analysis in electrical component manufacturing.

352. A capacitor in an RC circuit charges according to the equation $V(t) = V_s(1 - e^{-t/Rc})$, where V_s is the source voltage. If R = 100kΩ and C = 10μF, how long will it take for the capacitor to reach 90% of the source voltage?

a. 1.15 ms
b. 2.30 ms
c. 3.45 ms
d. 4.60 ms

Answer: b. 2.30 ms Explanation: Solve $0.9 = 1 - e^{-t/RC}$. Rearranging: $e^{-t/RC} = 0.1$. Taking natural log: $-t/RC = \ln(0.1)$. Solving for t: $t = -RC \ln(0.1) = -100,000 \times 10^{-5} \times \ln(0.1) \approx 0.00230$ s or 2.30 ms. This calculation is essential for designing timing circuits and understanding transient behavior in RC networks.

353. The intensity of an electromagnetic field decreases exponentially with distance from its source, following $I(x) = I_0 e^{-\mu x}$, where I_0 is the initial intensity, μ is the attenuation coefficient, and x is distance. If the intensity drops to 25% at 10 meters, what is the attenuation coefficient μ?
a. 0.0693 m^{-1}
b. 0.1386 m^{-1}
c. 0.2079 m^{-1}
d. 0.2772 m^{-1}

Answer: b. 0.1386 m^{-1} Explanation: Using the equation: $0.25 I_0 = I_0 e^{-10\mu}$. Simplifying: $0.25 = e^{-10\mu}$. Taking natural log: $\ln(0.25) = -10\mu$. Solving for μ: $\mu = -\ln(0.25)/10 \approx 0.1386$ m^{-1}. This exponential decay model is crucial for analyzing electromagnetic shielding and safety in high-power electrical environments.

354. The reliability of an electrical system over time is modeled by $R(t) = e^{-\lambda t}$, where λ is the failure rate. If a system has a 95% reliability after 1000 hours of operation, what is its Mean Time Between Failures (MTBF)?
a. 15,384 hours
b. 19,230 hours
c. 23,076 hours
d. 26,922 hours

Answer: b. 19,230 hours Explanation: First, find λ using $R(1000) = 0.95 = e^{-1000\lambda}$. Solving: $\lambda = -\ln(0.95)/1000 \approx 5.13 \times 10^{-5}$ hour^{-1}. MTBF is the reciprocal of λ: MTBF $= 1/\lambda \approx 19,230$ hours. This reliability modeling is essential for maintenance planning and system design in critical electrical infrastructure.

355. A single-phase AC voltage source is represented by the parametric equations $x = 120\sin(t)$, $y = 120\cos(t)$, where t is in radians. What is the standard form equation of this voltage source in the xy-plane?
a. $x^2 + y^2 = 120^2$
b. $x^2 + y^2 = 240^2$
c. $x^2 + y^2 = 14400$
d. $x^2 + y^2 = 28800$

Answer: c. $x^2 + y^2 = 14400$. Explanation: To convert from parametric to standard form, eliminate the parameter t. Squaring and adding the equations gives $x^2 + y^2 = 120^2\sin^2(t) + 120^2\cos^2(t) = 120^2(\sin^2(t) + \cos^2(t)) = 120^2 = 14400$. This tests understanding of converting parametric equations to standard form in the context of AC voltage representation.

356. The current and voltage in an AC circuit are given by the parametric equations $i = 10\sin(\omega t)$ and $v = 100\sin(\omega t + \pi/6)$, where ω is the angular frequency. What is the power factor of this circuit?
a. 0.866 leading
b. 0.866 lagging
c. 0.500 leading
d. 0.500 lagging

Answer: b. 0.866 lagging. Explanation: The power factor is $\cos(\phi)$, where ϕ is the phase difference between voltage and current. Here, $\phi = \pi/6$ radians or 30°. $\cos(30°) = 0.866$. The current lags the voltage, so the power factor is lagging. This tests application of parametric equations in power factor calculations.

357. An electrician's hand motion while bending conduit follows the parametric equations $x = 2t$, $y = t^2 - 4t$, where t is in seconds and x, y are in inches. What is the y-coordinate when x = 6 inches?
a. -6 inches
b. 0 inches
c. 3 inches
d. 6 inches

Answer: a. -6 inches. Explanation: When x = 6, t = 3 (since x = 2t). Substituting t = 3 into the equation for y: $y = 3^2 - 4(3) = 9 - 12 = -3$. This tests ability to work with parametric equations in practical motion problems.

358. The voltage and current in a nonlinear circuit element are described by the parametric equations $V = t^3 - 3t$ and $I = t^2 - 1$, where t is a parameter. What is the expression for the instantaneous power P in terms of I?
a. $P = I^3 - 3I^2 + 3I + 1$
b. $P = I^3 + 3I^2 - 3I - 1$
c. $P = I^3 - 3I^2 - 3I + 1$
d. $P = I^3 + 3I^2 + 3I - 1$

Answer: a. $P = I^3 - 3I^2 + 3I + 1$. Explanation: Power P = VI. We need to express V in terms of I. From $I = t^2 - 1$, we get $t = \sqrt{(I + 1)}$. Substituting this into the equation for V: $V = (\sqrt{(I + 1)})^3 - 3\sqrt{(I + 1)} = (I + 1)\sqrt{(I + 1)} - 3\sqrt{(I + 1)}$. Multiplying this by I gives the result. This tests ability to manipulate parametric equations in power calculations.

359. A three-phase generator's output voltages can be represented by the parametric equations $V_a = \sin(t)$, $V_b = \sin(t - 2\pi/3)$, $V_c = \sin(t - 4\pi/3)$, where t is in radians. What is the sum of these voltages at any instant?
a. 0
b. $\sqrt{3}$
c. 3/2
d. 3

Answer: a. 0. Explanation: In a balanced three-phase system, the sum of the instantaneous voltages is always zero. Mathematically, $\sin(t) + \sin(t - 2\pi/3) + \sin(t - 4\pi/3) = 0$ for all t. This tests understanding of three-phase systems and trigonometric identities.

360. The motion of an electron in a cathode ray tube is described by the parametric equations $x = at^2$ and $y = bt$, where a and b are constants and t is time. What is the equation of the electron's path in standard form?
a. $y = (b/2a)x$
b. $y = (b/\sqrt{a})\sqrt{x}$
c. $y = (b/2\sqrt{a})\sqrt{x}$
d. $y = (2b/a)x$

Answer: b. $y = (b/\sqrt{a})\sqrt{x}$. Explanation: To eliminate t, express t in terms of x: $t = \sqrt{(x/a)}$. Substitute this into the equation for y: $y = b\sqrt{(x/a)} = (b/\sqrt{a})\sqrt{x}$. This tests ability to convert parametric equations to standard form in electron motion problems.

361. A voltage surge in a power line follows the parametric equations $V = 100e^{-0.1t}\cos(\pi t)$ and $I = 10e^{-0.1t}\sin(\pi t)$, where t is in milliseconds. At what time does the instantaneous power reach its maximum value?
a. 0 ms
b. 2.5 ms
c. 5 ms
d. 7.5 ms

Answer: a. 0 ms. Explanation: Instantaneous power $P = VI = 1000e^{-0.2t}\cos(\pi t)\sin(\pi t) = 500e^{-0.2t}\sin(2\pi t)$. The maximum occurs when t = 0 due to the exponential decay term. This tests understanding of parametric equations in power surge analysis.

362. The current in a circuit is given by the parametric equations $i = 5\sin(2\pi t)$ and $di/dt = 10\pi\cos(2\pi t)$, where t is in seconds. What is the frequency of this current?
a. 0.5 Hz
b. 1 Hz
c. 2 Hz
d. 4 Hz

Answer: b. 1 Hz. Explanation: The period of the sine function is 1 second (2π radians = 1 second), so the frequency is 1 Hz. Alternatively, $\omega = 2\pi f$, where $\omega = 2\pi$ from the given equations, so f = 1 Hz. This tests understanding of frequency in parametric representations of AC circuits.

363. A motor's rotor position θ and angular velocity ω are given by the parametric equations $\theta = \pi t^2$ and $\omega = 2\pi t$, where t is in seconds. What is the motor's angular acceleration in rad/s²?

a. π rad/s²
b. 2π rad/s²
c. 4π rad/s²
d. 8π rad/s²

Answer: b. 2π rad/s². Explanation: Angular acceleration is dω/dt. From the given equation, dω/dt = 2π, which is constant. This tests understanding of derivatives in parametric equations for motor motion analysis.

364. The voltage and current in an RLC circuit during resonance are given by the parametric equations V = 100sin(ωt) and I = 2cos(ωt), where ω is the resonant frequency. What is the energy stored in the circuit as a function of time?
a. E = 100sin²(ωt)
b. E = 200sin(ωt)cos(ωt)
c. E = 100cos²(ωt)
d. E = 50sin(2ωt)

Answer: c. E = 100cos²(ωt). Explanation: In an RLC circuit at resonance, energy oscillates between the inductor and capacitor. The total energy is proportional to I², which is 4cos²(ωt). Scaling this to match the given voltage amplitude gives 100cos²(ωt). This tests understanding of energy storage in resonant circuits using parametric equations.

365. A directional antenna has a radiation pattern described by the polar equation r = 2 + 2cos(θ). What is the maximum distance (in arbitrary units) from the antenna at which the signal strength is non-zero?
a. 2
b. 3
c. 4
d. 5

Answer: c. 4 Explanation: The maximum value occurs when cos(θ) = 1, which is at θ = 0°. At this point, r = 2 + 2(1) = 4. This polar equation represents a cardioid pattern, common in many directional antennas. Understanding these patterns is crucial for optimizing wireless communication systems and reducing interference.

366. An electrician needs to install a circular bus bar with a radius of 0.5 meters. The connection point is located at rectangular coordinates (0.3, 0.4) meters relative to the center. What is the angular position of this connection point in polar coordinates?
a. 36.9°
b. 53.1°
c. 66.4°
d. 75.5°

Answer: b. 53.1° Explanation: To convert from rectangular (x, y) to polar (r, θ) coordinates, use θ = tan⁻¹(y/x). Here, θ = tan⁻¹(0.4/0.3) ≈ 53.1°. This calculation is essential for precise positioning of connections on circular bus bars, ensuring proper load distribution and minimizing impedance imbalances.

367. A power line sag is modeled by the polar equation r = 2sec(θ), where r is in meters and θ is measured from the vertical. What is the maximum sag of the power line?
a. 1 meter
b. 2 meters
c. 3 meters
d. 4 meters

Answer: b. 2 meters Explanation: The maximum sag occurs at θ = 90° (horizontal direction), where sec(90°) approaches infinity. As θ approaches 90°, r approaches 2 meters. This polar model helps in analyzing power line sag for safety clearances and structural load calculations.

368. An induction motor's magnetic field rotates in a circular pattern. At time t, the field vector is represented in polar coordinates as (5∠ωt), where ω is the angular velocity. If ω = 377 rad/s (corresponding to 60 Hz), what are the rectangular coordinates of the field vector at t = 2 ms?
a. (3.78, 3.28)
b. (3.28, -3.78)
c. (-3.28, 3.78)
d. (-3.78, -3.28)

Answer: a. (3.78, 3.28) Explanation: At t = 2 ms, θ = ωt = 377 × 0.002 = 0.754 rad. Converting to rectangular coordinates: x = 5cos(0.754) ≈ 3.78, y = 5sin(0.754) ≈ 3.28. This calculation is crucial for analyzing rotating magnetic fields in AC machines and understanding their time-varying nature.

369. A grounding electrode is driven into soil with varying resistivity. The resistance R as a function of depth d is given by the polar equation R = 10/(1 + 0.1d), where d is in meters and R in ohms. At what depth does the resistance reach 5Ω?
a. 5 meters
b. 10 meters
c. 15 meters
d. 20 meters

Answer: b. 10 meters Explanation: Solve 5 = 10/(1 + 0.1d) for d. Rearranging: 1 + 0.1d = 2, so d = 10 meters. This polar model helps in determining optimal grounding electrode depths for achieving target resistance values, crucial for electrical safety and lightning protection systems.

370. An electrician is analyzing harmonic distortion in a power system. The voltage waveform is represented in polar form as V(θ) = 220cos(θ) + 22cos(3θ) + 11cos(5θ) volts. What is the peak voltage of this waveform?
a. 220 V
b. 231 V
c. 242 V
d. 253 V

Answer: d. 253 V Explanation: The peak occurs when all harmonics align. Adding the magnitudes: 220 + 22 + 11 = 253 V. This polar representation of harmonics is useful for analyzing complex waveforms and assessing power quality in electrical systems.

371. A transformer's magnetic core has a B-H curve approximated by the polar equation $r = 2\theta/(\pi - \theta)$, where r represents the magnetic flux density B and θ the magnetic field strength H (both in arbitrary units). At what angle θ does the core begin to saturate, indicated by a rapid increase in r?
a. π/4 rad
b. π/3 rad
c. π/2 rad
d. 2π/3 rad

Answer: c. π/2 rad Explanation: As θ approaches π, r approaches infinity, indicating saturation. The knee of the curve, where saturation begins, is typically around π/2. This polar model of the B-H curve helps in analyzing transformer core behavior and designing efficient magnetic circuits.

372. An antenna array has a radiation pattern given by the polar equation $r = \sin^2(2\theta)$. How many main lobes does this pattern have?
a. 2
b. 3
c. 4
d. 5

Answer: c. 4 Explanation: The pattern repeats every π/2 radians (90°), resulting in four main lobes. This type of multi-lobe pattern is common in certain directional antenna arrays. Understanding these patterns is crucial for antenna design and optimizing signal coverage in communication systems.

373. A circular busbar carries a current I. The magnetic field strength H at a distance r from the center is given by the polar equation $H = I/(2\pi r)$. If I = 1000 A, at what distance from the center is H equal to 100 A/m?
a. 0.796 m
b. 1.592 m
c. 2.388 m
d. 3.184 m

Answer: b. 1.592 m Explanation: Solve 100 = 1000/(2πr) for r. This gives r = 1000/(2π × 100) ≈ 1.592 m. This polar relationship between current and magnetic field is fundamental in analyzing electromagnetic fields around conductors and designing safe clearances in high-current applications.

374. An electrical engineer is designing a spiral inductor on a printed circuit board. The spiral is described by the polar equation r = 0.1θ (r in cm, θ in radians). If the spiral makes 3 complete turns, what is the total length of the conductor?
a. 6.28 cm
b. 8.64 cm
c. 11.31 cm
d. 14.14 cm

Answer: c. 11.31 cm Explanation: For 3 turns, θ goes from 0 to 6π. The length is given by the integral of √(r² + (dr/dθ)²) dθ from 0 to 6π. Solving this gives approximately 11.31 cm. This application of polar coordinates in PCB design is crucial for creating compact, high-performance inductors in RF and power electronics.

375. A protective relay's time-current characteristic is given by t(I) = k / (I² - 1), where t is the trip time in seconds, I is the current in per-unit, and k is a constant. What is the limit of t(I) as I approaches 1 from the right?
a. 0
b. k/2
c. k
d. ∞

Answer: d. ∞. Explanation: As I approaches 1 from the right, I² - 1 approaches 0⁺, making the denominator infinitesimally small and t(I) approach infinity. This tests understanding of one-sided limits in protective relay characteristics.

376. The voltage across a capacitor during charging is given by V(t) = Vs(1 - e^(-t/RC)), where Vs is the source voltage, R is resistance, and C is capacitance. What is the limit of V(t) as t approaches infinity?
a. 0
b. Vs
c. Vs/2
d. Vs(1 - 1/e)

Answer: b. Vs. Explanation: As t approaches infinity, e^(-t/RC) approaches 0, so V(t) approaches Vs(1 - 0) = Vs. This tests understanding of limits involving exponential functions in capacitor charging circuits.

377. A power system's voltage stability is modeled by the function V(P) = √(1 - P/Pmax), where V is the bus voltage in per-unit, P is the active power, and Pmax is the maximum power. At what value of P is V(P) discontinuous?
a. 0
b. Pmax/2
c. Pmax
d. 2Pmax

Answer: c. Pmax. Explanation: The function is discontinuous when the expression under the square root becomes negative, which occurs when P > Pmax. At P = Pmax, the function is undefined. This tests understanding of domain and continuity in power system stability models.

378. The current through a nonlinear device is given by I(V) = {V²/10 for V ≤ 5; V - 3 for V > 5}. Is this function continuous at V = 5?
a. Yes, because both pieces evaluate to 2.5 at V = 5
b. No, because the derivative is discontinuous at V = 5
c. Yes, because the limit from both sides equals 2.5
d. No, because the function is piecewise defined

Answer: a. Yes, because both pieces evaluate to 2.5 at V = 5. Explanation: For continuity at V = 5, both pieces must evaluate to the same value. Left piece: 5²/10 = 2.5. Right piece: 5 - 3 = 2.5. Since these are equal, the function is continuous at V = 5. This tests understanding of continuity in piecewise functions representing device characteristics.

379. An induction motor's slip-torque characteristic is approximated by T(s) = 2s / (s² + 0.01) for 0 ≤ s ≤ 1, where T is torque and s is slip. What is the maximum torque and at what slip does it occur?
a. 10 at s = 0.1
b. 10 at s = 0.01
c. 5 at s = 0.1
d. 5 at s = 0.01

Answer: a. 10 at s = 0.1. Explanation: To find the maximum, differentiate T(s) and set to zero: dT/ds = (2s² + 0.02 - 4s²) / (s² + 0.01)² = 0. Solving gives s = 0.1. The maximum torque is T(0.1) = 2(0.1) / (0.1² + 0.01) = 10. This tests application of limits and derivatives in motor characteristics.

380. The impedance of a series RLC circuit near resonance is given by Z(ω) = R + j(ωL - 1/(ωC)). What is the limit of |Z(ω)| as ω approaches infinity?
a. R
b. ∞
c. √(R² + L²)
d. 0

Answer: b. ∞. Explanation: As ω approaches infinity, the inductive reactance ωL dominates, causing |Z(ω)| to approach infinity. This tests understanding of limits in complex impedance functions.

381. A voltage regulator's transfer function is H(s) = K / (s + K), where K is the gain. What is the limit of H(s) as s approaches 0, and what does this represent?
a. 1, representing the DC gain
b. K, representing the high-frequency gain
c. 0, representing perfect regulation
d. ∞, representing instability

Answer: a. 1, representing the DC gain. Explanation: lim(s→0) H(s) = K / (0 + K) = 1. This represents the DC gain of the regulator, indicating its steady-state behavior. This tests understanding of transfer function limits in control systems.

382. The magnetic flux density B in a ferromagnetic material as a function of magnetic field intensity H is given by B(H) = $\mu_0\mu_r$H / (1 + |H|/Hs), where Hs is the saturation field. What is the limit of B(H) as H approaches infinity?
a. 0
b. $\mu_0\mu_r$Hs
c. $\mu_0\mu_r$
d. ∞

Answer: b. $\mu_0\mu_r$Hs. Explanation: As H approaches infinity, |H|/Hs dominates in the denominator: lim(H→∞) B(H) = lim(H→∞) $\mu_0\mu_r$H / (H/Hs) = $\mu_0\mu_r$Hs. This represents the saturation flux density. This tests understanding of limits in magnetic material models.

383. A power electronic converter's output voltage as a function of control angle α is given by V(α) = Vm(1 + cosα) / 2 for 0 ≤ α ≤ π. Is this function continuous on its domain?
a. Yes, because it's a composition of continuous functions
b. No, because it's undefined at α = π
c. Yes, but only if Vm is constant
d. No, because it has a discontinuity at α = π/2

Answer: a. Yes, because it's a composition of continuous functions. Explanation: V(α) is composed of cosine and constant functions, which are continuous on all real numbers. The domain restriction doesn't introduce discontinuities. This tests understanding of continuity in power electronic control functions.

384. The transient current in an RL circuit is given by i(t) = (V/R)(1 - e^(-Rt/L)), where V is the applied voltage. What is the limit of di/dt as t approaches 0, and what does this represent?
a. V/L, representing the initial rate of current change
b. V/R, representing the steady-state current
c. ∞, representing an instantaneous current change
d. 0, representing a slow start

Answer: a. V/L, representing the initial rate of current change. Explanation: Differentiating i(t) gives di/dt = (V/L)e^(-Rt/L). As t approaches 0, this approaches V/L. This initial rate is determined by the circuit's inductance and applied voltage. This tests understanding of limits and derivatives in transient circuit analysis.

385. A voltage across a capacitor in an RC circuit is given by V(t) = 10(1 - $e^{-t/5}$) volts, where t is in seconds. What is the rate of change of voltage at t = 5 seconds?
a. 0.74 V/s

b. 0.82 V/s
c. 0.90 V/s
d. 0.98 V/s

Answer: a. 0.74 V/s Explanation: The rate of change is given by $dV/dt = 10(1/5)e^{-t/5}$. At t = 5, $dV/dt = 2e^{-1} \approx 0.74$ V/s. This calculation is crucial for understanding capacitor charging behavior and designing timing circuits. The derivative represents the instantaneous rate of voltage change, essential in analyzing transient responses in electrical systems.

386. An electrical motor's power output P (in watts) as a function of its angular velocity ω (in rad/s) is given by P(ω) = 1000ω - 2ω³. At what angular velocity does the motor reach its maximum power output?
a. 8.16 rad/s
b. 10.21 rad/s
c. 12.91 rad/s
d. 15.47 rad/s

Answer: c. 12.91 rad/s Explanation: To find the maximum, set dP/dω = 0. dP/dω = 1000 - 6ω². Solving 1000 - 6ω² = 0 gives ω = √(1000/6) ≈ 12.91 rad/s. This optimization problem is critical for determining the most efficient operating point of electric motors, balancing speed and power output.

387. The current in a conductor is given by I(t) = 5t² - 2t + 3 amperes, where t is in seconds. What is the rate of change of current at t = 2 seconds?
a. 14 A/s
b. 16 A/s
c. 18 A/s
d. 20 A/s

Answer: c. 18 A/s Explanation: The rate of change is dI/dt = 10t - 2. At t = 2, dI/dt = 10(2) - 2 = 18 A/s. This application of differentiation is essential in analyzing time-varying currents, particularly in circuit protection and electromagnetic field calculations.

388. A transformer's efficiency η as a function of load factor x is given by η(x) = 98 - 0.5x - 0.1x² percent. At what load factor is the efficiency maximum?
a. 1.25
b. 2.25
c. 2.50
d. 3.25

Answer: c. 2.50 Explanation: For maximum efficiency, set dη/dx = 0. dη/dx = -0.5 - 0.2x. Solving -0.5 - 0.2x = 0 gives x = 2.50. This optimization problem is crucial for determining the optimal operating point of transformers, balancing losses and load conditions.

389. The power factor of a circuit as a function of capacitance C (in µF) is given by PF(C) = 0.6 + 0.002C - 0.00001C². What capacitance value maximizes the power factor?
a. 75 µF
b. 100 µF
c. 125 µF
d. 150 µF

Answer: b. 100 µF Explanation: For maximum PF, set dPF/dC = 0. dPF/dC = 0.002 - 0.00002C. Solving 0.002 - 0.00002C = 0 gives C = 100 µF. This application of differentiation is essential in power factor correction, optimizing capacitor bank sizing for improved system efficiency.

390. The magnetic field B (in tesla) at a distance r (in meters) from a long straight wire carrying current I is given by B(r) = (μ_0I)/(2πr), where μ_0 is a constant. What is the rate of change of B with respect to r when r = 0.1 m and I = 100 A?
a. -318.3 T/m
b. -636.6 T/m
c. -954.9 T/m
d. -1273.2 T/m

Answer: c. -954.9 T/m Explanation: dB/dr = -(μ_0I)/(2πr²). With μ_0 = 4π × 10⁻⁷, I = 100, and r = 0.1, dB/dr = -(4π × 10⁻⁷ × 100)/(2π × 0.1²) ≈ -954.9 T/m. This calculation is crucial in analyzing magnetic field gradients around conductors, important for electromagnetic compatibility and safety considerations.

391. The instantaneous power in an AC circuit is given by P(t) = 200sin²(120πt) watts. What is the maximum rate of change of power?
a. 75,398 W/s
b. 90,478 W/s
c. 105,557 W/s
d. 120,637 W/s

Answer: a. 75,398 W/s Explanation: dP/dt = 400 × 120π × sin(120πt)cos(120πt). The maximum occurs when sin(2 × 120πt) = ±1, giving |dP/dt|max = 400 × 120π ≈ 75,398 W/s. This calculation is important for understanding power fluctuations in AC systems and designing appropriate control and protection mechanisms.

392. The voltage across an inductor during a transient is V(t) = 100e⁻⁵⁰ᵗsin(200t) volts. At what time does the voltage reach its maximum negative value in the first cycle?
a. 7.07 ms
b. 8.64 ms
c. 10.21 ms
d. 11.78 ms

Answer: b. 8.64 ms Explanation: The maximum negative value occurs when dV/dt = 0 and d²V/dt² > 0. Solving this gives t = (π + tan⁻¹(4))/(200) ≈ 8.64 ms. This application of derivatives is crucial in analyzing transient responses in inductive circuits, important for protection system design and power quality analysis.

393. A solar panel's output current I (in amperes) as a function of voltage V (in volts) is given by I(V) = 10 - 0.5V - 0.01V². At what voltage is the output power maximum?
a. 8.33 V
b. 9.17 V
c. 10.00 V
d. 10.83 V

Answer: b. 9.17 V Explanation: Power P = VI = V(10 - 0.5V - 0.01V²). For maximum power, dP/dV = 0. Solving this equation yields V ≈ 9.17 V. This optimization problem is critical in solar panel system design, determining the maximum power point for efficient energy harvesting.

394. The magnetic flux Φ through a coil varies with time t according to Φ(t) = 0.2sin(50t) + 0.1sin(100t) webers. What is the maximum induced EMF in the coil?
a. 10 V
b. 15 V
c. 20 V
d. 25 V

Answer: c. 20 V Explanation: The induced EMF is -dΦ/dt = -[10cos(50t) + 10cos(100t)]. The maximum occurs when both cosine terms equal ±1, giving a maximum magnitude of 20 V. This application of differentiation is fundamental in electromagnetic induction, crucial for transformer and generator design.

395. A variable speed drive's output voltage as a function of time during acceleration is given by V(t) = 20t² - 5t, where t is in seconds and V is in volts. What is the total energy delivered to the load over a 5-second interval, assuming a constant current of 10A?
a. 6250 J
b. 7500 J
c. 8333 J
d. 9166 J

Answer: c. 8333 J. Explanation: Energy E = ∫P dt = ∫VI dt = 10∫(20t² - 5t) dt from 0 to 5 seconds. Integrating: E = 10[20t³/3 - 5t²/2]₀⁵ = 10(833.33 - 62.5) = 8333 J (rounded). This tests application of definite integrals in energy calculations for variable speed drives.

396. The current in an RC circuit during discharge is given by i(t) = 5e^(-t/RC), where R = 100Ω and C = 50μF. What is the total charge that flows through the circuit from t = 0 to t = ∞?
a. 25 μC

b. 50 µC
c. 75 µC
d. 100 µC

Answer: a. 25 µC. Explanation: Total charge Q = ∫i(t) dt from 0 to ∞. Q = 5∫e^(-t/RC) dt = 5RC[e^(-t/RC)]₀^∞ = 5RC = 5(100)(50*10⁻⁶) = 25 µC. This tests understanding of indefinite integrals and their application in capacitor discharge problems.

397. A transformer's core loss as a function of flux density B is given by P(B) = kB^n, where k and n are constants. If the flux density varies sinusoidally as B(t) = Bm sin(ωt), what is the average core loss over one cycle?
a. kBm^n / π
b. 2kBm^n / π
c. kBm^n / 2
d. 2kBm^n

Answer: b. 2kBm^n / π. Explanation: Average loss = (1/T)∫P(B(t)) dt over one cycle, where T = 2π/ω. This becomes (ω/2π)∫k(Bm sin(ωt))^n dt from 0 to 2π/ω. Using the substitution u = ωt, this simplifies to (2kBm^n/π)∫|sin u|^n du from 0 to π, which equals 2kBm^n/π. This tests integration of nonlinear functions in magnetic core loss calculations.

398. The instantaneous power in an AC circuit is given by p(t) = 200 sin(ωt) cos(ωt) watts. What is the average power over one cycle?
a. 0 W
b. 50 W
c. 100 W
d. 200 W

Answer: c. 100 W. Explanation: Using the trigonometric identity sin(2x) = 2sin(x)cos(x), we can rewrite p(t) as 100 sin(2ωt). The average power is (1/T)∫p(t) dt over one cycle. Since the integral of sin(2ωt) over a full cycle is zero, the average power is 100 W. This tests understanding of power calculations in AC circuits using trigonometric integrals.

399. A variable inductor's inductance as a function of current is L(i) = L₀ + ki², where L₀ and k are constants. If the current varies as i(t) = Im sin(ωt), what is the expression for the instantaneous voltage across the inductor?
a. v(t) = L₀ωIm cos(ωt) + 2kIm³ω sin(ωt) cos(ωt)
b. v(t) = L₀ωIm cos(ωt) + kIm³ω sin³(ωt)
c. v(t) = L₀ωIm cos(ωt) + 3kIm³ω sin²(ωt) cos(ωt)
d. v(t) = L₀ωIm cos(ωt) + kIm³ω sin(ωt) cos²(ωt)

Answer: c. v(t) = L₀ωIm cos(ωt) + 3kIm³ω sin²(ωt) cos(ωt). Explanation: The voltage is given by v = L(di/dt) + i(dL/di)(di/dt). Differentiating i(t) and L(i), and substituting, we get the result. This tests application of the product rule and chain rule in nonlinear inductor analysis.

400. A capacitor bank's charging current is i(t) = 10e^(-t/τ) amperes. If the capacitor reaches 63.2% of its full charge in 5 seconds, what is the total charge stored in the capacitor?
a. 25 C
b. 50 C
c. 75 C
d. 100 C

Answer: b. 50 C. Explanation: The time constant τ is 5 seconds (63.2% is 1-1/e). Total charge Q = ∫i(t) dt from 0 to ∞ = 10∫e^(-t/5) dt = 10 * 5 = 50 C. This tests understanding of exponential decay and its integral in capacitor charging scenarios.

401. The force F required to push a heavy electrical cabinet across a floor is given by F(x) = 500 + 50x N, where x is the distance in meters. How much work is done in moving the cabinet 10 meters?
a. 5000 J
b. 6250 J
c. 7500 J
d. 8750 J

Answer: c. 7500 J. Explanation: Work W = ∫F(x) dx from 0 to 10 meters. W = ∫(500 + 50x) dx = [500x + 25x²]₀¹⁰ = 5000 + 2500 = 7500 J. This tests application of work integrals in practical scenarios.

402. A power line's temperature rise above ambient as a function of current is given by ΔT(I) = kI², where k is a constant. If the current varies sinusoidally as I(t) = Im sin(ωt), what is the average temperature rise over one cycle?
a. kIm² / 2
b. kIm² / √2
c. kIm² / 4
d. kIm² / 2√2

Answer: a. kIm² / 2. Explanation: Average temperature rise = (1/T)∫ΔT(I(t)) dt over one cycle. This becomes (k/2π)∫Im² sin²(ωt) dt from 0 to 2π. Using the identity sin²x = (1 - cos(2x))/2, this integrates to kIm² / 2. This tests integration of squared sinusoidal functions in thermal calculations.

403. The magnetic field H produced by a long straight wire carrying current I is given by H = I / (2πr), where r is the distance from the wire. What is the total magnetic flux through a rectangular loop of height h and width w, with one side parallel to the wire at a distance d?
a. (μ₀Ih/2π) ln(1 + w/d)
b. (μ₀Ih/π) ln(1 + w/d)
c. (μ₀Ih/2π) ln(w/d)
d. (μ₀Ih/π) ln(w/d)

Answer: a. $(\mu_0 Ih/2\pi) \ln(1 + w/d)$. Explanation: Flux $\Phi = \mu_0 \int H \, dr \, dz = \mu_0 Ih/(2\pi) \int dr/r$ from d to d+w. This integrates to $(\mu_0 Ih/2\pi) \ln(1 + w/d)$. This tests application of integration in electromagnetic field calculations.

404. A synchronous generator's excitation current during a step change is modeled by $i(t) = I_0(1 - e^{(-t/\tau)}) + I_1 e^{(-t/\tau)}$, where I_0, I_1, and τ are constants. What is the total charge that flows through the field winding from $t = 0$ to $t = \infty$?
a. $I_0 \tau$
b. $I_1 \tau$
c. $(I_0 + I_1)\tau$
d. $(I_0 - I_1)\tau$

Answer: c. $(I_0 + I_1)\tau$. Explanation: Total charge $Q = \int i(t) \, dt$ from 0 to ∞. Integrating, we get $Q = I_0 t - I_0 \tau e^{(-t/\tau)} - I_1 \tau e^{(-t/\tau)}$ evaluated from 0 to ∞. This yields $(I_0 + I_1)\tau$. This tests integration of exponential functions in generator excitation analysis.

405. A journeyman electrician needs to lift a 500-pound transformer using a lever system. The fulcrum is placed 2 feet from the load end of a 10-foot lever. What force must be applied to the other end to lift the transformer?
a. 83.3 pounds
b. 100 pounds
c. 125 pounds
d. 150 pounds

Answer: c. 125 pounds Explanation: Using the lever principle, (Force × Distance) on one side equals (Force × Distance) on the other. Here, 500 × 2 = F × 8, where F is the required force. Solving this gives F = 125 pounds. Understanding lever systems is crucial for safely handling heavy electrical equipment and optimizing mechanical advantage in various installation scenarios.

406. An electrician is using a compound pulley system to hoist a 200-pound electrical panel. The system consists of two fixed and two movable pulleys. Neglecting friction, what force is required to lift the panel?
a. 25 pounds
b. 50 pounds
c. 75 pounds
d. 100 pounds

Answer: b. 50 pounds Explanation: In a compound pulley system with n movable pulleys, the mechanical advantage is 2^n. Here, with 2 movable pulleys, the advantage is $2^2 = 4$. Therefore, the force required is 200/4 = 50 pounds. Proficiency in pulley systems is essential for safely and efficiently lifting heavy electrical equipment in various installation and maintenance scenarios.

407. A motor drives a gear train where the first gear has 20 teeth, the second has 60 teeth, and the third has 40 teeth. If the motor shaft rotates at 1800 RPM, what is the speed of the final gear?
a. 300 RPM
b. 450 RPM

c. 600 RPM
d. 900 RPM

Answer: c. 600 RPM Explanation: The gear ratio is calculated as (teeth of driven gear / teeth of driving gear). The overall ratio is (60/20) × (40/60) = 2. The final speed is 1800/2 = 900 RPM. Understanding gear ratios is crucial for electricians working with motor-driven systems, conveyor belts, and other mechanical applications in industrial settings.

408. An apprentice needs to determine the mechanical advantage of a block and tackle system used to lift a 600-pound electrical generator. If the system requires 150 pounds of force to lift the generator, what is the mechanical advantage?
a. 2
b. 3
c. 4
d. 5

Answer: c. 4 Explanation: Mechanical advantage (MA) is calculated as the load weight divided by the effort force. Here, MA = 600/150 = 4. This concept is vital for electricians to understand when dealing with heavy equipment installation, as it allows for efficient use of manpower and ensures safety in lifting operations.

409. A variable speed drive is connected to a gearbox with a ratio of 5:1. The motor's maximum speed is 3600 RPM. What is the minimum speed of the output shaft if the drive can reduce the motor's speed to 10% of its maximum?
a. 36 RPM
b. 72 RPM
c. 108 RPM
d. 144 RPM

Answer: b. 72 RPM Explanation: The motor's minimum speed is 10% of 3600 RPM, which is 360 RPM. With a 5:1 gear ratio, the output shaft speed is 360/5 = 72 RPM. This calculation is important for electricians working with variable speed drives and geared systems in industrial applications, ensuring proper speed control and system performance.

410. An electrician is using a chain hoist with a mechanical advantage of 6 to lift a 900-pound transformer. If the chain is pulled with a force of 160 pounds, what is the efficiency of the hoist system?
a. 87.5%
b. 90.0%
c. 93.75%
d. 96.25%

Answer: c. 93.75% Explanation: In an ideal system, a 150-pound force (900/6) would be required. The actual force is 160 pounds. Efficiency is calculated as (ideal force / actual force) × 100 = (150/160) × 100 = 93.75%. Understanding efficiency in mechanical systems is crucial for electricians to assess equipment performance and identify potential issues in lifting and moving heavy electrical components.

411. A conveyor belt system in a factory uses three gears in series. The first gear has 30 teeth, the second has 45 teeth, and the third has 60 teeth. If the input shaft rotates at 1200 RPM, what is the speed of the conveyor belt drive shaft?
a. 400 RPM
b. 500 RPM
c. 600 RPM
d. 700 RPM

Answer: a. 400 RPM Explanation: The gear ratio is (45/30) × (60/45) = 2/1 × 4/3 = 8/3. The final speed is 1200 × (3/8) = 450 RPM. Proper understanding of gear ratios is essential for electricians working in industrial settings, particularly when troubleshooting or maintaining motor-driven systems.

412. An electrician needs to lift a 300-pound electrical cabinet using a simple machine. The machine provides a mechanical advantage of 5. Assuming 80% efficiency, what force must be applied to lift the cabinet?
a. 60 pounds
b. 70 pounds
c. 75 pounds
d. 80 pounds

Answer: c. 75 pounds Explanation: In an ideal system, the force required would be 300/5 = 60 pounds. Accounting for 80% efficiency, the actual force needed is 60/0.8 = 75 pounds. This calculation demonstrates the importance of considering both mechanical advantage and efficiency in real-world applications, crucial for safe and effective handling of heavy electrical equipment.

413. A wind turbine's gearbox has a planetary gear system with a sun gear of 20 teeth, planet gears of 40 teeth each, and a ring gear of 100 teeth. If the turbine blades rotate at 15 RPM, what is the speed of the generator shaft connected to the sun gear?

a. 60 RPM
b. 75 RPM
c. 90 RPM
d. 105 RPM

Answer: b. 75 RPM Explanation: In a planetary gear system, the ratio is (teeth of ring gear + teeth of sun gear) / teeth of sun gear. Here, that's (100 + 20) / 20 = 6. So, the sun gear (and generator shaft) rotates 6 times faster than the input, giving 15 × 6 = 90 RPM. Understanding complex gear systems is crucial for electricians working with renewable energy systems and industrial power generation.

414. An electrician is designing a pulley system to lift a 1000-pound electrical transformer. The system needs to reduce the effort to 200 pounds or less. What is the minimum number of movable pulleys required in the system, assuming 100% efficiency?
a. 2 pulleys
b. 3 pulleys
c. 4 pulleys
d. 5 pulleys

Answer: b. 3 pulleys Explanation: The mechanical advantage needed is at least 1000/200 = 5. In a compound pulley system, the mechanical advantage is 2^n, where n is the number of movable pulleys. We need $2^n ≥ 5$. The smallest integer n that satisfies this is 3, as 2^3 = 8 > 5. This problem demonstrates the importance of understanding pulley systems for efficient and safe lifting of heavy electrical equipment.

415. A three-phase motor's terminal box has six connection points arranged in two rows of three. If the motor is rotated 180° around its vertical axis, which of the following correctly describes the new arrangement of terminals?
a. The order is reversed within each row
b. The rows are swapped, and the order is reversed within each row
c. The rows are swapped, but the order within each row remains the same
d. The arrangement remains unchanged

Answer: b. The rows are swapped, and the order is reversed within each row. Explanation: A 180° rotation around the vertical axis will swap the rows and reverse the order within each row. This tests understanding of rotational symmetry in electrical equipment configurations.

416. An electrician needs to bend a square duct into an L-shape for a 90° turn. If the duct is 6 inches wide and the bend radius is 3 inches, what is the length of the outer edge of the bend?
a. 4.71 inches
b. 9.42 inches
c. 14.14 inches
d. 18.85 inches

Answer: c. 14.14 inches. Explanation: The outer edge forms a quarter circle with radius 9 inches (6 + 3). The length of this arc is πr/2 = π * 9 / 2 ≈ 14.14 inches. This tests ability to visualize 3D bends and calculate arc lengths.

417. A cylindrical conduit with a diameter of 2 inches is cut at a 45° angle. What shape is formed at the cut surface?
a. Circle
b. Ellipse
c. Parabola
d. Hyperbola

Answer: b. Ellipse. Explanation: When a cylinder is cut at an angle other than 90°, the resulting cross-section is an ellipse. The more acute the angle, the more elongated the ellipse becomes. This tests understanding of 3D geometric intersections.

418. An electrician is installing a junction box in the corner where two walls meet the ceiling. If the box is 4 inches wide, 4 inches high, and 2 inches deep, what is the minimum volume of drywall that needs to be removed to accommodate the box?
a. 16 cubic inches
b. 24 cubic inches
c. 32 cubic inches
d. 40 cubic inches

Answer: c. 32 cubic inches. Explanation: The box occupies 4 * 4 * 2 = 32 cubic inches. However, it's positioned in the corner, so parts of it occupy space in the walls and ceiling, not just the drywall. The minimum volume to remove is still 32 cubic inches. This tests spatial reasoning in practical installation scenarios.

419. A coaxial cable is cut perpendicular to its axis. From innermost to outermost, the cross-section shows a solid circle, a ring, another ring, and another ring. What does each of these shapes represent?
a. Conductor, insulator, shield, jacket
b. Insulator, conductor, shield, jacket
c. Conductor, shield, insulator, jacket
d. Conductor, insulator, jacket, shield

Answer: a. Conductor, insulator, shield, jacket. Explanation: In a typical coaxial cable, the innermost part is the conductor, surrounded by an insulator, then a conductive shield, and finally an outer insulating jacket. This tests knowledge of cable construction and ability to visualize cross-sections.

420. An electrician needs to install a circular junction box in a triangular space formed by roof trusses. If the triangle has sides of 12, 16, and 20 inches, what is the maximum diameter of the circular box that can fit in this space?
a. 6.32 inches
b. 7.89 inches
c. 9.23 inches
d. 10.91 inches

Answer: c. 9.23 inches. Explanation: The largest circle that can fit in a triangle is the incircle. Its diameter is given by d = 2A/s, where A is the area of the triangle and s is the semi-perimeter. Using Heron's formula and calculating, we get approximately 9.23 inches. This tests advanced geometric reasoning in spatial constraints.

421. A three-phase transformer's core is built using E-I laminations. If each E-shaped lamination is rotated 180° and then flipped over for the next layer, how many distinct arrangements of the E-shaped laminations are there in the completed core?
a. 1

b. 2
c. 3
d. 4

Answer: b. 2. Explanation: There are two distinct arrangements: the original orientation and the 180° rotated orientation. Flipping over doesn't create a new arrangement because the E shape is symmetrical when viewed from either side. This tests understanding of symmetry and rotations in transformer core construction.

422. An electrician is wiring a cubical room with sides of 10 feet. If wires need to be run from one corner to the opposite corner (diagonally across the room), what is the shortest length of wire needed?
a. 10√2 feet
b. 10√3 feet
c. 20 feet
d. 30 feet

Answer: b. 10√3 feet. Explanation: The diagonal of a cube is given by a√3, where a is the length of a side. In this case, 10√3 ≈ 17.32 feet. This tests ability to visualize 3D diagonal paths and apply the appropriate geometric formula.

423. A cylindrical cable reel has a diameter of 24 inches and a width of 18 inches. If the cable has a diameter of 0.5 inches, what is the maximum length of cable that can be wound on this reel in a single layer?
a. 452.4 feet
b. 904.8 feet
c. 1357.2 feet
d. 1809.6 feet

Answer: b. 904.8 feet. Explanation: The number of turns is the width divided by the cable diameter: 18/0.5 = 36. The length per turn is the circumference of the reel: π * 24 = 75.4 inches. Total length is 36 * 75.4 = 2714.4 inches or 904.8 feet. This tests ability to calculate winding capacity considering spatial constraints.

424. An electrician needs to cut a hole in a spherical light fixture to install a switch. If the fixture has a diameter of 12 inches and the hole needs to be 2 inches from the edge, what is the diameter of the circular hole that will be formed?
a. 4.00 inches
b. 5.66 inches
c. 6.93 inches
d. 8.00 inches

Answer: c. 6.93 inches. Explanation: This forms a small circle on a sphere problem. The radius of the hole is given by r = √(R² - (R-h)²), where R is the radius of the sphere (6 inches) and h is the distance from the center to the plane of the cut (4 inches). This gives a diameter of approximately 6.93 inches. This tests advanced 3D geometric reasoning in practical applications.

425. An electrician observes that every time a specific circuit breaker trips, the lights in a certain area flicker before going out. The electrician concludes that the flickering lights are causing the circuit breaker to trip. What type of logical error is the electrician making?
a. False cause
b. Hasty generalization
c. Appeal to authority
d. Ad hominem fallacy

Answer: a. False cause Explanation: This is an example of the "false cause" fallacy, also known as "post hoc ergo propter hoc" (after this, therefore because of this). The electrician assumes that because the flickering precedes the tripping, it must be the cause. In reality, both symptoms likely stem from a common underlying issue, such as a loose connection or overloaded circuit. Recognizing this fallacy is crucial for accurate troubleshooting and avoiding misdiagnosis of electrical problems.

426. All GFCI outlets in a building are rated for 20 amperes. During an inspection, an electrician finds a GFCI outlet that has tripped. Which of the following conclusions can be logically deduced?
a. The circuit connected to this outlet was drawing more than 20 amperes
b. There is a ground fault in the circuit
c. The GFCI outlet is defective
d. None of the above conclusions can be definitively drawn

Answer: d. None of the above conclusions can be definitively drawn Explanation: This question tests deductive reasoning. While all the options are possible causes for a GFCI trip, none can be conclusively deduced from the given information. GFCI outlets can trip due to various reasons, including ground faults, overcurrent, or device malfunction. A proper investigation is required to determine the actual cause. This scenario emphasizes the importance of avoiding hasty conclusions and conducting thorough diagnostics in electrical troubleshooting.

427. An apprentice electrician notices that in the past week, every time they've worked on aluminum wiring, there have been issues with loose connections. The apprentice concludes that aluminum wiring is always problematic and should never be used. What type of reasoning error is the apprentice making?
a. Confirmation bias
b. Hasty generalization
c. Appeal to tradition
d. False dichotomy

Answer: b. Hasty generalization Explanation: The apprentice is making a hasty generalization based on a limited sample size and personal experience. While aluminum wiring can present challenges, it's not inherently problematic when properly installed and maintained. This type of reasoning error can lead to incorrect assumptions and potentially unsafe practices. Electricians must base their conclusions on comprehensive knowledge and established industry standards, not just personal, limited experiences.

428. A senior electrician states, "I've been doing this job for 30 years, so I know that this new safety procedure is unnecessary." What type of logical fallacy is present in this statement?
a. Appeal to authority
b. Ad hominem
c. Slippery slope
d. False equivalence

Answer: a. Appeal to authority Explanation: This is an example of an appeal to authority fallacy, specifically appealing to one's own authority or experience. While experience is valuable, it doesn't automatically invalidate new safety procedures, which are often based on updated research and regulations. Recognizing this fallacy is crucial in the electrical field, where adhering to the latest safety standards is paramount, regardless of personal experience.

429. If all properly functioning AFCI breakers detect arc faults, and a particular breaker in a panel is not detecting arc faults, what can be logically concluded?
a. The breaker is not an AFCI breaker
b. The breaker is not properly functioning
c. There are no arc faults in the circuit
d. The breaker needs to be replaced immediately

Answer: b. The breaker is not properly functioning Explanation: This question tests the application of deductive reasoning using a syllogism. Given that all properly functioning AFCI breakers detect arc faults, if this particular breaker is not detecting them, it logically follows that it is not properly functioning. Note that this doesn't necessarily mean it needs immediate replacement (it might need troubleshooting or repair), and we can't conclude it's not an AFCI breaker. This type of logical reasoning is crucial for accurate diagnosis of electrical system issues.

430. An electrician observes that in a sample of 100 LED bulbs from a specific manufacturer, 5 failed within the first month of installation. The electrician concludes that exactly 5% of all LED bulbs from this manufacturer will fail within a month. What type of reasoning is the electrician using, and what is the problem with this conclusion?
a. Deductive reasoning; the conclusion is too specific
b. Inductive reasoning; the sample size is too small
c. Abductive reasoning; the conclusion ignores other possibilities
d. Analogical reasoning; the comparison is not valid

Answer: b. Inductive reasoning; the sample size is too small Explanation: The electrician is using inductive reasoning, moving from specific observations to a general conclusion. However, the sample size of 100 is likely too small to make a definitive statement about all LED bulbs from the manufacturer. This scenario highlights the importance of understanding statistical significance and the limitations of small sample sizes when drawing conclusions about larger populations, a crucial skill in quality control and product evaluation.

431. A homeowner tells an electrician, "Either you can fix this wiring issue today, or I'll have to rewire the entire house." What type of logical fallacy is the homeowner committing?
a. False dilemma
b. Slippery slope

c. Begging the question
d. Red herring

Answer: a. False dilemma Explanation: This is an example of a false dilemma (also known as false dichotomy) fallacy. The homeowner presents only two extreme options, ignoring other possible solutions or timelines. In reality, there could be many other alternatives between these two extremes. Recognizing this fallacy is important for electricians when communicating with clients, as it helps in providing a more accurate and nuanced explanation of electrical issues and their solutions.

432. An electrical inspector reasons: "If the grounding system is properly installed, then the ground resistance test will pass. The ground resistance test has passed, therefore the grounding system is properly installed." Is this reasoning logically valid?
a. Yes, it's a valid form of modus ponens
b. No, it's an example of affirming the consequent
c. Yes, it's a valid form of modus tollens
d. No, it's an example of denying the antecedent

Answer: b. No, it's an example of affirming the consequent Explanation: This is a classic example of the logical fallacy known as "affirming the consequent." The structure is: If P, then Q. Q is true, therefore P must be true. This is not logically valid. While a properly installed grounding system will pass the test, passing the test doesn't necessarily mean the system is properly installed (there could be other factors influencing the test result). Understanding this distinction is crucial for thorough and accurate electrical inspections.

433. An electrician is troubleshooting a malfunctioning circuit. They have narrowed down the problem to either a faulty switch or a loose connection. After checking the switch and finding it functional, the electrician concludes that the loose connection must be the problem. What type of reasoning is the electrician using?
a. Inductive reasoning
b. Deductive reasoning
c. Abductive reasoning
d. Analogical reasoning

Answer: b. Deductive reasoning Explanation: This is an example of deductive reasoning, specifically a process of elimination. The electrician starts with a limited set of possibilities and systematically rules out options to arrive at a conclusion. This type of logical thinking is fundamental in electrical troubleshooting, allowing for efficient problem-solving by narrowing down potential causes. However, it's important to note that this method is only as reliable as the initial set of possibilities considered.

434. An article in an electrical trade magazine states, "80% of electricians prefer Brand X wire strippers. Therefore, Brand X wire strippers are the best on the market." What logical fallacy is present in this argument?
a. Bandwagon fallacy
b. False cause
c. Appeal to popularity
d. Hasty generalization

Answer: c. Appeal to popularity Explanation: This is an example of the appeal to popularity fallacy (also known as argumentum ad populum). The argument assumes that because a majority prefers something, it must be superior. However, popularity doesn't necessarily correlate with quality or effectiveness. In the electrical field, it's crucial to base tool and equipment choices on objective criteria such as performance, safety features, and suitability for specific tasks, rather than popularity alone. Recognizing this fallacy helps in making more informed and rational decisions in professional practice.

435. A technician is reviewing a section of a technical manual describing the operation of a three-phase motor starter. The manual explains that the primary function of the starter is to safely connect the motor to the power source, provide overload protection, and disconnect the motor in case of faults. It also mentions various components like the contactor, overload relay, and control circuit wiring, which support the starter's main operation. The final sentences discuss the importance of regular maintenance, such as cleaning the contacts and checking for wear. What is the main idea of this section?
a. The components that make up a motor starter
b. The importance of maintaining motor starters
c. The primary function of the motor starter
d. The wiring in a motor control circuit

Answer: c. The primary function of the motor starter. Explanation: The main idea of the section is centered on the primary function of the motor starter, which is to safely control the operation of the motor. Although components and maintenance are discussed, they are secondary to the core purpose of the starter itself.

436. A paragraph in a safety protocol describes the procedures to be followed when lockout/tagout (LOTO) is necessary. The paragraph opens by stating that LOTO is required when working on energized electrical systems. It goes on to describe the process of locking out a circuit breaker or switch and applying a tag to alert others that the equipment is being serviced. Additional details outline the steps for verifying that the equipment is de-energized before beginning work. Based on this structure, where is the topic sentence most likely located?
a. In the middle of the paragraph where the LOTO steps are listed
b. At the beginning of the paragraph before the process is explained
c. At the end of the paragraph summarizing the importance of safety
d. There is no clear topic sentence in this type of paragraph

Answer: b. At the beginning of the paragraph before the process is explained. Explanation: The topic sentence is typically located at the beginning of a paragraph, introducing the subject—in this case, the need for LOTO during electrical work. The rest of the paragraph supports and elaborates on this central idea.

437. A technical manual on electrical wiring systems describes the differences between copper and aluminum conductors. It explains that copper has better conductivity and is less prone to expansion and contraction, making it the preferred material for most installations. However, aluminum is lighter and less expensive, which can be beneficial for large-scale projects. The manual lists installation considerations, such as ensuring proper connections to prevent overheating with aluminum wire. What is the central concept of this section?
a. Aluminum conductors are cheaper than copper conductors

b. Copper is a better conductor than aluminum
c. The comparison between copper and aluminum conductors
d. Installation considerations for aluminum wiring

Answer: c. The comparison between copper and aluminum conductors. Explanation: The main concept is the comparison between the two types of conductors, highlighting the advantages and disadvantages of each material. The other options are details that support this comparison.

438. A technician is reading a specification sheet for a variable frequency drive (VFD). The sheet outlines the device's input voltage, output power rating, and environmental conditions such as maximum operating temperature and humidity. The document then lists additional features like built-in fault detection and communication capabilities with building management systems. In summarizing this information, which of the following would best capture the key points of the specification sheet?
a. The VFD's environmental operating conditions
b. The additional features like fault detection
c. The input voltage and output power rating
d. The technical specifications and additional features of the VFD

Answer: d. The technical specifications and additional features of the VFD. Explanation: A proper summary should cover both the core technical specifications and the extra features of the device, as these are the key points highlighted in the sheet.

439. A paragraph in a safety manual describes the use of personal protective equipment (PPE) in hazardous environments. It states that electricians should always wear insulated gloves, safety goggles, and steel-toed boots when working on or near live electrical systems. The paragraph then explains that, in certain environments, flame-resistant clothing may also be necessary. The final sentence mentions the importance of inspecting PPE before each use to ensure it is not damaged. What is the overarching theme of this section?
a. The necessity of inspecting PPE before use
b. Different types of PPE for electricians
c. When flame-resistant clothing is required
d. Safety protocols for working in hazardous environments

Answer: d. Safety protocols for working in hazardous environments. Explanation: The overarching theme is the safety protocols electricians should follow when working in hazardous environments, with a focus on appropriate PPE.

440. A technical manual on transformers explains that the primary winding receives power from the supply source, while the secondary winding delivers power to the load. It describes the core materials, insulation used between the windings, and the principles of electromagnetic induction that allow the transformer to step voltage up or down. The final part of the section discusses the importance of keeping the transformer cool to prevent overheating. What is the central idea of this section?
a. The insulation materials used in transformers
b. The role of electromagnetic induction in transformers
c. How the primary and secondary windings function

d. The function and operation of a transformer

Answer: d. The function and operation of a transformer. Explanation: The section explains the basic function and operation of a transformer, from the role of the windings to electromagnetic induction, with other details supporting this main idea.

441. In a section of a technical manual, the process of troubleshooting a malfunctioning motor is discussed. The manual begins by instructing the reader to check for any visible damage, such as burnt wires or loose connections. It then advises measuring the voltage supply to ensure it is within the motor's operating range, followed by testing the motor windings for continuity. Finally, it recommends checking the motor's insulation resistance. What is the main focus of this section?
a. Testing the motor windings for continuity
b. Ensuring the voltage supply is correct
c. Inspecting the motor for visible damage
d. The steps in troubleshooting a malfunctioning motor

Answer: d. The steps in troubleshooting a malfunctioning motor. Explanation: The main focus of the section is the overall process of troubleshooting the motor, which involves multiple steps, including checking for damage, testing voltage, and inspecting the windings.

442. An equipment specification document describes the design and function of an automatic transfer switch (ATS). The document explains that the ATS automatically transfers power to a backup generator when the utility power fails, ensuring continuous operation of critical systems. It also lists the various ratings, including the maximum load it can handle and the delay time before switching to the backup power source. How should this information be summarized?
a. The ATS ensures continuous operation by transferring power during utility failures
b. The ATS can handle a specific maximum load and has a configurable delay time
c. The ATS is essential for critical systems during power outages
d. The ATS automatically switches power and includes various ratings

Answer: d. The ATS automatically switches power and includes various ratings. Explanation: The best summary includes both the ATS's primary function of switching power and the detailed ratings, such as load capacity and delay times, mentioned in the document.

443. A technical manual explains that grounding is essential for the safety and proper operation of electrical systems. It discusses how grounding prevents dangerous voltage levels from building up and provides a safe path for fault currents to flow to the earth. The manual details different grounding methods, such as grounding rods and grounding plates, and the use of bonding to connect metal parts of the system. What is the central concept of this section?
a. The types of grounding methods used in electrical systems
b. The importance of grounding for safety and proper operation
c. How bonding works to connect metal parts in the system
d. The safe dissipation of fault currents to the earth

Answer: b. The importance of grounding for safety and proper operation. Explanation: The main concept is the importance of grounding for safety and proper system function, with the specific methods and bonding details supporting this idea.

444. In a manual on electrical safety protocols, a paragraph describes the steps to take when a worker encounters a person who has suffered an electric shock. It emphasizes not touching the victim until the power source is de-energized, followed by performing CPR if necessary. The paragraph then details how to call emergency services and use an automated external defibrillator (AED) if available. The last sentence reiterates the need to assess the scene for safety before helping the victim. What is the main idea of this paragraph?
a. How to perform CPR on an electric shock victim
b. The steps to follow when responding to an electric shock incident
c. The importance of using an AED after electric shock
d. The procedure for calling emergency services

Answer: b. The steps to follow when responding to an electric shock incident. Explanation: The paragraph outlines a series of steps to respond to an electric shock incident, making this the central idea.

445. A facility engineer receives a new single-line diagram for a medium-voltage switchgear system. The diagram includes three transformers, each stepping down from 13.8 kV to 480 V, and feeding into multiple motor control centers (MCCs). The MCCs distribute power to various industrial motors throughout the plant. The diagram shows implied connections from the transformers to the MCCs, but there are no detailed connections for the control wiring or protective relays. The engineer notes that each transformer has an associated 2000 A main breaker, but there is no detailed indication of any relay coordination for protection. Given this information, what can the engineer infer about the protection strategy of the system from the provided diagram?
a. The system likely employs current transformers for differential protection on each transformer.
b. The system likely lacks adequate protection since the relay details are not explicitly shown.
c. The system likely uses fuses for transformer protection instead of relays.
d. The system is likely protected by breaker trip settings and may rely on upstream relay coordination.

Answer: d. The system is likely protected by breaker trip settings and may rely on upstream relay coordination. Explanation: The lack of explicit relay information suggests the system may rely on breaker trip settings rather than detailed relay coordination. The 2000 A main breakers indicate some level of protection, and it's common for relay coordination to be handled upstream or in a centralized location.

446. A technician is reviewing a schematic diagram for a power distribution system in a commercial building. The diagram includes various lighting circuits, HVAC loads, and general-purpose outlets. The HVAC system is powered by a 50 kVA transformer, and the lighting circuits are connected to a separate 30 kVA transformer. The schematic shows a single grounding point for both transformers, located near the main distribution panel. However, there is no indication of whether separate grounding conductors are run to each transformer or if a shared grounding system is used. Based on the schematic, what can the technician infer about the grounding strategy used in this system?
a. The system likely uses a shared grounding conductor for both transformers, increasing the risk of ground loops.
b. The system likely uses separate grounding conductors for each transformer to prevent ground loops.
c. The system likely does not require grounding conductors because both transformers are small.

d. The system is likely improperly grounded due to the lack of detail in the schematic.

Answer: a. The system likely uses a shared grounding conductor for both transformers, increasing the risk of ground loops. Explanation: The single grounding point suggests a shared grounding system, which could lead to ground loops if not carefully managed. Ground loops can cause issues in sensitive electronic equipment due to potential differences between grounding points.

447. An electrician is troubleshooting an electrical fault in a large industrial facility. The facility's power distribution system consists of multiple feeders supplying different sections of the plant. A single-line diagram shows that each feeder is protected by an overcurrent relay, and the system is designed to handle a maximum load of 5000 kW. The current fault occurs when a new machine is brought online, causing one of the feeders to trip. The machine has a rated load of 800 kW, and the feeder in question has a capacity of 1000 kW. What is the most likely cause of the feeder tripping based on the available information?
a. The machine's load exceeds the feeder's capacity, causing the overcurrent relay to trip.
b. The feeder has an inadequate relay setting, causing it to trip prematurely.
c. The machine's startup current is causing the overcurrent relay to trip.
d. The system has a ground fault that is not shown on the single-line diagram.

Answer: c. The machine's startup current is causing the overcurrent relay to trip. Explanation: Large machines typically have high inrush currents during startup, which can cause overcurrent relays to trip even if the machine's steady-state load is within the feeder's capacity. Adjusting the relay settings for inrush current may resolve the issue.

448. A maintenance engineer is analyzing the wiring layout for a new automated control system. The system consists of multiple sensors and actuators connected to a programmable logic controller (PLC). The wiring layout shows several junction boxes where multiple control cables converge. However, the layout does not provide details on how the sensor signals are processed before reaching the PLC. The engineer is concerned about potential signal interference due to the long cable runs and the convergence of signals at the junction boxes. What can the engineer infer about the potential issues with the system from the wiring layout?
a. The system is likely to experience signal degradation due to excessive cable lengths.
b. The system is likely to experience signal interference due to inadequate shielding of the control cables.
c. The system is likely to experience ground faults due to improper grounding at the junction boxes.
d. The system is likely to experience no issues since the layout suggests proper routing of cables.

Answer: b. The system is likely to experience signal interference due to inadequate shielding of the control cables. Explanation: When control cables converge in junction boxes without proper shielding, there is a higher likelihood of signal interference, especially over long cable runs. Proper shielding and separation of signal and power cables are necessary to prevent interference.

449. An electrician is reviewing a single-line diagram for an emergency power system in a hospital. The diagram shows a 1000 kVA diesel generator connected to the hospital's critical loads via an automatic transfer switch (ATS). The system also includes a UPS system that provides short-term backup power during the transition between utility power and generator power. The single-line diagram does not show any surge protection devices (SPDs) installed in the system. What potential issue can the electrician infer from the absence of SPDs in the diagram?

a. The system is likely to experience frequent outages due to a lack of transient voltage protection.
b. The system is likely vulnerable to voltage surges that could damage sensitive medical equipment.
c. The system is likely to experience harmonic distortion due to the lack of power conditioning.
d. The system is likely designed without SPDs because the UPS provides adequate protection.

Answer: b. The system is likely vulnerable to voltage surges that could damage sensitive medical equipment. Explanation: Surge protection devices (SPDs) are essential in systems with sensitive equipment, such as medical devices, to protect against voltage spikes. While a UPS offers power conditioning, it does not replace the need for surge protection.

450. A power distribution diagram for a manufacturing plant shows multiple feeders supplying various production lines. Each production line has its own motor control center (MCC), which powers several motors. The diagram shows that each MCC is supplied by a dedicated 480V feeder from a 2000 kVA transformer. However, the diagram does not include details about the individual motor circuits or their protection devices. The plant engineer is trying to determine whether the system has adequate motor protection. Based on the diagram, what can the engineer conclude?
a. The system likely has adequate protection since each MCC is supplied by a dedicated feeder.
b. The system likely lacks adequate motor protection since the individual motor circuits are not shown.
c. The system likely relies on individual overload relays for motor protection, even though they are not shown.
d. The system is likely improperly protected due to the lack of detailed motor circuit information.

Answer: c. The system likely relies on individual overload relays for motor protection, even though they are not shown. Explanation: Motor control centers (MCCs) typically include overload relays and circuit breakers for each motor, even if these details are not explicitly shown on the single-line diagram. The dedicated feeders suggest sufficient capacity for the motors.

451. A facility manager is reviewing a load chart for a commercial building's electrical system. The chart lists various load types, including lighting, HVAC, and general power outlets. The total connected load is 600 kW, but the load chart indicates a diversity factor of 0.8. The building's main transformer has a rated capacity of 500 kVA. Based on this information, what can the facility manager infer about the system's capacity?
a. The transformer is undersized and will likely overload during peak demand periods.
b. The transformer is adequately sized, considering the diversity factor reduces the actual load.
c. The system is likely to experience voltage drops due to the transformer's limited capacity.
d. The load chart indicates that additional transformers are required to handle the building's load.

Answer: b. The transformer is adequately sized, considering the diversity factor reduces the actual load. Explanation: The diversity factor accounts for the fact that not all loads will be operating at their peak simultaneously. By applying the diversity factor (0.8), the actual load is 480 kW, which is within the transformer's 500 kVA capacity.

452. A contractor is reviewing a schematic for a photovoltaic (PV) system installed on a commercial building. The system consists of multiple PV arrays connected to an inverter, which feeds into the building's electrical system. The schematic shows that the inverter is rated for 500 kW, but the total output of the PV arrays is 550 kW. The contractor

is concerned about the potential for overloading the inverter. What can the contractor infer about the system based on this schematic?
a. The inverter is undersized and will likely be damaged by the PV array's output.
b. The inverter is appropriately sized, as PV output typically varies and does not consistently reach maximum capacity.
c. The system is likely to experience inefficiencies due to the mismatch between the PV output and inverter capacity.
d. The system will likely trip due to the overcapacity of the PV arrays.

Answer: b. The inverter is appropriately sized, as PV output typically varies and does not consistently reach maximum capacity. Explanation: PV systems rarely operate at maximum output continuously due to factors such as shading, temperature, and sunlight variability. An inverter with a slightly lower capacity than the total array output is common practice to maximize efficiency.

453. A facility supervisor is analyzing a wiring layout for a new office building. The layout includes several branch circuits supplying power to lighting, computers, and HVAC equipment. The layout shows multiple circuit breakers installed in the distribution panel, with each breaker rated for a specific load. However, the layout does not indicate whether any of the circuits share a neutral conductor. The supervisor is concerned about potential neutral conductor overloading. What can the supervisor infer from the wiring layout?
a. The system is likely designed with shared neutrals, which could lead to overloading and potential hazards.
b. The system likely uses separate neutral conductors for each circuit, preventing overload.
c. The system is likely designed with oversized neutral conductors to handle the combined load of multiple circuits.
d. The system likely does not require separate neutral conductors for each circuit, as indicated by the breaker ratings.

Answer: a. The system is likely designed with shared neutrals, which could lead to overloading and potential hazards. Explanation: In commercial buildings, it's common for circuits to share neutral conductors. However, if not properly sized, shared neutrals can lead to overloading, especially in systems with significant non-linear loads like computers and HVAC equipment.

454. An engineer is reviewing the electrical diagram for a new substation. The diagram shows multiple transformers and circuit breakers feeding various distribution lines. One section of the diagram shows a bus-tie breaker that connects two busbars. However, there is no indication of whether the bus-tie breaker is normally open or closed. The engineer is trying to determine the operational status of the bus-tie breaker. What can the engineer infer from the diagram?
a. The bus-tie breaker is likely normally open to prevent parallel operation of the two busbars.
b. The bus-tie breaker is likely normally closed to allow for load sharing between the busbars.
c. The bus-tie breaker is likely designed to operate automatically based on load conditions.
d. The bus-tie breaker is likely not operational based on the lack of detail in the diagram.

Answer: a. The bus-tie breaker is likely normally open to prevent parallel operation of the two busbars. Explanation: In many substation designs, bus-tie breakers are normally open to prevent parallel operation of busbars, which could lead to circulating currents and system instability. The breaker can be closed for load transfers or maintenance.

455. A section in a safety manual describes the installation process for an electrical panel. It begins by emphasizing the importance of following local codes and ensuring that the panel is installed level and securely mounted to prevent

shifting. The manual then discusses the necessity of using insulated tools when working on live circuits and outlines the proper procedures for testing the panel to ensure there are no loose connections before energizing the system. The section ends by cautioning electricians to double-check that the grounding is properly connected, as improper grounding can lead to serious safety hazards. What is the author's main purpose in this section?
a. To inform electricians about the steps for installing an electrical panel
b. To persuade electricians to use insulated tools at all times
c. To caution against improper grounding during panel installation
d. To explain the local codes involved in panel installation

Answer: a. To inform electricians about the steps for installing an electrical panel. Explanation: The section's primary focus is instructive, detailing the steps involved in installing an electrical panel, including safety precautions and proper techniques. Although grounding and tool usage are discussed, they support the larger purpose of outlining the installation process.

456. A safety communication sent to electricians discusses the proper use of lockout/tagout (LOTO) procedures. The communication explains that LOTO is not just a recommendation but a mandatory safety requirement for any electrical work involving live circuits or equipment maintenance. The memo uses bold, capitalized letters to stress the importance of isolating all energy sources before any work begins. It ends by reiterating that failure to follow LOTO procedures can lead to injury or death. Based on the format and language of the memo, what type of statement is being emphasized here?
a. Advisory recommendations for safe electrical work
b. A mandatory procedure that must be followed
c. A suggestion to improve overall workplace safety
d. A general guideline for preventing accidents

Answer: b. A mandatory procedure that must be followed. Explanation: The use of bold and capitalized letters emphasizes the importance of LOTO as a mandatory safety procedure. The language does not offer it as a suggestion or recommendation but as a required protocol, with serious consequences for non-compliance.

457. In a company-wide email, the safety manager urges electricians to report all near-miss incidents, even if no one was injured. The email explains that tracking near-misses helps identify patterns of unsafe behavior and prevents future accidents. It uses persuasive language, such as "critical to our safety culture" and "essential for protecting everyone on site." The email ends by encouraging employees to contribute to the safety culture and promises that all reports will be handled confidentially. What is the primary purpose of the safety manager's email?
a. To inform employees of their obligation to report all incidents
b. To persuade electricians to report near-miss incidents
c. To explain the confidentiality of incident reports
d. To describe patterns of unsafe behavior in the workplace

Answer: b. To persuade electricians to report near-miss incidents. Explanation: The email uses persuasive language to encourage employees to take part in the reporting process, highlighting its importance in building a safety culture. The mention of confidentiality and patterns supports the main goal, which is to persuade workers to report near-misses.

458. An electrician receives a flyer outlining the risks of arc flash incidents and the necessary personal protective equipment (PPE) required to mitigate those risks. The flyer begins with a brief description of arc flash hazards, including high temperatures and flying debris. It then lists the mandatory PPE, such as arc-rated clothing, face shields, and insulated gloves, before moving on to recommend regular equipment inspections and maintenance to prevent arc flashes from occurring. The flyer ends with a reminder that arc flash training is required annually. Which portion of the flyer can be classified as advisory rather than mandatory?
a. The requirement for arc-rated clothing
b. The recommendation for regular equipment inspections
c. The mandate for annual arc flash training
d. The need for insulated gloves during electrical work

Answer: b. The recommendation for regular equipment inspections. Explanation: The portion of the flyer that suggests regular inspections is advisory, providing a recommendation rather than a requirement. The other options relate to mandatory actions that electricians must follow to comply with safety regulations.

459. A section of a safety bulletin explains the proper use of extension cords on construction sites. It begins by noting that extension cords should only be used as a temporary solution and must meet specific criteria, including being rated for the equipment being powered. The bulletin stresses the importance of inspecting cords for damage before use and avoiding overloading them, as this could lead to overheating and electrical fires. The section is heavily cautionary in tone, particularly when it discusses avoiding daisy-chaining multiple extension cords, a practice that is strictly prohibited on job sites. How does the author emphasize the cautionary nature of this guidance?
a. By stating that daisy-chaining cords is strictly prohibited
b. By discussing the temporary nature of extension cords
c. By providing the criteria for selecting extension cords
d. By explaining the potential for overheating when cords are overloaded

Answer: a. By stating that daisy-chaining cords is strictly prohibited. Explanation: The strict prohibition against daisy-chaining, combined with the cautionary language about the dangers of overheating and fires, emphasizes the author's focus on preventing unsafe practices with extension cords.

460. In a section of an instructional manual on ladder safety, the author begins by explaining the different types of ladders, including step ladders and extension ladders, and their appropriate uses. The manual then shifts to the critical safety measures, such as ensuring that ladders are placed on stable ground, maintaining three points of contact, and never exceeding the weight limit specified on the ladder's label. It concludes by cautioning workers to avoid using metal ladders around electrical wiring, as they can conduct electricity. What is the author's purpose in the final part of this section?
a. To explain the weight limits on ladders
b. To advise workers on ladder placement techniques
c. To warn workers about the dangers of using metal ladders near electricity
d. To inform workers about the types of ladders available

Answer: c. To warn workers about the dangers of using metal ladders near electricity. Explanation: The final part of the section is clearly cautionary, warning workers of the specific risk posed by using metal ladders around electrical wiring. The rest of the section contains general safety advice, but the warning about metal ladders is emphasized as a serious hazard.

461. An electrician reads a safety guideline outlining the importance of wearing proper footwear on job sites. The guideline states that workers must wear boots with non-slip soles, puncture-resistant material, and steel toes to protect their feet from falling objects. It also mentions that wearing comfortable footwear can reduce fatigue, which helps maintain focus and productivity. The guideline ends by stating that no one is allowed on site without the required footwear. How does the author distinguish between mandatory and advisory statements in this guideline?
a. By describing the risks of wearing improper footwear
b. By stating that no one is allowed on site without the required boots
c. By recommending comfortable footwear to reduce fatigue
d. By explaining the importance of non-slip soles

Answer: b. By stating that no one is allowed on site without the required boots. Explanation: The mandatory nature of the footwear requirement is made clear by the statement that no one is permitted on site without it. The suggestion about comfort is advisory, aiming to improve well-being but not enforceable in the same way.

462. A technical manual for electrical installations provides a list of requirements for conduit bends. It emphasizes that all bends should be made using a proper conduit bender, and the radius of each bend must meet the minimum specifications outlined in the National Electrical Code (NEC). The section also advises that excessive bending can result in cable damage or difficulties pulling wires through the conduit. The section ends by repeating the minimum radius requirement in bold letters. How does the author emphasize the importance of this requirement?
a. By repeating the minimum radius requirement in bold letters
b. By discussing the risks of damaging cables
c. By advising the use of a proper conduit bender
d. By outlining the NEC specifications for conduit bends

Answer: a. By repeating the minimum radius requirement in bold letters. Explanation: The author uses formatting (bold letters) to emphasize the importance of meeting the minimum radius requirement for conduit bends, indicating that this is a critical safety and performance issue.

463. A paragraph in a safety manual describes the procedures for working in confined spaces. It explains that electricians must always have a confined space permit before entering and should test the atmosphere for hazardous gases or insufficient oxygen levels. The paragraph stresses that a trained observer must remain outside the confined space to monitor the worker's safety, and communication must be maintained at all times. It concludes by reiterating that confined space entry should never be done alone under any circumstances. What is the main method the author uses to emphasize the risks involved with confined spaces?
a. By discussing the importance of atmospheric testing
b. By stressing that entry should never be done alone
c. By requiring a confined space permit before entry
d. By ensuring a trained observer is present outside

Answer: b. By stressing that entry should never be done alone. Explanation: The emphasis is on the extreme danger of working in confined spaces alone, which is reiterated at the end of the paragraph as the most critical safety rule. This repetition serves to highlight the risk.

464. In a training manual for electrical apprentices, a section on fall protection describes the proper use of harnesses and lanyards. The manual outlines the steps for inspecting the equipment before use, including checking for frayed straps and damaged buckles. It explains that harnesses must be worn snugly to distribute the force of a fall evenly across the body and that lanyards should be anchored to a secure point capable of supporting at least 5,000 pounds. The section ends by reminding apprentices that fall protection is required at heights of six feet or more. How does the author balance mandatory and advisory content in this section?
a. By providing detailed steps for inspecting equipment
b. By stating that harnesses must be worn snugly
c. By setting a six-foot height requirement for fall protection
d. By recommending that lanyards be anchored to secure points

Answer: c. By setting a six-foot height requirement for fall protection. Explanation: The six-foot height requirement is a clear mandatory statement that aligns with OSHA regulations, while the inspection and snug fit recommendations offer advisory guidance to enhance safety and comfort.

465. While conducting a routine inspection in a manufacturing facility, an electrician noticed unusual wear and discoloration around a set of electrical connections in a motor control panel. The panel was responsible for controlling several 480V motors used in production, and the wear was most apparent near the connections for one of the larger motors. After investigating further, the electrician identified signs of overheating and arcing around the connections. A review of the maintenance logs showed that the motor had been serviced multiple times in the past year due to recurring tripping issues. The tripping had been attributed to overloads during peak production times, but the logs did not indicate any corrective actions related to the electrical connections themselves. Based on this incident, which factor is most likely the root cause of the electrical failure?
a. Overloading of the motor during peak production
b. Improper torque applied to the electrical connections during servicing
c. Use of incorrect wire sizing for the motor circuit
d. Faulty protective relays not responding to overload conditions

Answer: b. Improper torque applied to the electrical connections during servicing. Explanation: While overloading may contribute to the motor tripping, the wear and signs of overheating suggest a more immediate issue with the electrical connections. If the connections were not properly torqued, they could loosen over time, leading to arcing and overheating, which aligns with the observed damage.

466. During a repair of a distribution panel in an office building, a technician discovered that several breakers were damaged and showed signs of overheating. The damaged breakers were responsible for critical systems, including HVAC and lighting. An initial review of the incident report revealed that the building had experienced frequent breaker trips over the past few months, often during periods of high electrical demand. The panel had been replaced five years earlier, but no additional upgrades had been made since then. Despite the ongoing issues, the breakers had not been replaced until they failed. The incident report also noted that the panel was located in a confined space with limited ventilation. What is the most likely immediate cause of the breaker failure in this scenario?
a. Undersized conductors leading to excess current flow

b. Inadequate ventilation causing excessive heat buildup in the panel
c. Defective breakers that should have been replaced during the initial panel installation
d. Overloaded circuits due to the building's increased electrical demand

Answer: b. Inadequate ventilation causing excessive heat buildup in the panel. Explanation: While overloaded circuits could contribute to breaker tripping, the specific signs of overheating and the confined space with limited ventilation suggest that the main issue is heat buildup, which can lead to premature breaker failure. Proper ventilation is crucial to maintain safe operating temperatures in electrical panels.

467. A large industrial facility experienced a major electrical outage during a shift change, resulting in significant downtime. An incident investigation revealed that the outage occurred when a main feeder supplying power to several production areas tripped. The feeder was protected by an overcurrent relay, which activated after detecting a sudden surge in current. Further examination of the electrical system showed that one of the machines connected to the feeder had a damaged insulation layer on its power cables. The insulation failure caused a short circuit, which led to the surge in current. According to the investigation, the damaged cables had not been identified during the last routine inspection. What could be considered the underlying cause of this outage?
a. Inadequate inspection procedures that failed to identify the damaged cables
b. A fault in the overcurrent relay's sensitivity settings
c. A lack of surge protection on the main feeder
d. Excessive load demand from the machines connected to the feeder

Answer: a. Inadequate inspection procedures that failed to identify the damaged cables. Explanation: Although the damaged insulation directly caused the short circuit and resulting outage, the underlying cause is a failure in the inspection process. Proper inspection procedures would have identified the damaged cables before they caused a short circuit, preventing the outage.

468. A construction crew was installing a new electrical system in a commercial building when one of the workers sustained a minor shock while connecting wiring in a subpanel. The project manager reviewed the incident report and found that the subpanel had already been energized when the worker began making the connections, even though the lockout/tagout (LOTO) procedure had been followed for the main panel. The investigation showed that the subpanel was fed from a separate distribution point, which was not isolated during the LOTO process. As a result, the subpanel remained live. The worker was not seriously injured, but the incident highlighted a gap in the safety protocol. What is the most effective corrective action to prevent similar incidents in the future?
a. Install warning labels on subpanels to indicate when they are live
b. Train workers to verify that all panels are de-energized before starting work
c. Add additional steps to the LOTO procedure to include all distribution points
d. Replace the subpanel with a unit that has enhanced safety features

Answer: c. Add additional steps to the LOTO procedure to include all distribution points. Explanation: The root cause of this incident was the failure to isolate the subpanel, which was fed from a different distribution point. Modifying the LOTO procedure to account for all potential sources of power would prevent similar incidents in the future, addressing the gap in the safety protocol.

469. During an emergency response to an electrical failure in a large hospital, the maintenance team discovered that a critical feeder had failed, resulting in the loss of power to multiple life-support systems. The incident report indicated that the feeder was part of the hospital's backup power system, which relied on a diesel generator. The generator had started as expected, but the feeder failed due to excessive current draw when multiple large loads were connected simultaneously. The team identified that the feeder's ampacity was rated below the combined load of the connected systems, leading to an overload. What would be the most effective corrective action based on the root cause analysis?
a. Upgrade the feeder to handle the combined load of the connected systems
b. Install additional protective relays to monitor current draw on the feeder
c. Reduce the number of loads connected to the feeder during emergency operations
d. Replace the diesel generator with a unit of higher capacity

Answer: a. Upgrade the feeder to handle the combined load of the connected systems. Explanation: The root cause of the failure was the insufficient ampacity of the feeder relative to the connected loads. Upgrading the feeder to handle the load would prevent future overloads and ensure reliable operation of the backup power system during emergencies.

470. An electrical contractor was called to investigate a series of unexpected power outages at a warehouse facility. The incident report noted that the outages occurred whenever the HVAC system was turned on, particularly during peak summer months. The contractor reviewed the wiring diagram and found that the HVAC system and several other high-power devices were connected to the same 480V feeder. Upon further investigation, the contractor discovered that the feeder's load was nearing its maximum capacity, and the HVAC system's compressor had high inrush currents at startup. Based on this information, what is the likely cause of the outages?
a. Faulty wiring in the HVAC system causing short circuits
b. High inrush currents from the HVAC system exceeding the feeder's capacity
c. A defective feeder breaker not properly sized for the connected loads
d. Poor maintenance of the HVAC system causing equipment failure

Answer: b. High inrush currents from the HVAC system exceeding the feeder's capacity. Explanation: The high inrush current from the HVAC system's compressor startup is likely causing the feeder to exceed its capacity, leading to breaker trips and power outages. This issue is exacerbated during peak load periods, when the feeder is already near capacity.

471. An electrical supervisor at a chemical processing plant reviewed an incident where an operator received an electrical shock while operating a piece of equipment. The incident report indicated that the operator had been working near a control panel, and the equipment had a grounding issue. The report further stated that the panel's ground fault circuit interrupter (GFCI) had failed to trip during the incident. A closer investigation revealed that the GFCI had not been tested or maintained for over a year. Which action would best address both the immediate and underlying causes of this incident?
a. Replace the faulty GFCI and test it regularly
b. Install additional GFCI units to provide redundancy
c. Conduct more frequent inspections of all electrical equipment
d. Train operators to identify grounding issues before operating equipment

Answer: a. Replace the faulty GFCI and test it regularly. Explanation: The immediate cause of the incident was the failure of the GFCI to trip, likely due to a lack of maintenance. Replacing the faulty GFCI and ensuring regular testing would directly address both the immediate and underlying causes, ensuring future incidents are avoided.

472. During the commissioning of a new industrial facility, an incident occurred where a large motor failed during its first startup. The incident report noted that the motor had a soft starter installed to limit the inrush current, but the failure occurred immediately after the motor reached full speed. Further investigation revealed that the motor's protective relay settings had not been adjusted for the soft starter's characteristics, leading to an overcurrent condition once the motor transitioned to full speed. What is the most likely cause of the motor failure based on this information?
a. Incorrect relay settings that did not account for the soft starter
b. A defective soft starter that failed to limit the inrush current
c. Undersized conductors causing excessive voltage drop
d. A mechanical fault in the motor unrelated to electrical issues

Answer: a. Incorrect relay settings that did not account for the soft starter. Explanation: The overcurrent condition following the motor's transition to full speed indicates that the protective relay settings were not properly configured to work with the soft starter. Adjusting the relay settings would prevent overcurrent trips and protect the motor.

473. A food processing plant experienced an electrical fire in one of its production lines, resulting in significant equipment damage. The incident report indicated that the fire started in a junction box that housed multiple conductors feeding different pieces of equipment. The conductors were rated for 600V, and the system operated at 480V. However, the report also noted that several of the conductors were bundled together tightly, and there was no indication of temperature derating factors being applied. Based on this information, what is the most likely cause of the fire?
a. Faulty conductors that failed prematurely due to poor manufacturing
b. Bundling of conductors without proper derating, leading to overheating
c. A short circuit caused by damaged insulation in the junction box
d. Overvoltage conditions caused by a malfunction in the power supply

Answer: b. Bundling of conductors without proper derating, leading to overheating. Explanation: When conductors are bundled together, they can overheat due to the inability to dissipate heat properly. Without applying temperature derating factors, the conductors would be subjected to higher temperatures than they are rated for, leading to insulation failure and potentially causing a fire.

474. An electrical engineer was reviewing the design of a new data center's power distribution system when a power outage occurred during a load test. The incident report showed that the data center's UPS system failed to provide backup power when the main utility feed was disconnected. Upon further review, the engineer discovered that the UPS had been set to a manual bypass mode during testing, which allowed the outage to occur. What corrective action should the engineer implement to prevent similar incidents in the future?
a. Increase the UPS capacity to handle the data center's full load
b. Ensure that UPS systems are always set to automatic mode during load testing
c. Install additional generators to provide backup power in case the UPS fails
d. Schedule load tests during periods of low demand to minimize disruption

Answer: b. Ensure that UPS systems are always set to automatic mode during load testing. Explanation: The root cause of the outage was the manual bypass mode of the UPS during testing, which prevented the system from providing backup power. Ensuring the UPS is in automatic mode during testing would allow it to respond appropriately to utility feed disconnections.

475. A technical manual describes the installation requirements for two different types of electrical systems: a three-phase alternating current (AC) system and a direct current (DC) system. The AC system uses three conductors and one neutral wire, which allows it to efficiently distribute power across large commercial facilities. The manual emphasizes the ability of AC to easily transform voltages using transformers, making it more practical for long-distance power transmission. In contrast, the DC system requires only two conductors but is limited in its transmission distance because it cannot be easily stepped up or down in voltage. The manual also points out that DC systems are more efficient at delivering steady, consistent voltage to sensitive equipment such as data centers, which require minimal fluctuation. What is the primary advantage of AC systems over DC systems according to this manual?
a. AC systems provide more consistent voltage than DC systems
b. AC systems are easier to install than DC systems
c. AC systems allow for more efficient long-distance power transmission
d. AC systems use fewer conductors than DC systems

Answer: c. AC systems allow for more efficient long-distance power transmission. Explanation: The manual highlights that AC systems can easily transform voltages using transformers, which is critical for efficient long-distance transmission, a major advantage over DC systems that are limited in their ability to adjust voltage.

476. An electrician is comparing two methods of wiring: conduit-based wiring and cable tray systems. The installation manual states that conduit wiring involves running individual conductors through metal or PVC conduits, offering strong mechanical protection and grounding capabilities, but it is labor-intensive to install and difficult to modify once in place. In contrast, cable tray systems allow for quicker installation and easier modifications, especially in industrial settings where large amounts of cable need to be routed. However, cable trays provide less physical protection to the conductors and may require additional grounding methods. The manual also notes that cable trays are better suited for low-voltage or communication cables, while conduit is preferred for high-voltage systems. Based on the information, which of the following is a disadvantage of using cable trays compared to conduit wiring?
a. Cable trays are harder to modify after installation
b. Cable trays provide less mechanical protection to the conductors
c. Cable trays are more expensive to install than conduit systems
d. Cable trays require more conductors to be used for the same system

Answer: b. Cable trays provide less mechanical protection to the conductors. Explanation: The manual clearly states that cable trays offer less physical protection compared to conduit wiring, which is one of their disadvantages, particularly when handling sensitive or high-voltage conductors.

477. A section of a manual compares battery energy storage systems (BESS) with flywheel energy storage systems (FESS). BESS use chemical reactions to store energy, making them highly efficient in terms of energy density and capable of discharging power over long durations. However, they are sensitive to temperature variations and have limited lifespans, requiring regular maintenance and eventual replacement. FESS, on the other hand, store energy

mechanically by spinning a rotor in a vacuum. While FESS have virtually unlimited lifespans and are capable of rapid discharges, they are limited in the amount of energy they can store at any given time and are more appropriate for short-duration applications like grid frequency regulation. Which of the following is a drawback of battery energy storage systems compared to flywheel energy storage systems?
a. BESS have lower energy density than FESS
b. BESS are less suited for short-duration applications
c. BESS require more regular maintenance and eventual replacement
d. BESS are more suitable for grid frequency regulation than FESS

Answer: c. BESS require more regular maintenance and eventual replacement. Explanation: The manual explains that BESS have limited lifespans and need regular maintenance, which is a significant drawback compared to the virtually maintenance-free nature of FESS, which also have longer operational lifespans.

478. An electrician is working on a project involving both low-voltage and high-voltage circuits in an industrial facility. The project specifications explain that conduit wiring is recommended for high-voltage circuits due to its superior insulation and protection against physical damage. Low-voltage circuits, which control communication and automation systems, can be safely routed using cable trays, which provide easier access for maintenance and modifications. The specifications emphasize the importance of grounding all conduit and cable tray systems to prevent potential hazards. In this scenario, which is the most critical reason for using conduit wiring for high-voltage circuits?
a. Conduit wiring is more affordable for high-voltage installations
b. Conduit wiring allows for easier maintenance access
c. Conduit wiring provides better mechanical protection and insulation
d. Conduit wiring is required by code for all electrical installations

Answer: c. Conduit wiring provides better mechanical protection and insulation. Explanation: The specifications recommend conduit wiring for high-voltage circuits due to its superior mechanical protection and insulation capabilities, which are critical for the safe transmission of high-voltage power.

479. A paragraph in a technical guide discusses the differences between alternating current (AC) and direct current (DC) motors. AC motors are commonly used in applications where variable speed control is required, such as fans, pumps, and conveyors. They can be easily powered from standard electrical outlets and are more cost-effective for most industrial applications. DC motors, on the other hand, are preferred when precise control of motor speed is needed, as in robotics or electric vehicles. However, DC motors are more complex to maintain, often requiring brushes and commutators that can wear out over time. What is a key advantage of using a DC motor over an AC motor?
a. DC motors are less expensive to maintain than AC motors
b. DC motors provide more precise speed control than AC motors
c. DC motors are more commonly used in industrial settings than AC motors
d. DC motors are simpler to connect to standard power sources than AC motors

Answer: b. DC motors provide more precise speed control than AC motors. Explanation: The paragraph highlights that DC motors offer better speed control, which is essential in applications requiring precision, such as robotics and electric vehicles. AC motors, by contrast, are more suited for general industrial use.

480. An electrician is reviewing a section of a manual on emergency backup power systems. The manual contrasts the use of battery-based backup systems with diesel generators. Battery systems provide instantaneous power in the event of a grid failure and are ideal for sensitive equipment like data centers, as they produce no noise or emissions. However, battery systems have a limited runtime and need to be regularly recharged. Diesel generators, while slower to start, can run for extended periods as long as fuel is available and are more suitable for large industrial applications where long-term power outages are possible. The manual concludes by advising that both systems may be used together in critical applications to combine the advantages of both technologies. What is the primary advantage of diesel generators over battery-based backup systems?
a. Diesel generators can provide power instantly after a grid failure
b. Diesel generators are quieter and produce fewer emissions
c. Diesel generators can run for longer periods during power outages
d. Diesel generators are more suited for sensitive equipment like data centers

Answer: c. Diesel generators can run for longer periods during power outages. Explanation: The manual points out that diesel generators, with their ability to run for extended periods as long as fuel is available, have an advantage over battery systems, which are limited by their capacity and need for recharging.

481. A training manual for electricians outlines the differences between rigid metal conduit (RMC) and flexible metal conduit (FMC). RMC provides the highest level of mechanical protection and is ideal for outdoor installations or environments where the conduit is exposed to potential physical damage. FMC, while easier to install and modify in tight spaces, offers less protection against physical impacts and is generally used in indoor settings or in places where flexibility is more important than durability. The manual also highlights that both types of conduit must be grounded according to the National Electrical Code (NEC) to ensure proper safety. Based on this information, which of the following is a disadvantage of using FMC compared to RMC?
a. FMC requires more complex grounding procedures than RMC
b. FMC provides less mechanical protection than RMC
c. FMC cannot be used in outdoor installations
d. FMC is more difficult to install in confined spaces than RMC

Answer: b. FMC provides less mechanical protection than RMC. Explanation: The manual explains that while FMC is easier to install, it offers less mechanical protection, making it less suitable for environments where the conduit might be exposed to damage. This is a key disadvantage compared to RMC.

482. A specification sheet for two types of energy storage systems—lithium-ion batteries and lead-acid batteries—compares their efficiency, cost, and lifespan. Lithium-ion batteries are known for their high energy density, long cycle life, and rapid charging capabilities, making them ideal for modern applications such as renewable energy storage and electric vehicles. However, they are significantly more expensive than lead-acid batteries, which are cheaper but have a shorter lifespan and lower energy density. The sheet also points out that lead-acid batteries require more frequent maintenance and are less efficient in high-temperature environments. What is a key advantage of lithium-ion batteries over lead-acid batteries?
a. Lithium-ion batteries are more affordable than lead-acid batteries
b. Lithium-ion batteries have a longer lifespan and higher energy density
c. Lithium-ion batteries require more frequent maintenance than lead-acid batteries
d. Lithium-ion batteries are better suited for high-temperature environments

Answer: b. Lithium-ion batteries have a longer lifespan and higher energy density. Explanation: The specification sheet highlights that lithium-ion batteries offer a much longer lifespan and higher energy density than lead-acid batteries, which is a key advantage in modern energy storage applications.

483. An industrial manual describes the differences between using a transformer and an inverter in power conversion applications. Transformers are used to step up or step down AC voltage, making them essential for long-distance power transmission and distribution. They are efficient but can only work with AC power. Inverters, on the other hand, convert DC power into AC power and are commonly used in renewable energy systems where solar panels or batteries generate DC electricity. However, inverters are more complex and can experience power losses during conversion. The manual advises that transformers are the best choice when dealing solely with AC power, while inverters are necessary for systems involving DC generation. Based on this, what is a drawback of using an inverter instead of a transformer?
a. Inverters can only work with AC power
b. Inverters are less efficient due to power losses during conversion
c. Inverters cannot be used for long-distance power transmission
d. Inverters are more expensive than transformers in AC applications

Answer: b. Inverters are less efficient due to power losses during conversion. Explanation: The manual explains that inverters experience power losses when converting DC to AC, making them less efficient than transformers, which work directly with AC power and are more efficient in this context.

484. A section in a technical manual compares the use of single-phase and three-phase power systems in commercial applications. Single-phase systems are simpler and less expensive to install but are generally used for lower-power applications such as lighting or small appliances. Three-phase systems, while more costly and complex, provide more efficient power delivery and are used in large industrial settings where heavy machinery and motors are involved. The manual explains that three-phase systems provide smoother and more consistent power, which is critical for reducing wear on motors and ensuring reliable operation. Which of the following is a primary disadvantage of using a single-phase system compared to a three-phase system?
a. Single-phase systems are more expensive to install
b. Single-phase systems are more complex to maintain
c. Single-phase systems provide less efficient power delivery
d. Single-phase systems are not suitable for lighting applications

Answer: c. Single-phase systems provide less efficient power delivery. Explanation: The manual emphasizes that single-phase systems are less efficient in power delivery compared to three-phase systems, especially in large industrial applications where smoother and more reliable power is required.

485. A new technician at an industrial facility is tasked with starting up a large 600V motor for a conveyor system. The motor is controlled by a soft starter to limit inrush current and has a bypass contactor that engages once the motor reaches full speed. The startup procedure involves checking the control power indicator, setting the motor protection relay, and ensuring the disconnect switch is in the "on" position. The technician is instructed to press the "start" button to engage the soft starter, and the motor should ramp up to full speed within 10 seconds. If the motor fails to

reach full speed within that time, the instructions specify to check for any fault codes on the motor protection relay and reset the system before attempting to start again. After pressing the start button, the technician notices that the motor ramps up slowly but does not engage the bypass contactor. There are no fault codes displayed on the motor protection relay. What should the technician check next according to the startup procedure?
a. Verify that the soft starter settings match the motor's full load amperage
b. Reset the motor protection relay and try starting the motor again
c. Inspect the wiring connections for the bypass contactor for any loose connections
d. Check the condition of the motor windings for potential overheating

Answer: a. Verify that the soft starter settings match the motor's full load amperage. Explanation: Since the motor ramps up slowly but doesn't engage the bypass contactor, the issue could be due to incorrect soft starter settings, particularly the full load amperage setting. If this setting is incorrect, the motor may not reach full speed, and the bypass contactor won't engage. No fault codes indicate that the problem isn't with the protection relay.

486. A senior electrician is overseeing the shutdown procedure for a backup generator system at a data center. The generator is designed to automatically take over when utility power is lost. The written procedure states that after restoring utility power, the generator must be run for a cool-down period of five minutes under no load before completely shutting down. It also indicates that the fuel shutoff valve must be closed after the cool-down period, followed by turning the control panel switch to the "off" position. Finally, the transfer switch must be returned to the normal utility setting, ensuring no loads are connected to the generator. The electrician notices that after the generator has cooled down, the control panel switch is immediately turned off before the fuel shutoff valve is closed. According to the procedure, what potential issue might occur due to this deviation?
a. The generator may fail to start during the next power outage due to fuel system contamination
b. The generator could overheat because the cooling system remains inactive after shutdown
c. The transfer switch may fail to return to the utility power setting
d. The generator's fuel lines could become over-pressurized, causing a safety hazard

Answer: a. The generator may fail to start during the next power outage due to fuel system contamination. Explanation: By turning off the control panel switch before closing the fuel shutoff valve, the fuel could remain in the lines, leading to contamination or degradation over time. This could prevent the generator from starting properly in the future. The fuel shutoff valve should always be closed first according to procedure.

487. A technician is performing a routine maintenance check on a large air compressor system. The manufacturer's maintenance checklist specifies that the technician must first check the oil level, then inspect the air intake filters, and finally verify the system's operating pressure. If the operating pressure is too low, the checklist instructs to inspect the pressure regulator and the safety valve for proper function. The technician finds that the oil level is low and proceeds to top it up. Afterward, the air intake filters are clogged with debris and are replaced. Upon restarting the compressor, the system is still operating at lower than expected pressure. Following the maintenance checklist, what should the technician inspect next?
a. Check the compressor's discharge valve for blockages
b. Inspect the pressure regulator and safety valve for proper function
c. Replace the oil filter to improve system efficiency
d. Verify that the oil used was the correct grade for the compressor

Answer: b. Inspect the pressure regulator and safety valve for proper function. Explanation: According to the checklist, if the compressor is operating at low pressure after initial inspections, the next step is to check the pressure regulator and safety valve. These components control system pressure and can be the source of low pressure if they malfunction.

488. During a troubleshooting session, an electrician is examining a heating system that operates on a conditional control sequence. The system is designed to turn on the heating elements if the temperature drops below 50°F and the fan is confirmed to be operational. If the fan fails to start, the system will shut down the heating elements to prevent overheating. The troubleshooting guide for the system includes several conditional statements that outline potential fault scenarios. It first instructs the technician to check if the thermostat is functioning and set correctly. If the thermostat is correct, the next step is to verify whether the fan motor is receiving power. If the fan motor is not powered, the guide suggests inspecting the motor's wiring and control circuit. The electrician confirms that the thermostat is functioning, but the fan motor is not starting. Following the troubleshooting guide, what should the electrician do next?
a. Check the heating elements for signs of overheating or damage
b. Inspect the fan motor's wiring and control circuit for faults
c. Reset the thermostat to see if the system restarts
d. Test the heating element's circuit breaker for tripping

Answer: b. Inspect the fan motor's wiring and control circuit for faults. Explanation: According to the conditional troubleshooting guide, if the fan motor is not receiving power and the thermostat is functioning properly, the next logical step is to inspect the wiring and control circuit for the fan. Without the fan operating, the heating system will not engage as a safety precaution.

489. A maintenance team is responsible for shutting down a conveyor belt system in a manufacturing plant for routine inspection. The shutdown procedure emphasizes the importance of following the correct sequence to avoid mechanical damage. First, the control power must be deactivated, then the belt must be stopped by disengaging the motor. After that, the conveyor must be locked out to prevent accidental startup during maintenance. The team begins by shutting off the motor and then locks out the system without deactivating the control power. As the maintenance work begins, the control panel unexpectedly activates a nearby warning alarm, surprising the team. According to the shutdown procedure, what is the most likely reason the warning alarm activated?
a. The conveyor belt's motor was not properly locked out, leading to residual movement
b. The control power was not deactivated, allowing the panel to remain active
c. The shutdown sequence was too rapid, causing the system to enter an emergency state
d. The motor should have been disengaged first before locking out the conveyor

Answer: b. The control power was not deactivated, allowing the panel to remain active. Explanation: The shutdown procedure emphasizes that the control power must be deactivated first. By skipping this step, the control panel remains active, which could cause alarms to activate unexpectedly even though the motor is shut down.

490. A technician is following a maintenance manual for inspecting a large three-phase transformer that supplies power to an industrial facility. The manual specifies a step-by-step process, including de-energizing the transformer, verifying that all phases are grounded, and testing the insulation resistance before beginning any physical inspection. After completing the insulation resistance test, the manual instructs the technician to clean the transformer's cooling fins and check for any oil leaks. If oil leaks are found, the manual advises contacting an engineer for further

evaluation. During the inspection, the technician finds oil seeping from one of the transformer's cooling fins. Following the maintenance manual, what should the technician do next?
a. Patch the cooling fin leak temporarily to prevent further oil loss
b. Clean the cooling fins and continue the inspection
c. Contact an engineer to evaluate the severity of the oil leak
d. Increase the transformer's cooling capacity to prevent overheating

Answer: c. Contact an engineer to evaluate the severity of the oil leak. Explanation: The manual specifies that if oil leaks are discovered, the technician should contact an engineer. Oil leaks in transformers can indicate serious internal issues, such as degraded insulation or cooling problems, and should be evaluated by a professional.

491. An apprentice is tasked with performing a routine shutdown of an industrial chiller system. The shutdown procedure includes multiple steps, starting with reducing the system load by gradually lowering the chiller's setpoint, then stopping the compressor. After the compressor is stopped, the technician must allow the chiller's cooling tower to continue running for an additional 15 minutes to dissipate residual heat before shutting off the tower. However, the apprentice accidentally shuts down the cooling tower immediately after the compressor stops. What potential issue could arise from this error, based on the shutdown procedure?
a. The compressor may become damaged from overheating due to insufficient cooling
b. The chiller will not be able to restart without resetting the cooling tower
c. The system may experience a pressure buildup, leading to a safety valve release
d. The residual heat may damage the cooling tower's fan motors

Answer: a. The compressor may become damaged from overheating due to insufficient cooling. Explanation: The shutdown procedure specifies that the cooling tower must continue to run to dissipate residual heat. Shutting it down immediately could cause the compressor to overheat, as the system lacks sufficient cooling during the shutdown period.

492. An electrical contractor is reviewing the startup procedure for a new fire pump system in a high-rise building. The procedure requires checking the jockey pump's pressure settings, ensuring the main pump is filled with water, and verifying the power supply to the fire pump controller. The instructions emphasize that the fire pump should only be manually started if the jockey pump cannot maintain system pressure during a fire event. Once the fire pump is started, it cannot be turned off manually and will continue to run until the main control panel resets the system. During testing, the contractor manually starts the fire pump and allows it to run for several minutes. However, when attempting to stop the pump, the contractor is unable to turn it off from the local control panel. What does this behavior indicate based on the startup procedure?
a. The fire pump has a fault in the local control panel preventing shutdown
b. The fire pump's automatic shutdown system has been disabled during testing
c. The fire pump is functioning as expected, as it cannot be stopped manually
d. The jockey pump pressure is too low, causing the fire pump to stay on

Answer: c. The fire pump is functioning as expected, as it cannot be stopped manually. Explanation: The startup procedure clearly states that once the fire pump is manually started, it will continue to run until the main control panel resets the system. This is a safety feature to ensure the pump operates continuously during an emergency.

493. A team of electricians is responsible for restarting a cooling system in a data center following routine maintenance. The system includes multiple cooling units, each with its own compressor and evaporator fan. The restart procedure involves powering up the control panel, enabling the cooling units one at a time, and waiting for each unit to reach its setpoint temperature before activating the next. If a unit fails to reach the setpoint within 10 minutes, the procedure instructs the electricians to check the refrigerant levels and compressor performance before attempting to restart. After enabling the first cooling unit, the team notices that the unit is taking longer than expected to reach its setpoint. Following the procedure, what should the electricians do next?
a. Restart the control panel to reset the cooling system
b. Check the refrigerant levels and compressor performance for the first unit
c. Bypass the first unit and activate the second unit to maintain cooling
d. Increase the setpoint temperature to shorten the runtime

Answer: b. Check the refrigerant levels and compressor performance for the first unit. Explanation: The procedure specifies that if a cooling unit fails to reach its setpoint within the allocated time, the next step is to inspect the refrigerant levels and compressor performance. These are common causes of delays in reaching temperature setpoints.

494. A senior electrician is asked to interpret the shutdown sequence for a large centrifugal pump used in a water treatment plant. The sequence requires stopping the pump's motor, closing the discharge valve to prevent backflow, and draining the pump casing before locking out the system for maintenance. The discharge valve must be closed within 30 seconds of stopping the motor to avoid water hammer, which can damage the piping. However, during a recent shutdown, the discharge valve was not closed until two minutes after the motor stopped. According to the shutdown procedure, what potential issue could arise from this delay?
a. The pump motor may be damaged from backflow
b. The discharge valve could become stuck in the open position
c. Water hammer could damage the pump or piping system
d. The pump casing may not drain properly, leading to rust

Answer: c. Water hammer could damage the pump or piping system. Explanation: The shutdown procedure specifies closing the discharge valve within 30 seconds to prevent water hammer, a pressure surge that can occur when water flow is suddenly stopped or reversed. A delay in closing the valve increases the risk of damaging the pump and piping system.

495. An electrical contractor submits a proposal to a large industrial client arguing for the installation of LED lighting throughout their facility. The proposal claims that LED lighting will reduce energy consumption by 60% compared to the existing fluorescent fixtures. The contractor also suggests that LED fixtures will reduce maintenance costs, as they last up to 50,000 hours. As evidence, the proposal references case studies from other similar facilities that have seen energy savings. However, no specific data or cost-benefit analysis is provided for this particular facility. The proposal concludes by stating that "LEDs are the best choice for any modern facility." What is a weakness in the contractor's argument?
a. The case studies provide no useful information for this facility
b. The energy savings are exaggerated for LED fixtures
c. The lack of facility-specific data weakens the argument
d. The proposal's tone is overly technical

Answer: c. The lack of facility-specific data weakens the argument. Explanation: While the contractor references case studies, the absence of a specific cost-benefit analysis for the facility in question reduces the proposal's persuasiveness. General savings claims do not account for unique conditions, which could affect the accuracy of the energy savings.

496. A project manager presents a plan to install a new solar power system at a commercial site, arguing that it will cut energy costs by 80%. The manager supports this claim by citing the average peak sunlight hours for the region and the efficiency ratings of the selected solar panels. However, the plan does not mention the facility's existing electrical load or consider potential shading from nearby buildings. The manager ends by stating that solar energy is the "most efficient solution for all power needs." What type of logical fallacy is present in the final statement?
a. Hasty generalization
b. Appeal to authority
c. Slippery slope
d. Strawman argument

Answer: a. Hasty generalization. Explanation: The claim that solar energy is the "most efficient solution for all power needs" is a hasty generalization. The manager assumes that because solar works well in some situations, it must work well universally, without considering the specific circumstances of the site.

497. An engineering team proposes the use of a particular brand of uninterruptible power supply (UPS) for a new data center, arguing that it is "the most reliable choice" because it has the longest battery life. The proposal includes a chart comparing battery life across various UPS brands but does not provide any data on failure rates or maintenance requirements. Additionally, the proposal does not consider factors like the quality of customer support or warranty periods. The team insists that "longer battery life is the most important factor." Which of the following is a flaw in this argument?
a. The proposal lacks information about battery life
b. The proposal uses incorrect comparisons between UPS brands
c. The proposal overemphasizes battery life without considering other critical factors
d. The proposal does not offer a cost analysis

Answer: c. The proposal overemphasizes battery life without considering other critical factors. Explanation: While battery life is important, the argument is flawed because it ignores other factors like failure rates, maintenance, customer support, and warranties, which are also essential when choosing a reliable UPS for a data center.

498. A contractor submits a proposal to upgrade an electrical system in an older building, arguing that replacing all wiring with new copper conductors will improve safety and reduce energy losses. The proposal references outdated wiring standards and cites studies showing that modern copper wiring has lower resistance. However, the proposal does not provide data on the current state of the building's wiring or offer alternatives like rewiring only certain high-risk areas. It concludes by stating that "full rewiring is always the safest option." What aspect of the argument is unsupported by evidence?
a. The claim that copper wiring has lower resistance
b. The suggestion that rewiring is necessary for this building
c. The argument that modern standards improve safety

d. The data provided on outdated wiring standards

Answer: b. The suggestion that rewiring is necessary for this building. Explanation: The proposal assumes that full rewiring is necessary without presenting evidence about the condition of the current wiring system or considering partial rewiring as an option, making this aspect of the argument unsupported.

499. In a project proposal for a new electrical substation, the engineering firm argues that using aluminum conductors instead of copper will reduce costs by 20% while maintaining the same level of performance. The firm cites studies showing that aluminum is lighter and cheaper than copper. However, the proposal does not discuss the potential drawbacks of aluminum, such as the need for larger conductors to carry the same current or the risks of oxidation over time. The conclusion states that "aluminum is always a better choice due to cost savings." What is the main problem with the argument's conclusion?
a. It ignores the benefits of copper conductors
b. It fails to explain how aluminum can maintain performance levels
c. It overstates the cost savings of aluminum conductors
d. It disregards potential issues with aluminum conductors

Answer: d. It disregards potential issues with aluminum conductors. Explanation: The conclusion is flawed because it does not acknowledge the potential risks associated with aluminum conductors, such as oxidation and the need for larger wire sizes to carry the same current as copper, thus oversimplifying the choice based on cost alone.

500. An industrial energy audit report suggests replacing the facility's existing motors with high-efficiency models, claiming that this upgrade will reduce energy consumption by 40%. The report includes efficiency ratings for the new motors but does not analyze the existing load profile or factor in how often the motors are in operation. Additionally, the report does not consider the costs associated with downtime during installation. The conclusion asserts that the savings are "guaranteed based on motor efficiency alone." What is the primary flaw in this argument?
a. The report provides insufficient data on motor efficiency
b. The report overlooks the cost of purchasing new motors
c. The report fails to account for the facility's load profile and usage patterns
d. The report exaggerates the efficiency of high-efficiency motors

Answer: c. The report fails to account for the facility's load profile and usage patterns. Explanation: The argument is weakened by the omission of important factors like the load profile and actual usage of the motors. Efficiency savings depend on how frequently and under what conditions the motors are used, not just on the motor ratings.

501. A proposal for a new electrical distribution system argues that increasing the conductor size will reduce voltage drop and improve energy efficiency across the facility. The proposal includes calculations demonstrating reduced voltage drop with larger conductors but does not analyze the return on investment (ROI) for the increased cost of the larger conductors. The contractor concludes by stating that "investing in larger conductors always results in lower operating costs." What aspect of the argument is problematic?
a. The claim that voltage drop is reduced by larger conductors
b. The lack of calculations showing the impact on energy efficiency
c. The failure to consider the cost-benefit ratio of installing larger conductors

d. The assumption that conductor size is the only factor affecting operating costs

Answer: c. The failure to consider the cost-benefit ratio of installing larger conductors. Explanation: While larger conductors reduce voltage drop, the proposal fails to address whether the reduced energy losses will justify the increased material and installation costs. ROI analysis is critical in determining whether the investment is financially worthwhile.

502. An engineering consultant presents a plan for upgrading the electrical system of a manufacturing plant, recommending the use of variable frequency drives (VFDs) to control the motors. The consultant claims that installing VFDs will reduce energy usage by up to 30% and extends motor life. The proposal includes manufacturer data supporting energy savings but does not consider the upfront installation costs or the maintenance requirements of VFDs. It concludes by stating, "VFDs will save money in all situations." What is a key flaw in this argument?
a. The proposal fails to provide data on motor life extension
b. The consultant overestimates the energy savings from VFDs
c. The upfront installation and maintenance costs are ignored
d. The proposal incorrectly describes how VFDs work

Answer: c. The upfront installation and maintenance costs are ignored. Explanation: While the energy-saving potential of VFDs is well-documented, the proposal is flawed because it neglects to factor in the initial costs of installation and the ongoing maintenance requirements, which may affect the overall financial benefit.

503. A technical proposal for replacing the existing HVAC system in an office building argues that switching to a newer system will improve energy efficiency by 25%. The proposal cites studies from similar buildings but does not provide an analysis specific to the building in question. Additionally, the proposal does not account for the cost of upgrading the building's electrical infrastructure to support the new system. It concludes by saying, "This upgrade is guaranteed to reduce costs." What is the primary weakness in this conclusion?
a. The proposal provides insufficient data on energy efficiency improvements
b. The infrastructure upgrade costs are not considered
c. The 25% efficiency improvement is unrealistic for this type of system
d. The proposal fails to cite relevant studies for HVAC systems

Answer: b. The infrastructure upgrade costs are not considered. Explanation: The proposal's conclusion is problematic because it ignores the potential costs of upgrading the building's electrical infrastructure, which may negate or reduce the cost savings achieved by improved energy efficiency.

504. A manufacturer proposes a new control system for an automated production line, arguing that it will increase productivity by 15%. The proposal includes data showing increased throughput at similar facilities but fails to discuss the impact of downtime during installation or the potential learning curve for operators adapting to the new system. The proposal ends with the statement, "Productivity increases will be immediate and sustained." What type of logical fallacy does this statement represent?
a. False dilemma
b. Appeal to authority
c. Begging the question

d. Overgeneralization

Answer: d. Overgeneralization. Explanation: The statement assumes that productivity gains will be immediate and sustained without considering potential challenges like installation downtime or operator adaptation, making it an overgeneralization of the system's benefits across different environments.

505. An electrician is tasked with installing a new 480V motor in a manufacturing facility. The motor's manufacturer provides specific installation guidelines, which include torque specifications for the terminal connections and requirements for the size of the protective device. The facility's electrical engineer provides a specification sheet that lists a 100A circuit breaker for the motor protection. Additionally, the National Electrical Code (NEC) article for motor protection suggests that a motor of this size should have a breaker sized at 125% of the motor's full-load current. The electrician reviews the motor's nameplate, which shows a full-load current of 85A. However, the manufacturer's test report includes a note that the motor may draw up to 110A at startup. Given this information, what size circuit breaker should the electrician install?
a. 100A, as specified by the electrical engineer
b. 106A, following the NEC guideline of 125% of the motor's full-load current
c. 125A, to account for the motor's startup current
d. 150A, to ensure protection during both startup and continuous operation

Answer: b. 106A, following the NEC guideline of 125% of the motor's full-load current. Explanation: The NEC specifies that the circuit breaker should be sized at 125% of the motor's full-load current, which in this case is 85A. 125% of 85A equals 106.25A, so the closest standard breaker size would be 106A. While startup current can temporarily exceed full-load current, the breaker size is based on continuous operation rather than peak inrush.

506. An engineer is reviewing the electrical design for a new commercial building. The design includes lighting circuits, HVAC systems, and general power outlets. According to the manufacturer's guidelines, the HVAC system requires a dedicated circuit and must be fed by a 60A breaker. The electrical design specifies a 50A breaker for this system, based on the load calculations performed by the design team. The NEC recommends that all HVAC circuits be designed to handle 125% of the continuous load to avoid nuisance tripping. The engineer also checks the building load report, which indicates that the HVAC system runs continuously for long periods. What adjustment, if any, should the engineer make to the breaker size for the HVAC system?
a. No adjustment is needed since the design team's load calculation is correct
b. Increase the breaker size to 60A as recommended by the manufacturer's guidelines
c. Increase the breaker size to 75A to follow the NEC's 125% rule for continuous loads
d. Increase the breaker size to 100A to allow for future HVAC upgrades

Answer: c. Increase the breaker size to 75A to follow the NEC's 125% rule for continuous loads. Explanation: According to the NEC, circuits supplying continuous loads must be rated for 125% of the load to prevent nuisance tripping. Since the HVAC system runs continuously, the breaker should be increased to 75A (60A × 1.25).

507. A technician is troubleshooting an issue with a photovoltaic (PV) system at a solar farm. The system's inverters have been experiencing frequent overcurrent faults, which are causing the protective devices to trip. The technician reviews the installation specifications, which show that the inverters are rated for 500kW with a maximum input

current of 1000A. The NEC requires that conductors and overcurrent protection for PV systems be rated at 125% of the maximum continuous current. However, the manufacturer's documentation suggests sizing the overcurrent protection at 150% to account for environmental factors such as temperature. The technician finds that the system is currently protected by 1250A breakers. Based on this information, what is the most appropriate solution to prevent the overcurrent faults?
a. Increase the breaker size to 1500A as recommended by the manufacturer
b. Install cooling fans to lower the ambient temperature and reduce the inverter load
c. Replace the 1250A breakers with 1000A breakers to match the inverter's maximum current rating
d. Reconfigure the system to reduce the current draw from each inverter

Answer: a. Increase the breaker size to 1500A as recommended by the manufacturer. Explanation: The manufacturer's documentation suggests accounting for environmental factors by sizing overcurrent protection at 150% of the maximum continuous current, which would require a breaker size of 1500A (1000A × 1.5). This adjustment should prevent the frequent tripping.

508. A facility is undergoing an upgrade to its electrical distribution system, which involves replacing old switchgear. The electrical contractor is reviewing the existing switchgear specifications, the NEC guidelines, and the new manufacturer's requirements. The original switchgear had a short-circuit rating of 35kA, but the NEC suggests that for the facility's current load conditions, the switchgear should be rated at 50kA. The manufacturer's product sheet lists several options for short-circuit ratings, ranging from 40kA to 65kA, depending on the configuration. The contractor is also considering the facility's future load growth, which could increase fault current levels. Based on the available information, what short-circuit rating should the contractor choose for the new switchgear?
a. 35kA, matching the rating of the original switchgear
b. 40kA, to meet the manufacturer's minimum recommendation
c. 50kA, to comply with the NEC's current load requirements
d. 65kA, to allow for future load growth and increased fault current

Answer: d. 65kA, to allow for future load growth and increased fault current. Explanation: Given that the NEC recommends a 50kA rating for the current load and the facility is expected to experience load growth, selecting the higher 65kA rating would ensure the switchgear can handle future fault currents and remain compliant with safety standards.

509. An electrical engineer is reviewing the test report for a newly installed transformer at a power plant. The transformer has a nameplate rating of 15MVA with a primary voltage of 69kV and a secondary voltage of 13.8kV. The test report shows that the transformer passed all insulation resistance and polarity tests but failed the load test, where it overheated after running at 95% capacity for one hour. The manufacturer's datasheet recommends that the transformer operate at no more than 85% of its rated capacity for sustained periods to avoid overheating. The NEC also requires that transformers be loaded no more than 80% of their rated capacity under continuous operation. What recommendation should the engineer make to ensure the transformer operates reliably?
a. Operate the transformer at 85% of its rated capacity as per the manufacturer's recommendation
b. Reduce the load to 80% of the transformer's rated capacity in accordance with the NEC
c. Replace the transformer with a unit that has a higher MVA rating
d. Install additional cooling fans to prevent overheating during high loads

Answer: b. Reduce the load to 80% of the transformer's rated capacity in accordance with the NEC. Explanation: The NEC requires transformers to be loaded no more than 80% under continuous operation to prevent overheating. Although the manufacturer allows for 85%, following the NEC guideline ensures compliance and reduces the risk of overheating.

510. A commercial building is being equipped with a new fire alarm system, and the installation team must follow both the manufacturer's installation guide and local building codes. The manufacturer specifies that all control panels must have a dedicated 120V circuit with a 20A breaker, while the local building code requires fire alarm systems to be installed on circuits that are monitored and backed up by an emergency power supply. The installation team also reviews the NEC, which states that fire alarm circuits must be clearly labeled and accessible for emergency shutoff. The team finds that the building's emergency power supply is limited and does not have sufficient capacity for additional loads. What should the installation team do to ensure the fire alarm system is compliant with all regulations?
a. Connect the fire alarm panels to the existing emergency power supply, despite the limited capacity
b. Install a dedicated 120V circuit with a 20A breaker as per the manufacturer's guidelines
c. Upgrade the building's emergency power supply to handle the additional load from the fire alarm system
d. Label the fire alarm circuit as "non-emergency" and install it without connecting to the backup system

Answer: c. Upgrade the building's emergency power supply to handle the additional load from the fire alarm system. Explanation: To comply with local building codes and the NEC, the fire alarm system must be backed up by an emergency power supply. The manufacturer's guidelines for a dedicated circuit must also be followed, but the priority is ensuring the emergency power supply can support the additional load.

511. An industrial facility is reviewing the grounding system for its new power distribution network. The manufacturer's installation instructions for the switchgear specify a minimum grounding conductor size of 4/0 AWG for the main grounding electrode. However, the NEC specifies that the grounding conductor size must be based on the size of the service-entrance conductors, and in this case, the service conductors are 600 kcmil copper. The NEC provides a table indicating that a 2/0 AWG copper conductor is sufficient for grounding service-entrance conductors up to 600 kcmil. The facility also has an internal guideline that recommends using oversized conductors to ensure low impedance grounding. Given these conflicting sources of information, what grounding conductor size should be used?
a. 2/0 AWG, following the NEC's minimum requirement
b. 4/0 AWG, as specified by the manufacturer
c. 600 kcmil, to match the size of the service-entrance conductors
d. 500 kcmil, to follow the facility's internal guidelines for oversized conductors

Answer: b. 4/0 AWG, as specified by the manufacturer. Explanation: While the NEC provides a minimum requirement of 2/0 AWG based on the service conductors, the manufacturer's installation instructions take precedence because they are tailored to the specific switchgear. Using a larger 4/0 AWG conductor also aligns with the facility's guideline for low impedance grounding.

512. A contractor is evaluating the installation of a new 2000A busway system for a factory expansion project. The manufacturer's guidelines recommend that the busway be installed with at least 18 inches of clearance from any combustible materials and that the temperature in the busway's vicinity be maintained below 40°C. The NEC requires that the busway be installed with appropriate fire-rated barriers if it passes through walls or floors and that it be sized to handle the calculated load at 125% for continuous use. The contractor's load calculations show that the busway

will carry a continuous load of 1600A. What actions should the contractor take to ensure the installation meets code and manufacturer specifications?
a. Install a 1600A busway and ensure it passes through fire-rated barriers
b. Install a 2000A busway and ensure it has 18 inches of clearance from combustibles
c. Install a 2500A busway to handle future load increases and maintain a temperature below 40°C
d. Install a 1600A busway with additional cooling fans to prevent overheating

Answer: b. Install a 2000A busway and ensure it has 18 inches of clearance from combustibles. Explanation: The load calculations show a continuous load of 1600A, and the NEC requires that the busway be sized for 125% of the continuous load. Therefore, a 2000A busway is appropriate. Additionally, the manufacturer's clearance requirement from combustible materials must be met.

513. A field engineer is tasked with reviewing the installation of a generator system for a data center. The generator is rated for 1500kW, and the manufacturer specifies that the fuel system should be designed to provide continuous operation for at least 48 hours under full load. The installation design, however, has provided a fuel tank with a capacity for only 36 hours of operation. The local building code requires that all backup generator systems have sufficient fuel for a minimum of 24 hours of continuous operation. The NEC does not specify a minimum fuel requirement but mandates that the generator's fuel system must meet the operational demands of the equipment it supports. What should the field engineer recommend regarding the fuel system design?
a. Increase the fuel tank capacity to meet the manufacturer's 48-hour specification
b. Leave the fuel tank as designed, since it exceeds the local building code's requirement
c. Increase the fuel tank capacity to meet the NEC's demand requirements
d. Install an additional fuel tank to meet both the NEC and local code requirements

Answer: a. Increase the fuel tank capacity to meet the manufacturer's 48-hour specification. Explanation: The manufacturer's specifications require the generator to have fuel for 48 hours of continuous operation under full load. Although the local code only requires 24 hours, following the manufacturer's guidelines ensures the system operates as intended in critical situations.

514. A project manager is overseeing the installation of a UPS (uninterruptible power supply) system for a hospital's critical care unit. The manufacturer's documentation specifies that the UPS must be connected to an isolated ground to prevent electrical noise from interfering with sensitive medical equipment. The NEC requires that the UPS be grounded according to Article 250, which allows for the use of a common grounding electrode system shared with other electrical equipment. However, the hospital's internal guidelines call for separate grounds for all critical equipment. The project manager reviews the electrical plans, which show that the UPS is connected to the common grounding system used by the facility's non-critical equipment. What corrective action should the project manager take?
a. Leave the grounding system as is, since it complies with the NEC
b. Install an isolated ground for the UPS, following the manufacturer's guidelines
c. Use the facility's common grounding system, but increase the size of the grounding conductor
d. Install a separate ground rod for the UPS, as per the hospital's internal guidelines

Answer: b. Install an isolated ground for the UPS, following the manufacturer's guidelines. Explanation: The manufacturer specifies that the UPS should be connected to an isolated ground to avoid electrical noise, which is critical in a hospital setting with sensitive equipment. Following the manufacturer's guidelines ensures reliable operation.

515. A technical manual explains electrical grounding by using the analogy of water flowing through pipes. The manual states, "Just as water flows to the lowest point, electrical current follows the path of least resistance to ground." It describes how grounding provides a safe path for excess current, preventing dangerous voltage from building up in a circuit. The analogy is extended by comparing ungrounded systems to "dammed rivers" that could overflow and cause damage if not properly controlled. What does the analogy of water flowing through pipes represent in this context?
a. The distribution of voltage in a circuit
b. The flow of current to a safe grounding point
c. The control of current in high-voltage systems
d. The buildup of resistance in conductors

Answer: b. The flow of current to a safe grounding point. Explanation: The analogy compares the flow of water to the flow of electrical current, emphasizing that grounding provides a safe path for excess current, similar to how water flows to the lowest point to avoid overflow or damage.

516. In a section describing surge protectors, a technical document states, "A surge protector is like a gatekeeper, allowing only a safe amount of electricity to pass through while blocking dangerous spikes in voltage." The document explains how surge protectors protect sensitive electronics from power surges caused by lightning strikes or power grid fluctuations. It further explains that without surge protectors, electrical spikes can cause significant damage to equipment. What does the "gatekeeper" metaphor in this description refer to?
a. The ability of surge protectors to completely eliminate all voltage surges
b. The process of regulating the amount of current flowing through a circuit
c. The function of surge protectors in allowing safe voltage levels to pass
d. The blocking of all incoming current during a power surge

Answer: c. The function of surge protectors in allowing safe voltage levels to pass. Explanation: The "gatekeeper" metaphor highlights the surge protector's role in allowing safe levels of voltage to pass while blocking harmful voltage spikes, rather than eliminating all current or blocking all surges.

517. A technical manual describing the behavior of current in alternating current (AC) systems uses the metaphor, "The current in an AC system is like a pendulum, swinging back and forth as it alternates between positive and negative cycles." The document explains how current in AC systems constantly changes direction, unlike direct current (DC), which flows steadily in one direction. The metaphor helps illustrate how AC operates on sinusoidal waveforms, alternating between peaks and valleys of voltage. What does the "pendulum" in the metaphor represent in the context of AC systems?
a. The generation of electrical power in an AC system
b. The constant fluctuation in voltage and direction of current flow
c. The speed at which current moves through a circuit
d. The unchanging nature of current in a DC system

Answer: b. The constant fluctuation in voltage and direction of current flow. Explanation: The "pendulum" metaphor represents how AC current alternates between positive and negative cycles, illustrating the constant changes in voltage and direction within an AC system.

518. A technical training document on electrical load balancing uses the idiom, "Don't put all your eggs in one basket," to explain the importance of distributing electrical loads evenly across circuits. It warns that placing too much load on a single circuit can cause overheating, tripped breakers, or even equipment failure. The document advises spreading the load across multiple circuits to ensure safety and prevent system overloads. What is the meaning of the idiom "Don't put all your eggs in one basket" in this technical context?
a. Avoid using a single type of circuit for different electrical loads
b. Spread the electrical load evenly across multiple circuits
c. Ensure that all circuits are capable of handling maximum load
d. Use higher-rated circuits to prevent overloads

Answer: b. Spread the electrical load evenly across multiple circuits. Explanation: The idiom "Don't put all your eggs in one basket" in this context advises against overloading a single circuit, instead encouraging the distribution of electrical loads to prevent overheating or system failure.

519. In a section of a technical manual on transformers, the author describes high-voltage power transmission by saying, "Electricity flows like a river through power lines, but transformers act like dams, controlling the voltage and ensuring the current is delivered at the correct level downstream." The manual explains that transformers increase voltage for long-distance transmission and then step it down at distribution points. What role do the "dams" in the analogy represent in the context of transformers?
a. The blocking of excess current to prevent overloading
b. The control and regulation of voltage as it flows through power lines
c. The generation of electrical power in high-voltage systems
d. The conversion of electrical energy into mechanical energy

Answer: b. The control and regulation of voltage as it flows through power lines. Explanation: The "dams" in the analogy refer to transformers' role in regulating voltage, stepping it up for transmission and stepping it down at distribution points to ensure safe delivery of electricity, just as dams control water flow in a river.

520. In a discussion about short circuits, a safety guide describes a short as "a shortcut that bypasses the intended path, allowing electricity to rush through unchecked, like water bursting through a broken dam." The guide warns that this uncontrolled flow of electricity can lead to equipment damage, fires, or personal injury. It recommends properly insulating wires and regularly checking for wear and tear to prevent short circuits. What does the comparison to "water bursting through a broken dam" illustrate in the description of a short circuit?
a. The loss of electrical resistance in a circuit
b. The rapid and uncontrolled flow of current during a short circuit
c. The prevention of electrical overload in a properly grounded system
d. The steady flow of current in a functioning electrical circuit

Answer: b. The rapid and uncontrolled flow of current during a short circuit. Explanation: The comparison to "water bursting through a broken dam" illustrates the uncontrolled and dangerous flow of electricity that occurs in a short circuit, bypassing the intended pathway and potentially causing damage.

521. In a manual about motor control systems, the author uses the phrase "the heart of the system" to describe the role of the motor controller. The manual explains that the motor controller regulates the speed, torque, and direction of the motor, much like how the heart regulates blood flow in the body. It also outlines the importance of maintaining the motor controller to ensure the smooth operation of the entire system. What does the metaphor "the heart of the system" suggest about the motor controller's role?
a. The motor controller is responsible for generating power in the system
b. The motor controller plays a central and vital role in regulating the motor
c. The motor controller is the largest component of the electrical system
d. The motor controller is responsible for monitoring electrical resistance

Answer: b. The motor controller plays a central and vital role in regulating the motor. Explanation: Describing the motor controller as "the heart of the system" suggests that it is a critical component responsible for controlling the motor's operation, just as the heart is essential for regulating blood flow in the body.

522. A technical guide on power factor correction compares reactive power to "a tug of war between voltage and current." The guide explains that when voltage and current are not in phase, the system has reactive power, which reduces overall efficiency. It recommends installing power factor correction devices to minimize this inefficiency and ensure that voltage and current remain aligned. What does the "tug of war" analogy describe in this explanation?
a. The balance between resistance and capacitance in a circuit
b. The struggle between voltage and current when they are out of phase
c. The competition between different circuits for electrical power
d. The difficulty in measuring power in an unbalanced system

Answer: b. The struggle between voltage and current when they are out of phase. Explanation: The "tug of war" analogy describes the situation where voltage and current are out of phase, leading to reactive power and reduced system efficiency. Power factor correction helps align them, improving performance.

523. In a troubleshooting guide for photovoltaic (PV) systems, the author describes solar panels as "the fuel tanks" of a solar energy system, holding the potential energy that will eventually be converted into electricity. The guide explains that just as a car cannot run without fuel, a PV system cannot generate power without sunlight absorbed by the panels. It also discusses how panel orientation and tilt affect the "fuel" they collect. What does the metaphor "the fuel tanks" represent in this context?
a. The efficiency of energy storage in solar batteries
b. The ability of PV panels to store electrical energy for later use
c. The capacity of solar panels to absorb and store sunlight for conversion
d. The rate at which solar panels convert sunlight into electricity

Answer: c. The capacity of solar panels to absorb and store sunlight for conversion. Explanation: In this metaphor, the "fuel tanks" represent the solar panels' role in absorbing sunlight, which is then converted into usable electrical energy. Just as fuel is needed for a car to operate, sunlight is essential for PV systems to generate power.

524. A manual on electrical safety procedures warns that "working without proper grounding is like walking a tightrope without a safety net." The manual stresses the dangers of electrical shock or fire when systems are not grounded properly and describes grounding as a critical safety measure to protect workers and equipment. It advises checking grounding systems regularly and ensuring that all circuits are correctly grounded before beginning any work. What does the metaphor "walking a tightrope without a safety net" illustrate about improper grounding?
a. The difficulty of maintaining balance in electrical circuits without grounding
b. The high level of skill required to install grounding systems
c. The extreme risk and danger involved in working without grounding
d. The reliance on advanced technology to ensure proper grounding

Answer: c. The extreme risk and danger involved in working without grounding. Explanation: The metaphor "walking a tightrope without a safety net" conveys the significant danger of working without proper grounding, suggesting that without this safety measure, there is a high risk of serious injury or damage to equipment.

525. During a site visit to a hydroelectric plant, a technician encounters an issue where the main turbine generator repeatedly shuts down during peak load periods. The troubleshooting guide provided by the manufacturer is organized in a problem-solution format, listing common faults and corresponding corrective actions. The guide first recommends verifying whether the governor control system is responding to load changes appropriately. If the governor system is functioning normally, the next step is to check for overheating in the generator windings, as excessive heat could trigger the protective relays. The technician observes that the governor system appears to be responding correctly, and the control panel shows no temperature warnings. However, the guide also notes that some shutdowns can be caused by harmonic distortions in the generator's output, which are not immediately apparent without specialized equipment. Based on this troubleshooting guide, what should the technician do next?
a. Reset the protective relays and restart the generator
b. Conduct a harmonic analysis of the generator's output to check for distortions
c. Increase the cooling system's capacity to reduce potential overheating
d. Adjust the governor system's sensitivity to better handle peak load changes

Answer: b. Conduct a harmonic analysis of the generator's output to check for distortions. Explanation: Since the governor system is functioning and there are no signs of overheating, the next logical step, based on the guide's problem-solution structure, is to check for harmonic distortions in the generator's output. Harmonics can cause malfunctions in electrical equipment without triggering obvious fault indicators.

526. A team of electricians is reviewing a procedure manual for the installation of a medium-voltage switchgear system. The manual is organized in a strict chronological format, with each step building on the previous one. Step one involves placing the switchgear in its final location and securing it to the foundation. Step two requires connecting the grounding system before any other electrical connections are made. Step three involves verifying that all required cable lugs and terminations are installed before proceeding to the power connections. During installation, the team accidentally connects the power cables before completing the grounding connections. According to the manual's structure, what potential risk does this error introduce?
a. The switchgear may be incorrectly aligned, causing misoperation

b. The system may not pass inspection due to incomplete documentation
c. The lack of grounding could result in an unsafe condition during energization
d. The power cables may be improperly sized for the connected load

Answer: c. The lack of grounding could result in an unsafe condition during energization. Explanation: The chronological organization of the manual indicates that grounding must be completed before any power connections. Skipping this step introduces a significant safety risk, as an ungrounded system could cause electrical hazards during operation.

527. An industrial facility is reviewing a failure analysis report after a transformer malfunctioned, causing an unexpected power outage. The report is structured in a cause-effect format, detailing how an undetected fault in the transformer's insulation led to a gradual degradation of its windings, eventually resulting in a short circuit. The report compares this failure to a similar incident in another facility, where overheating caused by poor ventilation led to a transformer failure. The report concludes by recommending regular insulation resistance testing to prevent future failures, emphasizing the importance of early detection. What key takeaway should the facility's maintenance team prioritize based on the report's structure?
a. Implement a more robust cooling system to prevent overheating
b. Perform routine insulation resistance testing to detect faults early
c. Install a larger transformer to handle future load increases
d. Ensure that all electrical equipment is properly grounded to avoid short circuits

Answer: b. Perform routine insulation resistance testing to detect faults early. Explanation: The cause-effect structure of the report identifies the transformer's insulation failure as the root cause of the outage. The recommendation to prioritize insulation testing is directly related to preventing similar faults from going undetected in the future.

528. A contractor is evaluating two different brands of motor control centers (MCCs) for use in a new industrial project. The contractor refers to a product comparison chart that is organized in a compare-contrast format, listing each MCC's features side by side. Brand A offers higher short-circuit protection ratings but requires more space for installation. Brand B has a smaller footprint but is rated for lower fault currents. Both brands meet the project's minimum requirements for voltage and load capacity. The contractor's primary concern is fitting the MCC into a confined electrical room while still ensuring adequate fault protection for the equipment. Based on the comparison chart, which option should the contractor choose?
a. Brand A, because its higher short-circuit protection is crucial for safety
b. Brand B, because its smaller footprint will fit into the confined space
c. Brand A, because it offers more protection despite requiring additional space
d. Brand B, because its lower fault rating is sufficient for the project's requirements

Answer: b. Brand B, because its smaller footprint will fit into the confined space. Explanation: The contractor's priority is fitting the MCC into a confined space, and Brand B's smaller footprint meets this need. Although Brand A offers higher short-circuit protection, Brand B still meets the project's minimum requirements, making it the more practical choice.

529. An engineer is tasked with troubleshooting an issue in an automated assembly line where several motors are failing to start. The troubleshooting guide is organized in a problem-solution structure, with each problem linked to a potential cause and solution. The guide first advises checking the motor control circuits for power. If power is present, the next step is to verify the integrity of the control wiring. If the wiring is intact, the guide recommends checking for overload conditions on the motor starters. The engineer confirms that power is reaching the motors and the control wiring is undamaged. What should the engineer check next according to the guide's problem-solution structure?
a. Inspect the motor windings for damage
b. Test the motor starters for overload conditions
c. Check the control panel for any fault codes
d. Verify that the motors are properly grounded

Answer: b. Test the motor starters for overload conditions. Explanation: Following the problem-solution structure of the guide, once power and wiring are confirmed to be in good condition, the next logical step is to check for overload conditions on the motor starters, which could be preventing the motors from starting.

530. A building's electrical system recently underwent an upgrade, which included installing energy-efficient lighting and a new HVAC system. A failure analysis report was issued after the HVAC system tripped several times during peak usage. The report is structured to first explain the sequence of events, then identify the root cause of the failure, and finally recommend corrective actions. The report attributes the HVAC system's failure to insufficient power supply due to the combined load of the new lighting and HVAC equipment. The recommendation is to install a dedicated circuit for the HVAC system to prevent overload. Based on the structure of this report, what should the building's management prioritize as the next step?
a. Revert to the previous lighting system to reduce the overall load
b. Install a dedicated circuit for the HVAC system to avoid overload
c. Increase the capacity of the main electrical service to handle both systems
d. Schedule regular maintenance checks to prevent future tripping

Answer: b. Install a dedicated circuit for the HVAC system to avoid overload. Explanation: The cause-effect structure of the report identifies the combined load of the new systems as the root cause of the HVAC tripping. Installing a dedicated circuit is the recommended solution to prevent further issues.

531. An electrical contractor is tasked with choosing between two different UPS (uninterruptible power supply) systems for a critical data center application. The product comparison document is organized using a compare-contrast structure, detailing each UPS's battery life, power capacity, and response time during power outages. System A offers longer battery life and faster response time but at a higher cost. System B is more affordable but provides a shorter battery life and a slower response time. Both systems meet the data center's minimum requirements for power capacity. The contractor's primary goal is to ensure maximum uptime during power interruptions. Based on this comparison, which UPS should the contractor choose?
a. System A, because its faster response time ensures better protection during outages
b. System B, because it meets the minimum requirements at a lower cost
c. System A, because its longer battery life will maximize uptime
d. System B, because the slower response time is still acceptable for the application

Answer: c. System A, because its longer battery life will maximize uptime. Explanation: The contractor's priority is ensuring maximum uptime, and System A's longer battery life directly supports that goal. While both systems meet the power capacity requirements, System A offers better performance for this critical application.

532. During an annual inspection at a manufacturing facility, an electrician reviews a failure analysis report on the plant's primary transformer. The report is organized in a cause-effect structure, showing how a small oil leak in the transformer's cooling system led to a gradual increase in operating temperature. The rising temperature caused the transformer's insulation to deteriorate over time, eventually resulting in a complete failure. The report recommends more frequent inspections of the cooling system and temperature monitoring to prevent similar issues. What preventive measure should the electrician prioritize based on the report's structure?
a. Replace the transformer with a higher-rated unit to avoid overheating
b. Increase the transformer's load to test its current capacity
c. Perform regular cooling system inspections and temperature monitoring
d. Install a new cooling system with a higher efficiency rating

Answer: c. Perform regular cooling system inspections and temperature monitoring. Explanation: The cause-effect structure of the report identifies the cooling system failure as the root cause of the transformer's failure. Prioritizing cooling system inspections and temperature monitoring will address the issue and help prevent future failures.

533. A facility is upgrading its backup generator system, and the installation manual is structured chronologically, with specific steps that must be followed in order. The first step involves checking the fuel system for leaks and ensuring that the fuel tank is filled. The second step is verifying that the generator's battery is fully charged and that the control panel is operational. The third step requires testing the automatic transfer switch (ATS) to ensure it will engage when power is lost. However, during installation, the contractor skips the ATS test and proceeds to the generator load test. What potential issue could arise from skipping this step, according to the manual's structure?
a. The generator may not start when utility power is lost
b. The generator may overheat during the load test
c. The control panel could malfunction and require resetting
d. The fuel system could fail to deliver enough fuel under load

Answer: a. The generator may not start when utility power is lost. Explanation: The chronological structure of the manual emphasizes testing the ATS to ensure it engages when power is lost. Skipping this step could result in the generator failing to start when utility power fails, defeating the purpose of the backup system.

534. An electrician is troubleshooting a conveyor system at a factory where the motor repeatedly trips under heavy load. The troubleshooting guide provided by the motor manufacturer is organized in a problem-solution format, listing potential causes of motor tripping. The guide first recommends checking for overload conditions by measuring the current draw during operation. If the current exceeds the motor's rated capacity, the next step is to reduce the load on the conveyor or install a larger motor. If the current is within the motor's capacity, the guide suggests inspecting the motor's thermal protection devices for faults. The electrician measures the current and finds it to be within the motor's rating. What should the electrician check next according to the guide's structure?
a. Check for loose wiring connections at the motor terminals
b. Inspect the motor's thermal protection devices for faults
c. Replace the motor with a larger unit to handle the load
d. Reset the motor's protective relays and attempt a restart

Answer: b. Inspect the motor's thermal protection devices for faults. Explanation: Following the problem-solution format of the guide, the next logical step after confirming that the motor is not overloaded is to check the thermal protection devices, which could be causing the motor to trip unnecessarily.

535. An electrician is performing an insulation resistance test on a motor winding using a megohmmeter. The initial reading shows 500 megohms, and after 10 minutes of applying the test voltage, the resistance has dropped to 250 megohms. The test conditions include stable temperature and humidity. The manual states that a significant decrease in insulation resistance over time can indicate the presence of moisture or contaminants within the insulation. However, the motor was recently cleaned and dried. Based on the test data and conditions, what is the most likely conclusion about the insulation's condition?
a. The insulation is in excellent condition with no issues
b. The insulation has absorbed moisture despite recent cleaning
c. The insulation is degrading, potentially due to age or wear
d. The temperature during testing caused the resistance drop

Answer: c. The insulation is degrading, potentially due to age or wear. Explanation: The significant drop in insulation resistance suggests degradation, which could be due to factors such as aging or wear, despite recent cleaning. Moisture would have shown a more immediate drop, and stable temperature means thermal effects can be ruled out.

536. A power quality analysis is conducted at an industrial facility, revealing frequent voltage sags during peak hours of operation. Measurements indicate that the voltage regularly drops below 90% of the nominal level for short periods. The equipment being used includes large motors, compressors, and HVAC systems that demand high inrush current. The power quality report suggests that these voltage sags are likely caused by the equipment's high starting currents. Given this data, what is the most appropriate action to improve power quality at the facility?
a. Replace all large motors with more efficient models
b. Install capacitor banks to improve power factor
c. Implement soft starters or VFDs on large motors to reduce inrush current
d. Upgrade the entire electrical system to a higher voltage

Answer: c. Implement soft starters or VFDs on large motors to reduce inrush current. Explanation: The voltage sags are likely due to high inrush currents when starting large motors. Soft starters or variable frequency drives (VFDs) can help reduce these currents, minimizing the voltage dips and improving overall power quality.

537. An energy efficiency study of a commercial building compares the energy consumption of two different HVAC systems over the course of a year. System A, a standard air-cooled unit, shows a seasonal efficiency ratio (SEER) of 12, while System B, a newer geothermal system, has a SEER of 25. Despite the significantly higher efficiency rating, System B only reduced energy consumption by 30%, whereas the study initially predicted a 50% reduction. All other operating conditions were kept the same. Based on the data, what conclusion can be drawn about the performance of the geothermal system?
a. The geothermal system is malfunctioning and needs repair
b. The building's thermal load is higher than anticipated, affecting the expected savings
c. The geothermal system's efficiency is overstated, and its real SEER is closer to 12

d. The initial energy savings estimate did not account for variable operating conditions

Answer: d. The initial energy savings estimate did not account for variable operating conditions. Explanation: While the geothermal system performs better than the older unit, the predicted savings were not met, likely due to variations in real-world operating conditions that were not fully accounted for in the initial estimate. This highlights the difference between theoretical and actual performance.

538. A technician is reviewing predictive maintenance data for a transformer and notes that over the past six months, dissolved gas analysis (DGA) has shown increasing levels of acetylene and ethylene. These gases are commonly associated with arcing and overheating within the transformer. However, no significant temperature changes or operational anomalies have been observed during regular thermal imaging inspections. Based on the data trends, what is the most likely conclusion regarding the health of the transformer?
a. The transformer is operating normally, and the gas levels are irrelevant
b. The increasing gas levels indicate a developing fault that may lead to failure
c. The transformer is suffering from poor cooling, and fans should be upgraded
d. The gas levels are due to external environmental factors, not internal issues

Answer: b. The increasing gas levels indicate a developing fault that may lead to failure. Explanation: The rise in acetylene and ethylene suggests that internal arcing or overheating is occurring, despite no immediate external temperature anomalies. DGA results are a strong indicator of developing internal faults in transformers, and proactive measures should be taken.

539. An energy audit for a large warehouse examines lighting systems before and after the installation of LED fixtures. The audit shows that energy consumption for lighting dropped by 40% after the retrofit, as expected. However, total energy costs for the building only decreased by 10%. The audit notes that the HVAC system still relies on older, inefficient technology, and the warehouse experiences high heating and cooling loads due to its size and structure. Based on these findings, what is the most reasonable conclusion?
a. The LED retrofit was ineffective, and the old lighting system should be reinstalled
b. The majority of energy consumption is from the HVAC system, not lighting
c. The audit overestimated the energy savings from the LED retrofit
d. Energy savings from lighting are negligible compared to the building's overall consumption

Answer: b. The majority of energy consumption is from the HVAC system, not lighting. Explanation: While the LED retrofit effectively reduced lighting energy consumption, the small overall reduction in energy costs suggests that the HVAC system is responsible for the majority of the building's energy use. Addressing HVAC inefficiencies could lead to greater overall savings.

540. A technician measures harmonic distortion levels on a three-phase power system supplying several pieces of sensitive electronic equipment. The total harmonic distortion (THD) is recorded at 10%, which exceeds the recommended limit for the equipment, leading to overheating and malfunctioning of devices. To mitigate this, the technician recommends the installation of harmonic filters. A follow-up measurement after the filters are installed shows the THD reduced to 3%. What conclusion can be drawn from these results?
a. The harmonic filters were ineffective and did not reduce THD sufficiently

b. The reduction in THD to 3% demonstrates that the filters are working effectively
c. The equipment malfunction was not related to harmonic distortion after all
d. Harmonic filters are only partially effective and need to be replaced with a new system

Answer: b. The reduction in THD to 3% demonstrates that the filters are working effectively. Explanation: The installation of harmonic filters successfully reduced the THD to acceptable levels (below 5%), showing that the filters addressed the issue and reduced the risk of equipment malfunction.

541. During a load test of a backup generator, a facility manager observes that the generator's output voltage drops by 15% under full load conditions. According to the manufacturer's specifications, the voltage drop should not exceed 5% at full load. The test also reveals that the generator's engine is running below the rated speed. What is the most likely cause of the excessive voltage drop?
a. The generator is overloaded beyond its capacity
b. The generator's voltage regulator is set too high
c. The engine's reduced speed is causing the voltage drop
d. The fuel quality is too low for efficient generator operation

Answer: c. The engine's reduced speed is causing the voltage drop. Explanation: The voltage output of a generator is closely tied to its engine speed. A reduction in speed will lead to a proportional drop in voltage, explaining why the voltage falls under full load conditions.

542. A predictive maintenance system uses vibration analysis to monitor the condition of a motor. The data shows a gradual increase in vibration levels over several months, particularly in the frequency range associated with bearing wear. However, no other operational parameters, such as temperature or load, have changed significantly during this period. What is the most likely conclusion about the motor's condition?
a. The motor is likely experiencing a misalignment issue
b. The bearings are wearing out and should be inspected or replaced soon
c. The increase in vibration is normal and not a cause for concern
d. The motor's foundation is unstable, causing excessive vibration

Answer: b. The bearings are wearing out and should be inspected or replaced soon. Explanation: The increase in vibration specifically in the frequency range associated with bearing wear suggests that the motor's bearings are likely deteriorating and should be inspected to prevent future failure.

543. A building manager conducts an energy audit to evaluate the performance of two different heating systems in a facility: a gas furnace and an electric heat pump. Over the course of the winter, the audit shows that while the gas furnace consumed more total energy, the heat pump's coefficient of performance (COP) remained stable at 3.5. Despite this, the heat pump contributed to higher energy costs. The audit concludes that the heat pump's performance is affected by the region's colder-than-average temperatures, which reduced its efficiency in extremely cold weather. What is the most likely reason for the heat pump's higher energy costs?
a. The heat pump operates more efficiently than the furnace
b. The heat pump's COP decreased in colder temperatures, reducing efficiency
c. The furnace was improperly sized, leading to higher energy use

d. The audit incorrectly measured the furnace's total energy consumption

Answer: b. The heat pump's COP decreased in colder temperatures, reducing efficiency. Explanation: Heat pumps are less efficient in colder temperatures, as their ability to extract heat from the outside air is diminished. This reduced COP in colder conditions explains the higher energy costs despite the heat pump's stable performance in moderate temperatures.

544. An industrial plant uses an online monitoring system to track motor temperature and operating hours to predict maintenance needs. Over the last three months, the data shows a gradual increase in motor temperature during normal operation, even though the workload and ambient temperature remain constant. No alarms have been triggered, and the motor continues to operate within safe limits. Based on this trend, what is the most likely conclusion regarding the motor?
a. The motor is operating normally and no action is required
b. The motor is beginning to overheat and should be taken offline immediately
c. The motor is experiencing early signs of wear, and maintenance should be scheduled soon
d. The temperature sensor is faulty and should be replaced

Answer: c. The motor is experiencing early signs of wear, and maintenance should be scheduled soon. Explanation: The gradual increase in temperature despite consistent workload and ambient conditions suggests that the motor is beginning to show signs of wear, likely due to internal friction or component degradation. Maintenance should be scheduled before the problem escalates.

545. A contractor is reviewing a series of product brochures from different vendors offering surge protection devices (SPDs) for industrial applications. Vendor A's brochure prominently emphasizes that their SPDs comply with the latest UL 1449 standards but fails to mention how their products perform under sustained low-voltage conditions, which is critical for the contractor's project. Vendor B's brochure focuses heavily on product performance in high-voltage environments but lacks detailed information on their SPD's maintenance requirements. Vendor C highlights that their products are the most cost-effective solution on the market, offering significant discounts for bulk orders but does not include any data on product lifespan or reliability. The contractor needs to determine which SPD to recommend for a facility that prioritizes long-term reliability over initial cost. Based on this vendor literature, what bias should the contractor be most cautious about when reviewing Vendor C's claims?
a. Bias toward regulatory compliance with UL standards
b. Bias toward high-voltage performance data
c. Bias toward cost-effectiveness, potentially overlooking long-term reliability
d. Bias toward product maintenance requirements over performance

Answer: c. Bias toward cost-effectiveness, potentially overlooking long-term reliability. Explanation: Vendor C's literature heavily emphasizes cost-effectiveness, which may overshadow the more critical aspects such as the product's reliability and longevity. This bias could lead the contractor to focus too much on initial savings rather than the SPD's performance over time.

546. An electrical engineer is reviewing a technical report issued by a regulatory body regarding new safety standards for arc flash protection in commercial buildings. The report emphasizes the need for stricter regulations, citing

multiple incidents where insufficient arc flash protection led to serious injuries. However, the engineer notices that many of the incidents referenced in the report occurred in older buildings with outdated electrical infrastructure, while newer buildings with modern systems seem to have significantly lower incident rates. The report does not make any distinctions between the two categories of buildings. What type of bias is most likely present in this regulatory document?
a. Vendor bias favoring manufacturers of arc flash protection equipment
b. Regulatory bias promoting stricter safety standards across all buildings
c. Advocacy bias pushing for the complete overhaul of all electrical systems
d. Performance bias highlighting only outdated infrastructure failures

Answer: b. Regulatory bias promoting stricter safety standards across all buildings. Explanation: The report does not distinguish between older and newer buildings, potentially pushing for unnecessary regulatory changes across the board. This suggests a regulatory bias aimed at enforcing stricter standards universally, even in cases where they may not be warranted.

547. A facility manager is reading an article in a trade journal discussing the advantages of switching to LED lighting for industrial applications. The article argues that LED lighting systems are superior to traditional fluorescent lighting in all respects, including energy efficiency, maintenance, and overall cost savings. However, the manager notices that the article was written by a representative of a major LED lighting manufacturer, and the data provided does not include comparisons of LED performance in high-temperature environments, which is a significant concern for the manager's facility. What type of bias should the facility manager be aware of in this article?
a. Advocacy bias promoting energy efficiency over other considerations
b. Vendor bias favoring the author's company's LED products
c. Regulatory bias focusing on compliance with energy standards
d. Market bias pushing for the reduction of traditional lighting options

Answer: b. Vendor bias favoring the author's company's LED products. Explanation: Since the article is written by a representative from an LED manufacturer and lacks critical performance data in specific conditions, it is likely to exhibit vendor bias. This bias may lead the author to emphasize only the positive aspects of their products while omitting potential drawbacks.

548. An electrician is comparing two technical reports on grounding methods for photovoltaic (PV) systems. Report A is produced by an independent engineering firm and discusses various grounding options, providing detailed case studies on both single-point and multi-point grounding techniques in different climates. Report B is sponsored by a PV system component manufacturer and emphasizes that multi-point grounding is the best option, focusing on its performance in hot climates, where the manufacturer's components have been used. Report B provides less information on performance in cold or humid environments, which are relevant to the electrician's region. What bias is most evident in Report B?
a. Advocacy bias promoting multi-point grounding in all environments
b. Performance bias highlighting component effectiveness in specific climates
c. Vendor bias favoring the manufacturer's products over other grounding solutions
d. Regulatory bias ignoring code-compliant alternatives to multi-point grounding

Answer: c. Vendor bias favoring the manufacturer's products over other grounding solutions. Explanation: Report B was sponsored by a component manufacturer and heavily promotes multi-point grounding, particularly in conditions favorable to the manufacturer's products. This suggests a vendor bias that could overlook other effective grounding methods for different environments.

549. A power systems consultant is reading a trade journal article that advocates for stricter environmental regulations on coal-fired power plants. The article cites several studies on the negative environmental impacts of coal plants but does not include any data on the advancements in emissions control technologies that have been implemented in newer plants. The consultant knows that recent installations have significantly reduced emissions, making coal plants cleaner than the article suggests. What bias might the consultant be encountering in this article?
a. Regulatory bias supporting outdated environmental standards
b. Vendor bias pushing for alternative energy solutions
c. Advocacy bias against coal power without acknowledging recent improvements
d. Market bias promoting new technology over traditional energy sources

Answer: c. Advocacy bias against coal power without acknowledging recent improvements. Explanation: The article seems to focus on the negative aspects of coal power while ignoring advancements in emissions control. This suggests an advocacy bias aimed at opposing coal power without considering the impact of newer technologies.

550. An industrial maintenance manager is reviewing a white paper published by a major equipment vendor, which discusses the importance of regular maintenance for motor control centers (MCCs). The white paper emphasizes that the vendor's MCCs require less maintenance compared to competitors' models, citing proprietary design improvements. However, the paper does not include any third-party studies or comparisons and primarily relies on internal data produced by the vendor. The manager is concerned about the objectivity of the white paper. What type of bias is likely influencing the content of this document?
a. Advocacy bias pushing for reduced maintenance schedules
b. Vendor bias promoting the superiority of the vendor's MCC products
c. Regulatory bias emphasizing compliance with industry standards
d. Market bias encouraging the adoption of new maintenance practices

Answer: b. Vendor bias promoting the superiority of the vendor's MCC products. Explanation: The white paper relies on internal data and lacks third-party validation, which suggests that the vendor is biased in promoting its own products as superior without providing objective comparisons.

551. A government regulatory agency publishes a report recommending increased inspections of electrical substations to ensure compliance with safety standards. The report argues that many substations have fallen out of compliance, but the data is primarily based on inspections of older substations, some of which were built decades ago. There is little mention of newer substations that were constructed according to modern safety standards. What kind of bias might this regulatory report exhibit?
a. Vendor bias pushing for the sale of new safety inspection equipment
b. Performance bias emphasizing failures in older substations
c. Advocacy bias for increasing regulatory inspections across all substations
d. Regulatory bias promoting the same safety measures for all substation types

Answer: d. Regulatory bias promoting the same safety measures for all substation types. Explanation: The report seems to recommend increased inspections based on data from older substations, potentially ignoring the fact that newer substations may already comply with modern standards. This suggests a regulatory bias favoring uniform safety measures across the board.

552. An engineer is reading a technical review of different types of battery energy storage systems (BESS) used in grid applications. The review discusses various chemistries, including lithium-ion, lead-acid, and flow batteries, comparing their performance in terms of efficiency, cost, and lifespan. The section on lithium-ion batteries highlights their superior energy density and lower operational costs but makes no mention of safety concerns such as the risk of thermal runaway, which the engineer knows is a significant factor in some applications. What type of bias may be present in this technical review?
a. Vendor bias in favor of lithium-ion battery manufacturers
b. Performance bias focusing on efficiency and cost over safety
c. Regulatory bias downplaying safety standards for newer technologies
d. Market bias emphasizing the need for energy storage across the grid

Answer: b. Performance bias focusing on efficiency and cost over safety. Explanation: The review highlights the performance benefits of lithium-ion batteries without addressing known safety concerns. This suggests a performance bias that emphasizes efficiency and cost at the expense of discussing safety risks.

553. A utility company issues a report discussing its decision to invest in smart grid technology. The report is framed as an objective assessment of the benefits of smart grid systems, including improved reliability and reduced operational costs. However, the report fails to address the significant upfront costs and potential cybersecurity risks associated with smart grid implementation, both of which have been well-documented in independent studies. What kind of bias is most likely influencing the utility company's report?
a. Regulatory bias advocating for compliance with new technology standards
b. Advocacy bias supporting smart grid technology while ignoring its drawbacks
c. Vendor bias promoting products sold by smart grid technology providers
d. Market bias encouraging widespread adoption of smart grid systems

Answer: b. Advocacy bias supporting smart grid technology while ignoring its drawbacks. Explanation: The report presents an overwhelmingly positive view of smart grid technology without addressing significant challenges like upfront costs and cybersecurity risks, indicating an advocacy bias aimed at promoting the technology without a balanced assessment.

554. An electrician is comparing two safety compliance documents from different regulatory agencies regarding arc flash hazards. Document A, published by a national standards body, includes detailed tables on incident energy levels and specific requirements for personal protective equipment (PPE) based on voltage and task type. Document B, issued by a regional safety organization, provides general recommendations for arc flash protection but lacks the detailed data found in Document A. Instead, Document B emphasizes the importance of ongoing safety training and awareness programs. The electrician is trying to determine which document to prioritize for a new facility's safety protocols. What bias might be present in Document B that could affect the electrician's decision?
a. Advocacy bias promoting safety training over technical compliance
b. Vendor bias favoring PPE manufacturers

c. Regulatory bias encouraging the adoption of local safety practices
d. Performance bias focusing on energy levels over practical safety measures

Answer: a. Advocacy bias promoting safety training over technical compliance. Explanation: Document B emphasizes safety training and awareness programs over providing technical data, suggesting an advocacy bias that promotes education as a primary safety measure, potentially at the expense of more detailed, technical compliance guidelines found in Document A.

555. A facility manager is reviewing a bar graph comparing monthly energy consumption between two systems: System A and System B. The graph shows that System A consistently uses more energy than System B across all months, with the largest gap occurring in July when System A consumed 20,000 kWh compared to System B's 10,000 kWh. In the winter months, the difference narrows, with System A using 8,000 kWh in January and System B using 7,000 kWh. The graph is part of a presentation recommending an upgrade to System B due to its lower energy consumption year-round. Based on the graph, what conclusion can the facility manager reasonably draw about System A?
a. System A is less efficient and requires more energy year-round, particularly in summer
b. System A performs better in colder months but struggles in the summer
c. The energy consumption difference is negligible, making both systems equally efficient
d. System A experiences technical issues in July, leading to abnormally high energy use

Answer: a. System A is less efficient and requires more energy year-round, particularly in summer. Explanation: The bar graph clearly shows that System A uses more energy than System B throughout the year, with a significant increase in the summer. This suggests System A is less efficient, especially in hotter months when its energy consumption spikes.

556. An electrician is studying a line chart that tracks voltage fluctuations in a commercial building's electrical system over a 24-hour period. The chart shows a steady voltage of 240V for most of the day, but from 5 p.m. to 8 p.m., the voltage drops to 220V, then gradually returns to normal levels. The load on the system increases during this time due to the operation of heavy machinery in the building. The electrician is tasked with preventing future voltage drops during peak hours. What does the line chart most likely indicate as the cause of the voltage fluctuations?
a. External power grid issues causing voltage instability
b. Overloading of the building's electrical system during peak usage hours
c. Poor wiring causing intermittent voltage drops
d. The presence of faulty transformers on the power lines

Answer: b. Overloading of the building's electrical system during peak usage hours. Explanation: The drop in voltage coincides with the increased operation of heavy machinery, suggesting that the building's electrical system is being overloaded during these hours, which causes the voltage to drop below the normal level.

557. A pie chart is shown in a technical presentation on power distribution at an industrial plant. The chart breaks down power consumption by equipment: 50% for motors, 20% for HVAC systems, 15% for lighting, and 15% for office equipment. The presenter is recommending power factor correction for the motors to reduce the overall energy bill. Based on the pie chart, why are motors the focus of the recommendation?

a. Motors are the largest consumers of power and improving their efficiency will have the most impact
b. Motors contribute the least to the power consumption, so they should be upgraded first
c. Office equipment and lighting are already optimized, leaving motors as the next target
d. HVAC systems are too complex to improve, so motors are an easier target for optimization

Answer: a. Motors are the largest consumers of power and improving their efficiency will have the most impact. Explanation: The pie chart shows that motors account for 50% of the power consumption, making them the most significant target for energy savings. Optimizing motor efficiency would have the greatest impact on reducing the overall energy usage.

558. A technical photograph shows the installation of a cable tray in an industrial facility. The tray appears to be filled with cables, with several visible junctions and splices. Upon reviewing the image, an inspector notes that there is very little separation between power cables and control cables, which can lead to electromagnetic interference (EMI). What corrective action should the inspector recommend based on the photograph?
a. Install shielded cables to prevent electrical fires
b. Separate the power and control cables to minimize the risk of EMI
c. Replace all visible splices and junctions with new ones
d. Increase the cable tray size to accommodate more cables

Answer: b. Separate the power and control cables to minimize the risk of EMI. Explanation: The lack of separation between power and control cables, as observed in the photograph, increases the potential for electromagnetic interference. Separating these cables will help mitigate this issue and ensure proper signal integrity for control systems.

559. A bar graph comparing energy consumption before and after the installation of variable frequency drives (VFDs) on industrial motors shows a 25% reduction in energy use after the VFDs were installed. However, the graph also shows a slight increase in energy consumption during startup periods when the motors are ramping up. What conclusion can be drawn from the data presented in the bar graph?
a. VFDs are ineffective and increase energy use during motor startup
b. VFDs reduce overall energy consumption but require more energy during startup
c. The energy savings from VFDs are negligible compared to the increased startup energy
d. VFDs cause fluctuations in energy use that make them unreliable

Answer: b. VFDs reduce overall energy consumption but require more energy during startup. Explanation: The bar graph indicates that although VFDs reduce total energy consumption, there is an increase in energy use during the startup phase, which is normal. The overall reduction in energy usage demonstrates that VFDs are effective despite the slight increase during startup.

560. A line chart in a technical report illustrates voltage levels in a residential area over a 7-day period. The chart shows consistent voltage levels of 120V, except for a sharp spike to 135V on the third day, lasting for 2 hours. The report attributes the spike to a sudden drop in local demand, causing the voltage to rise temporarily. What is the most appropriate conclusion based on the line chart data?
a. The voltage increase indicates a permanent fault in the electrical system

b. The voltage spike was due to an external event and is not a recurring issue
c. The electrical system is unstable and needs to be upgraded
d. Voltage fluctuations like these are common and require no further action

Answer: b. The voltage spike was due to an external event and is not a recurring issue. Explanation: The line chart shows a one-time spike in voltage, which the report attributes to a drop in demand. This suggests the spike was caused by an external event and does not indicate an ongoing or recurring fault in the system.

561. A pie chart presented in a power quality audit shows the causes of equipment malfunctions in a manufacturing plant: 40% from harmonic distortion, 30% from voltage sags, 20% from transients, and 10% from grounding issues. Based on the pie chart, which issue should be prioritized for immediate corrective action?
a. Grounding issues, since they are the most dangerous
b. Harmonic distortion, since it accounts for the largest percentage of malfunctions
c. Transients, since they cause sudden equipment failure
d. Voltage sags, since they are most common in manufacturing environments

Answer: b. Harmonic distortion, since it accounts for the largest percentage of malfunctions. Explanation: Harmonic distortion accounts for 40% of the malfunctions, making it the primary cause of equipment issues. Correcting harmonic distortion would address the largest contributor to equipment failures and improve overall system reliability.

562. A technician is reviewing a photograph of a panelboard installation. The image shows multiple circuits connected to the busbars, but several of the circuit breakers are labeled with different ratings than the wires connected to them. The technician knows that this can create a fire hazard due to mismatched wire and breaker ratings. What is the correct conclusion based on this photograph?
a. The circuit breakers need to be upgraded to match the wire ratings
b. The wires need to be replaced with ones that match the circuit breaker ratings
c. The panelboard is installed correctly, and no changes are necessary
d. The busbars should be resized to accommodate the circuit load

Answer: b. The wires need to be replaced with ones that match the circuit breaker ratings. Explanation: The photograph reveals that the wire sizes are mismatched with the circuit breaker ratings. To prevent overheating or fire hazards, the wires need to be replaced with appropriately rated ones to match the breakers.

563. A line chart displays the harmonic distortion levels of a facility's electrical system over a week. The chart shows a steady level of 3% distortion throughout the first five days, followed by a sudden spike to 8% on the sixth day. The spike coincides with the operation of a new piece of equipment. Based on the chart, what is the most likely cause of the increased harmonic distortion?
a. The new equipment generates significant harmonic distortion
b. The overall electrical load increased on the sixth day
c. The spike indicates a power quality issue from the utility provider
d. The distortion spike is unrelated to the new equipment and likely a random occurrence

Answer: a. The new equipment generates significant harmonic distortion. Explanation: The sudden spike in harmonic distortion coincides with the operation of the new equipment, suggesting that it is the source of the increased distortion. Further investigation into the equipment's harmonics is needed to address the issue.

564. A bar graph compares the energy consumption of three different HVAC systems over a six-month period. System A shows the highest energy use, while System C shows the lowest. However, the accompanying photograph shows that System C has a larger number of air handling units than System A, despite its lower energy consumption. What conclusion can be drawn from this comparison?
a. System A is more efficient than System C despite its higher energy consumption
b. System C has a more efficient design, allowing for greater capacity with less energy use
c. The graph is incorrect, as more air handling units should consume more energy
d. Both systems are equally efficient, and the difference is due to seasonal variations

Answer: b. System C has a more efficient design, allowing for greater capacity with less energy use. Explanation: Despite having more air handling units, System C consumes less energy, suggesting that its design is more efficient. This allows it to operate more units while still using less energy than System A.

565. A commercial facility plans to upgrade its HVAC system to a more energy-efficient model. The new system is expected to operate at 80% of the energy consumption of the existing unit while providing the same cooling capacity. The facility currently spends approximately $50,000 annually on electricity for HVAC operation, and the cost of electricity is $0.10 per kWh. Based on the manufacturer's data, the new system will operate 8,000 hours per year. The facility manager is trying to predict the total annual savings after the system upgrade. What will the estimated annual savings be?
a. $8,000
b. $10,000
c. $12,000
d. $15,000

Answer: b. $10,000. Explanation: The current system consumes $50,000 of electricity annually. With the new system operating at 80% of the current consumption, the facility will save 20%. Therefore, $50,000 × 0.20 = $10,000 in estimated annual savings.

566. A manufacturing plant is planning to increase production, which will add an additional 300 kW of load to its electrical distribution system. The plant's existing transformer is rated for 750 kVA with a 0.9 power factor, and the current load on the system is 600 kW. The plant engineer needs to determine if the current transformer can handle the increased load. What will the approximate total load be after the production increase, and will the transformer be sufficient?
a. 750 kW; the transformer will be sufficient
b. 780 kW; the transformer will be insufficient
c. 900 kW; the transformer will be insufficient
d. 660 kW; the transformer will be sufficient

Answer: b. 780 kW; the transformer will be insufficient. Explanation: The current load is 600 kW, and with an additional 300 kW, the total load becomes 900 kW. At a power factor of 0.9, the transformer can supply 675 kW (750 kVA × 0.9), meaning it will be insufficient for the increased load.

567. A facility is upgrading its lighting system by replacing traditional fluorescent fixtures with LED fixtures. The existing system uses 1,000 fluorescent fixtures, each rated at 100W. The new LED fixtures are rated at 40W each and will operate for 10 hours per day, 365 days per year. The facility's electricity cost is $0.12 per kWh. The facility manager needs to estimate the total energy savings from this upgrade. What is the approximate annual energy savings in kilowatt-hours?
a. 109,500 kWh
b. 87,600 kWh
c. 219,000 kWh
d. 131,400 kWh

Answer: c. 219,000 kWh. Explanation: The current system consumes 100W × 1,000 fixtures = 100 kW. The new system consumes 40W × 1,000 fixtures = 40 kW. The difference is 60 kW. Over 10 hours per day for 365 days, the annual savings is 60 kW × 10 hours × 365 days = 219,000 kWh.

568. A power distribution system is being upgraded at a chemical processing plant. The plant's existing circuit breaker panels are rated at 1,000A, and the proposed upgrade will involve adding new equipment that will increase the total load by 180A. The plant engineer must ensure that the total load does not exceed 80% of the breaker panel's capacity to comply with NEC guidelines. Currently, the panels are loaded at 600A. Will the engineer need to upgrade the circuit breaker panels to accommodate the new equipment?
a. No, the panels will remain within safe operating limits
b. Yes, the new load will exceed 80% of the panel's capacity
c. No, but the panels will be operating near their limit
d. Yes, the NEC requires an upgrade if any additional load is added

Answer: b. Yes, the new load will exceed 80% of the panel's capacity. Explanation: The existing load is 600A, and the new load adds 180A, bringing the total to 780A. The breaker panel's 80% capacity is 1,000A × 0.80 = 800A, so the new load will exceed the safe operating limit.

569. A data center is considering upgrading its backup generator system to meet future power demands. The current generator is rated at 500 kW, and the data center's current load is 400 kW. The expected load increase is 25% due to expansion. The facility engineer needs to determine if the existing generator can handle the increased load or if a larger generator is necessary. What will the new load be, and will the existing generator be sufficient?
a. 450 kW; the generator will be sufficient
b. 500 kW; the generator will be sufficient
c. 525 kW; the generator will be insufficient
d. 480 kW; the generator will be sufficient

Answer: c. 525 kW; the generator will be insufficient. Explanation: The current load is 400 kW, and a 25% increase results in 400 kW × 1.25 = 500 kW. Since this load matches the generator's full rating, it would operate at or beyond capacity, making it insufficient to handle any additional load or account for inrush currents.

570. A manufacturing facility is upgrading its motor control center (MCC) to support higher horsepower motors. The existing MCC was designed to accommodate motors with a combined load of 600 HP. The new system will increase the combined load to 750 HP. The facility's main electrical service is rated for 480V at 1,200A. Assuming an efficiency of 95% and a power factor of 0.9, will the existing electrical service be adequate for the new combined motor load?
a. Yes, the service will be adequate with a comfortable margin
b. No, the service will be slightly over its capacity
c. Yes, but the service will be operating near its limit
d. No, the service will need to be upgraded to handle the increased load

Answer: c. Yes, but the service will be operating near its limit. Explanation: The total power required for 750 HP is approximately 750 × 746 W/HP ÷ (480 V × 1.732 × 0.9 × 0.95) = 1,135A. This is close to the 1,200A service capacity, leaving little margin for additional load or fluctuations.

571. A utility company is forecasting maintenance needs for its electrical grid, which supports a large urban area. The system includes numerous aging transformers, some of which are over 30 years old. The company has observed an increase in transformer failures during summer months when demand is highest. By analyzing temperature data and historical failure rates, the company predicts that transformers operating at 80% of their capacity in temperatures above 90°F are five times more likely to fail. What preventive measure would most likely reduce the likelihood of transformer failure?
a. Increase the transformers' capacity by adding parallel units
b. Upgrade the transformers to handle higher loads and higher temperatures
c. Reduce the demand on each transformer by implementing load shedding during peak times
d. Increase the frequency of maintenance checks during the summer months

Answer: c. Reduce the demand on each transformer by implementing load shedding during peak times. Explanation: Reducing the load on transformers during high-demand periods would lower the risk of overheating and failure, as the transformers are most vulnerable when operating near capacity in high temperatures.

572. A university campus is installing a solar photovoltaic (PV) system to reduce its energy costs. The system is rated at 500 kW and will operate an average of 5 hours per day, 365 days per year. The current annual energy consumption of the campus is 2 million kWh. The facility manager wants to estimate the percentage of the campus's annual energy consumption that will be offset by the solar system. What percentage of the total energy consumption will be offset by the PV system?
a. 20%
b. 25%
c. 12.5%
d. 30%

Answer: a. 20%. Explanation: The PV system will generate 500 kW × 5 hours/day × 365 days/year = 912,500 kWh annually. The campus consumes 2,000,000 kWh annually, so the offset is 912,500 ÷ 2,000,000 = 0.456, or 20%.

573. A distribution center is evaluating the impact of installing a new automated conveyor system on its overall energy usage. The new system will run 16 hours per day and is expected to consume 250 kWh per hour. The facility currently consumes 1,200,000 kWh annually. The energy cost is $0.08 per kWh. How much will the facility's energy cost increase annually due to the installation of the new conveyor system?
a. $112,000
b. $117,600
c. $102,400
d. $92,000

Answer: c. $102,400. Explanation: The new system will consume 250 kWh/hour × 16 hours/day × 365 days/year = 1,460,000 kWh annually. At $0.08 per kWh, the additional cost will be 1,460,000 kWh × $0.08 = $102,400 annually.

574. A utility company is implementing a demand-response program to manage energy usage during peak periods. As part of the program, large industrial customers are incentivized to reduce their electrical load by 20% when called upon. One industrial customer typically operates at a load of 5 MW. During a demand-response event, the customer agrees to reduce their load by the full 20%. How much power will the customer still be consuming during the demand-response event?
a. 3.5 MW
b. 4.0 MW
c. 4.5 MW
d. 3.0 MW

Answer: b. 4.0 MW. Explanation: The customer typically operates at 5 MW, and a 20% reduction would be 5 MW × 0.20 = 1 MW. Therefore, during the demand-response event, the customer will still consume 5 MW - 1 MW = 4 MW.

575. An electrician receives a safety bulletin from the site manager regarding the recent increase in near-miss incidents involving overhead power lines. The bulletin emphasizes the urgency of reporting any such incidents immediately and following all safety protocols when working around live lines. It includes phrases like "near-miss incidents are serious warnings," "this is an immediate concern," and "delayed reporting could lead to fatal accidents." The bulletin closes by stating that any failure to comply with safety procedures will result in disciplinary action. What is the tone of this safety bulletin?
a. Casual and informative
b. Urgent and authoritative
c. Encouraging and optimistic
d. Formal and celebratory

Answer: b. Urgent and authoritative. Explanation: The repeated emphasis on immediacy, the use of serious language regarding the consequences of near-miss incidents, and the threat of disciplinary action all contribute to an urgent and authoritative tone.

576. In a company-wide email, the training manager writes, "We know you've all been working hard to implement the new wiring techniques, and your dedication has not gone unnoticed. We appreciate the extra effort you've all put in to learn the new methods, and we're here to support you every step of the way." The email then details the next phase of training, encouraging the team to continue progressing and offering additional resources for help. What is the primary tone of this email?
a. Critical and formal
b. Encouraging and supportive
c. Urgent and demanding
d. Detached and impersonal

Answer: b. Encouraging and supportive. Explanation: The language is designed to boost morale, expressing appreciation and offering support. Phrases like "dedication has not gone unnoticed" and "we're here to support you" show encouragement and motivation.

577. A project manager sends a technical memo to an electrical contractor, outlining the expectations for an upcoming installation. The memo includes specific instructions for conduit placement, required material specifications, and deadlines. Phrases like "ensure compliance with all listed standards," "adherence to these guidelines is non-negotiable," and "failure to meet deadlines will result in penalties" are used throughout. What is the tone of this correspondence?
a. Formal and directive
b. Friendly and conversational
c. Apologetic and regretful
d. Collaborative and inclusive

Answer: a. Formal and directive. Explanation: The memo uses formal language with a strong emphasis on following standards and meeting deadlines, indicating a directive tone focused on clear instructions and consequences.

578. A training manual on electrical safety introduces a section with the following: "Before entering confined spaces, remember: safety is your first priority. Always double-check your equipment, monitor oxygen levels, and never skip a step in the safety checklist. Your life may depend on it." The manual uses bold font to highlight key warnings and reminders throughout the section. What is the tone used in this section of the manual?
a. Cautionary and serious
b. Optimistic and casual
c. Informative and relaxed
d. Urgent but celebratory

Answer: a. Cautionary and serious. Explanation: The manual stresses the importance of safety with phrases like "your life may depend on it," indicating a serious and cautionary tone that emphasizes the potential risks involved.

579. An electrical engineer writes a letter to a client proposing an energy efficiency upgrade to their facility. The letter explains the long-term cost savings, the environmental benefits, and the relatively low initial investment required. It ends with, "We're confident this upgrade will not only reduce your energy consumption but also improve the overall value of your operations. Let's move forward to ensure you're getting the most out of your energy system." What tone does the letter primarily convey?
a. Persuasive and positive
b. Formal and distant
c. Urgent and demanding
d. Neutral and factual

Answer: a. Persuasive and positive. Explanation: The letter aims to persuade the client by focusing on the benefits and using positive, confident language like "we're confident" and "improve the overall value," creating a tone of optimism and encouragement toward making a decision.

580. A warning label on a new electrical control panel reads: "DANGER: High Voltage. Do not open this panel without proper authorization and protective equipment. Serious injury or death may result if these warnings are not followed." The label uses red coloring and bold text to highlight the most critical parts of the message. What tone does the label convey?
a. Informative and instructional
b. Cautionary and severe
c. Encouraging and supportive
d. Formal and neutral

Answer: b. Cautionary and severe. Explanation: The label uses strong language like "serious injury or death" and visual cues like red text to create a severe, cautionary tone, underscoring the dangerous nature of the equipment.

581. An electrician receives a progress report from a supervisor detailing the team's performance on a large commercial wiring project. The report states, "While there have been some delays due to supply chain issues, the team has done an excellent job of maintaining quality and staying on track with critical deadlines. Your hard work is noticed and appreciated, and we're confident the final phases will be completed on time." What is the tone of this report?
a. Critical and demanding
b. Appreciative and reassuring
c. Neutral and factual
d. Informal and dismissive

Answer: b. Appreciative and reassuring. Explanation: The supervisor expresses appreciation for the team's efforts and offers reassurance that the project is progressing well despite challenges, making the tone both supportive and positive.

582. A technical proposal for a new electrical distribution system contains the following passage: "This design follows all necessary industry standards and provides an optimal balance of cost, efficiency, and safety. It is strongly

recommended that this configuration be implemented without modifications to ensure the highest level of reliability." What is the tone of this proposal passage?
a. Formal and advisory
b. Casual and speculative
c. Encouraging and flexible
d. Critical and harsh

Answer: a. Formal and advisory. Explanation: The passage uses formal language and offers strong recommendations, indicating an advisory tone. Phrases like "strongly recommended" and "highest level of reliability" reflect professional, careful guidance.

583. An internal email from the safety officer states, "Our current protocol for equipment lockout/tagout must be adhered to with no exceptions. Recent inspections have shown a lapse in compliance, and this needs to be addressed immediately. Any future violations will be met with strict disciplinary action." What is the tone of this email?
a. Strict and urgent
b. Neutral and factual
c. Encouraging and supportive
d. Optimistic and celebratory

Answer: a. Strict and urgent. Explanation: The use of terms like "must be adhered to with no exceptions" and "immediately" indicates an urgent need for action, while the mention of disciplinary measures suggests a strict tone.

584. A company handbook outlines the procedures for reporting safety violations. It reads, "If you witness any unsafe conditions or practices, please report them immediately using the designated forms. Your quick action can prevent accidents and keep everyone safe. Remember, it is everyone's responsibility to maintain a safe work environment." What tone does this handbook section convey?
a. Cautionary and severe
b. Encouraging and proactive
c. Dismissive and casual
d. Formal and impersonal

Answer: b. Encouraging and proactive. Explanation: The section encourages employees to take action, using positive and proactive language such as "your quick action" and "everyone's responsibility," which reflects an encouraging tone designed to motivate participation in safety practices.

585. An electrical contractor is tasked with installing a backup power generator system for a hospital, and they must adhere to specific National Electrical Code (NEC) guidelines. The NEC requires that emergency systems in healthcare facilities have automatic transfer switches (ATS) to ensure critical loads, such as life-support systems, have continuous power. The manual for the generator specifies that the ATS must be tested every 12 months to ensure functionality, but local regulations require testing every six months. In addition, the manual outlines detailed steps for isolating the generator during maintenance and resetting the system after a power failure. The contractor must condense this information for the facility's operations team, highlighting the most critical aspects of both the NEC code and the

manufacturer's guidelines. Which of the following should be emphasized as the key point for ensuring code compliance and operational safety?
a. Conducting monthly tests of the generator to ensure it starts automatically
b. Testing the ATS every six months in compliance with local regulations
c. Replacing the generator every five years as part of preventive maintenance
d. Installing an additional ATS to support non-essential loads during emergencies

Answer: b. Testing the ATS every six months in compliance with local regulations. Explanation: The key compliance requirement is to test the ATS every six months as per local regulations, even though the manufacturer's guideline specifies 12 months. This ensures the system is ready to switch automatically during power outages, which is crucial for life-support systems.

586. A plant manager receives a research paper on the use of variable frequency drives (VFDs) to improve energy efficiency in industrial motor applications. The paper explains that VFDs can reduce the amount of power consumed by adjusting the motor speed to match load requirements, particularly in applications like pumps and fans where demand fluctuates. The paper also includes technical data showing energy savings of up to 30% in systems that operate at partial load for extended periods. The manager wants a summary that focuses on the practical benefits and limitations of using VFDs. What should be highlighted as the primary advantage of VFDs based on the research paper's findings?
a. VFDs increase the motor lifespan by reducing wear and tear on the motor windings
b. VFDs are most effective in systems with high constant loads, improving overall power factor
c. VFDs can significantly reduce energy consumption by optimizing motor speed for varying loads
d. VFDs eliminate the need for regular maintenance, lowering operational costs

Answer: c. VFDs can significantly reduce energy consumption by optimizing motor speed for varying loads. Explanation: The research paper emphasizes that VFDs adjust motor speed based on load requirements, resulting in substantial energy savings, particularly in systems that operate under variable loads.

587. An electrical engineer is preparing a summary of complex grounding and bonding requirements for a new data center based on the NEC and IEEE standards. The data center will house sensitive IT equipment, so the grounding system must minimize electrical noise and protect against transient voltage surges. The standards specify that a single-point grounding system should be used, with all equipment bonded to a common ground to prevent ground loops. The engineer needs to distill these requirements into a concise checklist for the construction team. Which of the following points should be considered the most critical for ensuring compliance with the grounding standards?
a. Ensuring that each piece of equipment is grounded separately to reduce interference
b. Installing surge protection devices at all service entrances to the data center
c. Using a single-point grounding system to prevent ground loops and electrical noise
d. Implementing a multi-point grounding system to improve fault current dissipation

Answer: c. Using a single-point grounding system to prevent ground loops and electrical noise. Explanation: The primary requirement for a data center is to minimize electrical noise and prevent ground loops, which is best achieved through a single-point grounding system, as specified by the NEC and IEEE standards.

588. A facility supervisor is reviewing the operations manual for a new fire pump system to be installed in a high-rise building. The manual details a complex series of steps for testing the fire pump's automatic start function, verifying that the pressure switch engages correctly when the system detects a drop in water pressure. Additionally, the manual outlines the importance of testing the pump under full load conditions, ensuring that it can provide the required water flow rate. The supervisor must create a simplified procedure for the maintenance team to follow during routine inspections. Which key step should be highlighted as the most essential in ensuring the system's reliability?
a. Checking the pump's oil levels before every test
b. Verifying that the pressure switch engages when water pressure drops
c. Conducting a visual inspection of the pump's exterior for signs of wear
d. Running the pump under full load to test its performance

Answer: b. Verifying that the pressure switch engages when water pressure drops. Explanation: The pressure switch's correct engagement is critical for the automatic operation of the fire pump, ensuring that it starts when needed during an emergency. This should be a priority in any routine inspection.

589. A construction engineer is summarizing the code requirements for installing photovoltaic (PV) systems on commercial buildings. The NEC specifies that PV systems must be installed with appropriate disconnecting means, such as switches, to isolate the system from the utility grid during maintenance or emergencies. Furthermore, the NEC requires that the disconnecting means be located at a readily accessible site and clearly labeled to prevent accidental re-energization. The engineer needs to distill these details into a few critical points for the installation crew. Which point should be the top priority to ensure both safety and compliance?
a. Installing additional surge protection devices on the PV system
b. Verifying that all wiring connections are rated for outdoor use
c. Ensuring the disconnecting means is accessible and clearly labeled
d. Installing backup battery storage to maintain power during grid outages

Answer: c. Ensuring the disconnecting means is accessible and clearly labeled. Explanation: According to the NEC, the disconnecting means must be easily accessible and properly labeled to ensure safe operation and maintenance of the PV system. This is crucial for safety and compliance during emergencies or repairs.

590. A utility company is conducting a review of its transformer maintenance procedures and finds that the current documentation includes complex steps for performing insulation resistance tests and oil analysis. The company wants to streamline the procedure by focusing on the most critical preventive measures that will extend transformer life and prevent failures. After reviewing industry best practices, the engineer responsible for the update must summarize the key maintenance tasks that should be prioritized. Which of the following tasks is most important to include in the revised maintenance procedure?
a. Performing thermal imaging scans to detect hot spots in the transformer windings
b. Regularly replacing the transformer's cooling fans to prevent overheating
c. Conducting insulation resistance testing to detect early signs of insulation breakdown
d. Upgrading the transformer to a higher capacity model to handle future loads

Answer: c. Conducting insulation resistance testing to detect early signs of insulation breakdown. Explanation: Insulation resistance testing is a key preventive measure that can detect early signs of insulation failure, which is a common cause of transformer breakdowns. This should be prioritized in the maintenance procedure.

591. An industrial plant is installing a new control panel that integrates multiple motor starters and programmable logic controllers (PLCs). The installation manual provides detailed wiring diagrams, voltage ratings, and step-by-step instructions for connecting the control panel to the plant's power distribution system. The manual also includes specific guidelines for grounding the PLCs to prevent electrical noise from interfering with their operation. The plant's lead electrician is responsible for creating a summary of the installation process for the crew. Which key aspect of the installation should be highlighted to ensure the system operates without interference?
a. Ensuring all wiring connections are properly secured to prevent voltage drops
b. Grounding the PLCs correctly to avoid electrical noise affecting their performance
c. Installing backup power systems to prevent PLC data loss during power outages
d. Verifying the current rating of each motor starter to ensure they match the load requirements

Answer: b. Grounding the PLCs correctly to avoid electrical noise affecting their performance. Explanation: Proper grounding is critical for ensuring that the PLCs function correctly without interference from electrical noise. This step should be highlighted to ensure reliable system operation.

592. A project manager is overseeing the installation of a large industrial chiller and is summarizing the equipment manual, which contains lengthy descriptions of the chiller's operating conditions, maintenance intervals, and troubleshooting steps. The manual emphasizes the importance of regular condenser coil cleaning to prevent efficiency losses due to dust and debris accumulation. It also includes instructions for adjusting the refrigerant levels to optimize performance during varying load conditions. The project manager must create a simplified maintenance guide for the facility's staff. What should be the primary focus of the maintenance guide to ensure long-term efficiency of the chiller?
a. Checking refrigerant levels monthly to ensure optimal performance
b. Cleaning the condenser coils regularly to prevent efficiency losses
c. Verifying that all electrical connections are secure after each shutdown
d. Adjusting the chiller's compressor settings based on seasonal changes

Answer: b. Cleaning the condenser coils regularly to prevent efficiency losses. Explanation: The manual highlights the importance of keeping the condenser coils clean, as dust and debris accumulation can significantly reduce the chiller's efficiency over time. This should be the focus of the simplified maintenance guide.

593. A municipal power authority is evaluating the installation of a new substation to support a growing residential area. The project's technical report includes detailed load forecasts, equipment specifications, and environmental impact assessments. The report explains that the substation will operate at 33 kV and must be designed to handle load growth over the next 20 years. Additionally, the report emphasizes the need for voltage regulation equipment to maintain power quality as the load fluctuates. The lead engineer is tasked with condensing the report into a summary for city officials. What key point should be included in the summary to ensure city officials understand the long-term benefits of the project?
a. The substation will be able to accommodate future load growth for the next 20 years
b. The substation will reduce power costs for residents by operating at higher efficiency
c. The substation will require minimal maintenance due to its advanced design

d. The substation will improve the reliability of the city's emergency power systems

Answer: a. The substation will be able to accommodate future load growth for the next 20 years. Explanation: The report emphasizes that the substation is designed to handle load growth over the next two decades, which is a key consideration for city officials planning long-term infrastructure development.

594. An electrical inspector is reviewing the NEC code requirements for grounding of metal-clad (MC) cables in industrial applications. The NEC specifies that MC cables must have an effective grounding path, and the cable's metallic sheath can serve as this grounding path if it meets certain conditions. The inspector is summarizing the code to ensure electricians understand how to comply when installing MC cables in the facility. Which key point should be included to ensure code compliance in this scenario?
a. The MC cable's metallic sheath must be bonded to the building's steel structure
b. A separate grounding conductor must be run inside the MC cable for all installations
c. The metallic sheath of the MC cable can be used as the grounding path if it meets NEC requirements
d. MC cables should not be used in applications where grounding is required

Answer: c. The metallic sheath of the MC cable can be used as the grounding path if it meets NEC requirements. Explanation: According to the NEC, the metallic sheath of MC cables can serve as the grounding path under certain conditions, which should be highlighted to ensure proper grounding compliance in industrial installations.

595. An electrician reviews an energy usage report for a manufacturing facility over the course of a year. The report shows a clear pattern of increased energy consumption in the summer months, with usage peaking in July and August. In the winter months, energy consumption drops significantly, reaching its lowest point in January. This trend has repeated for the past three years, correlating with the increased use of HVAC systems to cool the facility during the summer. Based on this pattern, what is the most likely explanation for the seasonal changes in energy usage?
a. Increased lighting usage in the summer
b. Additional production shifts during the summer
c. Higher HVAC system demand in the summer
d. Poor insulation causing energy loss in winter

Answer: c. Higher HVAC system demand in the summer. Explanation: The significant rise in energy consumption during the summer months corresponds with the increased demand for cooling provided by the HVAC system. The pattern is consistent and correlates with the known need for more cooling in hotter months, making this the most likely explanation.

596. A power quality engineer is analyzing the load profile of a commercial building over a week. The data shows that the load spikes sharply between 7 a.m. and 9 a.m., remains relatively stable throughout the day, and then drops off after 6 p.m. This pattern repeats every weekday, but the weekends show much lower and more stable energy use throughout the day. Based on this load profile, what pattern is the engineer most likely observing?
a. Power fluctuations caused by unreliable grid supply
b. Peak load times corresponding to normal business hours
c. Cyclical loads due to HVAC system malfunction
d. Irregular load caused by equipment failures during the day

Answer: b. Peak load times corresponding to normal business hours. Explanation: The spike in the morning, followed by steady load during the day and a drop-off after business hours, is typical of a commercial building's energy consumption pattern, with the weekends showing less usage when the building is not fully operational.

597. A maintenance log for an industrial facility records motor failures that seem to occur more frequently in January and February each year. The failures are often due to issues with lubrication and increased wear on the bearings. The facility operates continuously year-round, but these failures are not as common in the summer months. What is the most likely reason for the seasonal pattern in motor failures?
a. Overloading of motors in winter due to increased production
b. Colder temperatures affecting lubrication performance and motor wear
c. Higher humidity levels causing electrical faults in the motors
d. Inconsistent maintenance practices during the winter months

Answer: b. Colder temperatures affecting lubrication performance and motor wear. Explanation: Colder temperatures can cause lubrication to thicken, leading to increased wear on motor bearings and higher rates of failure during the winter months. This explains why failures are more frequent during January and February.

598. An energy usage report for a residential area shows an anomaly in the data: on one day in April, there is a sudden and sharp increase in power consumption that does not fit with the usual pattern of energy use in the area. The report notes that this spike lasted for only a few hours before returning to normal. After checking the weather and local news reports, it is found that no extreme weather or outages occurred on this day. What is the most likely explanation for the anomaly?
a. An equipment failure at the local power plant
b. An increase in solar energy production causing reverse power flow
c. A temporary surge in residential electricity demand, possibly due to a special event
d. A problem with the data logging equipment used in the report

Answer: c. A temporary surge in residential electricity demand, possibly due to a special event. Explanation: A sharp, temporary increase in energy use without any weather-related issues could be due to a community event or specific activity that caused a short-term spike in demand, such as a large gathering or local celebration.

599. A facility manager is reviewing performance metrics for two HVAC systems: System A and System B. Over the past six months, both systems show consistent energy usage, but System B shows a gradual decrease in efficiency, consuming more energy to maintain the same temperature levels. The maintenance log indicates that System B was last serviced over a year ago, while System A was serviced six months ago. What is the most likely correlation between the performance of System B and its maintenance history?
a. The decrease in efficiency is due to outdated equipment in System B
b. System B is operating under a heavier load than System A
c. The lack of recent maintenance for System B is causing a decline in efficiency
d. System B's location in the facility exposes it to higher temperatures

Answer: c. The lack of recent maintenance for System B is causing a decline in efficiency. Explanation: The gradual decrease in System B's efficiency, along with the fact that it has not been serviced recently, suggests that regular maintenance, such as cleaning and inspection, is needed to restore its performance.

600. A performance analysis of a facility's electrical distribution system reveals that energy losses increase significantly whenever the load exceeds 80% of the system's capacity. The losses seem to correlate with higher conductor temperatures and lower power factors during these high-load periods. What is the most likely explanation for the increased energy losses at high loads?
a. Excessive current flow causing conductor heating and resistive losses
b. Voltage fluctuations due to poor power quality from the utility provider
c. Insufficient grounding leading to electrical noise and signal interference
d. Faulty equipment causing sudden surges and voltage spikes

Answer: a. Excessive current flow causing conductor heating and resistive losses. Explanation: Higher loads cause more current to flow through the conductors, which increases their temperature and resistance, leading to greater energy losses in the form of heat, particularly when the system is operating near capacity.

601. A predictive maintenance system at a manufacturing plant records vibration data for several critical motors. One motor shows a distinct pattern of increasing vibration levels over a period of months, reaching a critical point right before the motor was taken offline for repairs. A closer look at the data reveals that the increase in vibration was closely tied to spikes in load on the motor. What conclusion can be drawn from the relationship between the load and the vibration data?
a. The motor is improperly aligned, causing excessive vibration regardless of load
b. Increased vibration levels are directly related to the higher loads placed on the motor
c. The predictive maintenance system is not calibrated correctly, leading to false data
d. The motor requires more frequent lubrication to prevent vibration at high loads

Answer: b. Increased vibration levels are directly related to the higher loads placed on the motor. Explanation: The data shows a clear correlation between the spikes in load and the increased vibration levels, indicating that higher loads are putting additional strain on the motor, which leads to the excessive vibration.

602. An energy consumption report for a manufacturing plant shows a consistent pattern of increased energy use during the first week of each month, followed by a gradual decrease in energy consumption until the end of the month. The report notes that the plant's production schedule is consistent, with no significant changes in output throughout the month. Based on this pattern, what is the most likely reason for the fluctuation in energy consumption?
a. The plant increases production at the start of each month
b. Employees work longer hours at the beginning of each month
c. Energy usage spikes at the beginning of the month due to equipment calibration
d. The plant performs energy-intensive maintenance tasks at the start of each month

Answer: d. The plant performs energy-intensive maintenance tasks at the start of each month. Explanation: The consistent increase in energy consumption at the beginning of each month, followed by a decrease, suggests that regular maintenance or testing activities that require significant energy are conducted during this time.

603. An analysis of a building's lighting system shows that energy usage has steadily increased over the past year, despite no changes in occupancy or lighting schedules. The report notes that the building uses primarily fluorescent lighting and has not undergone a lighting upgrade in over a decade. What is the most likely explanation for the gradual increase in energy consumption?
a. A malfunction in the building's lighting controls causing lights to stay on longer
b. Degradation in the efficiency of the fluorescent lighting due to aging components
c. Increased use of the building's HVAC system affecting lighting energy consumption
d. A recent spike in energy costs that coincides with the increased consumption

Answer: b. Degradation in the efficiency of the fluorescent lighting due to aging components. Explanation: Fluorescent lighting systems lose efficiency as they age, which can cause a gradual increase in energy consumption even if usage patterns remain unchanged.

604. A data set tracking the performance of a solar power system shows that energy production follows a cyclical pattern, with peaks in the summer months and lower production in the winter months. However, the report notes that production during the past winter was significantly lower than in previous years, despite similar weather conditions. What is the most likely cause of the reduced energy production?
a. A degradation of the solar panels leading to reduced efficiency
b. An increase in overall energy demand in the winter months
c. The tilt of the solar panels was incorrectly adjusted for winter conditions
d. Power outages in the area causing interruptions in energy production

Answer: a. A degradation of the solar panels leading to reduced efficiency. Explanation: The reduced energy production during the past winter, despite normal weather conditions, suggests that the solar panels may be experiencing degradation over time, reducing their ability to generate electricity efficiently.

605. A plant maintenance crew is undergoing safety training for working in confined spaces, and the training material presents a hypothetical situation. In this scenario, two electricians are tasked with repairing a fault in an underground utility vault. Before entering, they check the atmosphere with a gas detector and find oxygen levels to be normal, but no test was done for flammable gases. Midway through the work, one of the electricians notices a faint odor of gasoline but dismisses it. Soon after, a spark from a tool causes an explosion, injuring both workers. Based on this scenario, what was the critical safety error that contributed to the accident?
a. The workers failed to wear appropriate personal protective equipment (PPE) for confined spaces
b. The workers neglected to lockout/tagout the electrical equipment before beginning work
c. The workers did not test for flammable gases before entering the confined space
d. The workers failed to follow proper evacuation procedures when they detected the gasoline odor

Answer: c. The workers did not test for flammable gases before entering the confined space. Explanation: The critical error was the failure to test for flammable gases before entering the confined space. Proper confined space entry procedures require testing for oxygen and potential flammable or toxic gases. The explosion was caused by the presence of a flammable gas, which could have been detected with the appropriate test.

606. During a troubleshooting training session, an electrician is presented with a hypothetical case study where a large motor in a factory repeatedly trips its breaker during startup. The motor is part of a conveyor system that operates under heavy load conditions, and it has been in service for several years without major issues. The technician who installed the motor had recently replaced the motor's bearings but did not perform any electrical tests after the replacement. The breaker trips immediately upon startup, but resets without issue each time. Based on this scenario, what is the most likely cause of the motor tripping?
a. The motor is experiencing an overload due to increased production demands
b. The motor's breaker is undersized for the current operating conditions
c. The motor's windings have been damaged during the recent bearing replacement
d. The motor's inrush current during startup is exceeding the breaker's rating

Answer: d. The motor's inrush current during startup is exceeding the breaker's rating. Explanation: Motors experience high inrush current during startup, which can trip a breaker if the breaker rating is not sufficient to handle the surge. Given that the motor trips immediately upon startup and resets without issue, this points to inrush current as the likely cause.

607. In a system design training exercise, participants are asked to evaluate the reliability of a backup generator system for a hospital. The hypothetical scenario describes a generator that powers critical systems, including life-support machines, during a power outage. The generator is equipped with an automatic transfer switch (ATS) that detects power loss and engages the generator within 10 seconds. However, during a recent power outage, the ATS failed to engage, and the hospital experienced a 30-second delay before manually switching to backup power. Upon inspection, no faults were found in the ATS, but the generator had not been tested in over a year. What is the most likely cause of the delayed power restoration in this scenario?
a. The ATS malfunctioned due to poor wiring connections
b. The generator's startup sequence failed due to a lack of regular testing
c. The hospital's electrical load exceeded the generator's capacity, delaying startup
d. The manual override switch was incorrectly set, preventing automatic engagement

Answer: b. The generator's startup sequence failed due to a lack of regular testing. Explanation: Regular testing is critical for ensuring that the generator's automatic systems, including the ATS and startup sequence, function properly. In this case, the delay in switching to backup power is likely due to the generator not being tested for an extended period, causing startup issues.

608. In a training module on power distribution systems, electricians are given a scenario where a utility substation experiences a failure in one of its transformers. The transformer is part of a system that serves multiple residential neighborhoods, and its failure causes an outage affecting thousands of customers. The training material presents several potential causes for the transformer failure, including insulation degradation, overloading during peak demand, and poor maintenance. The substation's load records show that the transformer was operating at 95% of its rated capacity during a heatwave at the time of failure. Based on this information, what is the most likely cause of the transformer failure?
a. The transformer was undersized for the load it was serving
b. The transformer experienced insulation degradation due to aging

c. The transformer failed due to overloading during peak demand in high temperatures
d. The transformer's failure was caused by inadequate preventive maintenance

Answer: c. The transformer failed due to overloading during peak demand in high temperatures. Explanation: Transformers are more likely to fail when operating near their capacity, especially during high-temperature conditions. The heatwave would have increased the load on the transformer, likely causing an overload and subsequent failure.

609. A scenario in a troubleshooting exercise presents an issue at a manufacturing facility where a conveyor system intermittently shuts down during operation. The system includes several motors controlled by variable frequency drives (VFDs), and each motor is protected by overload relays. The shutdowns occur randomly, and the facility's maintenance team has ruled out mechanical faults. A review of the control panel shows no fault codes, and the overload relays have not tripped. The VFDs are programmed to ramp the motors up and down based on production demand. Based on this scenario, what is the most likely cause of the intermittent shutdowns?
a. The motors are overheating due to inadequate ventilation
b. The VFDs are incorrectly programmed, causing the motors to stall
c. The overload relays are set too low, causing unnecessary shutdowns
d. The system is experiencing voltage fluctuations that are affecting the VFDs

Answer: d. The system is experiencing voltage fluctuations that are affecting the VFDs. Explanation: Voltage fluctuations can cause VFDs to malfunction, leading to intermittent shutdowns of the motors. Since no mechanical faults or overload relay trips were observed, voltage instability is the most likely cause.

610. During a safety training session, workers are presented with a hypothetical "what-if" situation where an electrical technician must work on live equipment due to an emergency situation. The technician is following the lockout/tagout (LOTO) procedure but realizes that the equipment cannot be fully de-energized without interrupting critical hospital operations. The training material asks participants to evaluate the risks involved and propose a course of action. Based on this scenario, what should the technician do to minimize risk while working on the live equipment?
a. Use insulated tools and wear high-voltage-rated gloves and protective equipment
b. Bypass the LOTO procedure since the equipment must remain energized
c. Increase the distance from the live parts by using remote operating tools
d. Temporarily disconnect non-critical loads to reduce the overall system load

Answer: a. Use insulated tools and wear high-voltage-rated gloves and protective equipment. Explanation: When working on live equipment, proper personal protective equipment (PPE) and insulated tools are essential to minimize the risk of electrical shock. Following strict safety protocols, even in emergency situations, is critical.

611. An electrical apprentice is presented with a case study in a training exercise where a commercial building's lighting system experiences frequent circuit breaker trips. The building is fitted with multiple lighting panels, each controlled by separate breakers, and the issues only occur during peak operational hours. The breakers are sized according to the National Electrical Code (NEC), and no equipment failures have been identified. The training asks the

apprentice to hypothesize why the breakers are tripping. Based on the case study, what is the most likely cause of the issue?
a. The lighting system is drawing more current during peak hours due to increased usage
b. The circuit breakers are defective and need to be replaced
c. The building's wiring is too old to handle the lighting system's load
d. The lighting panels are incorrectly grounded, causing electrical shorts

Answer: a. The lighting system is drawing more current during peak hours due to increased usage. Explanation: Peak operational hours likely correspond to times when all lights are on, increasing the current draw and tripping breakers that are sized for lower, non-peak loads. This would explain why the issue occurs only at certain times.

612. A training scenario in a maintenance course describes a critical piece of equipment that operates continuously in a manufacturing plant. The equipment's motor is showing signs of wear, including occasional overheating and excessive vibration. The motor has not been serviced in over two years, and its performance has gradually declined. The course asks participants to evaluate the situation and determine the best preventive maintenance strategy. Based on the scenario, what should the maintenance team prioritize?
a. Immediately replace the motor with a higher-rated model
b. Perform vibration analysis and lubricate the motor bearings
c. Reduce the motor's operating hours to prevent further wear
d. Increase the motor's operating voltage to improve efficiency

Answer: b. Perform vibration analysis and lubricate the motor bearings. Explanation: Excessive vibration and overheating are common signs of worn or damaged motor bearings. Lubricating the bearings and performing a vibration analysis will help extend the motor's life and restore proper performance.

613. In a certification prep scenario, candidates are asked to assess the potential failure of a power distribution system in a high-rise office building. The scenario describes a situation where the building's electrical load has steadily increased over the past decade, but the main service transformer has not been upgraded. The transformer is now operating at 95% of its rated capacity, and summer heatwaves have caused multiple brownouts in the building. The building management is concerned about a potential system failure. What should be the first step in addressing the issue based on the information provided?
a. Install additional transformers to share the building's electrical load
b. Perform thermal imaging scans to detect hot spots in the transformer
c. Reduce the building's electrical load by upgrading to more efficient systems
d. Increase the transformer's cooling capacity to handle the summer heat

Answer: a. Install additional transformers to share the building's electrical load. Explanation: Since the transformer is already operating near its maximum capacity, adding additional transformers to distribute the load will reduce strain on the existing system and help prevent future brownouts.

614. A case study presented in a training module describes a scenario where a factory's conveyor system experiences a complete shutdown after a power surge. The conveyor motors are protected by surge protectors, but the system's control panel was directly exposed to the surge. After the surge, the control panel displayed fault codes and refused

to reset. The surge protection devices were installed only on the motors and not the control circuits. The training asks participants to determine the primary reason for the shutdown. Based on the case study, what was the critical oversight in the system's protection?
a. The surge protection devices installed on the motors were undersized
b. The control panel was not adequately protected from power surges
c. The conveyor motors failed, causing a chain reaction that shut down the system
d. The power surge was too large for the system's breakers to handle

Answer: b. The control panel was not adequately protected from power surges. Explanation: Although the motors were protected by surge devices, the control panel was directly exposed to the surge, leading to a shutdown. Surge protection for control circuits is just as important as for the motors to ensure full system protection.

615. An article in an electrical industry journal discusses the rise of smart grid technology and its impact on energy distribution. The author states, "Smart grids are revolutionizing the way we manage electricity, offering unprecedented efficiency and reliability. With real-time monitoring and automatic fault detection, smart grids drastically reduce outage times and energy waste. I believe that within the next decade, every utility will have adopted this technology to some extent, as the advantages are undeniable. The future of energy is undoubtedly smart." Which part of the passage contains an opinion rather than a verifiable fact?
a. Smart grids offer real-time monitoring and automatic fault detection
b. Smart grids drastically reduce outage times and energy waste
c. Every utility will adopt smart grid technology within the next decade
d. Smart grids are revolutionizing energy management

Answer: c. Every utility will adopt smart grid technology within the next decade. Explanation: The prediction about the future adoption of smart grids is an opinion, as it cannot be verified at present. The other statements are based on current technology and its benefits, which can be confirmed with data.

616. In a review of a new high-efficiency motor, an equipment supplier writes, "This motor is the most cost-effective solution available on the market today. It offers a 15% improvement in energy efficiency over traditional motors, making it a top choice for industrial applications. Many of our clients have reported significant savings on their energy bills after switching to this model. While there are other options, none deliver the same combination of performance and value." Which part of the review is an opinion rather than a factual claim?
a. The motor offers a 15% improvement in energy efficiency over traditional models
b. Many clients have reported significant savings on energy bills
c. This motor is the most cost-effective solution available on the market today
d. The motor is a top choice for industrial applications

Answer: c. This motor is the most cost-effective solution available on the market today. Explanation: The claim that this motor is the "most cost-effective" is subjective and based on the reviewer's opinion. It cannot be universally verified. The other statements refer to measurable improvements and customer feedback, which can be supported by evidence.

617. A technical debate over the use of copper vs. aluminum conductors highlights different viewpoints. One engineer argues, "Copper is far superior due to its higher conductivity and lower resistance, which results in less power loss. While aluminum is cheaper, it's also more prone to oxidation and has lower conductivity, meaning you need thicker wires to handle the same current load. In my experience, copper should always be the material of choice for high-stakes applications, especially in mission-critical systems." Which part of the engineer's statement is based on personal opinion rather than verifiable fact?
a. Copper has higher conductivity than aluminum
b. Aluminum is more prone to oxidation than copper
c. Copper should always be the material of choice for high-stakes applications
d. Aluminum requires thicker wires to handle the same current load

Answer: c. Copper should always be the material of choice for high-stakes applications. Explanation: The claim that copper "should always" be used is a subjective opinion based on the engineer's personal experience. The other statements are factual and can be verified through material properties and technical standards.

618. In an industry forecast, a market analyst writes, "The demand for electric vehicle (EV) charging stations will increase exponentially over the next five years, driven by government incentives and widespread adoption of EVs. The current growth trend shows no signs of slowing, and many automakers have already committed to electrifying their fleets. This, combined with a growing focus on sustainability, makes it certain that we will see a massive build-out of charging infrastructure in both urban and rural areas." Which statement in this forecast is an opinion rather than a fact?
a. Automakers have committed to electrifying their fleets
b. Government incentives are driving demand for EV charging stations
c. The demand for EV charging stations will increase exponentially over the next five years
d. The current growth trend shows no signs of slowing

Answer: c. The demand for EV charging stations will increase exponentially over the next five years. Explanation: This is a prediction and, while based on current trends, it cannot be verified as a fact at this time. The other statements refer to current events and observable trends that can be supported by data.

619. A white paper on renewable energy integration argues, "Solar power has become one of the fastest-growing energy sources worldwide, with installations increasing by over 20% annually in many regions. However, solar energy's intermittent nature limits its effectiveness without reliable energy storage solutions. Despite these challenges, I'm convinced that solar will surpass all other energy sources in both growth and capacity within the next two decades." Which part of the argument is an opinion rather than a verifiable fact?
a. Solar power is growing by over 20% annually in many regions
b. Solar energy's intermittent nature limits its effectiveness without storage
c. Solar will surpass all other energy sources in both growth and capacity within two decades
d. Energy storage is required to make solar power more reliable

Answer: c. Solar will surpass all other energy sources in both growth and capacity within two decades. Explanation: This statement is speculative and represents the author's personal belief about the future of solar power. The other statements refer to current trends and technical limitations, which can be verified.

620. An article in a trade publication discussing automation in electrical systems states, "Automation will soon dominate the industry, transforming how electricians work. Automated systems reduce human error, improve efficiency, and lower operational costs. According to recent studies, facilities that adopt automation experience a 30% decrease in downtime. There's no question that automation is the future, and those who don't adapt will be left behind." Which part of this statement is opinion rather than fact?

a. Automation reduces human error and improves efficiency
b. Facilities that adopt automation experience a 30% decrease in downtime
c. Automation will soon dominate the industry
d. Automated systems lower operational costs

Answer: c. Automation will soon dominate the industry. Explanation: This is a prediction about the future and reflects the author's belief. The other statements can be supported by data from studies on automation's effects on efficiency and cost.

621. In a discussion about energy-efficient building designs, a consultant writes, "Green building standards like LEED have set the benchmark for sustainability, offering guidelines that improve energy efficiency and reduce environmental impact. The benefits are clear: buildings designed to LEED standards consume less energy, which leads to long-term cost savings and reduced carbon footprints. While LEED certification is not necessary for every project, I believe it should be the standard for all new commercial buildings." Which statement reflects the consultant's opinion rather than a fact?
a. LEED standards improve energy efficiency and reduce environmental impact
b. Buildings designed to LEED standards consume less energy
c. LEED certification should be the standard for all new commercial buildings
d. Green building standards set the benchmark for sustainability

Answer: c. LEED certification should be the standard for all new commercial buildings. Explanation: This is a subjective recommendation based on the consultant's belief. The other statements describe measurable benefits and widely accepted facts about LEED standards and their impact.

622. A debate arises at a trade conference over the potential of hydrogen fuel cells. One speaker argues, "Hydrogen fuel cells are the cleanest option available, as they produce only water vapor as a byproduct. They also offer higher energy efficiency compared to traditional combustion engines. However, I don't think hydrogen will replace electric batteries in the transportation sector any time soon due to infrastructure challenges and cost. Battery technology is still far ahead in terms of accessibility and development." Which part of the speaker's statement is an opinion rather than a fact?
a. Hydrogen fuel cells produce only water vapor as a byproduct
b. Hydrogen fuel cells offer higher energy efficiency than combustion engines
c. Hydrogen will not replace electric batteries in the transportation sector any time soon
d. Battery technology is ahead in terms of accessibility and development

Answer: c. Hydrogen will not replace electric batteries in the transportation sector any time soon. Explanation: This is a subjective prediction about the future of hydrogen fuel cells versus electric batteries, and while infrastructure challenges exist, this specific outcome cannot be verified as fact.

623. In a review of battery storage technologies, a technical analyst writes, "Lithium-ion batteries remain the dominant technology due to their high energy density and relatively low cost. However, they are prone to thermal runaway, which poses significant safety concerns, especially in large-scale installations. Alternatives like solid-state batteries are on the horizon, but I expect lithium-ion to remain the standard for the foreseeable future as the market continues to mature." Which statement in the review is an opinion rather than a fact?
a. Lithium-ion batteries are prone to thermal runaway
b. Solid-state batteries are on the horizon as an alternative
c. Lithium-ion will remain the standard for the foreseeable future
d. Lithium-ion batteries have high energy density and relatively low cost

Answer: c. Lithium-ion will remain the standard for the foreseeable future. Explanation: This is the analyst's opinion based on current trends but cannot be definitively verified. The other statements refer to technical characteristics and emerging technologies, which can be confirmed with current data.

624. An industry report on power grid resilience states, "As more renewable energy sources like wind and solar are integrated into the grid, the variability in energy supply becomes a challenge. Grid operators must adapt to these fluctuations by implementing advanced storage solutions and real-time monitoring systems. While some argue that these challenges are too great, I believe that technological advancements will soon allow for seamless integration of renewables, ensuring grid stability and sustainability." Which part of this report reflects the author's opinion rather than fact?
a. Renewable energy sources like wind and solar increase variability in energy supply
b. Grid operators must implement storage solutions and real-time monitoring to adapt
c. Technological advancements will soon allow for seamless integration of renewables
d. The variability of renewable energy is a challenge for grid stability

Answer: c. Technological advancements will soon allow for seamless integration of renewables. Explanation: This is the author's belief about future technological capabilities and cannot be proven at present. The other statements highlight current technical challenges and operational requirements that can be verified.

625. A plant engineer is reviewing the specifications for a new 600V motor that will be installed as part of a large conveyor system. The technical data sheet includes several abbreviations, such as "FLA," "RPM," and "NEMA," which are critical for ensuring that the motor is compatible with the existing electrical infrastructure. The motor is rated for 175 FLA and operates at 1,200 RPM, with a NEMA enclosure type 4X. The engineer needs to determine if the motor will operate within the plant's existing breaker and wiring limits. Based on this data, what does "FLA" refer to, and why is it important in this context?
a. Full Load Amps, indicating the maximum current the motor will draw under full load
b. Frequency Load Allowance, specifying the allowable frequency variation for the motor
c. Fast Line Acceleration, representing the time it takes for the motor to reach full speed
d. Final Load Adjustment, showing the motor's current rating after calibration

Answer: a. Full Load Amps, indicating the maximum current the motor will draw under full load. Explanation: "FLA" stands for Full Load Amps, which refers to the current that the motor will draw when operating at full load. This is crucial for determining whether the existing breakers and wiring can handle the motor's electrical demands.

626. An electrician is interpreting a wiring diagram for a three-phase motor control center (MCC) in an industrial facility. The diagram includes several abbreviations such as "NO," "NC," and "OL." The motor is protected by an overload relay (OL), and the control circuit features normally open (NO) and normally closed (NC) contacts. In this context, the electrician needs to understand the function of the "NO" and "NC" contacts in controlling the motor. What do these abbreviations stand for, and what role do they play in motor control?
a. "NO" stands for Normally Open, and "NC" stands for Normally Closed; they control the flow of current in the motor's safety circuit
b. "NO" refers to Normal Operation, and "NC" refers to No Control; they indicate different modes of motor operation
c. "NO" means Non-operational, and "NC" means Non-compliant; they are used to indicate faulty contacts
d. "NO" represents No Output, and "NC" stands for No Current; they are associated with power failure conditions

Answer: a. "NO" stands for Normally Open, and "NC" stands for Normally Closed; they control the flow of current in the motor's safety circuit. Explanation: In motor control systems, "NO" and "NC" contacts are essential for controlling the flow of current. "NO" contacts only close when activated, allowing current to flow, while "NC" contacts remain closed until activated, interrupting the current when needed.

627. During a safety training session, a team of electricians is briefed on various personal protective equipment (PPE) standards and the associated acronyms used in safety protocols. One of the acronyms discussed is "ARC," which is frequently mentioned in the context of electrical safety gear. The training materials emphasize the importance of selecting PPE with an appropriate "ARC rating" when working on live electrical equipment. What does the acronym "ARC" stand for, and why is the "ARC rating" crucial for safety?
a. Arc-Resistant Coating, which refers to a protective layer on PPE that prevents electrical burns
b. Arc-Rated Clothing, which indicates the level of protection the PPE provides against arc flash events
c. Amperage Resistance Capability, specifying the amount of current the PPE can withstand
d. Anti-Risk Certification, ensuring that the equipment meets minimum safety standards for hazardous environments

Answer: b. Arc-Rated Clothing, which indicates the level of protection the PPE provides against arc flash events. Explanation: "ARC" stands for Arc-Rated Clothing, which is designed to protect workers from the intense heat and energy produced during an arc flash event. The ARC rating specifies the amount of protection offered by the clothing, making it a critical consideration in electrical safety.

628. A project manager is reviewing the electrical plans for a new commercial building and notices the abbreviation "THHN" in the specifications for the building's wiring. The plans indicate that all conductors must be "THHN" and rated for use in dry locations. The project manager needs to ensure that the selected wiring meets the building's electrical code requirements. What does "THHN" stand for, and what does it indicate about the properties of the wiring?
a. Thermoplastic High Heat-resistant Nylon-coated, indicating the wire's ability to withstand high temperatures in dry environments
b. Triple High Heat Neoprene, specifying a three-layer insulation system for extreme environments

c. Thermosetting Hard Nylon, meaning the wire is designed for applications requiring flexible installation in both wet and dry environments
d. Temperature Humidity High Neutral, which describes a wire that balances temperature and humidity control in electrical systems

Answer: a. Thermoplastic High Heat-resistant Nylon-coated, indicating the wire's ability to withstand high temperatures in dry environments. Explanation: "THHN" stands for Thermoplastic High Heat-resistant Nylon-coated, which describes wiring designed for high-temperature applications in dry locations. The nylon coating provides additional protection and ensures compliance with code requirements for dry areas.

629. In a training course on power systems, technicians are introduced to the acronym "kVA" when discussing transformer ratings. A transformer in the training material is rated at 500 kVA, and the technicians are tasked with calculating the load that the transformer can support. Understanding the unit abbreviation is essential for performing accurate load calculations. What does "kVA" stand for, and how is it relevant to transformer capacity?
a. Kilovolt Amperes, representing the apparent power capacity of the transformer
b. Kinetic Voltage Amplitude, describing the energy efficiency of the transformer under load
c. Kilowatt Amperes, specifying the real power output of the transformer
d. Kinetic Voltage Analysis, used to determine the efficiency of power distribution in the transformer

Answer: a. Kilovolt Amperes, representing the apparent power capacity of the transformer. Explanation: "kVA" stands for Kilovolt Amperes, which is a measure of the apparent power capacity of a transformer. It represents both the real power and reactive power that the transformer can handle, making it a key factor in determining load capacity.

630. An electrical inspector is reviewing a facility's grounding system and sees the abbreviation "GEC" in the system documentation. The facility uses a grounding electrode conductor (GEC) to connect the electrical system to the earth, as required by the NEC. The inspector must confirm that the correct size and type of conductor are used to ensure a safe and compliant installation. What does "GEC" stand for, and why is it important in this context?
a. Grounding Electrode Conduit, indicating the protective conduit used to shield the grounding system
b. Grounding Equipment Connection, specifying the point where equipment is bonded to the ground
c. Grounding Electrode Conductor, which connects the electrical system to the grounding electrode
d. Ground Electrode Coupler, describing a device used to join multiple grounding electrodes

Answer: c. Grounding Electrode Conductor, which connects the electrical system to the grounding electrode. Explanation: "GEC" stands for Grounding Electrode Conductor, which is the conductor that connects the electrical system to the earth via the grounding electrode. It ensures the safe dissipation of fault currents and compliance with NEC grounding requirements.

631. In a troubleshooting exercise, an electrician must diagnose a fault in a motor control circuit. The wiring diagram includes the abbreviation "RMS" in reference to the voltage measurements taken at various points in the circuit. The electrician knows that RMS voltage readings are critical for understanding the actual power delivered to the motor. What does "RMS" stand for, and why is it important in electrical measurements?
a. Root Mean Square, representing the effective value of an AC voltage or current
b. Reactive Mean Signal, indicating the average reactive power in the circuit

c. Real Mean Supply, describing the total real power available in the system
d. Rated Maximum Strength, specifying the maximum voltage tolerance of the components

Answer: a. Root Mean Square, representing the effective value of an AC voltage or current. Explanation: "RMS" stands for Root Mean Square, which is a mathematical value used to represent the effective voltage or current in an AC circuit. It is essential for calculating the actual power delivered to devices like motors.

632. A technician is reviewing a manual for the installation of a photovoltaic (PV) system and sees several abbreviations, including "MPPT," which refers to a critical component in the system's power management. The manual explains that the MPPT optimizes the voltage and current output from the solar panels to increase efficiency. Understanding this abbreviation is essential for correctly installing and configuring the system. What does "MPPT" stand for, and what is its function in the PV system?
a. Maximum Power Point Tracker, which optimizes the power output from solar panels
b. Multi-phase Power Transfer, describing a method of distributing power across multiple circuits
c. Maximum Phase Potential Test, used to verify voltage levels during installation
d. Multi-Power Protection Transfer, which safeguards the system against overvoltage conditions

Answer: a. Maximum Power Point Tracker, which optimizes the power output from solar panels. Explanation: "MPPT" stands for Maximum Power Point Tracker, a device that continuously adjusts the voltage and current from solar panels to ensure they operate at their most efficient power point.

633. An industrial facility is installing a new emergency power system, and the technical drawings include the abbreviation "ATS." The ATS is a critical component that automatically transfers the load to the backup generator in the event of a power failure. The facility's electricians need to fully understand the function of the ATS to ensure proper installation and operation. What does "ATS" stand for, and what is its role in the emergency power system?
a. Automatic Transfer Switch, which transfers the electrical load from the utility to the generator
b. Automated Time Synchronizer, ensuring that all systems remain synchronized during power outages
c. Alternate Transmission System, providing a secondary route for power distribution
d. Advanced Testing Sequence, used to check the readiness of backup power systems

Answer: a. Automatic Transfer Switch, which transfers the electrical load from the utility to the generator. Explanation: "ATS" stands for Automatic Transfer Switch, which automatically transfers the load to the backup generator when it detects a power outage. This is crucial for ensuring continuous power to critical systems during emergencies.

634. In a training course on electrical safety, workers are introduced to the term "GFCI," which is commonly used in construction sites and wet environments. The training explains that GFCI devices are required by the NEC in certain locations to protect workers from electrical shock hazards. The workers must understand where and how to install these devices. What does "GFCI" stand for, and why is it important in electrical safety?
a. Ground Fault Circuit Interrupter, which disconnects the circuit when a ground fault is detected
b. General Fault Current Indicator, which alerts workers to potential electrical issues
c. Grounded Frame Contact Indicator, used to test the integrity of electrical enclosures
d. Generator Fault Control Interface, which manages fault conditions in portable generators

Answer: a. Ground Fault Circuit Interrupter, which disconnects the circuit when a ground fault is detected. Explanation: "GFCI" stands for Ground Fault Circuit Interrupter, a device that detects ground faults and interrupts the circuit to prevent electrical shock. GFCIs are especially important in areas where there is a higher risk of shock, such as wet environments.

635. In an engineering report justifying the use of aluminum conductors over copper in a high-voltage power distribution project, the author argues, "Aluminum conductors provide the same current-carrying capacity as copper when sized correctly, but at a significantly lower cost. Numerous industry studies have demonstrated that aluminum is the cost-effective alternative without compromising safety or performance. Major utility companies, such as XYZ Power and ABC Electric, have transitioned to aluminum conductors in similar projects with great success. Aluminum is the future of power distribution." What rhetorical strategy is primarily used in the mention of major utility companies?
a. Appeal to emotion
b. Appeal to authority
c. Logical appeal (logos)
d. Repetition for emphasis

Answer: b. Appeal to authority. Explanation: The mention of major utility companies adopting aluminum conductors serves as an appeal to authority, leveraging the credibility and success of well-known organizations to strengthen the argument for aluminum conductors.

636. A safety communication sent to electrical workers states, "Every year, countless electricians are injured or killed because they did not follow lockout/tagout procedures. Imagine the devastation your family would feel if you failed to take this simple, life-saving precaution. This is not just about compliance with regulations; it's about ensuring you return home safely at the end of each day. Don't let a moment's carelessness destroy lives." What rhetorical strategy is being used in the communication?

a. Appeal to logic
b. Appeal to authority
c. Appeal to emotion
d. Repetition for emphasis

Answer: c. Appeal to emotion. Explanation: The communication invokes fear and concern for family well-being to persuade the workers to follow safety procedures, focusing on the emotional consequences of neglecting safety, rather than purely logical reasoning.

637. In a technical manual explaining the National Electrical Code (NEC) requirements for grounding and bonding, the author states, "According to the NEC, grounding is essential for reducing the risk of electrical shock and protecting equipment from surges. All grounding must follow the procedures outlined in Article 250 of the NEC, which has been developed and approved by leading industry experts to ensure the highest level of safety and reliability." How is the appeal to authority being used in this explanation?
a. By citing electrical codes created by industry experts

b. By emphasizing the emotional consequences of improper grounding
c. By repeating the word "safety" for emphasis
d. By listing potential hazards of failing to ground properly

Answer: a. By citing electrical codes created by industry experts. Explanation: The explanation appeals to authority by referencing the NEC and the expertise of industry professionals who developed the standards, adding credibility to the importance of following grounding procedures.

638. In a project proposal for upgrading a building's electrical system, the author repeatedly uses the phrase "cost-effective" when describing each component of the proposal. "Our proposed solution is cost-effective, offering significant savings over time. By upgrading to LED lighting, which is both energy-efficient and cost-effective, the building will reduce operating costs by 30%. Additionally, we recommend the installation of a cost-effective smart control system to optimize energy usage." What rhetorical strategy is being used here?
a. Appeal to authority
b. Appeal to emotion
c. Repetition for emphasis
d. Appeal to logic

Answer: c. Repetition for emphasis. Explanation: The repeated use of "cost-effective" serves to emphasize the affordability and economic benefits of the proposed solutions, reinforcing the idea that these options provide financial advantages.

639. A technical article discussing the risks of improper grounding emphasizes, "Without proper grounding, the consequences can be catastrophic. Electrical faults could lead to fires, damage to equipment, and even loss of life. Fault currents must be directed safely to ground, or the results could be devastating." The article repeats the term "catastrophic" multiple times when referring to potential failures. What rhetorical strategy is being employed in this passage?
a. Appeal to authority
b. Repetition for emphasis
c. Appeal to logic
d. Appeal to authority

Answer: b. Repetition for emphasis. Explanation: The repeated use of the word "catastrophic" highlights the seriousness of the issue and stresses the potential consequences of improper grounding, using repetition to drive the point home.

640. In an argument for the use of arc-fault circuit interrupters (AFCIs) in residential electrical systems, an engineer writes, "AFCIs are now required by the National Electrical Code for most circuits in homes because they prevent fires caused by arc faults. Leading electrical safety organizations, including the National Fire Protection Association (NFPA), recommend AFCIs as a critical component of modern electrical safety. Failure to install AFCIs not only violates code but increases the risk of fire." What rhetorical strategy is primarily used in referencing the NFPA?
a. Appeal to logic
b. Repetition for emphasis

c. Appeal to authority
d. Appeal to emotion

Answer: c. Appeal to authority. Explanation: The author uses the endorsement of a respected organization, the NFPA, to lend authority and credibility to the argument for installing AFCIs, making it more persuasive by associating it with a well-known safety organization.

641. A white paper promoting renewable energy integration argues, "By investing in renewable energy technologies like wind and solar, we can not only reduce our carbon footprint but also cut long-term energy costs. Studies have shown that renewable systems pay for themselves within 10 years, offering a financial return on investment while helping the planet. We owe it to future generations to transition to sustainable energy sources before it's too late." Which rhetorical strategy is used in the final sentence of this passage?
a. Appeal to authority
b. Appeal to logic
c. Appeal to emotion
d. Repetition for emphasis

Answer: c. Appeal to emotion. Explanation: The final sentence appeals to the reader's emotions by focusing on the moral responsibility to future generations, invoking a sense of urgency and ethical obligation to support renewable energy.

642. In an equipment catalog, a supplier describes a new circuit breaker, stating, "This breaker is built with the highest quality materials and meets all current safety standards. It has been approved by the Underwriters Laboratories (UL) for its exceptional durability and performance. When it comes to safety and reliability, UL certification is the gold standard in the industry." How is the appeal to authority used in this passage?
a. By emphasizing the potential hazards of non-certified equipment
b. By referencing UL certification to support the breaker's reliability
c. By explaining how the breaker meets customer needs
d. By highlighting the materials used in the breaker

Answer: b. By referencing UL certification to support the breaker's reliability. Explanation: The author uses the certification from a reputable organization, Underwriters Laboratories, to build credibility and trust in the breaker's safety and performance, appealing to authority.

643. In a presentation on job site safety, the trainer states, "We've all seen the statistics. Every year, thousands of workers are injured because safety protocols were ignored. The numbers don't lie: following proper lockout/tagout procedures reduces injury rates by 40%. If you care about your health and the health of your coworkers, you must make safety your top priority." What rhetorical strategy is used when the trainer says, "The numbers don't lie"?
a. Appeal to authority
b. Appeal to logic
c. Appeal to emotion
d. Repetition for emphasis

Answer: b. Appeal to logic. Explanation: By stating "the numbers don't lie," the trainer appeals to logic, using statistical evidence to reinforce the argument that following safety protocols is essential for reducing injuries.

644. An engineering report on transformer maintenance includes the following: "Regular transformer oil testing is critical to detecting problems early. Leading industry experts recommend testing at least once a year to check for moisture, oxidation, and contamination, which can severely degrade performance. Failure to follow this advice can lead to expensive repairs and costly downtime. Industry best practices are clear: preventive maintenance saves both time and money." How does the appeal to authority function in this passage?
a. By focusing on the financial consequences of poor maintenance
b. By referencing industry experts to support the importance of oil testing
c. By explaining the technical process of oil testing in transformers
d. By highlighting the potential for equipment failure

Answer: b. By referencing industry experts to support the importance of oil testing. Explanation: The author appeals to authority by mentioning the recommendations of "leading industry experts," which adds credibility to the advice given about regular transformer maintenance.

645. In the early 1900s, Thomas Edison's development of direct current (DC) systems helped electrify parts of cities, but these systems faced limitations, particularly in transmitting power over long distances. Around the same time, Nikola Tesla's alternating current (AC) systems began to gain traction because they allowed for more efficient long-distance transmission by stepping up voltage through transformers. Eventually, AC systems became the standard for most electrical grids. However, modern technologies such as renewable energy sources and high-voltage direct current (HVDC) lines are again emphasizing DC for certain applications, due to its efficiency in specific contexts. Based on this historical context, what is one key reason why AC systems became more dominant over DC systems in the early 20th century?
a. AC systems required less maintenance compared to DC systems
b. AC systems allowed for easier voltage transformation, making long-distance transmission more efficient
c. AC systems were more compatible with industrial machinery of the time
d. AC systems provided better power quality for household lighting and appliances

Answer: b. AC systems allowed for easier voltage transformation, making long-distance transmission more efficient. Explanation: AC systems could use transformers to step up voltage for long-distance transmission and step it down for local use, a major advantage over DC systems, which faced significant losses over long distances.

646. The National Electrical Code (NEC) was first published in 1897, and over the years, it has evolved significantly to address emerging electrical technologies and safety concerns. Early editions focused primarily on preventing fires caused by faulty wiring, but later editions expanded to include safety requirements for grounding, overcurrent protection, and more. In the 1970s, ground fault circuit interrupters (GFCIs) were introduced into the code as a safety measure for wet areas, which reduced the risk of electrical shock. What is the primary reason the NEC introduced GFCI requirements in the 1970s?
a. To address rising concerns about electrical fires in industrial settings
b. To improve grounding practices in residential and commercial buildings
c. To reduce the risk of electrical shock in environments prone to moisture

d. To prevent overloads in circuits with sensitive electronic equipment

Answer: c. To reduce the risk of electrical shock in environments prone to moisture. Explanation: GFCIs were introduced in the NEC to protect against electrical shock by quickly disconnecting power when a ground fault is detected, especially in areas such as bathrooms, kitchens, and outdoor locations where moisture is present.

647. The development of high-voltage transmission systems in the mid-20th century played a critical role in expanding the reach of electrical power across the country. One significant advancement was the introduction of high-voltage alternating current (HVAC) systems, which allowed utilities to transmit electricity over long distances with minimal loss. In contrast, earlier low-voltage systems could only transmit power a few miles before suffering significant energy losses. In modern times, high-voltage direct current (HVDC) lines are becoming increasingly popular for very long-distance transmission. What is one major reason for using HVDC lines instead of HVAC lines in modern power grids?
a. HVDC lines are less expensive to construct and maintain than HVAC lines
b. HVDC lines offer more efficient long-distance transmission with lower losses
c. HVDC lines are safer to install in densely populated urban areas
d. HVDC lines are more compatible with renewable energy sources like wind and solar

Answer: b. HVDC lines offer more efficient long-distance transmission with lower losses. Explanation: HVDC lines are more efficient for very long-distance power transmission because they experience lower energy losses compared to HVAC lines, making them a preferred option for connecting distant power sources to load centers.

648. Electrical safety standards have changed dramatically since the early days of electrification. For example, early electrical systems often used ungrounded wiring, which increased the risk of electric shock and fires. In the mid-20th century, grounding requirements were added to electrical codes to provide a safer path for fault currents and protect people from electrocution. Modern codes now require extensive grounding and bonding systems for safety. Why is grounding considered a critical component of electrical safety in modern installations?
a. Grounding helps reduce the overall energy consumption of electrical systems
b. Grounding provides a low-resistance path for fault currents to prevent electric shock
c. Grounding improves the efficiency of power transmission in high-voltage lines
d. Grounding prevents circuit breakers from tripping under normal operating conditions

Answer: b. Grounding provides a low-resistance path for fault currents to prevent electric shock. Explanation: Grounding is essential for electrical safety because it ensures that fault currents are safely directed to the ground, reducing the risk of electric shock and equipment damage.

649. One of the most significant advancements in electrical safety came with the development of overcurrent protection devices like circuit breakers and fuses in the early 20th century. Before these devices were widely used, electrical systems often relied on simple disconnect switches that provided no automatic protection against overloads. Modern electrical systems use circuit breakers that can trip automatically to prevent damage to wiring and equipment. What is the primary function of a circuit breaker in an electrical system?
a. To monitor voltage levels and adjust power distribution accordingly
b. To automatically disconnect the circuit in the event of an overload or short circuit

c. To regulate the current flow in high-demand areas of the electrical system
d. To prevent power surges from reaching sensitive electronic equipment

Answer: b. To automatically disconnect the circuit in the event of an overload or short circuit. Explanation: Circuit breakers protect electrical systems by automatically disconnecting power when they detect an overload or short circuit, preventing damage to wiring and equipment, and reducing the risk of fires.

650. In the 1930s, the theory of electrical resonance gained attention in both academic and industrial circles. Electrical resonance occurs when the inductive reactance and capacitive reactance in a circuit are equal, allowing the circuit to operate at maximum efficiency. Resonance plays a critical role in radio frequency circuits, transformers, and other AC applications. However, resonance can also lead to voltage surges if not properly managed. How does electrical resonance affect the performance of an AC circuit when used intentionally?
a. It increases the resistance in the circuit, making it less efficient
b. It allows the circuit to transfer energy more efficiently at a specific frequency
c. It causes the circuit to overheat and fail due to excessive current
d. It limits the amount of current that can pass through the circuit, reducing power output

Answer: b. It allows the circuit to transfer energy more efficiently at a specific frequency. Explanation: Electrical resonance occurs when the inductive and capacitive reactances are balanced, allowing energy to be transferred efficiently at a specific frequency, which is beneficial in many AC applications.

651. Over the years, electrical codes have evolved to account for new technologies and safety concerns. For example, early codes focused primarily on protecting against fire hazards, but modern codes now also address issues like arc flash, electromagnetic interference (EMI), and equipment grounding. The addition of arc flash protection requirements was particularly significant, as arc flash events can cause severe injuries and equipment damage. What is the purpose of arc flash protection in electrical systems?
a. To prevent short circuits from damaging sensitive electronic components
b. To minimize the risk of fire by containing electrical faults within conduits
c. To reduce the risk of injury by limiting exposure to the high heat and energy of an arc flash
d. To improve the efficiency of electrical circuits by reducing energy losses

Answer: c. To reduce the risk of injury by limiting exposure to the high heat and energy of an arc flash. Explanation: Arc flash protection is designed to reduce the risk of injury or death by limiting exposure to the intense heat, light, and energy released during an arc flash event. This is crucial in environments with high-voltage equipment.

652. The concept of grounding for electrical systems was not always a standard practice. In the early days of electricity, systems were often ungrounded, which led to a higher risk of electrical shock and equipment damage. By the mid-20th century, grounding became a standard requirement in electrical codes to ensure a safer and more reliable electrical system. Grounding provides a safe path for fault currents and helps stabilize voltage levels. What is one of the main purposes of grounding in an electrical system?
a. To improve the energy efficiency of the electrical system
b. To provide a path for fault currents to reduce the risk of shock and equipment damage
c. To enhance the performance of electrical equipment by reducing impedance

d. To ensure that all electrical devices receive the same amount of current

Answer: b. To provide a path for fault currents to reduce the risk of shock and equipment damage. Explanation: Grounding is essential in electrical systems because it provides a safe, low-resistance path for fault currents, protecting both people and equipment from electrical shock and damage.

653. The invention of the transformer in the late 19th century revolutionized the ability to transmit electricity over long distances. Transformers enabled the voltage of electricity to be stepped up for transmission and stepped down for safe use in homes and businesses. This development was critical for the widespread distribution of AC power. Modern electrical systems still rely on transformers, though modern designs are much more efficient and reliable. How does a transformer function in an electrical power distribution system?
a. It converts alternating current (AC) to direct current (DC) for use in specific applications
b. It stores electrical energy and releases it as needed to balance supply and demand
c. It changes the voltage levels of electrical power to enable efficient transmission and safe distribution
d. It monitors the frequency of the electrical system to prevent fluctuations in voltage

Answer: c. It changes the voltage levels of electrical power to enable efficient transmission and safe distribution. Explanation: Transformers are used to step up voltage for efficient long-distance transmission and step it down for safe use in homes and businesses, making them a key component of modern power distribution systems.

654. In the 19th century, early experiments with electricity led to the development of basic electrical theories, including Ohm's Law, which describes the relationship between voltage, current, and resistance in a circuit. This fundamental theory remains essential for understanding electrical systems and troubleshooting issues in circuits. Ohm's Law states that the current in a circuit is directly proportional to the voltage and inversely proportional to the resistance. What is the formula for Ohm's Law?
a. $I = V/R$
b. $V = IR$
c. $R = VI$
d. $P = IV$

Answer: a. $I = V/R$. Explanation: Ohm's Law is expressed as $I = V/R$, where I is the current in amperes, V is the voltage in volts, and R is the resistance in ohms. It is a foundational principle in electrical engineering for analyzing circuits.

655. An electrician is reading a research paper on the effectiveness of photovoltaic (PV) systems in different climate conditions. The author, Dr. Paul Gregson, holds a Ph.D. in electrical engineering and has published numerous articles on renewable energy systems. The paper cites a combination of peer-reviewed studies, government energy reports, and third-party evaluations from private companies. It includes detailed data tables from field tests in multiple locations, showing the energy output of PV systems in sunny, cloudy, and rainy environments. Based on this information, how should the electrician assess the credibility of this research paper?
a. The paper is credible because it includes peer-reviewed studies and is authored by a well-qualified expert
b. The paper lacks credibility because it includes third-party evaluations from private companies
c. The paper is credible only if all sources are government reports
d. The paper lacks credibility because it relies on climate data from different locations

Answer: a. The paper is credible because it includes peer-reviewed studies and is authored by a well-qualified expert. Explanation: The author's qualifications, use of peer-reviewed studies, and inclusion of government reports contribute to the paper's credibility. The use of third-party evaluations does not necessarily undermine the credibility if they are used alongside reliable sources.

656. An online article discusses new trends in electrical safety equipment and highlights the advantages of smart personal protective equipment (PPE). The article is published by an electrical tool manufacturer and includes quotes from the company's CEO, along with data from their in-house testing labs. The article also makes claims that the company's smart PPE outperforms other models on the market. How should an electrician evaluate the reliability of this online resource?
a. The resource is reliable because it contains data from the company's testing labs
b. The resource is unreliable because it is produced by a company with a vested interest in selling its products
c. The resource is reliable because it includes quotes from the company's CEO, an industry expert
d. The resource is unreliable because it doesn't include any peer-reviewed research

Answer: b. The resource is unreliable because it is produced by a company with a vested interest in selling its products. Explanation: Since the article is produced by a manufacturer promoting its own products, it may be biased. While it includes data from in-house testing, the lack of independent or peer-reviewed sources reduces its reliability.

657. An electrician is reviewing two documents about transformer maintenance. The first document is a peer-reviewed article published in a respected engineering journal, outlining transformer oil testing procedures. The second document is a technical guide written by a transformer manufacturer that outlines similar procedures but is not peer-reviewed. Both documents contain technical details, but the manufacturer's guide also includes promotional language encouraging the use of their specific testing kits. Which source is likely more credible?
a. The peer-reviewed article, because it has undergone rigorous academic review
b. The manufacturer's guide, because it comes from a company that specializes in transformers
c. Both sources are equally credible because they contain the same technical information
d. The manufacturer's guide, because it includes detailed product recommendations

Answer: a. The peer-reviewed article, because it has undergone rigorous academic review. Explanation: Peer-reviewed articles are more credible because they are evaluated by experts in the field for accuracy and reliability. The manufacturer's guide, while informative, may contain bias and promotional content that affects its credibility.

658. An engineer is reading a technical report on grounding systems that cites multiple sources, including articles from trade publications, government standards, and textbooks written by electrical experts. The report also includes data from case studies conducted by the engineer's firm. Which of the following sources in the report is a primary source?
a. The textbooks written by electrical experts
b. The articles from trade publications
c. The data from case studies conducted by the engineer's firm
d. The government standards referenced in the report

Answer: c. The data from case studies conducted by the engineer's firm. Explanation: The case study data generated by the engineer's firm is a primary source, as it provides original data and analysis. The other references, such as textbooks and articles, are secondary sources that interpret or compile information from other works.

659. An electrician is using an online forum to research troubleshooting techniques for variable frequency drives (VFDs). The forum includes posts from a variety of users, including industry professionals and hobbyists. One user claims to be an electrical engineer with 20 years of experience and offers a solution to a specific VFD issue, but does not provide any external references or documentation. How should the electrician assess the credibility of this forum post?
a. The post is credible because the user claims to have 20 years of experience
b. The post is not credible because the forum format is informal and lacks peer review
c. The post is credible if other users on the forum agree with the solution provided
d. The post is not credible unless the user provides references to verified sources

Answer: d. The post is not credible unless the user provides references to verified sources. Explanation: While the user claims to have extensive experience, the lack of external references or documentation reduces the post's credibility. Verified sources would provide additional support for the user's claims.

660. A company newsletter discusses a new innovation in electrical cable design, claiming that the company's patented technology will reduce energy losses by 25% compared to traditional designs. The article does not include any data from third-party testing but references the company's internal research department. How should an experienced electrician evaluate the reliability of this claim?
a. The claim is reliable because it comes from the company's internal research department
b. The claim is unreliable because it lacks data from independent, third-party testing
c. The claim is reliable if the company has previously produced similar innovations
d. The claim is unreliable because it discusses an untested technology

Answer: b. The claim is unreliable because it lacks data from independent, third-party testing. Explanation: Claims made solely on the basis of internal research are less reliable, especially without independent verification. Independent testing would help confirm the validity of the company's energy loss reduction claim.

661. A journal article presents the results of a study on electrical arc flash hazards in industrial environments. The author, a professor of electrical engineering, includes references to multiple peer-reviewed studies on arc flash incidents and standards from the Occupational Safety and Health Administration (OSHA). The article concludes with recommendations for improving workplace safety based on the study's findings. How credible is this source?
a. Highly credible due to the peer-reviewed nature of the article and the author's qualifications
b. Somewhat credible because it includes peer-reviewed sources but lacks firsthand data
c. Not credible because the author is an academic and not a practicing electrician
d. Somewhat credible because it references OSHA standards but lacks product-specific data

Answer: a. Highly credible due to the peer-reviewed nature of the article and the author's qualifications. Explanation: The combination of peer-reviewed sources, authoritative standards (OSHA), and the author's qualifications make this article highly credible. Peer review ensures that the content has been vetted by other experts in the field.

662. An electrical contractor is reading a blog post about new developments in battery storage technology. The post provides a broad overview of different types of batteries but does not include citations or references to any external research. The author of the blog is not listed, and the website is not affiliated with any known technical organizations. How should the contractor assess the credibility of this blog post?
a. The post is credible because it provides a broad overview of battery storage technology
b. The post is not credible because it lacks citations, references, and author credentials
c. The post is credible if the website frequently publishes technical content
d. The post is not credible because it discusses battery technology, which is not widely understood

Answer: b. The post is not credible because it lacks citations, references, and author credentials. Explanation: Without citations, references, or author credentials, the blog post lacks the necessary components of a reliable technical source. Its credibility is significantly reduced by these omissions.

663. A technical article discussing the installation of solar inverters cites a peer-reviewed study from a renewable energy journal, a manufacturer's installation manual, and an online product review site. Which of these sources is the least reliable in terms of providing technical accuracy?
a. The peer-reviewed study from the renewable energy journal
b. The manufacturer's installation manual
c. The online product review site
d. All sources are equally reliable

Answer: c. The online product review site. Explanation: Online product review sites typically feature subjective opinions and are not peer-reviewed or verified for technical accuracy. They are less reliable than peer-reviewed studies or manufacturer documentation, which are based on expert knowledge or product specifications.

664. An electrical engineer is evaluating two reports on the performance of a new type of underground cable insulation. The first report is a peer-reviewed study published in a scientific journal, containing laboratory test results and long-term field data. The second report is a marketing brochure from the insulation manufacturer, highlighting the benefits of the product but offering no test data. Which report should the engineer consider more credible, and why?
a. The peer-reviewed study, because it includes test results and field data
b. The marketing brochure, because it highlights the product's benefits
c. Both reports are equally credible, as they discuss the same product
d. The marketing brochure, because it is published by the manufacturer

Answer: a. The peer-reviewed study, because it includes test results and field data. Explanation: The peer-reviewed study is more credible because it includes verified test results and data, providing objective analysis. The marketing brochure, while informative, is promotional and lacks the technical rigor found in peer-reviewed research.

665. A construction company has installed a new switchgear unit provided by a manufacturer, and the switchgear comes with a five-year warranty. The warranty document states that the manufacturer will cover defects in materials and workmanship, but excludes any failures caused by improper installation, external factors such as power surges, or normal wear and tear. Additionally, the warranty specifies that any modifications made to the equipment will void the warranty. Six months after installation, the switchgear fails due to a power surge caused by a nearby lightning strike. The construction company attempts to file a warranty claim with the manufacturer for repairs. Based on the warranty language, how is the manufacturer likely to respond to the claim?
a. The manufacturer will deny the claim because the failure was caused by a power surge, which is excluded from coverage
b. The manufacturer will approve the claim because the failure occurred within the five-year warranty period
c. The manufacturer will approve the claim if the switchgear was properly installed according to their guidelines
d. The manufacturer will deny the claim due to modifications made during installation

Answer: a. The manufacturer will deny the claim because the failure was caused by a power surge, which is excluded from coverage. Explanation: The warranty specifically excludes coverage for failures caused by external factors such as power surges. Since the failure was due to a lightning-induced surge, it falls under the exclusions listed in the warranty.

666. A contractor purchases a series of industrial motors from a supplier. The product documentation includes a disclaimer stating that the supplier is not responsible for any damages resulting from improper use, including overloading, operation beyond the motor's rated capacity, or installation in unsuitable environmental conditions. The contractor installs the motors in a facility where they are regularly subjected to higher-than-rated loads for extended periods. After six months, several motors fail, and the contractor contacts the supplier to seek a refund or replacement. How is the supplier most likely to respond, based on the disclaimer?
a. The supplier will replace the motors because they failed within a reasonable period of time
b. The supplier will deny any responsibility for the motor failures due to improper use, as outlined in the disclaimer
c. The supplier will issue a partial refund for the motors but not cover installation costs
d. The supplier will offer to repair the motors at a reduced cost as a gesture of goodwill

Answer: b. The supplier will deny any responsibility for the motor failures due to improper use, as outlined in the disclaimer. Explanation: The disclaimer in the product documentation clearly states that the supplier is not liable for damages resulting from improper use, including overloading the motors. Since the motors were operated beyond their rated capacity, the supplier is not responsible for their failure.

667. A maintenance company enters into a service agreement with a client to provide regular inspections of electrical equipment. The agreement includes a liability clause stating that the maintenance company will not be held liable for any consequential damages, including lost production or profits, arising from equipment failures. The agreement also includes an indemnification provision requiring the client to indemnify the maintenance company against any third-party claims related to the service provided. After a power outage caused by equipment failure, the client sues the maintenance company for lost production. Based on the liability clause, how is the maintenance company likely to defend itself?
a. The maintenance company will argue that the indemnification provision protects it from any claims by the client
b. The maintenance company will accept liability but argue that damages should be reduced because of proper inspections
c. The maintenance company will claim that the client is responsible for third-party claims only, not direct claims

d. The maintenance company will deny liability for the client's lost production, citing the consequential damages exclusion in the contract

Answer: d. The maintenance company will deny liability for the client's lost production, citing the consequential damages exclusion in the contract. Explanation: The liability clause in the service agreement excludes consequential damages, such as lost production or profits. Therefore, the maintenance company is not liable for these damages as per the contract terms.

668. A facility manager is reviewing a warranty for a new UPS (Uninterruptible Power Supply) system. The warranty states that the manufacturer's liability is limited to repair or replacement of defective components and that the manufacturer will not be responsible for any incidental or consequential damages, including data loss, downtime, or lost revenue. Six months after installation, the UPS fails during a critical power outage, resulting in significant data loss and system downtime. The facility manager contacts the manufacturer to seek compensation for the data loss and downtime. Based on the warranty terms, what will the manufacturer's response most likely be?
a. The manufacturer will compensate the facility for both the data loss and downtime
b. The manufacturer will replace the UPS system but not compensate for the data loss or downtime
c. The manufacturer will refund the purchase price of the UPS but not cover any other damages
d. The manufacturer will offer partial compensation for the data loss but not for the downtime

Answer: b. The manufacturer will replace the UPS system but not compensate for the data loss or downtime. Explanation: The warranty limits the manufacturer's liability to repair or replacement of defective components and specifically excludes compensation for incidental or consequential damages, such as data loss or downtime.

669. An electrical contractor signs a service contract to maintain a facility's power distribution system. The contract includes an indemnification clause in which the facility owner agrees to indemnify the contractor against any claims arising from the contractor's performance of the work, except for claims resulting from the contractor's own negligence. During routine maintenance, the contractor accidentally damages a critical transformer, leading to significant power outages. The facility owner attempts to seek damages from the contractor for the cost of repairs and lost business. How will the indemnification clause likely impact the contractor's liability?
a. The contractor will be fully protected by the indemnification clause and not liable for any damages
b. The contractor will be responsible for the damages because the claim resulted from the contractor's negligence
c. The contractor will be partially liable for the damages but the indemnification clause will limit the total amount
d. The contractor will be protected from all claims because the clause does not specify a dollar limit for liability

Answer: b. The contractor will be responsible for the damages because the claim resulted from the contractor's negligence. Explanation: The indemnification clause excludes claims resulting from the contractor's own negligence, so the contractor remains liable for the damages caused by their negligent actions during the maintenance work.

670. A manufacturer's warranty for an electrical panel specifies that the warranty covers defects in materials and workmanship for three years from the date of installation. However, the warranty also includes a clause stating that it does not cover damages resulting from installation by an unlicensed contractor, improper use, or failure to follow the manufacturer's installation guidelines. A licensed contractor installs the panel correctly, but the panel fails after 18

months due to excessive exposure to moisture in the installation location, which was not recommended by the manufacturer. Based on the warranty terms, how is the manufacturer likely to respond to the warranty claim?
a. The manufacturer will replace the panel because it failed within the three-year warranty period
b. The manufacturer will deny the claim due to improper installation by an unlicensed contractor
c. The manufacturer will deny the claim due to failure to follow the installation guidelines
d. The manufacturer will repair the panel but not cover any additional costs related to the failure

Answer: c. The manufacturer will deny the claim due to failure to follow the installation guidelines. Explanation: The manufacturer's warranty excludes damages resulting from failure to follow installation guidelines. Since the panel was exposed to moisture, which was not recommended, the manufacturer is not responsible for the failure.

671. An electrical equipment rental company includes a clause in its rental agreements stating that the renter assumes all responsibility for damages to the equipment during the rental period. The agreement also includes a disclaimer that the rental company is not liable for any injuries or damages resulting from the use of the equipment, regardless of the condition in which it was provided. A renter uses a defective generator that malfunctions and causes a small fire, resulting in property damage. The renter claims the rental company should be responsible for the damages because the equipment was provided in faulty condition. Based on the rental agreement, how is the rental company most likely to respond?
a. The rental company will accept liability for the damages because the generator was defective
b. The rental company will deny liability, citing the disclaimer in the rental agreement
c. The rental company will offer partial compensation to avoid legal action
d. The rental company will repair the generator but not cover any damages to property

Answer: b. The rental company will deny liability, citing the disclaimer in the rental agreement. Explanation: The rental agreement includes a disclaimer that absolves the company of liability for damages or injuries resulting from the use of the equipment, even if it was defective. The renter assumed responsibility for any damages during the rental period.

672. A service provider's contract for maintaining electrical systems includes a section on "limitation of liability" that specifies the provider's total liability will not exceed the amount paid for the service in the past year. In the event of a service failure that causes damage to customer property, the provider will not be responsible for any indirect or consequential damages, such as lost profits or downtime. A customer experiences a significant service failure, leading to $500,000 in property damage and $1 million in lost profits. The customer paid the service provider $50,000 over the past year and now seeks full compensation. Based on the limitation of liability clause, what compensation is the customer likely to receive?
a. The customer will receive $500,000 to cover the property damage
b. The customer will receive $1 million for the lost profits only
c. The customer will receive $50,000, the maximum allowable under the contract
d. The customer will receive no compensation due to the exclusion of property damage in the contract

Answer: c. The customer will receive $50,000, the maximum allowable under the contract. Explanation: The limitation of liability clause caps the provider's total liability at the amount paid for the service in the past year, which is $50,000. The provider is not responsible for consequential damages like lost profits or downtime.

673. A utility company is reviewing an indemnification provision in a contract with a third-party contractor responsible for installing power lines. The contract specifies that the contractor will indemnify the utility company against any claims arising from accidents or damages caused by the contractor's work. However, the provision also states that the utility company must notify the contractor of any potential claims within 30 days. After an accident, the utility company waits 45 days to notify the contractor of a potential claim. The contractor disputes the claim based on the notification delay. What impact will the late notification likely have on the indemnification provision?
a. The contractor will still be required to indemnify the utility company for the full claim amount
b. The contractor will not be required to indemnify the utility company due to the late notification
c. The contractor will be required to indemnify the utility company for partial damages
d. The indemnification provision will be voided, and the utility company will be liable for all damages

Answer: b. The contractor will not be required to indemnify the utility company due to the late notification.
Explanation: The indemnification provision requires the utility company to notify the contractor within 30 days of a potential claim. Since the utility company failed to meet this requirement, the contractor is not obligated to provide indemnification.

674. A building owner signs a contract with an electrical service provider for emergency repairs. The contract includes a "force majeure" clause, which relieves both parties from liability in the event of unforeseen circumstances beyond their control, such as natural disasters, war, or labor strikes. Shortly after signing the contract, a major flood damages the electrical system, but the service provider is unable to perform the repairs because their facilities were also affected by the flood. The building owner demands compensation for the delayed repairs, arguing that the service provider should have had backup systems in place. How will the force majeure clause likely affect the provider's liability?
a. The provider will be held liable because they did not have backup systems in place
b. The provider will be excused from liability because the flood is covered under the force majeure clause
c. The provider will be required to provide partial compensation for the delays but not full damages
d. The provider will only be liable for repairs to the building owner's electrical system, not for delays

Answer: b. The provider will be excused from liability because the flood is covered under the force majeure clause.
Explanation: The force majeure clause excuses both parties from liability for events beyond their control, such as natural disasters. Since the flood qualifies as a force majeure event, the service provider is not liable for the delayed repairs.

675. A newly published section of the National Electrical Code (NEC) introduces requirements for energy storage systems (ESS) in residential installations, mandating that all ESS must be installed with overcurrent protection and disconnecting means that are "readily accessible." The code states that the disconnecting means should be located "within sight" of the energy storage system and allow for easy manual operation. It also adds that ESS installations must comply with local jurisdictional amendments that may add additional safety measures. The NEC revision does not explicitly state what constitutes "readily accessible" or "within sight," leaving interpretation to the local authority. What is the likely implication of this code change for electricians installing energy storage systems?
a. Electricians must install ESS disconnects within 5 feet of the system
b. Electricians will need to consult local building codes to determine acceptable disconnect locations
c. ESS installations are exempt from local code requirements if the NEC is followed
d. Electricians can ignore the new rule if they have installed ESS without disconnects in the past

Answer: b. Electricians will need to consult local building codes to determine acceptable disconnect locations. Explanation: The NEC leaves "readily accessible" and "within sight" open to interpretation, so electricians will need to verify with local authorities to ensure their installations meet specific local safety requirements, as these terms may vary by jurisdiction.

676. A city has adopted an amendment to its electrical code that strengthens safety requirements for commercial electrical installations in wet locations. The amendment now requires that all GFCI (Ground Fault Circuit Interrupter) outlets in such areas must be rated for industrial use and feature weatherproof covers, even if the outlets are located indoors. The amendment doesn't explicitly state whether this rule applies to outlets that are protected by upstream GFCIs. However, it does mention that the goal is to reduce the risk of electrocution in all wet or damp environments. What is the likely implication of this local amendment for electricians working in the area?
a. GFCI protection is no longer required in wet areas
b. The rule only applies to outdoor outlets and not those indoors
c. All GFCI outlets, even those upstream, need industrial ratings and weatherproof covers
d. Electricians can install standard GFCIs as long as they are located indoors

Answer: c. All GFCI outlets, even those upstream, need industrial ratings and weatherproof covers. Explanation: Since the amendment's intent is to improve safety in wet environments, it likely requires that all GFCIs in such areas meet higher safety standards, regardless of whether the protection is upstream or the outlets are indoors.

677. The Occupational Safety and Health Administration (OSHA) releases a new standard requiring that all lockout/tagout (LOTO) procedures for electrical equipment include a documented annual audit to verify compliance. The audit must be conducted by an authorized individual who is not involved in the day-to-day operation of the equipment. The regulation does not specify penalties for failing to conduct the audit but emphasizes that non-compliance may result in "serious violations" under OSHA's broader safety enforcement policies. What is the most likely consequence of failing to implement these LOTO audit requirements?
a. There will be no consequences since no penalties are explicitly listed
b. A one-time fine may be imposed, but the company can still be in compliance without the audit
c. Failure to conduct the audit could result in penalties for serious OSHA safety violations
d. The rule only applies to companies with more than 50 employees

Answer: c. Failure to conduct the audit could result in penalties for serious OSHA safety violations. Explanation: Although specific penalties are not outlined, the mention of "serious violations" implies that non-compliance could lead to penalties under OSHA's general safety enforcement, meaning it is essential to follow the audit requirement.

678. A recent code change in a major city requires that all newly installed lighting systems in commercial buildings must use "energy-efficient technology that meets or exceeds 2025 energy standards." The code does not specify what technologies qualify but states that the intent is to promote sustainability and long-term energy savings for the city. The change also mentions that all systems should be designed with the capability to integrate with future smart grid technology. What is the most likely implied requirement for electricians working in this jurisdiction?
a. Only LED lighting can be installed in commercial buildings
b. All lighting systems must be designed to connect to a smart grid in the future
c. Electricians must wait until 2025 to install new lighting systems

d. The code applies only to outdoor lighting systems

Answer: b. All lighting systems must be designed to connect to a smart grid in the future. Explanation: The code mentions future integration with smart grid technology, implying that any lighting systems installed must have the capability to interface with such systems when available, in addition to meeting current energy efficiency standards.

679. The National Fire Protection Association (NFPA) has updated its guidelines for emergency power systems in healthcare facilities. The update mandates that backup generators must be tested monthly under load for a minimum of 30 minutes and that the test results must be documented. Although the guideline mentions that compliance is strongly recommended, it does not specify whether failure to comply would result in direct penalties. However, the guideline is referenced in both federal and state healthcare facility regulations. What is the most likely implication of failing to adhere to these guidelines?
a. There will be no immediate consequences since no penalties are stated
b. Healthcare facilities may face penalties or citations from state or federal authorities for non-compliance
c. The guideline only applies to hospitals with more than 100 beds
d. The monthly testing requirement can be ignored as long as the facility performs annual tests

Answer: b. Healthcare facilities may face penalties or citations from state or federal authorities for non-compliance. Explanation: Although the NFPA does not directly impose penalties, its guidelines are incorporated into federal and state regulations, meaning failure to follow the monthly testing requirement could result in penalties under those governing bodies.

680. A state electrical code revision specifies that all residential solar photovoltaic (PV) systems must have rapid shutdown capabilities in case of an emergency. The new code also requires that any PV system components installed on or after the revision's effective date must be clearly labeled with shutdown instructions for first responders. The code does not provide a grace period for systems installed before the revision. What is the likely consequence for electricians working on existing systems after the code's effective date?
a. Existing PV systems installed before the revision must be retrofitted with rapid shutdown capabilities
b. Only new PV systems require labeling and rapid shutdown features
c. Electricians can ignore the rapid shutdown requirement for systems installed before the code revision
d. PV systems installed within the past year are exempt from the new requirements

Answer: a. Existing PV systems installed before the revision must be retrofitted with rapid shutdown capabilities. Explanation: Since the code does not provide a grace period, it likely implies that all systems, including those installed before the revision, must be brought into compliance with the new safety feature requirements.

681. A new building code amendment requires that all commercial electrical installations in high-rise buildings include arc-fault circuit interrupters (AFCIs) for all 15- and 20-amp branch circuits supplying outlets in office areas. The code states that AFCIs are required to prevent electrical fires but does not explicitly state whether retrofitting is necessary for existing buildings. The amendment, however, notes that the intent is to maximize fire prevention in all office spaces. What is the most likely implication for electricians working in existing high-rise office buildings?
a. Existing office buildings are exempt from the AFCI requirement
b. Electricians must retrofit all 15- and 20-amp circuits in office areas with AFCIs

c. The AFCI requirement only applies to newly constructed office buildings
d. AFCI installation is only required in residential portions of the building

Answer: b. Electricians must retrofit all 15- and 20-amp circuits in office areas with AFCIs. Explanation: The intent to prevent fires in all office spaces likely implies that existing buildings must also comply with the AFCI requirement, even though the code does not explicitly mention retrofitting.

682. A new code provision states that all electrical wiring in hazardous (classified) locations, such as chemical plants, must be installed using explosion-proof enclosures and conduits rated for the specific hazard class. The code specifies that materials must comply with standards set by recognized national testing laboratories but does not detail what specific materials or products must be used. The provision emphasizes that safety and preventing ignition are the highest priorities. What is the most likely implied requirement for electricians in these locations?
a. Electricians must install explosion-proof wiring in all parts of the facility
b. Electricians must consult national testing laboratories to verify material suitability
c. Electricians can install standard wiring as long as it meets the facility's internal guidelines
d. The requirement applies only to outdoor installations in hazardous locations

Answer: b. Electricians must consult national testing laboratories to verify material suitability. Explanation: Since the code refers to standards set by national testing laboratories, electricians will need to verify that the materials they install meet these specific standards to ensure compliance and safety in hazardous environments.

683. A local electrical code has been amended to require energy monitoring systems in all new commercial buildings over 10,000 square feet. These systems must measure and report real-time energy usage for lighting, HVAC, and plug loads, but the amendment does not specify which brands or types of monitoring systems are acceptable. The amendment also notes that future local regulations may mandate that the data from these systems be integrated with city-wide energy management platforms. What is the most likely implication for electricians installing these systems?
a. Electricians must ensure that the monitoring systems can be integrated with future city platforms
b. The amendment only applies to buildings over 50,000 square feet
c. Electricians must install monitoring systems that track energy usage but not in real-time
d. The amendment requires only the installation of monitoring systems for lighting loads

Answer: a. Electricians must ensure that the monitoring systems can be integrated with future city platforms. Explanation: The reference to future local regulations implies that electricians should choose systems capable of integration with city-wide platforms, even though current requirements do not mandate this level of integration.

684. A recent OSHA regulation on confined space entry in electrical vaults emphasizes that before any entry, a full atmospheric test must be conducted, including oxygen levels, explosive gases, and toxic substances. The regulation states that the atmospheric test results must be documented, but it does not specify the consequences of failing to conduct or document the test. The regulation also highlights that improper atmospheric testing could lead to serious worker injuries or fatalities. What is the most likely consequence of not conducting the required atmospheric tests before entering an electrical vault?
a. No consequence, as OSHA does not specify penalties in the regulation

b. Penalties or citations could be issued for non-compliance with OSHA safety standards
c. The rule only applies to confined spaces with known gas leaks
d. The regulation is only enforceable in facilities with more than 100 employees

Answer: b. Penalties or citations could be issued for non-compliance with OSHA safety standards. Explanation: Even though the regulation does not outline specific penalties, OSHA's enforcement policies typically apply when safety requirements are violated, meaning failure to conduct the required tests could result in fines or other penalties under general safety standards.

685. A utility company is conducting a risk assessment for a new high-voltage substation. The report outlines potential hazards, including electrical arcing and equipment failure, with each risk rated by probability and severity. The probability of an arc flash event is rated as "unlikely," with an estimated occurrence of once every 20 years. However, the severity is classified as "catastrophic," meaning such an event could result in serious injury or death to personnel, along with significant damage to equipment. The company is considering installing additional arc flash protective barriers, which would reduce the severity rating to "marginal." The cost of these barriers is significant, and the report includes a cost-benefit analysis. Based on this assessment, what is the main reason the company should consider installing the barriers?
a. The barriers will completely eliminate the possibility of an arc flash event
b. The barriers will lower the probability of an arc flash event to "impossible"
c. The barriers will reduce the severity of an arc flash event to prevent catastrophic outcomes
d. The barriers are required by law for all new substation installations, regardless of risk

Answer: c. The barriers will reduce the severity of an arc flash event to prevent catastrophic outcomes. Explanation: While the probability of an arc flash event is low, the severity is rated as catastrophic, meaning the consequences of such an event would be severe. Installing the protective barriers mitigates the risk by reducing the severity, even though it does not eliminate the probability of an arc flash.

686. A construction project is undergoing a risk assessment for the installation of a rooftop solar photovoltaic (PV) system. The project plan outlines various risks, including the potential for roof leaks caused by improper installation of PV mounting hardware. The probability of a leak is rated as "moderate," while the severity is classified as "significant," meaning a leak could cause water damage to the building's interior. The project team suggests using a more expensive mounting system that minimizes the need for roof penetrations, thereby lowering the probability of leaks. The increased cost is noted in the risk management report, but the team believes it is justified. What is the primary benefit of using the more expensive mounting system?
a. It will reduce both the probability and severity of leaks
b. It will eliminate the possibility of roof leaks altogether
c. It will lower the probability of leaks, though the severity remains significant
d. It will improve the overall efficiency of the PV system by reducing energy loss

Answer: c. It will lower the probability of leaks, though the severity remains significant. Explanation: The more expensive mounting system reduces the likelihood of roof leaks by minimizing roof penetrations, but if a leak were to occur, the severity of damage could still be significant. Therefore, the primary benefit is reducing the probability of leaks.

687. An electrical contractor is evaluating risk mitigation strategies for working on live electrical panels in a commercial building. The risk assessment identifies "electric shock" as a primary hazard, with a probability rating of "low" and a severity rating of "severe." The contractor's safety plan includes the use of personal protective equipment (PPE) such as insulated gloves, as well as insulated tools and a safety lockout/tagout procedure. The report also evaluates the costs associated with PPE and training for proper lockout/tagout procedures. Based on this analysis, which of the following is the most effective way to reduce the risk of electric shock?
a. Reducing the probability rating by providing more extensive training for workers
b. Increasing the severity rating to reflect the actual dangers of electric shock
c. Improving PPE and enforcing lockout/tagout procedures to mitigate the risk
d. Relying on the existing safety protocols and accepting the risk as low

Answer: c. Improving PPE and enforcing lockout/tagout procedures to mitigate the risk. Explanation: Using appropriate PPE and following lockout/tagout procedures are essential risk mitigation strategies for reducing both the probability and potential severity of electric shock when working on live electrical panels.

688. A large industrial plant is assessing the risk of failure for its main electrical distribution transformer. The risk assessment classifies the probability of transformer failure as "unlikely," but the severity is considered "critical" due to the potential for plant-wide power loss and expensive downtime. The plant's management is considering replacing the transformer as a preventive measure. The cost of replacement is high, but the report also highlights the cost of downtime if the transformer fails unexpectedly. What should the plant's management prioritize in its decision-making process?
a. The immediate cost savings from not replacing the transformer
b. The critical severity of a transformer failure and its impact on plant operations
c. The probability of failure being "unlikely," justifying no immediate action
d. The potential to reduce insurance premiums by replacing the transformer

Answer: b. The critical severity of a transformer failure and its impact on plant operations. Explanation: While the probability of failure is "unlikely," the severity is critical. Management should prioritize mitigating the impact of a potential transformer failure because the consequences would be severe, including significant downtime and financial losses.

689. A contractor is preparing a risk management plan for the installation of high-voltage cables in a residential area. The risk assessment identifies several hazards, including "accidental contact with live wires" during installation. The probability of such an event is rated as "low," but the severity is classified as "extreme," with the potential for fatal injuries. The contractor's plan proposes several mitigation measures, such as marking live cables clearly, using insulated tools, and scheduling work during low-traffic hours. However, these measures will increase the project cost. How should the contractor justify the additional cost of the mitigation measures?
a. The mitigation measures will reduce the probability of accidental contact to zero
b. The mitigation measures are required by local building codes, making them unavoidable
c. The mitigation measures will minimize risk and ensure worker safety, despite the low probability
d. The mitigation measures will improve the overall efficiency of the installation process

Answer: c. The mitigation measures will minimize risk and ensure worker safety, despite the low probability. Explanation: Even though the probability of accidental contact is low, the severity is extreme, meaning the consequences would be fatal. Justifying the additional cost for safety measures is essential to minimize this high-risk hazard and ensure worker safety.

690. An engineering firm is performing a cost-benefit analysis for upgrading an old electrical system in a manufacturing facility. The risk assessment identifies several hazards, including outdated circuit breakers that may fail during an overload. The probability of failure is rated as "moderate," and the severity is classified as "high" due to the potential for equipment damage and fire. Upgrading the system will significantly reduce the probability of failure, but the cost of the upgrade is high. The report recommends the upgrade but leaves the final decision to the facility's management. What is the primary benefit of proceeding with the system upgrade?
a. It will reduce both the probability and severity of equipment failure
b. It will lower the probability of failure, but the severity of a fire remains high
c. It will eliminate the need for further maintenance of the electrical system
d. It will reduce insurance premiums by improving safety compliance

Answer: b. It will lower the probability of failure, but the severity of a fire remains high. Explanation: Upgrading the electrical system will reduce the likelihood of circuit breaker failure, but if a fire were to occur, the severity would still be high. The main benefit of the upgrade is reducing the probability of failure.

691. A power utility company is conducting a hazard analysis for a major substation upgrade. The analysis identifies risks such as equipment overload and environmental damage from oil leaks in the transformers. The probability of an overload is rated as "low," while the severity is classified as "severe" due to the potential for widespread outages. Oil leaks are rated as having a "moderate" probability and "moderate" severity, with the potential for environmental contamination. The project manager recommends replacing the oil-filled transformers with newer models that use eco-friendly insulating fluids. How will replacing the transformers mitigate the identified risks?
a. It will reduce the probability of equipment overload by increasing system capacity
b. It will eliminate the risk of environmental contamination from oil leaks
c. It will lower both the probability and severity of oil leaks, while maintaining system capacity
d. It will improve the transformer efficiency but not address the overload risk

Answer: c. It will lower both the probability and severity of oil leaks, while maintaining system capacity. Explanation: Replacing oil-filled transformers with eco-friendly models reduces both the likelihood and impact of environmental contamination from leaks, while maintaining the necessary capacity to manage equipment overload risks.

692. A building manager is reviewing a risk management report for installing a backup power generator system. The report highlights the risk of fuel spills during refueling, which is rated as having a "moderate" probability and "moderate" severity due to the potential for environmental damage. The report suggests implementing mitigation measures, such as secondary containment systems and regular maintenance checks, to lower the probability of spills. These measures will increase the installation cost by 15%. Based on the cost-benefit analysis in the report, why should the manager consider implementing the mitigation measures?
a. The mitigation measures will completely eliminate the risk of fuel spills
b. The mitigation measures will reduce the probability of fuel spills and the severity of environmental damage
c. The mitigation measures will lower the cost of future generator maintenance
d. The mitigation measures are legally required for all generator installations

Answer: b. The mitigation measures will reduce the probability of fuel spills and the severity of environmental damage. Explanation: While the mitigation measures may not eliminate the risk of spills, they reduce both the probability of an event occurring and the severity of potential environmental damage, justifying the increased cost.

693. A project team is developing a risk assessment for the installation of a wind turbine near a populated area. The assessment identifies the risk of turbine blade failure, which is rated as having a "very low" probability but a "high" severity due to the potential for injury to nearby residents. The team suggests several mitigation strategies, including installing monitoring systems to detect blade defects early and placing barriers around the turbine base to protect people. However, the cost of these mitigation strategies is significant. What should be the primary consideration in deciding whether to implement the mitigation strategies?
a. The monitoring systems will completely eliminate the risk of blade failure
b. The low probability of blade failure justifies not implementing the mitigation strategies
c. The high severity of blade failure makes mitigation necessary despite the low probability
d. The mitigation strategies will increase the turbine's energy efficiency and justify the cost

Answer: c. The high severity of blade failure makes mitigation necessary despite the low probability. Explanation: Even though the probability of blade failure is very low, the potential consequences are severe. Mitigation strategies are necessary to address the high severity of the risk and ensure public safety.

694. A company is performing a risk assessment for installing new electrical equipment in a facility prone to lightning strikes. The assessment rates the probability of lightning-induced power surges as "moderate" and the severity as "critical," with the potential for extensive equipment damage and fires. The company considers installing surge protection devices (SPDs) to reduce the probability of surge damage. The cost of installing SPDs is substantial, but the report outlines the potential financial losses from unprotected equipment. What is the most important factor the company should consider when deciding whether to install SPDs?
a. The SPDs will eliminate the risk of power surges entirely
b. The critical severity of surge damage justifies the cost of installing SPDs
c. The moderate probability of surges means SPDs are not necessary
d. The company can reduce insurance premiums by installing SPDs

Answer: b. The critical severity of surge damage justifies the cost of installing SPDs. Explanation: The severity of lightning-induced power surges is critical, meaning the consequences could be devastating. Installing SPDs reduces the probability of surge damage, making the investment worthwhile despite the moderate probability of an event occurring.

695. A project proposal for a new electrical system installation in a large manufacturing facility includes a cost breakdown, showing labor, materials, and contingency costs. The proposal states that the total cost for the project is estimated at $1.2 million, with labor accounting for 45% of the total, materials for 40%, and contingency for 15%. It also notes that the contingency budget is set aside to cover any unexpected increases in material costs or additional labor. However, the materials section includes a footnote stating that material prices have fluctuated by up to 10% over the past six months. Given this, how much of the project cost could potentially be affected by material price fluctuations?

a. $540,000
b. $120,000
c. $48,000
d. $60,000

Answer: d. $48,000. Explanation: The material costs account for 40% of the total project cost, which is $480,000 (40% of $1.2 million). A 10% fluctuation in material prices would affect $48,000 (10% of $480,000). Therefore, up to $48,000 of the project cost could be impacted by material price changes.

696. An engineer is evaluating the load factor for a commercial building's electrical system. The peak load of the building is measured at 500 kW, but the average load over a year is recorded at 300 kW. The utility company uses the load factor to assess whether the electrical capacity of the building is being used efficiently. The load factor is calculated as the ratio of the average load to the peak load. What is the building's load factor, and what does it suggest about the efficiency of its electrical usage?

a. 1.67, indicating highly efficient electrical usage
b. 0.60, indicating moderately efficient electrical usage
c. 0.90, indicating near-optimal electrical usage
d. 0.50, indicating inefficient electrical usage

Answer: b. 0.60, indicating moderately efficient electrical usage. Explanation: The load factor is calculated by dividing the average load (300 kW) by the peak load (500 kW), giving a load factor of 0.60. A load factor of 0.60 suggests that the electrical system is being used moderately efficiently, but there is room for improvement in reducing peak demand or increasing average usage to better utilize the system's capacity.

697. A technical specification for a motor states that its efficiency is 92%, meaning that 92% of the electrical energy supplied to the motor is converted into mechanical energy, while the remaining 8% is lost as heat. The motor is part of a critical system that operates 24 hours a day, consuming 100 kW of power continuously. Based on this efficiency rating, how much power is being lost as heat, and what are the potential implications for the system's cooling requirements?
a. 8 kW, suggesting that the system's cooling requirements will be minimal
b. 92 kW, indicating significant power losses and high cooling requirements
c. 12 kW, suggesting moderate cooling requirements
d. 8 kW, indicating that additional cooling capacity may be needed to handle heat dissipation

Answer: d. 8 kW, indicating that additional cooling capacity may be needed to handle heat dissipation. Explanation: The motor's efficiency of 92% means that 8% of the power, or 8 kW, is lost as heat (8% of 100 kW = 8 kW). While 8 kW may seem small compared to the total power consumption, this heat is generated continuously, which could increase the system's cooling requirements, especially in a 24-hour operation.

698. A solar power installation proposal for a commercial building includes projections for energy savings over 20 years. The system is expected to generate 300,000 kWh per year, which will offset 70% of the building's annual energy consumption. The utility company charges $0.12 per kWh, and the system's installation cost is $400,000.

Based on these figures, what is the projected monetary savings in the first year, and how long will it take to recoup the installation cost?
a. $36,000 in savings, with a payback period of 11.1 years
b. $25,200 in savings, with a payback period of 15.9 years
c. $21,000 in savings, with a payback period of 19.0 years
d. $29,000 in savings, with a payback period of 13.8 years

Answer: b. $25,200 in savings, with a payback period of 15.9 years. Explanation: The system generates 300,000 kWh annually, and the utility rate is $0.12 per kWh, resulting in first-year savings of $25,200 (300,000 kWh * $0.12 = $36,000, but only 70% of this = $25,200). To recoup the $400,000 installation cost, the payback period is approximately 15.9 years ($400,000 ÷ $25,200 ≈ 15.9 years).

699. A manufacturer's datasheet for an industrial generator specifies that the acceptable operating voltage tolerance is ±5% of the nominal voltage of 480V. The generator is used to supply power to sensitive equipment that can only tolerate voltage fluctuations within ±2% of the nominal voltage. If the generator's output voltage fluctuates within its acceptable range, what is the risk to the sensitive equipment?
a. No risk, as the generator's voltage tolerance is within the equipment's range
b. Low risk, as the generator's voltage tolerance overlaps slightly with the equipment's tolerance
c. High risk, as the generator's voltage tolerance exceeds the equipment's tolerance
d. No risk, as the equipment has built-in voltage regulation

Answer: c. High risk, as the generator's voltage tolerance exceeds the equipment's tolerance. Explanation: The generator allows for a ±5% voltage fluctuation (480V ± 24V), which means the voltage could range from 456V to 504V. However, the sensitive equipment can only tolerate a ±2% fluctuation (480V ± 9.6V), meaning its acceptable range is from 470.4V to 489.6V. Therefore, there is a significant risk of damaging the equipment if the generator operates outside this narrower range.

700. A specification sheet for a commercial HVAC unit lists the unit's cooling capacity as 120,000 BTU per hour with a SEER (Seasonal Energy Efficiency Ratio) of 14. The SEER rating represents the cooling output divided by the energy consumed in watt-hours. If the unit operates for 1,000 hours in a year, how much energy will it consume, and what is the significance of the SEER rating in terms of energy efficiency?
a. The unit will consume 8,571 kWh, and the SEER rating indicates low efficiency
b. The unit will consume 12,000 kWh, and the SEER rating indicates high efficiency
c. The unit will consume 8,571 kWh, and the SEER rating indicates moderate efficiency
d. The unit will consume 10,000 kWh, and the SEER rating indicates very high efficiency

Answer: c. The unit will consume 8,571 kWh, and the SEER rating indicates moderate efficiency. Explanation: The SEER rating is 14, so for every watt-hour consumed, the unit provides 14 BTU of cooling. Over 1,000 hours, the total energy consumption is (120,000 BTU ÷ 14 SEER) * 1,000 = 8,571 kWh. A SEER of 14 is considered moderately efficient for commercial systems.

701. An electrical contractor is reviewing the specifications for a power distribution panel that will supply three-phase power to multiple machines. The panel is rated for 800A and must be de-rated by 20% due to high ambient

temperature conditions. After the de-rating is applied, what is the maximum allowable current the panel can safely handle, and what implications does this have for the contractor's load calculations?
a. 640A, meaning the contractor must reduce the load to avoid overloading the panel
b. 720A, meaning the contractor can proceed with the original load calculation
c. 680A, meaning the contractor needs to install a larger panel
d. 800A, meaning no de-rating is necessary for high temperatures

Answer: a. 640A, meaning the contractor must reduce the load to avoid overloading the panel. Explanation: A 20% de-rating means the panel's maximum allowable current is reduced to 640A (800A * 0.80). This lower current capacity requires the contractor to adjust the load calculations to ensure the panel is not overloaded.

702. A report on the electrical consumption of an industrial facility shows that the facility's demand has been steadily increasing, and the facility is now operating at 85% of its maximum capacity. The report recommends that the facility expand its electrical capacity to avoid overloading its system during peak demand periods. If the facility's total available capacity is 1,500 kW, how much of the remaining capacity is available, and what might happen if the facility does not expand its capacity?
a. 225 kW is available, and failure to expand could result in equipment shutdowns during peak times
b. 375 kW is available, and failure to expand could result in higher electricity bills
c. 225 kW is available, and failure to expand could result in reduced system efficiency
d. 150 kW is available, and failure to expand could result in overheating of electrical equipment

Answer: a. 225 kW is available, and failure to expand could result in equipment shutdowns during peak times. Explanation: At 85% of its 1,500 kW capacity, the facility is using 1,275 kW, leaving 225 kW available. Operating so close to maximum capacity could lead to equipment overloads or shutdowns during peak demand periods if the system is not expanded.

703. A technical specification for a circuit breaker lists its interrupting rating at 65,000 AIC (Amps Interrupting Capacity) and states that it is suitable for installation in systems where the available fault current does not exceed this rating. The electrician is installing the breaker in a system where the available fault current is calculated to be 70,000A. What is the most likely consequence of using this breaker, and what should the electrician do?
a. The breaker will handle the fault current without issues, so no action is needed
b. The breaker may fail to interrupt the fault current, so the electrician should select a breaker with a higher AIC rating
c. The breaker will trip at lower currents, so the system will be overly sensitive
d. The breaker's AIC rating is irrelevant if the system voltage is low

Answer: b. The breaker may fail to interrupt the fault current, so the electrician should select a breaker with a higher AIC rating. Explanation: The available fault current of 70,000A exceeds the breaker's 65,000 AIC rating, meaning the breaker may not be able to safely interrupt the fault current, leading to potential failure. The electrician should select a breaker with an AIC rating that meets or exceeds the available fault current.

704. A project manager is defending a decision to install a 1,500 kVA transformer for a new commercial building. The manager argues that based on the building's current electrical load profile and projected future expansion, the

transformer will handle all anticipated loads. However, the argument assumes that the future load will grow at a linear rate, similar to the past growth observed in the building's electrical usage. The manager does not account for potential changes in energy efficiency measures, such as the installation of LED lighting and more efficient HVAC systems, which could reduce the overall demand on the transformer. What is the unstated assumption in the project manager's argument, and how does it affect the validity of the decision?
a. The assumption is that energy efficiency improvements will offset future load growth, making the transformer size excessive
b. The assumption is that future electrical loads will continue to grow at a similar rate, potentially making the transformer undersized
c. The assumption is that the transformer will operate continuously at full capacity, requiring additional cooling systems
d. The assumption is that future building occupancy rates will remain the same, reducing the need for additional electrical capacity

Answer: b. The assumption is that future electrical loads will continue to grow at a similar rate, potentially making the transformer undersized. Explanation: The project manager assumes that electrical loads will grow in the future at the same rate as past growth, without considering that energy efficiency improvements may reduce overall demand. This could result in the transformer being larger than necessary, but more importantly, it assumes a linear growth without factoring in potential changes in energy consumption patterns.

705. A contractor is tasked with installing a backup generator for a hospital's critical systems. The contractor argues that a 1,000 kW generator is sufficient, based on the hospital's current emergency load. However, the argument does not consider the possibility that additional equipment could be added to the emergency system in the future, increasing the load. Additionally, the argument assumes that the generator will operate at 100% capacity during outages without significant derating due to environmental factors like temperature or altitude. What is the unstated assumption, and how might it impact the system's long-term reliability?
a. The assumption is that the generator will always operate at peak efficiency, which may not be realistic under actual conditions
b. The assumption is that the hospital will never expand its critical systems, leading to potential generator overload in the future
c. The assumption is that the generator can handle minor load increases, which may cause system instability during an outage
d. The assumption is that the generator's fuel supply will be continuous, preventing any interruptions during outages

Answer: a. The assumption is that the generator will always operate at peak efficiency, which may not be realistic under actual conditions. Explanation: The unstated assumption here is that the generator will not experience any performance derating, which could occur due to environmental conditions like heat or altitude. Additionally, the contractor doesn't consider future load increases that could stress the generator beyond its capacity.

706. An electrical engineer is evaluating a proposal to use copper-clad aluminum conductors in a new data center's electrical system. The engineer claims that these conductors will provide the same level of performance as solid copper conductors, but at a lower cost. The proposal focuses on the cost savings and the weight reduction benefits of copper-clad aluminum, without discussing potential issues such as increased resistance and thermal expansion differences between copper and aluminum. What unstated assumption underlies the engineer's argument, and why might it be problematic?
a. The assumption is that copper-clad aluminum conductors are always a better choice because of cost savings

b. The assumption is that the conductors will perform identically to solid copper under all load conditions, ignoring performance differences
c. The assumption is that the weight reduction will not affect the overall installation process or require special handling
d. The assumption is that the data center's load profile will never exceed the rated capacity of the copper-clad aluminum conductors

Answer: b. The assumption is that the conductors will perform identically to solid copper under all load conditions, ignoring performance differences. Explanation: The engineer's argument assumes that copper-clad aluminum will perform as well as solid copper, but it ignores important factors like increased resistance and potential thermal expansion issues, which could affect performance under high loads or varying temperatures.

707. In a presentation to upper management, an electrical supervisor advocates for delaying the replacement of aging switchgear, citing that it has operated reliably for the past 25 years without significant failure. The supervisor suggests that the switchgear can continue to function for several more years, and the expense of early replacement is unnecessary. However, the argument assumes that past performance is an indicator of future reliability and does not consider the possibility of catastrophic failure due to aging components. What is the unstated assumption, and how does it affect the risk assessment?
a. The assumption is that aging electrical equipment has a predictable failure curve, which may lead to unforeseen downtime
b. The assumption is that management will prioritize cost savings over system reliability, potentially causing longer-term issues
c. The assumption is that past reliability guarantees future performance, overlooking the risk of component failure due to age
d. The assumption is that maintenance costs will remain low even as the equipment ages, which may underestimate future expenses

Answer: c. The assumption is that past reliability guarantees future performance, overlooking the risk of component failure due to age. Explanation: The supervisor's argument assumes that because the switchgear has performed well in the past, it will continue to do so. However, this overlooks the increasing risk of failure as components age, which could result in unplanned downtime and costly repairs.

708. A manufacturing facility is planning to install a new motor control center (MCC) to support its expanded operations. The proposal recommends a standard MCC design that has worked well in other facilities. However, the proposal does not consider the facility's unique environmental conditions, including high humidity and the presence of corrosive chemicals in the air, which could affect the longevity of the MCC components. What unstated assumption is present in the proposal, and how might it impact the decision to move forward with the installation?
a. The assumption is that the environmental conditions are consistent with other facilities, leading to potential corrosion issues
b. The assumption is that the MCC design will require frequent maintenance due to the harsh environment
c. The assumption is that the expanded operations will not place additional strain on the electrical system
d. The assumption is that high humidity and corrosive chemicals will improve the efficiency of the MCC components

Answer: a. The assumption is that the environmental conditions are consistent with other facilities, leading to potential corrosion issues. Explanation: The proposal assumes that the standard MCC design will perform well in the facility without considering the specific environmental factors, such as humidity and corrosive chemicals, which could lead to corrosion and reduced equipment lifespan.

709. During a feasibility study for a solar power installation at a manufacturing plant, the consultant assumes that the current utility rates will remain stable over the next 20 years, making solar power a cost-effective alternative. The report does not account for possible fluctuations in utility rates, which could affect the overall cost savings of the solar installation. What is the unstated assumption in the consultant's argument, and how does it influence the analysis?
a. The assumption is that utility rates will increase significantly, making solar power less attractive
b. The assumption is that utility rates will remain constant, which may not reflect real-world volatility
c. The assumption is that solar power will be more efficient than grid electricity over the long term
d. The assumption is that solar panel efficiency will improve, offsetting any future increases in utility rates

Answer: b. The assumption is that utility rates will remain constant, which may not reflect real-world volatility. Explanation: The consultant's analysis assumes that utility rates will remain stable, which may not be the case. If utility rates fluctuate or decrease, the projected cost savings from solar power could be less than anticipated, affecting the feasibility of the project.

710. An industrial client is considering an upgrade to their electrical distribution system and is presented with a report that recommends using oversized conductors to handle future load growth. The report assumes that the increased cost of the oversized conductors will be offset by the future load increases. However, it does not account for the possibility that energy efficiency improvements or changes in production may reduce the overall load on the system. What is the unstated assumption, and how might it affect the client's decision?
a. The assumption is that future load growth is guaranteed, making oversized conductors necessary
b. The assumption is that energy efficiency improvements will not be implemented, leading to higher future loads
c. The assumption is that production levels will remain constant, justifying the need for oversized conductors
d. The assumption is that the conductors will improve overall system efficiency, regardless of future load growth

Answer: a. The assumption is that future load growth is guaranteed, making oversized conductors necessary. Explanation: The report assumes that the client's future load will increase, which justifies the need for oversized conductors. However, it does not consider the possibility that energy efficiency improvements or changes in production could reduce the future load, making the oversized conductors unnecessary.

711. A facilities manager is reviewing a recommendation to replace the existing lighting system with LED fixtures. The recommendation focuses on the long-term energy savings and reduced maintenance costs associated with LED lighting, but it assumes that the initial installation costs are within the facility's current budget. The report does not address the facility's current financial constraints or the possibility of phasing in the LED fixtures over time to spread out the costs. What is the unstated assumption, and how does it affect the feasibility of the recommendation?
a. The assumption is that the facility's budget will increase in the near future, allowing for the full installation
b. The assumption is that the initial installation costs are manageable, which may not align with current financial constraints
c. The assumption is that LED lighting will require less maintenance, which has not been confirmed by the facility's maintenance team

d. The assumption is that the LED fixtures will improve worker productivity, justifying the installation costs

Answer: b. The assumption is that the initial installation costs are manageable, which may not align with current financial constraints. Explanation: The recommendation assumes that the facility can afford the upfront installation costs of LED lighting, but it does not account for the possibility that the budget may be limited. This affects the feasibility of the project if the facility cannot cover the full cost of installation at once.

712. An electrical contractor is proposing a new power distribution system for a warehouse. The contractor argues that the system will improve overall reliability and reduce the frequency of outages. However, the argument assumes that the current outages are primarily caused by issues within the existing distribution system. The proposal does not investigate whether external factors, such as utility service reliability or environmental conditions, may be contributing to the outages. What is the unstated assumption, and why is it important for the contractor to address?
a. The assumption is that external factors are responsible for the outages, making the upgrade unnecessary
b. The assumption is that the new system will improve power quality, even if external factors are causing the outages
c. The assumption is that the current outages are caused by internal distribution issues, which may overlook external factors
d. The assumption is that the new system will eliminate all outages, regardless of the cause

Answer: c. The assumption is that the current outages are caused by internal distribution issues, which may overlook external factors. Explanation: The contractor assumes that the existing distribution system is responsible for the outages without fully investigating other potential causes, such as issues with the utility service. If external factors are contributing to the outages, the proposed upgrade may not fully resolve the problem.

713. A data center is evaluating the decision to add a secondary backup generator to ensure continuous operation during power outages. The recommendation assumes that the additional generator will always be available during an outage, without considering potential mechanical failures or fuel supply issues. The report also does not address the need for regular maintenance and testing of the secondary generator to ensure reliability. What is the unstated assumption in the recommendation, and how might it affect the data center's emergency preparedness?
a. The assumption is that the primary generator will fail more frequently, justifying the need for a secondary generator
b. The assumption is that fuel supply will always be available, which may not be realistic during extended outages
c. The assumption is that the secondary generator will always function as intended, ignoring potential maintenance issues
d. The assumption is that the data center's energy needs will decrease over time, reducing the strain on both generators

Answer: c. The assumption is that the secondary generator will always function as intended, ignoring potential maintenance issues. Explanation: The recommendation assumes that the secondary generator will be available whenever needed, without accounting for possible mechanical failures or the need for regular maintenance and testing. This assumption could impact the reliability of the data center's emergency power system if the generator is not properly maintained.

714. A new section of the National Electrical Code (NEC) regarding emergency lighting systems states, "If the emergency lighting system is installed in a building exceeding four stories, then the system must be equipped with a battery backup capable of providing power for a minimum of 90 minutes. However, if the system is connected to an on-site generator, then the battery backup requirement is waived, provided the generator is tested monthly and is capable of automatic startup within 10 seconds of power loss." An electrical contractor is installing an emergency lighting system in a six-story building that has an on-site generator, but the building owner does not conduct monthly generator tests. What is the most accurate interpretation of the code for this installation?
a. The contractor does not need to install a battery backup because the building has a generator
b. The contractor must install a battery backup because the generator is not tested monthly
c. The contractor can bypass both the battery backup and generator testing requirements
d. The contractor must install a generator and perform monthly tests, but no battery backup is required

Answer: b. The contractor must install a battery backup because the generator is not tested monthly. Explanation: The code specifies that the battery backup requirement is waived only if the generator is tested monthly and can start automatically within 10 seconds. Since the building owner does not conduct monthly tests, the battery backup must be installed.

715. A state electrical code includes the following provision for grounding: "If metallic water pipes are present and extend at least 10 feet into the ground, then they shall be used as the grounding electrode. However, if a plastic water service is installed, or if the metallic pipe is coated in a non-conductive material, then an alternative grounding electrode system shall be used in accordance with NEC Article 250. If multiple grounding electrodes are required, they must be bonded together." An electrician is working on a building where the water service is metallic but coated in a non-conductive material. What grounding method must be followed?
a. Use the metallic water pipe as the grounding electrode since it extends into the ground
b. Use a plastic water service as the grounding electrode
c. Install an alternative grounding system in accordance with NEC Article 250
d. No grounding electrode is required since the pipe is metallic

Answer: c. Install an alternative grounding system in accordance with NEC Article 250. Explanation: Since the metallic water pipe is coated with non-conductive material, the code requires an alternative grounding system. The condition about metallic water pipes applies only if they are uncoated and conductive.

716. A new electrical safety regulation for commercial kitchens reads: "If an appliance with a power rating of 50 amps or greater is installed, then a dedicated branch circuit shall be provided for that appliance. Additionally, if the appliance is within 6 feet of a water source, it must be protected by a ground-fault circuit interrupter (GFCI). However, if the appliance is permanently hardwired and installed more than 6 feet from a water source, then the GFCI requirement is waived." A contractor is installing a 60-amp commercial oven that is hardwired and located 5 feet from a sink. What code requirements must be followed?
a. A dedicated branch circuit must be provided, but no GFCI is required
b. A dedicated branch circuit and GFCI protection are both required
c. Only GFCI protection is required, no dedicated branch circuit is necessary
d. No additional requirements apply since the oven is hardwired

Answer: b. A dedicated branch circuit and GFCI protection are both required. Explanation: The oven exceeds 50 amps, so a dedicated branch circuit is required. Since it is within 6 feet of a water source, GFCI protection is also required, despite being hardwired.

717. An update to the electrical code states, "If a dwelling is equipped with a photovoltaic (PV) system, then it must be installed with rapid shutdown functionality in accordance with NEC 690.12. However, if the PV system is smaller than 10 kW and is located on a detached structure more than 20 feet from the main building, then the rapid shutdown requirement is optional." An electrician is installing an 8 kW PV system on a detached garage located 15 feet from the main house. What is the correct interpretation of the rapid shutdown requirement?
a. Rapid shutdown is not required since the system is under 10 kW
b. Rapid shutdown is required because the detached garage is within 20 feet of the main house
c. Rapid shutdown is optional since the system is on a detached structure
d. Rapid shutdown is required regardless of system size or location

Answer: b. Rapid shutdown is required because the detached garage is within 20 feet of the main house. Explanation: Although the system is under 10 kW, it is located within 20 feet of the main house, meaning the rapid shutdown requirement applies as specified in the code.

718. A new electrical code provision states: "If a residential service panel exceeds 200 amps, then surge protection must be installed at the main panel. In addition, if more than one sub-panel is installed, surge protection must be provided for each sub-panel as well. If the sub-panel supplies sensitive electronic equipment, the surge protection device must be rated for Type 2 protection." An electrician is installing a 250-amp service panel with one sub-panel that supplies kitchen appliances. What must the electrician install to comply with the code?
a. Surge protection at the main panel and sub-panel, with Type 2 protection for the sub-panel
b. Surge protection only at the main panel since only one sub-panel is installed
c. Surge protection only at the sub-panel since it supplies appliances
d. Surge protection at the main panel and sub-panel, but Type 2 protection is not required

Answer: a. Surge protection at the main panel and sub-panel, with Type 2 protection for the sub-panel. Explanation: The main panel exceeds 200 amps, so surge protection is required at the main panel. Since the sub-panel supplies sensitive kitchen equipment, Type 2 protection is also required.

719. An energy efficiency code for commercial buildings states, "If a building exceeds 50,000 square feet, then it must include an automated lighting control system. Additionally, if the building operates 24 hours a day, occupancy sensors must be installed in all non-essential areas to reduce energy consumption. However, if the building is primarily a data center, the occupancy sensor requirement is waived." An electrical contractor is installing a lighting system in a 60,000-square-foot data center that operates 24/7. What does the code require for the lighting control system?
a. Automated lighting control and occupancy sensors are both required
b. Only automated lighting control is required, but occupancy sensors are waived
c. Occupancy sensors are required, but automated lighting control is optional
d. No lighting control system is required since the building is a data center

Answer: b. Only automated lighting control is required, but occupancy sensors are waived. Explanation: The building exceeds 50,000 square feet, so an automated lighting control system is mandatory. However, since the building is a data center, the occupancy sensor requirement is waived.

720. The NEC includes the following provision regarding grounding conductors: "If an equipment grounding conductor is installed in a raceway with current-carrying conductors, it must be insulated or bare. However, if the raceway is installed in an area subject to corrosive conditions, then the grounding conductor must be insulated and corrosion-resistant. If no grounding conductor is installed, the raceway itself may serve as the grounding means." An electrician is installing a raceway in a chemical plant where corrosive chemicals are used. What is the correct method for grounding?
a. The raceway itself can serve as the grounding conductor, and no further action is needed
b. Install a bare equipment grounding conductor inside the raceway
c. Install an insulated, corrosion-resistant grounding conductor in the raceway
d. No grounding conductor is needed as long as the current-carrying conductors are insulated

Answer: c. Install an insulated, corrosion-resistant grounding conductor in the raceway. Explanation: Since the raceway is being installed in a corrosive environment, the code requires the grounding conductor to be insulated and corrosion-resistant.

721. A city electrical ordinance states: "If an electrical contractor installs outdoor lighting in a commercial parking lot, then all lighting must comply with the city's Dark Sky Initiative, which limits light pollution by requiring full-cutoff fixtures. However, if the parking lot is smaller than 10,000 square feet, the requirement for full-cutoff fixtures is waived, but energy-efficient lighting must still be installed." A contractor is installing lighting for a 12,000-square-foot parking lot. What does the code require for the lighting fixtures?
a. Full-cutoff fixtures must be installed to comply with the Dark Sky Initiative
b. Energy-efficient lighting must be installed, but full-cutoff fixtures are optional
c. No specific lighting requirements apply since the parking lot is larger than 10,000 square feet
d. Full-cutoff fixtures are only required if the lighting is above a certain wattage

Answer: a. Full-cutoff fixtures must be installed to comply with the Dark Sky Initiative. Explanation: Since the parking lot exceeds 10,000 square feet, the waiver for full-cutoff fixtures does not apply, meaning the lighting must comply with the Dark Sky Initiative.

722. A new electrical code for industrial facilities states, "If an arc-flash analysis indicates a potential hazard, personal protective equipment (PPE) rated for the incident energy level must be provided to all personnel working within the arc-flash boundary. Additionally, if the incident energy exceeds 12 cal/cm², flame-resistant clothing must also be worn. If the hazard is mitigated through engineering controls, the PPE requirement may be reduced." An arc-flash analysis for a facility shows an incident energy of 14 cal/cm², but the facility has installed arc-flash barriers. What is required for personnel working near the equipment?
a. Only flame-resistant clothing is required since barriers have been installed
b. No PPE is required since the barriers mitigate the hazard
c. Personnel must wear flame-resistant clothing and PPE rated for 14 cal/cm²
d. Standard PPE rated for 8 cal/cm² is sufficient due to the barriers

Answer: c. Personnel must wear flame-resistant clothing and PPE rated for 14 cal/cm². Explanation: Although the facility has installed arc-flash barriers, the incident energy exceeds 12 cal/cm², so flame-resistant clothing and PPE rated for the specific energy level are still required.

723. A municipal electrical code reads: "If solar panels are installed on a residential building, they must be grounded in accordance with NEC requirements. Additionally, if the system is larger than 5 kW, an additional grounding electrode must be installed. However, if the building already has a supplemental grounding system in place, this requirement is waived." A contractor is installing a 7 kW solar system on a home that does not have a supplemental grounding system. What does the contractor need to do to comply with the code?
a. No additional grounding electrode is required since the system is under 10 kW
b. Install an additional grounding electrode due to the system size
c. Only standard NEC grounding is required since this is a residential building
d. The code applies only to commercial solar installations

Answer: b. Install an additional grounding electrode due to the system size. Explanation: Since the system exceeds 5 kW and there is no supplemental grounding system in place, the contractor must install an additional grounding electrode to comply with the code.

724. A facility manager is reviewing the manual for a newly installed variable frequency drive (VFD) used to control a large HVAC system. The manual includes a detailed explanation of the drive's control parameters, wiring schematics, maintenance schedules, and troubleshooting steps. It also contains information on the manufacturer's history, safety certifications, and installation guidelines for various climates, although the building is located in a temperate zone. The manager is only concerned with ensuring proper operation and maintenance of the VFD. Based on this scenario, which section of the manual contains non-critical information for the manager's current needs?
a. Troubleshooting steps for common VFD faults
b. Maintenance schedules for the VFD's components
c. Manufacturer's history and climate-specific installation guidelines
d. Wiring schematics detailing how the VFD connects to the HVAC system

Answer: c. Manufacturer's history and climate-specific installation guidelines. Explanation: The manual's sections on the manufacturer's history and installation guidelines for other climates are not critical to the manager, whose primary focus is on maintaining the VFD's operation and resolving any potential faults. These details do not contribute directly to ensuring proper functionality of the system.

725. A technical report outlines the performance of several types of transformers used in industrial settings, listing efficiency ratings, cooling methods, and maintenance intervals. The report also includes a section on the visual design of the transformers and historical background on their development over the past 50 years. An electrical engineer reviewing the report is tasked with selecting a transformer that maximizes energy efficiency while requiring minimal maintenance. What information in the report is extraneous for the engineer's decision-making process?
a. Cooling methods and efficiency ratings of the transformers
b. Historical background on the development of transformer designs
c. Maintenance intervals for each type of transformer
d. Specifications comparing the energy efficiency of each transformer

Answer: b. Historical background on the development of transformer designs. Explanation: The historical background on the development of transformers is not relevant to the engineer's current task, which is focused on selecting a transformer based on performance and maintenance factors. The key data points for this decision include efficiency ratings and maintenance intervals.

726. An electrician is troubleshooting a complex control system that powers an assembly line in a manufacturing facility. The system's manual provides detailed circuit diagrams, component specifications, recommended tools for repairs, and a brief section on the history of the assembly line's design. The electrician needs to quickly locate a wiring issue that is causing intermittent power failures. Which section of the manual should the electrician prioritize to resolve the issue?
a. Component specifications to check the system's operating tolerances
b. The history of the assembly line's design to understand its evolution
c. The detailed circuit diagrams to trace the wiring and identify the fault
d. Recommended tools for repairs to ensure proper equipment is used

Answer: c. The detailed circuit diagrams to trace the wiring and identify the fault. Explanation: To locate and resolve the wiring issue, the electrician should focus on the circuit diagrams, which will help identify the specific location of the fault in the system. The other sections provide useful but non-essential information for this immediate task.

727. A maintenance supervisor is reviewing a large dataset from a predictive maintenance system monitoring a facility's motor control centers (MCCs). The dataset includes vibration readings, temperature data, and power consumption trends for each MCC. Additionally, the dataset contains general site information, such as the facility's square footage, staff schedules, and the age of unrelated equipment. The supervisor's goal is to identify motors that may be at risk of failure due to overheating. What information is critical for the supervisor's analysis?
a. Vibration readings for each MCC
b. Temperature data for each MCC
c. Staff schedules and square footage of the facility
d. The age of unrelated equipment in the facility

Answer: b. Temperature data for each MCC. Explanation: The supervisor is specifically looking for signs of overheating, making temperature data the critical information needed to assess the risk of motor failure. The other data points, while potentially useful for broader maintenance planning, are not directly relevant to this specific task.

728. A consultant is reviewing a technical document detailing the installation process for a new energy management system (EMS). The document includes step-by-step installation instructions, a list of required tools and materials, troubleshooting guides, and a lengthy introduction discussing the benefits of energy management in reducing costs and improving system efficiency. The consultant's task is to assess the installation process and ensure the system will integrate with the building's existing infrastructure. Which part of the document is extraneous for the consultant's assessment?
a. The list of required tools and materials for the EMS installation
b. The step-by-step installation instructions for the EMS
c. The introduction discussing the benefits of energy management
d. The troubleshooting guide in case of system malfunctions

Answer: c. The introduction discussing the benefits of energy management. Explanation: The introduction about the benefits of energy management is not necessary for the consultant's focus, which is on the technical aspects of installing and integrating the system. The consultant should prioritize sections related to the actual installation process.

729. An engineering team is tasked with upgrading the electrical system for a large office building. They are reviewing a technical report that provides data on power usage trends, equipment capacities, and the projected growth of the building's electrical load. The report also includes a detailed analysis of energy-saving strategies implemented in similar buildings. The team's immediate goal is to ensure that the new system can handle future electrical loads without overloading the existing infrastructure. Which section of the report is most critical for this purpose?
a. Detailed analysis of energy-saving strategies in other buildings
b. Power usage trends and projected growth of the building's electrical load
c. Equipment capacities and specifications for the current electrical system
d. Recommendations for integrating solar power into the electrical system

Answer: b. Power usage trends and projected growth of the building's electrical load. Explanation: The team's goal is to ensure that the electrical system can handle future loads, so the most critical information is the projected growth of the building's electrical load. This data will help determine the system's capacity requirements.

730. A field technician is repairing a malfunctioning automated conveyor system. The technical manual includes a detailed troubleshooting section, diagrams of the conveyor's mechanical and electrical components, and a description of the conveyor's intended applications in various industries. The technician needs to resolve a control panel error that is causing the conveyor to stop intermittently. Which section of the manual is non-essential for addressing the immediate problem?
a. Troubleshooting section addressing common control panel errors
b. Electrical component diagrams showing the conveyor's wiring
c. Mechanical component diagrams for identifying part replacements
d. Description of the conveyor's intended applications in various industries

Answer: d. Description of the conveyor's intended applications in various industries. Explanation: The technician's task is to resolve the control panel error, so the information on the conveyor's applications in various industries is irrelevant. The technician should focus on the troubleshooting section and electrical component diagrams.

731. An electrical contractor is preparing a bid for a project to install new lighting systems in a warehouse. The project documents include a specification sheet for the lighting fixtures, the building's electrical plans, a summary of local energy efficiency incentives, and a section discussing the history of lighting design. The contractor is primarily concerned with ensuring that the new system meets the warehouse's lighting needs and complies with local electrical codes. Which section of the documents is least relevant to the contractor's concerns?
a. The specification sheet for the lighting fixtures
b. The building's electrical plans for the new system
c. The summary of local energy efficiency incentives
d. The section discussing the history of lighting design

Answer: d. The section discussing the history of lighting design. Explanation: The history of lighting design is not relevant to the contractor's goal of ensuring compliance with electrical codes and meeting the warehouse's lighting requirements. The contractor should focus on the specification sheet and electrical plans.

732. A team of engineers is reviewing a troubleshooting guide for a malfunctioning wind turbine. The guide includes detailed diagnostic procedures for each turbine component, descriptions of common error codes, and a lengthy introduction on the history of wind power development. The engineers need to quickly identify the cause of a specific fault that is causing the turbine to stop generating power intermittently. Which part of the troubleshooting guide is unnecessary for the engineers' current task?
a. Diagnostic procedures for the turbine components
b. Descriptions of common error codes related to turbine performance
c. The history of wind power development
d. Steps for resolving specific fault conditions in the turbine

Answer: c. The history of wind power development. Explanation: The history of wind power development is irrelevant to the engineers' immediate need to diagnose and resolve the fault causing the turbine to malfunction. They should focus on the diagnostic procedures and error code descriptions.

733. A project manager is tasked with implementing a new power distribution system in a commercial building. The technical documentation for the system includes performance data, installation instructions, a comparison of the system with alternative technologies, and safety guidelines for installation and maintenance. The manager's primary goal is to ensure that the system is installed correctly and safely. Which section of the documentation is extraneous for the manager's current focus?
a. Performance data for the power distribution system
b. Installation instructions detailing the steps for a correct installation
c. Safety guidelines for handling the equipment during installation
d. Comparison of the system with alternative technologies

Answer: d. Comparison of the system with alternative technologies. Explanation: Since the manager's focus is on ensuring proper installation and safety, the comparison with alternative technologies is not immediately relevant. The manager should concentrate on the installation instructions and safety guidelines.

734. A project manager sends an email to the electrical contractor regarding an ongoing high-rise building installation: "As you know, we're entering the final stages of the project, and it's critical that we remain on schedule. We've received a lot of attention from upper management due to the visibility of this project. They're expecting us to complete the electrical work within the next two weeks to align with the general contractor's schedule. I trust your team will prioritize this and ensure that we avoid any further delays, as missing this deadline could cause significant issues for everyone involved." What is the underlying message the project manager is conveying to the contractor?
a. The project schedule is flexible, and minor delays will be acceptable
b. The contractor has already delayed the project, and any further delays will not be tolerated
c. The electrical work is not the main concern of upper management, so it can be deprioritized
d. The contractor is doing an excellent job, and the timeline is secondary to quality

Answer: b. The contractor has already delayed the project, and any further delays will not be tolerated. Explanation: The project manager's message emphasizes the importance of staying on schedule and implies that previous delays have already occurred. The mention of upper management's attention and the phrase "significant issues for everyone involved" subtly convey that missing the deadline could have serious consequences, signaling an underlying concern about further delays.

735. A client sends a message to the electrical team working on a major office renovation: "We're pleased with the progress so far, but there's one thing that's been on our minds. Some of our staff have raised concerns about the timeline for the next phase of installation, particularly regarding the integration of the lighting control systems. Could you provide us with an update on how you plan to address any potential scheduling conflicts? We understand these things can be complex, but we want to avoid any surprises down the line." What is the client's primary concern?
a. The quality of the installation work being done by the electrical team
b. A potential delay in the integration of the lighting control systems
c. The cost of the next phase of the electrical work
d. Whether the electrical team can meet the original project specifications

Answer: b. A potential delay in the integration of the lighting control systems. Explanation: The client's concern is subtly expressed through the mention of "scheduling conflicts" and "avoiding surprises," which suggests they are worried about potential delays, specifically in the lighting control system phase. The message reflects a focus on timeline management rather than quality or cost.

736. A senior electrician provides feedback to an apprentice working on a commercial wiring project: "You've been doing well with most of the tasks, but there's something I want to bring up before it becomes an issue. I've noticed a couple of small mistakes in your wiring connections that could lead to bigger problems down the line. It's nothing major right now, but I'd suggest paying closer attention during the final checks. If you're unsure about anything, don't hesitate to ask for guidance." What subtle warning is the senior electrician giving the apprentice?
a. The apprentice is doing excellent work and does not need improvement
b. The apprentice's mistakes are not serious and can be ignored
c. The apprentice's small mistakes could cause significant problems if not corrected
d. The apprentice is working too slowly and needs to speed up

Answer: c. The apprentice's small mistakes could cause significant problems if not corrected. Explanation: The senior electrician is subtly warning the apprentice that while the current mistakes are small, they could lead to bigger issues if not addressed. The advice to "pay closer attention" and ask for guidance implies that the apprentice's work requires improvement to avoid potential future problems.

737. A company posts a job description for a journeyman electrician position: "We're looking for a detail-oriented and self-motivated journeyman electrician to join our growing team. The ideal candidate will be comfortable working independently on both residential and commercial projects. While direct supervision will be minimal, candidates should demonstrate a proactive approach to problem-solving and take ownership of their projects. Experience in project management is a plus, as is the ability to manage time effectively under tight deadlines." What unspoken expectation is implied in this job description?

a. The journeyman will work primarily under close supervision
b. The journeyman will need to manage projects independently without much oversight
c. The job will have flexible deadlines and minimal pressure
d. The journeyman will be focused solely on residential electrical work

Answer: b. The journeyman will need to manage projects independently without much oversight. Explanation: The phrases "minimal supervision" and "take ownership of their projects" imply that the company expects the electrician to manage their work independently. The mention of project management and working under tight deadlines suggests the company is looking for someone who can handle responsibility without needing constant direction.

738. A general contractor sends a memo to all subcontractors, including the electrical team, regarding safety protocols on-site: "We've had a great track record with safety so far, and I want to keep it that way. That being said, there's been a recent uptick in minor incidents related to improper PPE usage. I'm not naming names here, but we all know how critical it is to follow these safety protocols to the letter. Please ensure your teams are adhering to all safety requirements, as we cannot afford any serious accidents on this project." What is the implied message to the electrical team in this memo?
a. The electrical team has been fully compliant with all safety protocols
b. There have been minor safety violations within the electrical team that need correction
c. The electrical team should ignore safety protocols since the violations are minor
d. The contractor is satisfied with the electrical team's safety performance and has no concerns

Answer: b. There have been minor safety violations within the electrical team that need correction. Explanation: The mention of "minor incidents" and "not naming names" implies that some teams, possibly including the electrical team, have not been fully compliant with safety protocols. The contractor is warning all teams to improve their adherence to safety rules without directly calling out specific violations.

739. An electrical supervisor sends a message to the project manager: "We've managed to stay on top of most of the project tasks, but I've noticed we're running a bit behind on getting the wiring for the HVAC systems up to code. I don't think it's anything to be overly concerned about just yet, but I wanted to make sure it was on your radar. It might be worth allocating a bit more manpower to that task over the next few days, just to avoid falling further behind." What is the supervisor subtly asking the project manager to do?
a. Ignore the wiring issue for now and focus on other tasks
b. Assign additional resources to speed up the HVAC wiring work
c. Extend the project deadline to allow for the wiring work to catch up
d. Reduce the quality checks on the wiring to save time

Answer: b. Assign additional resources to speed up the HVAC wiring work. Explanation: The supervisor is subtly indicating that the HVAC wiring is behind schedule and suggests that the project manager "allocate more manpower" to prevent further delays. The underlying message is a request for more resources to stay on track.

740. A client sends an email to the electrical contractor working on their warehouse renovation: "We're happy with the progress so far, but we've noticed that the lighting in the storage areas seems a bit dimmer than we expected based on the initial plans. We're not overly concerned at this stage, but we wanted to check whether there's any

room for adjustment as we move forward. Please advise on whether any changes are possible." What concern is the client subtly expressing?
a. They are concerned about the overall project timeline
b. They are dissatisfied with the electrical contractor's work quality
c. They are worried that the lighting design may not meet their expectations
d. They are satisfied with the lighting and just want confirmation

Answer: c. They are worried that the lighting design may not meet their expectations. Explanation: The client mentions that the lighting seems dimmer than expected, indicating a subtle concern that the lighting may not meet their needs. The request for advice on potential changes suggests they are looking for reassurance or adjustments to address this issue.

741. A senior project manager provides feedback to a junior electrician: "I've been reviewing your work on the last few projects, and overall, it's been solid. However, there are a few areas where I think you could improve, especially when it comes to time management. It's important to keep an eye on the clock and ensure that you're balancing quality with efficiency. I know you're focused on doing things right, but we also need to keep pace with the project timelines. Let's work on finding that balance moving forward." What is the project manager's primary concern?
a. The electrician is rushing through tasks without attention to detail
b. The electrician is not managing their time efficiently, causing delays
c. The electrician is taking shortcuts that affect the quality of work
d. The electrician is not following project specifications

Answer: b. The electrician is not managing their time efficiently, causing delays. Explanation: The project manager's feedback focuses on the need for better time management, indicating that while the electrician's work is good, it is taking too long. The emphasis on "balancing quality with efficiency" suggests that the electrician needs to improve in managing time without sacrificing workmanship.

742. A contractor sends a progress report to a property developer: "The electrical work is coming along as expected, but we've had a couple of days where bad weather slowed things down a bit. I don't think this will impact the final delivery date, but I wanted to give you a heads-up just in case we need to make some minor adjustments to the schedule. We're still aiming to meet the original deadline, but it's something to keep in mind if the delays start to add up." What is the contractor subtly warning the developer about?
a. The project will be delayed significantly due to the weather
b. The project may require an extension if more delays occur
c. The project is ahead of schedule and can be finished early
d. The contractor is facing labor shortages and may need additional workers

Answer: b. The project may require an extension if more delays occur. Explanation: The contractor is subtly warning the developer that while they still aim to meet the original deadline, the recent delays due to weather could result in minor adjustments to the schedule if further delays occur. The message is preparing the developer for the possibility of a timeline extension.

743. An electrical apprentice receives a performance review from their supervisor: "You've been making steady progress, and I've seen improvement in your technical skills. That being said, I've noticed that you sometimes struggle to keep up with the pace of the job site, especially when we're under tight deadlines. It's something that I believe you'll get better at with more experience, but I'd recommend focusing on speeding things up a little while still maintaining the quality of your work." What is the supervisor subtly advising the apprentice to focus on?
a. Improving technical knowledge and skill level
b. Prioritizing speed and meeting deadlines without losing quality
c. Slowing down to ensure higher quality work
d. Asking more questions about technical tasks to avoid mistakes

Answer: b. Prioritizing speed and meeting deadlines without losing quality. Explanation: The supervisor acknowledges the apprentice's technical progress but emphasizes the need to improve speed, especially under tight deadlines. The suggestion to "speed things up" while maintaining quality indicates that the supervisor wants the apprentice to work more efficiently.

744. A project engineer submits a proposal to replace the existing motor control center (MCC) in a manufacturing facility. The proposal argues that the current MCC is outdated and that replacing it will improve energy efficiency, reduce downtime, and provide better diagnostics for future troubleshooting. The engineer provides data showing that the new MCC will operate at 20% greater efficiency and offers remote monitoring capabilities. However, the proposal also assumes that the new system will not require any major modifications to the existing infrastructure. The engineer suggests that the long-term energy savings will offset the initial cost of installation within five years. Based on the structure of the argument, what is the main conclusion the engineer is trying to support?
a. The existing MCC is outdated and inefficient.
b. The new MCC will operate with 20% greater efficiency than the old one.
c. The initial installation cost will be offset by energy savings in five years.
d. Replacing the MCC will reduce downtime and improve diagnostics.

Answer: c. The initial installation cost will be offset by energy savings in five years. Explanation: The proposal's main conclusion is that the long-term energy savings will justify the initial investment within five years. The other points about efficiency and downtime serve as supporting premises for this conclusion.

745. A utility company is evaluating an engineering proposal to upgrade the transmission lines between two substations. The proposal argues that the current lines are reaching their capacity limits and that upgrading to higher voltage lines will improve transmission efficiency and prevent overloading. The engineer provides data showing that the current lines experience a 10% loss of power due to heat dissipation and resistance, while the new lines will reduce these losses to 3%. The proposal also notes that the upgrade will require minimal downtime and only a moderate increase in installation costs. What piece of evidence primarily supports the engineer's argument for upgrading the transmission lines?
a. The minimal downtime required for installation
b. The reduction of power loss from 10% to 3%
c. The moderate increase in installation costs
d. The current lines reaching capacity limits

Answer: b. The reduction of power loss from 10% to 3%. Explanation: The primary evidence supporting the argument for upgrading the transmission lines is the significant reduction in power loss, which directly improves efficiency. The other factors, such as downtime and cost, are secondary considerations.

746. An electrical contractor is troubleshooting an industrial pump control system that repeatedly trips its circuit breaker. The contractor follows a logical troubleshooting process, checking for wiring faults, inspecting the motor for signs of damage, and measuring the pump's current draw. Each step provides useful data, but the final solution involves adjusting the motor's overload settings, which had been incorrectly configured during installation. The contractor concludes that the incorrect settings were causing the system to draw excessive current under load. Which part of the troubleshooting procedure represents the conclusion of the argument?
a. Checking for wiring faults
b. Measuring the pump's current draw
c. Adjusting the motor's overload settings
d. Inspecting the motor for signs of damage

Answer: c. Adjusting the motor's overload settings. Explanation: The conclusion of the troubleshooting process is the adjustment of the overload settings, which resolves the issue. The other steps are part of the logical flow of the procedure but lead up to this final conclusion.

747. A manufacturing plant is considering implementing a new power distribution system, and the proposal argues that the current system is inefficient and prone to outages. The engineer outlines three premises: first, the current system experiences frequent power losses due to outdated equipment; second, the new system will allow for real-time monitoring and fault detection, reducing downtime; and third, the initial cost of the system will be recovered through energy savings over ten years. Which of these premises directly supports the claim that the new system will reduce outages?
a. The current system experiences frequent power losses due to outdated equipment
b. The new system will allow for real-time monitoring and fault detection
c. The initial cost of the system will be recovered through energy savings
d. The new system will require a significant initial investment

Answer: b. The new system will allow for real-time monitoring and fault detection. Explanation: The premise about real-time monitoring and fault detection directly supports the claim that the new system will reduce outages. The other premises address different aspects of the proposal, such as costs and efficiency.

748. In a case study analyzing the failure of a large power transformer, the investigation report concludes that inadequate cooling was the primary cause of the failure. The report outlines the following sequence: the transformer experienced increased load, the cooling system failed to maintain proper oil temperatures, and the winding insulation deteriorated as a result. The report also includes data showing that the transformer had been operating near its maximum capacity for extended periods. What part of the report serves as the conclusion of the argument?
a. The transformer experienced increased load
b. The winding insulation deteriorated
c. Inadequate cooling was the primary cause of the failure
d. The transformer operated near its maximum capacity

Answer: c. Inadequate cooling was the primary cause of the failure. Explanation: The report's conclusion is that inadequate cooling led to the transformer's failure. The other elements are part of the reasoning that supports this conclusion.

749. An industrial facility is evaluating a proposal to install a new generator for emergency backup power. The engineer argues that the current backup generator is undersized, resulting in frequent overloading during outages. The proposal suggests installing a larger generator with additional capacity to handle future load growth. The engineer presents data showing that the facility's power demand has increased by 15% over the past five years and is projected to continue growing. The engineer also notes that the new generator will operate more efficiently under partial load compared to the current one. What is the main conclusion of the engineer's proposal?
a. The facility's power demand has increased by 15% over the past five years
b. The current generator is undersized and frequently overloaded
c. The new generator will operate more efficiently under partial load
d. Installing a larger generator will accommodate future load growth

Answer: d. Installing a larger generator will accommodate future load growth. Explanation: The main conclusion of the proposal is that a larger generator is needed to handle the facility's increasing power demand and future growth. The other points serve as supporting premises for this conclusion.

750. A technical report justifies the installation of surge protection devices (SPDs) in a commercial building by citing recent data on lightning strikes in the area and electrical surges caused by power grid fluctuations. The report argues that without SPDs, the building's sensitive equipment is at risk of damage, which could lead to costly repairs and downtime. The report includes evidence showing that facilities with SPDs installed have experienced a 70% reduction in surge-related equipment failures. What part of the report represents the key evidence supporting the argument for installing SPDs?
a. The data on lightning strikes and power grid fluctuations
b. The evidence of a 70% reduction in surge-related equipment failures
c. The potential cost of equipment repairs and downtime
d. The sensitivity of the building's equipment to electrical surges

Answer: b. The evidence of a 70% reduction in surge-related equipment failures. Explanation: The key evidence supporting the argument for installing SPDs is the data showing a significant reduction in equipment failures in facilities with SPDs, demonstrating the effectiveness of the devices.

751. A proposal to modernize an electrical distribution system at a data center presents the following argument: the current system is more than 20 years old and does not support real-time monitoring or remote diagnostics. The engineer argues that installing a new system with advanced monitoring capabilities will improve reliability and reduce maintenance costs. Additionally, the proposal notes that the new system will allow for predictive maintenance, which can prevent failures before they occur. What is the conclusion of this argument?
a. The current system is more than 20 years old
b. The new system will improve reliability and reduce maintenance costs
c. The new system will support predictive maintenance
d. The new system includes advanced monitoring capabilities

Answer: b. The new system will improve reliability and reduce maintenance costs. Explanation: The conclusion of the argument is that installing the new system will lead to improved reliability and reduced maintenance costs. The other points are premises supporting this conclusion.

752. An electrical contractor is reviewing a proposal for installing energy-efficient LED lighting in a warehouse. The proposal argues that replacing the existing fluorescent lights with LEDs will reduce energy consumption by 50%, lowering the building's energy costs. The engineer also provides data from a similar project, showing that the LED installation paid for itself within three years through energy savings. Additionally, the proposal highlights that LED lighting has a longer lifespan and requires less maintenance than fluorescent fixtures. What part of the argument supports the cost-benefit analysis of installing LED lighting?
a. The data from a similar project showing that the installation paid for itself in three years
b. The 50% reduction in energy consumption
c. The longer lifespan and lower maintenance requirements of LED lighting
d. The energy cost savings associated with LED lighting

Answer: a. The data from a similar project showing that the installation paid for itself in three years. Explanation: The cost-benefit analysis is supported by the data from a similar project, which provides concrete evidence of how quickly the investment in LED lighting can be recouped through energy savings.

753. A plant manager is justifying the purchase of a new power monitoring system for the facility's electrical distribution network. The argument is that the current system lacks detailed analytics, which makes it difficult to pinpoint inefficiencies and areas of excessive energy consumption. The manager claims that the new system will provide granular data on energy usage, allowing for targeted improvements in operational efficiency. The proposal includes an estimate that energy costs could be reduced by 10% annually. What is the conclusion of the manager's argument?
a. The current system lacks detailed analytics
b. The new system will allow for targeted improvements in operational efficiency
c. The facility's energy costs could be reduced by 10% annually
d. The new system will provide granular data on energy usage

Answer: b. The new system will allow for targeted improvements in operational efficiency. Explanation: The conclusion of the manager's argument is that the new power monitoring system will improve operational efficiency by providing detailed data on energy usage. The other points serve as premises supporting this conclusion.

754. In an electrical training session, the instructor explains voltage and current using the analogy of water flowing through a pipe: "Think of electrical current as water flowing through a pipe, with voltage being the pressure pushing the water. The higher the voltage, the more pressure, and the faster the water (or current) moves. If you increase the size of the pipe, representing resistance, the water can flow more freely, meaning the current will increase. But if the pipe narrows, representing higher resistance, the flow of water is restricted, which reduces the current." Based on this analogy, what would increasing resistance in an electrical circuit be equivalent to in the water flow analogy?
a. Increasing the pressure in the pipe
b. Narrowing the pipe
c. Increasing the size of the pipe

d. Adding more water to the system

Answer: b. Narrowing the pipe. Explanation: In this analogy, resistance is represented by the size of the pipe. Narrowing the pipe restricts water flow, just as increasing resistance in a circuit reduces the flow of current.

755. An electrical engineer is discussing heat dissipation in conductors and compares it to a hot stovetop: "When a conductor carries current, it heats up just like a stovetop does when you turn the burner on. The more current flowing through the conductor, the hotter it becomes. If you have poor ventilation, the heat has nowhere to go, and the stovetop (or conductor) overheats. But if there's proper ventilation, the heat can dissipate into the surrounding air, preventing overheating." In this analogy, what does the ventilation represent in terms of electrical systems?
a. The amount of current flowing through the conductor
b. The thermal insulation surrounding the conductor
c. The ability of the system to dissipate heat
d. The voltage applied to the system

Answer: c. The ability of the system to dissipate heat. Explanation: Just as ventilation allows heat from a stovetop to dissipate, heat dissipation in electrical systems refers to how effectively the system can release heat to avoid overheating.

756. A senior technician is explaining the relationship between power and resistance in a circuit, using a mechanical analogy: "Imagine you're riding a bike uphill. The steeper the hill, the more resistance you're facing, which means you have to pedal harder to maintain the same speed. In a circuit, higher resistance is like a steeper hill—it requires more energy (or power) to push the current through the resistance. If you reduce the resistance, it's like flattening the hill, making it easier for the current to flow with less power." In this analogy, what does the hill represent?
a. The voltage in the circuit
b. The power supply of the circuit
c. The resistance in the circuit
d. The speed of the current

Answer: c. The resistance in the circuit. Explanation: The steeper hill represents higher resistance, requiring more power to overcome. Similarly, increased resistance in a circuit requires more energy to maintain the same current flow.

757. An instructor uses a car analogy to describe a parallel circuit: "Think of a parallel circuit like multiple roads leading to the same destination. Each road is a path for cars to travel on, and each path can handle a certain number of cars (current). If one road gets blocked, cars can still reach the destination using the other paths, just like in a parallel circuit, where current can still flow even if one path is interrupted." Based on this analogy, what does the destination represent in the context of the circuit?
a. The power source in the circuit
b. The load or device being powered in the circuit
c. The total resistance in the circuit
d. The voltage applied to the circuit

Answer: b. The load or device being powered in the circuit. Explanation: The destination in the analogy represents the load or device that receives power in the circuit. Each path (or branch) of the parallel circuit leads to this load.

758. In a discussion about voltage drop, a master electrician uses the analogy of a waterfall: "Voltage drop is like the height of a waterfall. The higher the waterfall, the more energy the water has as it falls. But as the water flows downstream, it loses some of that energy due to friction with the riverbed (resistance). Similarly, as current flows through a long wire, some voltage is 'lost' due to resistance, resulting in a voltage drop." According to this analogy, what does the riverbed represent in the electrical system?
a. The power supply of the system
b. The length and material of the wire in the circuit
c. The total current flowing through the circuit
d. The efficiency of the system

Answer: b. The length and material of the wire in the circuit. Explanation: The riverbed, which causes friction and energy loss, represents the wire in the circuit. The wire's resistance (due to its length and material) causes the voltage drop as current flows through it.

759. A trainer uses a hose analogy to explain the concept of electrical resistance: "Think of a garden hose with water flowing through it. If the hose is smooth and wide, water flows easily. But if the hose has kinks or blockages, water flow slows down, which increases resistance. Electrical resistance works the same way—the easier it is for current to flow through a conductor, the lower the resistance. If there are 'kinks' in the form of impurities or small conductors, the current flow slows down." What do the kinks or blockages in the hose represent in an electrical circuit?
a. Points of low voltage in the circuit
b. Areas of increased current flow
c. Impurities or limitations in the conductor that increase resistance
d. The total power consumed by the circuit

Answer: c. Impurities or limitations in the conductor that increase resistance. Explanation: The kinks or blockages represent factors like impurities or poor-quality conductors that increase resistance, making it harder for current to flow, just as kinks reduce water flow in a hose.

760. An engineer uses the analogy of a dam to explain capacitance: "Capacitance is like a dam holding back water. The dam can store a certain amount of water (charge), and the higher the water level (voltage), the more pressure it creates on the dam. If the dam reaches its limit, it will release the excess water downstream. Similarly, a capacitor stores electrical charge, and once it reaches its capacity, it can release the stored energy." In this analogy, what does the dam represent in the electrical circuit?
a. The resistor
b. The capacitor
c. The power source
d. The current flow

Answer: b. The capacitor. Explanation: The dam represents the capacitor, which stores electrical charge like the dam stores water. When the capacitor reaches its limit, it releases the stored energy, similar to a dam releasing water.

761. A discussion on electrical insulation compares it to thermal insulation in a house: "Just like insulation in your home keeps heat from escaping in the winter, electrical insulation prevents electricity from leaking out of a conductor. The better the insulation, the more efficient the system is because less energy is lost. If there are gaps or breaks in the insulation, it's like leaving a window open in winter—you'll lose a lot of energy." What does leaving the window open represent in an electrical system?

a. High resistance in a circuit
b. Voltage drop across a component
c. Energy loss due to poor insulation
d. Increased power supply to the system

Answer: c. Energy loss due to poor insulation. Explanation: In this analogy, leaving a window open represents gaps or faults in the electrical insulation, leading to energy loss. Just as heat escapes through an open window, electricity "leaks" through poor insulation.

762. A senior electrician explains series circuits using a train analogy: "Imagine a train with multiple cars connected in a straight line. The engine at the front is like the power source, and the train cars are like the resistors in a series circuit. If one car gets disconnected, the whole train comes to a stop because they're all linked together. Similarly, in a series circuit, if one component fails, the entire circuit stops working." According to this analogy, what does each train car represent in the electrical circuit?
a. Each train car represents the power source
b. Each train car represents a resistor or load in the circuit
c. Each train car represents the voltage in the circuit
d. Each train car represents the current in the circuit

Answer: b. Each train car represents a resistor or load in the circuit. Explanation: In the analogy, each train car represents a resistor or load in a series circuit. If one component (car) is removed, the entire circuit (train) is interrupted.

763. An instructor uses a highway analogy to explain how a fuse works: "A fuse in a circuit is like a toll booth on a highway. The toll booth limits the number of cars (current) that can pass through at one time. If too many cars try to go through at once, the toll booth will close to prevent a traffic jam. Similarly, a fuse 'blows' if too much current flows through it, stopping the current to protect the circuit." Based on this analogy, what would closing the toll booth represent in the context of a fuse?

a. Increasing the voltage to the circuit
b. Allowing more current to flow through the circuit
c. The fuse blowing and stopping the flow of current
d. Decreasing the resistance in the circuit

Answer: c. The fuse blowing and stopping the flow of current. Explanation: Closing the toll booth represents the fuse "blowing," which stops the flow of current to protect the circuit, just as the toll booth stops cars from entering the highway when there's too much traffic.

764. A solar panel manufacturer provides a specification sheet for its latest high-efficiency panels. The sheet lists the panels' power output as "up to 400 watts under standard test conditions (STC)." However, the sheet also notes that actual performance may vary depending on environmental factors such as temperature, shading, and orientation. The efficiency rating is given as 22%, but the sheet specifies that this is a "typical" value, not a minimum. A commercial installer reviewing the specification sheet is tasked with designing a system that guarantees a minimum output. Based on the qualifying language in the specifications, how should the installer approach the project to ensure reliable power output?
a. Assume that each panel will consistently generate 400 watts in most conditions
b. Design the system based on the 22% efficiency as the minimum performance standard
c. Factor in potential losses due to environmental conditions and use a lower expected output per panel
d. Ignore the environmental caveats since they will not significantly impact the panel's performance

Answer: c. Factor in potential losses due to environmental conditions and use a lower expected output per panel. Explanation: The manufacturer specifies that 400 watts is the maximum output "under standard test conditions," meaning the actual output may be lower depending on real-world factors. The 22% efficiency is described as typical, not guaranteed, so the installer should consider losses due to shading, temperature, and orientation when designing the system.

765. A datasheet for a high-performance circuit breaker lists its current rating as "up to 2000 A" and states that it operates within "typical ambient temperatures." The sheet also includes a performance guarantee, noting that the breaker will function as expected only if installed according to the manufacturer's guidelines. In the footnotes, the datasheet mentions that in environments with temperatures above 40°C, the breaker may need to be derated by 15%. An engineer reviewing the document is planning to install the breaker in a facility that regularly experiences temperatures of 45°C. How should the engineer proceed with the installation?
a. Install the breaker as rated for 2000 A, since typical ambient temperatures apply
b. Derate the breaker by 15% to accommodate the higher ambient temperature
c. Ignore the temperature footnote, as the facility's temperature rarely exceeds 45°C
d. Select a breaker rated for 2200 A to compensate for any potential temperature-related issues

Answer: b. Derate the breaker by 15% to accommodate the higher ambient temperature. Explanation: The datasheet specifies that the breaker should be derated in environments exceeding 40°C, and since the facility regularly experiences 45°C, the engineer should reduce the breaker's rating accordingly to ensure safe and reliable operation.

766. A manufacturer of industrial motors includes the following in their product specifications: "This motor is rated for continuous operation at its full load capacity of 50 HP, but under certain conditions—such as high ambient temperatures or prolonged operation above the rated voltage—performance may decrease." The manufacturer also highlights that the efficiency rating of the motor is 95%, which is labeled as "nominal" efficiency. A plant manager reviewing these specifications is considering using the motor in a high-temperature area of the plant where ambient temperatures can reach 35°C, with occasional voltage surges above the rated values. What should the plant manager consider based on the motor's specifications?
a. The motor will always operate at 95% efficiency, regardless of conditions

b. The motor will operate at its full capacity continuously, even under high temperature and voltage surge conditions
c. The motor's efficiency and performance may decrease under high temperatures and voltage surges
d. The motor will not be affected by ambient temperatures or voltage fluctuations

Answer: c. The motor's efficiency and performance may decrease under high temperatures and voltage surges. Explanation: The manufacturer clearly states that performance may decrease under conditions such as high ambient temperatures or voltage surges, which are relevant to the plant's operating environment. The "nominal" efficiency of 95% may not be maintained under these conditions.

767. A specification for an energy-efficient HVAC system claims that the unit can "reduce energy consumption by up to 30% under optimal conditions." The specification also notes that actual performance will vary based on installation, climate, and system load. The facility manager is reviewing this system for an office building located in a region with extreme seasonal temperature fluctuations and heavy cooling loads during the summer months. Based on the qualifying language in the specification, what should the facility manager consider before selecting this system?
a. The HVAC system will consistently reduce energy consumption by 30% regardless of load and climate conditions
b. The 30% energy reduction can be guaranteed under all operating conditions, including extreme weather
c. The energy savings will likely be lower during periods of heavy cooling load and extreme temperature fluctuations
d. The system's energy efficiency will be unaffected by climate and installation variables

Answer: c. The energy savings will likely be lower during periods of heavy cooling load and extreme temperature fluctuations. Explanation: The "up to 30%" energy reduction refers to optimal conditions, but the specification acknowledges that actual performance will vary depending on factors like load and climate. In a region with extreme temperature fluctuations and heavy loads, energy savings may be lower.

768. A manufacturer provides a performance guarantee for a new type of uninterruptible power supply (UPS), claiming that it will deliver "up to 100% power capacity for 30 minutes during an outage." The fine print, however, mentions that this capacity depends on battery health and operating temperature, with reduced performance in temperatures above 30°C. The manufacturer also states that regular maintenance is required to ensure battery longevity. The UPS is being considered for a server room that operates at 32°C year-round. What should the IT manager keep in mind regarding the performance guarantee?
a. The UPS will provide full power capacity for 30 minutes, regardless of the server room's temperature
b. The UPS will need regular battery replacements to maintain full capacity in higher temperatures
c. The UPS will need to be derated due to the operating temperature, which may reduce its performance time
d. The UPS's power capacity will not be affected by battery health or maintenance schedules

Answer: c. The UPS will need to be derated due to the operating temperature, which may reduce its performance time. Explanation: Since the server room operates above the specified 30°C threshold, the UPS's performance will likely be reduced. The IT manager should factor in the operating temperature when assessing the expected backup time.

769. A technical document for a new three-phase motor describes its performance as "up to 98% efficient under ideal conditions." However, the document also specifies that efficiency can drop when the motor operates under partial load or in environments where temperatures exceed 25°C. Additionally, the manufacturer advises regular

maintenance to ensure optimal performance. A contractor is reviewing this motor for use in a factory where the motor will frequently run at partial load and in temperatures up to 30°C. Based on the qualifying language in the document, what should the contractor expect?
a. The motor will maintain 98% efficiency under all load conditions
b. The motor's efficiency will decrease when operating under partial load and in higher temperatures
c. The motor's performance will be unaffected by variations in load and temperature
d. The motor will not require regular maintenance to maintain its efficiency

Answer: b. The motor's efficiency will decrease when operating under partial load and in higher temperatures. Explanation: The document specifies that the 98% efficiency rating applies under ideal conditions, and that efficiency may drop under partial loads or higher temperatures. Given the operating environment, the contractor should expect reduced efficiency.

770. A specification sheet for a new electrical panel lists its operational temperature range as "0°C to 40°C" and its maximum load capacity as "2000 A." However, the sheet also states that if the panel is operated near its maximum load for extended periods, additional cooling may be required to maintain performance, especially in temperatures above 35°C. An industrial electrician is considering this panel for a facility that often operates near 2000 A with ambient temperatures averaging 38°C. How should the electrician interpret the performance limitations of this panel?
a. The panel will operate at full capacity without additional cooling
b. The panel will need additional cooling to operate reliably near its maximum load in this temperature range
c. The panel's performance will not be affected by operating temperature or load conditions
d. The panel's load capacity can be increased by reducing the ambient temperature below 35°C

Answer: b. The panel will need additional cooling to operate reliably near its maximum load in this temperature range. Explanation: The specification sheet clearly indicates that additional cooling is required when operating near the maximum load in temperatures above 35°C. Given the facility's high load and temperature, cooling measures should be implemented.

771. A manufacturer claims that their advanced insulation material "reduces thermal losses by up to 40% compared to standard insulation materials." The product datasheet specifies that this figure is based on laboratory tests conducted under controlled conditions. It also notes that real-world performance may vary depending on installation quality and environmental factors such as humidity and temperature. A facility manager is considering using this insulation for an industrial building in a humid coastal region. Based on the qualifying language in the datasheet, what should the facility manager consider when evaluating the material's effectiveness?
a. The insulation will reduce thermal losses by exactly 40% in all environments
b. The insulation's effectiveness will likely be lower due to the humid coastal environment
c. The product will perform equally well in both controlled and real-world conditions
d. The quality of installation will not affect the insulation's performance

Answer: b. The insulation's effectiveness will likely be lower due to the humid coastal environment. Explanation: The datasheet notes that performance may vary based on environmental factors like humidity. In a humid coastal region, the insulation may not achieve the full 40% reduction in thermal losses seen in controlled laboratory conditions.

772. A wind turbine manufacturer claims that its new model can generate "up to 3 MW of power" under optimal wind conditions. The technical documentation states that the turbine's power output is directly proportional to wind speed, with the maximum output only achievable at wind speeds of 12 m/s. The documentation also indicates that in lower wind speeds, the power output will decrease significantly. An energy consultant is reviewing the turbine for use in an area where wind speeds typically average 8 m/s. What should the consultant expect in terms of the turbine's actual power output?
a. The turbine will generate 3 MW of power in typical wind conditions
b. The turbine's power output will be lower than 3 MW due to the lower average wind speed
c. The turbine's power output will not be affected by variations in wind speed
d. The turbine will consistently operate at 90% of its maximum power output, regardless of wind speed

Answer: b. The turbine's power output will be lower than 3 MW due to the lower average wind speed. Explanation: The turbine's power output depends on wind speed, and since the average wind speed in the area is below the optimal 12 m/s, the consultant should expect lower output than the maximum 3 MW.

773. A manufacturer's catalog for a new high-efficiency water heater states that it can provide "up to 20% energy savings" compared to standard models. The fine print clarifies that the savings depend on the water heater's usage patterns, the temperature of the incoming water, and the building's overall energy efficiency. A building manager is reviewing this heater for a residential complex where water demand fluctuates significantly throughout the day. How should the building manager interpret the manufacturer's energy savings claim?
a. The water heater will save 20% on energy costs regardless of usage patterns
b. The water heater's energy savings will likely vary depending on the complex's water usage and temperature patterns
c. The water heater will always perform at its peak efficiency, even during periods of high water demand
d. The water heater's energy savings will not be affected by the building's overall energy efficiency

Answer: b. The water heater's energy savings will likely vary depending on the complex's water usage and temperature patterns. Explanation: The fine print clarifies that the energy savings are dependent on factors like usage patterns and incoming water temperature, meaning the 20% savings may not be consistently achievable in real-world conditions.

774. A technical manual for installing an electrical panel includes the following instructions: "First, ensure the main breaker is in the OFF position before starting any work. Next, remove the panel cover to access the internal wiring. After removing the cover, verify that the service conductors are de-energized by using an appropriate testing device. Once you've confirmed no power is present, begin connecting the branch circuit wires to the breakers. Finally, double-check all connections and fasten the panel cover back in place." What transition word in the passage signals that one step must be completed before another can begin?
a. after
b. first
c. finally
d. next

Answer: a. after. Explanation: "After" indicates a sequence where the preceding action (removing the panel cover) must be completed before the following action (verifying de-energization) can occur. The word implies that certain steps must occur in a specific order.

775. In a proposal comparing two types of conduit for a wiring project, the following statement is made: "Although steel conduit offers greater durability in harsh environments, PVC conduit is lighter, easier to install, and less expensive. On the other hand, steel conduit provides superior protection against physical damage and is often required in industrial settings." Which transition word highlights the contrasting characteristics between steel and PVC conduit?
a. although
b. on the other hand
c. superior
d. and

Answer: b. on the other hand. Explanation: The phrase "on the other hand" is used to introduce a contrast between two options, in this case, highlighting the different advantages of steel conduit compared to PVC conduit.

776. An electrical safety guideline explains the importance of grounding: "Grounding is crucial to ensuring electrical systems are safe and reliable. Consequently, failure to properly ground equipment can result in dangerous voltage buildup, which could cause electrical shock or equipment damage. Therefore, all grounding connections must meet the requirements specified by the National Electrical Code (NEC)." What transition word signals the cause-and-effect relationship in this passage?
a. therefore
b. dangerous
c. consequently
d. failure

Answer: c. consequently. Explanation: "Consequently" indicates a cause-and-effect relationship between the failure to properly ground equipment and the resulting danger of voltage buildup, showing that one action leads to specific consequences.

777. In a discussion on power factor correction methods, a report states: "To improve power factor, either capacitors can be added to the circuit or inductive loads can be reduced. First, determine the existing power factor using a power analyzer. Then, decide which method is most appropriate based on the load characteristics. Finally, implement the chosen solution and monitor the system's performance over time to ensure the desired improvement is achieved." Which transition word or phrase indicates the final step in the process?
a. either
b. then
c. finally
d. first

Answer: c. finally. Explanation: "Finally" signals the last step in the procedure, indicating that the process has reached its conclusion and all previous steps should have been completed before moving on.

778. A technical article on alternating current (AC) and direct current (DC) systems includes the following comparison: "AC systems are typically used for long-distance power transmission because they can easily be transformed to higher or lower voltages. In contrast, DC systems are commonly used in electronic devices and battery-powered equipment due to their consistent voltage output." What transition phrase is used to introduce the contrast between AC and DC systems?
a. due to
b. in contrast
c. typically
d. because

Answer: b. in contrast. Explanation: "In contrast" introduces a comparison between AC and DC systems, highlighting their differences in applications and characteristics.

779. An instruction manual for testing circuit breakers states: "Before conducting any tests, always make sure the power is off to avoid electrical shock. Additionally, wear appropriate personal protective equipment (PPE) to ensure your safety during testing. After completing the initial tests, record the results and compare them to the manufacturer's specifications." Which transition word indicates an additional requirement for safety during testing?
a. before
b. additionally
c. after
d. always

Answer: b. additionally. Explanation: "Additionally" introduces an extra safety requirement—wearing PPE—on top of the initial instruction to turn off the power, adding further emphasis on safety.

780. A code review document outlines the reasons for upgrading an outdated electrical system: "The current system is no longer compliant with the latest NEC standards. Furthermore, its capacity is insufficient to handle the increased load demands, which could lead to frequent tripping of breakers and potential equipment failures. Therefore, upgrading the system is essential to ensure compliance and reliability." What transition word introduces an additional reason for upgrading the system?
a. insufficient
b. furthermore
c. therefore
d. potential

Answer: b. furthermore. Explanation: "Furthermore" adds another reason for upgrading the system (inadequate capacity), building on the previous reason of non-compliance with NEC standards.

781. A training module on electrical load calculations contains the following explanation: "Calculating the total load on a circuit is essential for ensuring that it operates safely and efficiently. First, identify all the devices connected to the circuit and their individual power ratings. Next, sum the power ratings to determine the total load. If the total

exceeds the circuit's capacity, you must redistribute the load or upgrade the circuit to prevent overload." What transition word indicates the introduction of a necessary condition to prevent overload?
a. if
b. first
c. next
d. prevent

Answer: a. if. Explanation: "If" introduces a conditional statement that outlines a specific requirement (redistributing the load or upgrading the circuit) only when the total load exceeds the circuit's capacity.

782. In a troubleshooting guide for industrial motors, the following advice is given: "If the motor fails to start, check the power supply and ensure that all connections are secure. If these are functioning properly, examine the motor windings for signs of damage. Additionally, verify that the thermal overload protection has not been triggered. Only after all these checks have been completed should you attempt to restart the motor." What transition word signals the inclusion of another troubleshooting step?
a. only
b. additionally
c. if
d. verify

Answer: b. additionally. Explanation: "Additionally" signals that another step—verifying the thermal overload protection—should be included in the troubleshooting process, expanding on the previously listed steps.

783. A project plan for upgrading a facility's electrical distribution system includes the following sequence: "To begin, assess the current load capacity of the facility's transformers. Then, determine the peak load demand over the past year to identify any discrepancies. Once this data has been gathered, evaluate the need for additional transformers or higher-rated equipment. Finally, present your findings and recommendations to the project manager for approval." Which transition word indicates that the evaluation should occur only after data has been collected?
a. to begin
b. once
c. finally
d. then

Answer: b. once. Explanation: "Once" introduces a condition that must be fulfilled before moving on to the next step, indicating that the evaluation of equipment needs should only happen after the necessary data has been collected.

784. A recent inspection report for a manufacturing facility states that the electrical distribution system is "sufficient for current operations but may benefit from further evaluation under increased demand." The report also notes that "certain components of the system have shown signs of wear consistent with age" and that "proactive attention to these areas is advised to ensure continued reliable performance." The plant manager is considering whether to schedule a full electrical audit based on this report. How should the manager interpret the language in the report?
a. The system is operating perfectly, and no immediate action is necessary.
b. The system is likely to fail soon and requires immediate replacement.

c. The system is adequate for now, but upgrades or repairs may be needed if demand increases or aging components deteriorate further.
d. The report is overly cautious, and the manager can delay any action for several years.

Answer: c. The system is adequate for now, but upgrades or repairs may be needed if demand increases or aging components deteriorate further. Explanation: The report uses softened language to indicate potential issues without outright stating that immediate action is required. Phrases like "may benefit from further evaluation" and "proactive attention is advised" imply that the system could face problems in the future, especially under increased load or as aging components continue to degrade.

785. A performance evaluation for an apprentice electrician includes the following statement: "While the apprentice consistently completes assigned tasks, there is room for growth in terms of independent decision-making and initiative in troubleshooting." The supervisor also notes that "communication with senior staff is generally effective, though there is an opportunity to improve responsiveness under tight deadlines." How should the apprentice interpret this feedback?
a. The apprentice is meeting all expectations with no significant areas for improvement.
b. The apprentice needs to work on being more proactive and responsive, especially in fast-paced situations.
c. The feedback suggests the apprentice is not suited for independent work and should avoid troubleshooting.
d. The feedback is purely positive, and the apprentice should continue working as before.

Answer: b. The apprentice needs to work on being more proactive and responsive, especially in fast-paced situations. Explanation: The phrases "room for growth" and "opportunity to improve" indicate areas where the apprentice could develop further, particularly in taking initiative during troubleshooting and improving responsiveness under tight deadlines. These are indirect suggestions for improvement rather than outright criticisms.

786. A safety bulletin issued by an electrical equipment manufacturer states that "routine maintenance of circuit breakers should be conducted to ensure optimal performance." It also mentions that "delaying maintenance could potentially lead to reduced system reliability over time." The bulletin does not mention any specific risks of failure. How should a facility's safety officer interpret this language?
a. The equipment will function reliably without regular maintenance.
b. The system is prone to immediate failure if maintenance is delayed.
c. Delaying maintenance increases the risk of system issues, but the problem is not urgent.
d. There are no significant risks, and the maintenance recommendations can be ignored.

Answer: c. Delaying maintenance increases the risk of system issues, but the problem is not urgent. Explanation: The bulletin uses indirect language such as "potentially" and "reduced reliability over time," indicating that while regular maintenance is important for long-term system health, it does not suggest an immediate risk of failure. The safety officer should recognize this as a subtle warning to ensure routine maintenance.

787. In a client communication regarding a project delay, the contractor writes, "We are working diligently to meet the revised schedule, and we appreciate your understanding as we navigate these unforeseen challenges." The email also states that "certain external factors beyond our control have contributed to the timeline adjustment." How should the client interpret this language?

a. The contractor is likely to miss the revised deadline as well.
b. The contractor is blaming the client for the delays.
c. The contractor is experiencing delays due to factors they cannot control but is still committed to completing the project.
d. The project is on track, and no further delays are expected.

Answer: c. The contractor is experiencing delays due to factors they cannot control but is still committed to completing the project. Explanation: Phrases like "external factors beyond our control" and "appreciate your understanding" suggest that while the contractor is dealing with delays, they are committed to the revised schedule. This is a diplomatic way of explaining a problem without assigning blame or creating alarm.

788. A technical inspection report for an electrical installation notes that "while the overall system performance meets industry standards, there are areas where efficiency could be improved." The report also states that "certain sections of the wiring exhibit characteristics that may warrant further review in the next maintenance cycle." How should the facility manager interpret this report?
a. The system is functioning well and no action is required in the near future.
b. The system has serious performance issues that require immediate attention.
c. The system is operating within acceptable limits, but there are areas that may need improvement or review during future maintenance.
d. The inspection was inconclusive, and another inspection is needed immediately.

Answer: c. The system is operating within acceptable limits, but there are areas that may need improvement or review during future maintenance. Explanation: The language "meets industry standards" and "may warrant further review" suggests that the system is performing adequately for now, but there are areas that could benefit from improvements during future maintenance. This is indirect language indicating non-urgent concerns.

789. In an inspection report for a newly installed industrial transformer, the inspector notes that "the installation conforms to the manufacturer's guidelines, though adjustments to cable routing could enhance long-term reliability." The report also mentions that "no immediate issues were detected, though periodic monitoring is advised to ensure continued optimal performance." How should the project engineer interpret this report?
a. The installation has major issues that require immediate correction.
b. The installation is fully compliant, but minor adjustments could improve reliability over time.
c. The transformer is likely to fail unless significant changes are made.
d. The report indicates that future inspections are unnecessary.

Answer: b. The installation is fully compliant, but minor adjustments could improve reliability over time. Explanation: Phrases like "conforms to the manufacturer's guidelines" and "enhance long-term reliability" indicate that the installation is acceptable but could benefit from minor improvements to ensure optimal long-term performance. This is a suggestion for enhancement, not a warning of imminent failure.

790. A client receives a progress update from a contractor, stating that "substantial progress has been made on the project, and we are confident that the remaining work can be completed in a timely manner." The update also

mentions that "a few minor adjustments to the schedule have been made to accommodate unforeseen developments." How should the client interpret this update?
a. The project is significantly delayed, and more major adjustments are likely needed.
b. The project is progressing well, but there have been minor delays that the contractor has addressed.
c. The project is nearly finished and will be completed ahead of schedule.
d. The contractor is struggling to keep up and the project is likely to fall behind.

Answer: b. The project is progressing well, but there have been minor delays that the contractor has addressed. Explanation: The language "substantial progress" and "minor adjustments" suggests that the project is moving forward but has encountered small delays, which the contractor believes are manageable. The overall tone remains positive, indicating confidence in timely completion.

791. A performance review for a journeyman electrician includes the statement: "The electrician demonstrates a strong understanding of electrical systems and consistently performs tasks to standard. However, there is room for improvement in time management during larger, more complex projects." The review also notes that "feedback from colleagues indicates a willingness to assist others, though more assertiveness in decision-making could be beneficial." How should the journeyman interpret this feedback?
a. The electrician is failing to meet expectations and needs to improve in all areas.
b. The electrician performs well but needs to focus on improving time management and decision-making.
c. The feedback is negative, and the electrician should reconsider their approach to teamwork.
d. The review is entirely positive, and no improvements are necessary.

Answer: b. The electrician performs well but needs to focus on improving time management and decision-making. Explanation: The language "room for improvement" and "more assertiveness could be beneficial" points to specific areas where the electrician can grow, while the overall tone is supportive and acknowledges competence in other areas.

792. In a safety bulletin for a construction site, the safety officer writes, "Personnel are reminded to consistently wear PPE, as there have been instances of non-compliance observed during routine checks. While no incidents have occurred as a result, it is critical to maintain vigilance to prevent future risks." The bulletin also states, "continued non-compliance may necessitate further corrective action." How should site workers interpret this bulletin?
a. The current level of PPE usage is acceptable, and no changes are needed.
b. There have been several safety incidents caused by non-compliance with PPE requirements.
c. PPE compliance is not being enforced and will not be until an incident occurs.
d. Non-compliance with PPE requirements has been observed, and stricter enforcement may follow if the issue persists.

Answer: d. Non-compliance with PPE requirements has been observed, and stricter enforcement may follow if the issue persists. Explanation: The bulletin uses indirect language to point out that non-compliance has been observed, and although no incidents have occurred yet, the tone suggests that stricter measures may be implemented if the issue continues.

793. A utility company sends an email to a customer regarding upcoming maintenance, stating that "scheduled maintenance will result in a brief disruption of service, expected to last no longer than 30 minutes." The email also notes that "while every effort will be made to minimize inconvenience, we appreciate your patience as we complete these necessary upgrades." How should the customer interpret this message?
a. The service disruption will likely last much longer than 30 minutes.
b. The utility company is uncertain about the length of the disruption and may extend it if needed.
c. The disruption will be brief, but the company acknowledges there may be minor inconveniences.
d. The maintenance is optional, and the customer can opt out of the service disruption.

Answer: c. The disruption will be brief, but the company acknowledges there may be minor inconveniences.
Explanation: The language "brief disruption" and "no longer than 30 minutes" suggests the company expects a short interruption. Phrases like "appreciate your patience" indicate that minor inconveniences could occur, but the overall message is intended to reassure the customer that the disruption will be minimal.

794. A technical guide on transformer maintenance includes the following paragraph: "Transformer oil testing is critical for ensuring the longevity and performance of the equipment. The oil serves as both a coolant and an insulator, making it a key component of the system. Over time, contaminants such as moisture, acids, and sludge can accumulate in the oil, reducing its effectiveness. Regular testing helps to detect these contaminants before they cause significant damage. In addition, oil testing can reveal the presence of gases, which are often indicators of internal arcing or overheating. By monitoring these factors, technicians can schedule maintenance before costly failures occur." What is the topic sentence of this paragraph?
a. Transformer oil testing is critical for ensuring the longevity and performance of the equipment.
b. Regular testing helps to detect these contaminants before they cause significant damage.
c. The oil serves as both a coolant and an insulator, making it a key component of the system.
d. In addition, oil testing can reveal the presence of gases, which are often indicators of internal arcing or overheating.

Answer: a. Transformer oil testing is critical for ensuring the longevity and performance of the equipment.
Explanation: The topic sentence introduces the main idea of the paragraph—why transformer oil testing is essential. The rest of the paragraph supports this statement with details about oil functions and contaminants.

795. An excerpt from a manual on electrical safety procedures reads: "Before beginning any work on energized equipment, technicians must first verify that proper lockout/tagout (LOTO) procedures are in place. This involves isolating the energy source and applying locks to prevent accidental re-energization. Additionally, every team member working on the system must apply their own lock and tag to ensure that no one is exposed to electrical hazards. Once the equipment has been locked out, the technician should test the system to verify that it is fully de-energized. Only after confirming that the system is safe should work proceed." What is the concluding statement of this paragraph?
a. Technicians must first verify that proper lockout/tagout (LOTO) procedures are in place.
b. Once the equipment has been locked out, the technician should test the system.
c. Only after confirming that the system is safe should work proceed.
d. Every team member working on the system must apply their own lock and tag.

Answer: c. Only after confirming that the system is safe should work proceed. Explanation: The concluding statement wraps up the paragraph by emphasizing the importance of verifying safety before beginning work, reinforcing the sequence of steps described earlier.

796. A technical paragraph on grounding systems explains: "Grounding systems are designed to protect both personnel and equipment from electrical faults. A properly grounded system ensures that excess current from a fault condition is directed safely to the earth, preventing injury or damage. Grounding also stabilizes the voltage levels during normal operation, which helps protect sensitive equipment from voltage fluctuations. Without effective grounding, electrical faults can lead to dangerous conditions such as electrical shock, equipment failure, or fire." Which sentence provides supporting details about how grounding protects sensitive equipment?
a. Grounding systems are designed to protect both personnel and equipment from electrical faults.
b. A properly grounded system ensures that excess current from a fault condition is directed safely to the earth.
c. Grounding also stabilizes the voltage levels during normal operation, which helps protect sensitive equipment from voltage fluctuations.
d. Without effective grounding, electrical faults can lead to dangerous conditions such as electrical shock, equipment failure, or fire.

Answer: c. Grounding also stabilizes the voltage levels during normal operation, which helps protect sensitive equipment from voltage fluctuations. Explanation: This sentence specifically explains how grounding protects sensitive equipment, adding depth to the explanation of grounding's benefits beyond safety from faults.

797. An instructional document about conduit installations includes the following text: "The selection of conduit material depends on the environment in which it will be installed. For example, rigid metal conduit (RMC) is ideal for industrial settings where physical protection is necessary. On the other hand, PVC conduit is commonly used in environments where corrosion resistance is a higher priority. Additionally, flexible metal conduit (FMC) can be used in areas where vibration or movement may affect the installation. The key to choosing the right conduit is to understand the environmental challenges and select a material that can withstand them." Which sentence serves as the topic sentence of the paragraph?
a. The selection of conduit material depends on the environment in which it will be installed.
b. Rigid metal conduit (RMC) is ideal for industrial settings where physical protection is necessary.
c. PVC conduit is commonly used in environments where corrosion resistance is a higher priority.
d. The key to choosing the right conduit is to understand the environmental challenges.

Answer: a. The selection of conduit material depends on the environment in which it will be installed. Explanation: This sentence introduces the main idea that the choice of conduit material varies based on the installation environment. The rest of the paragraph provides examples and supporting details.

798. An article on electrical system design states: "When designing an electrical system, load calculations are critical for ensuring that the system can handle the anticipated electrical demand. First, identify the types of equipment that will be powered by the system. Next, determine the total wattage required by adding the individual power ratings of each device. Then, factor in a safety margin to account for potential future load increases or equipment upgrades. Finally, compare the calculated load with the system's rated capacity to ensure it meets the requirements." How does the paragraph maintain cohesion?
a. By explaining the role of each piece of equipment in the system
b. By listing the steps in a logical sequence for performing load calculations

c. By focusing on the safety margin and its impact on system design
d. By comparing different types of electrical equipment

Answer: b. By listing the steps in a logical sequence for performing load calculations. Explanation: The paragraph maintains cohesion by clearly organizing the steps involved in calculating an electrical system's load, ensuring a logical flow of information from one point to the next.

799. In a section on the importance of insulation in electrical systems, the following passage is given: "Electrical insulation prevents the flow of unwanted current and helps maintain the integrity of the system. Insulating materials, such as rubber or plastic, are selected based on their resistance to heat and electrical conductivity. Additionally, proper insulation reduces the risk of electrical shock and minimizes energy loss in the system. The effectiveness of insulation depends on both the quality of the material and the installation process." What role does the last sentence play in the paragraph?
a. It introduces a new idea about insulation material.
b. It summarizes the key factors that influence the effectiveness of insulation.
c. It provides a specific example of insulation used in electrical systems.
d. It contrasts insulation materials with conductors.

Answer: b. It summarizes the key factors that influence the effectiveness of insulation. Explanation: The final sentence ties together the discussion of insulation by summarizing that both material quality and installation affect its effectiveness, reinforcing the main points of the paragraph.

800. A section of an electrical safety guide reads: "Lockout/tagout procedures are essential for preventing accidents during maintenance. These procedures ensure that energy sources are isolated and cannot be accidentally re-energized. Workers must be trained to apply and remove locks and tags in accordance with company policies. Regular audits of lockout/tagout practices should be conducted to ensure compliance and identify areas for improvement. Non-compliance with lockout/tagout procedures can lead to severe penalties, including fines or injuries." Which sentence provides a concluding statement summarizing the importance of the procedure?
a. Workers must be trained to apply and remove locks and tags in accordance with company policies.
b. Non-compliance with lockout/tagout procedures can lead to severe penalties, including fines or injuries.
c. Regular audits of lockout/tagout practices should be conducted to ensure compliance.
d. These procedures ensure that energy sources are isolated and cannot be accidentally re-energized.

Answer: b. Non-compliance with lockout/tagout procedures can lead to severe penalties, including fines or injuries. Explanation: This sentence concludes the paragraph by emphasizing the serious consequences of failing to follow lockout/tagout procedures, reinforcing their importance.

801. In an article about surge protection devices (SPDs), the following is written: "SPDs are designed to protect electrical systems from transient voltage spikes. These devices work by diverting excess voltage away from sensitive components and into the grounding system. They are most commonly used in areas where lightning strikes or power surges are a regular occurrence. It's important to install SPDs at key points in the system to provide comprehensive protection, especially where critical equipment is involved." Which sentence contains a supporting detail that explains how SPDs work?

a. SPDs are designed to protect electrical systems from transient voltage spikes.
b. They are most commonly used in areas where lightning strikes or power surges are a regular occurrence.
c. These devices work by diverting excess voltage away from sensitive components and into the grounding system.
d. It's important to install SPDs at key points in the system to provide comprehensive protection.

Answer: c. These devices work by diverting excess voltage away from sensitive components and into the grounding system. Explanation: This sentence provides a specific explanation of how surge protection devices operate, supporting the general statement that they protect against voltage spikes.

802. An engineering report on electrical distribution efficiency reads: "Distribution transformers play a vital role in reducing energy losses in electrical systems. By stepping down voltage levels, they ensure that power is delivered safely to homes and businesses. High-efficiency transformers can significantly reduce energy waste, especially in large-scale installations. Furthermore, they contribute to lower operating costs and improved system reliability. With ongoing advances in transformer technology, electrical systems are becoming more efficient and environmentally friendly." Which sentence signals the introduction of an additional benefit of high-efficiency transformers?
a. High-efficiency transformers can significantly reduce energy waste.
b. Distribution transformers play a vital role in reducing energy losses.
c. By stepping down voltage levels, they ensure that power is delivered safely.
d. Furthermore, they contribute to lower operating costs and improved system reliability.

Answer: d. Furthermore, they contribute to lower operating costs and improved system reliability. Explanation: The word "furthermore" introduces an additional point, highlighting another benefit of high-efficiency transformers—lower operating costs and better reliability—after the initial discussion of energy waste reduction.

803. A manual on electrical grounding systems includes the following explanation: "Ground rods are the most common method for grounding electrical systems. These rods are typically made of copper or steel and are driven deep into the earth to provide a low-resistance path for fault currents. The effectiveness of a grounding system depends on soil conditions, the depth of the ground rod, and the material used. In areas with rocky or dry soil, alternative methods such as ground plates or chemical electrodes may be necessary to achieve proper grounding." Which sentence introduces a potential limitation of standard grounding methods?
a. Ground rods are the most common method for grounding electrical systems.
b. These rods are typically made of copper or steel and are driven deep into the earth.
c. The effectiveness of a grounding system depends on soil conditions.
d. In areas with rocky or dry soil, alternative methods may be necessary.

Answer: d. In areas with rocky or dry soil, alternative methods may be necessary. Explanation: This sentence introduces a limitation of using standard ground rods by explaining that in certain soil conditions, other methods may be required for effective grounding.

804. A manufacturing plant receives a recommendation from an electrical engineering firm to replace its existing transformers with higher-efficiency models. The recommendation states that these new transformers will reduce energy losses by 10% and result in long-term energy cost savings. However, the report also mentions that installation will require modifications to the existing switchgear and may involve a temporary shutdown of part of the facility. The

firm projects that the energy savings will offset the cost of the new transformers within eight years. The plant's management must decide whether to move forward with the recommendation. Based on the implications of the recommendation, what is the most significant unstated impact the management should consider?
a. The initial cost of the transformers may exceed the projected energy savings
b. The temporary shutdown could disrupt production and lead to additional costs
c. The facility's existing transformers are functioning properly and do not need to be replaced
d. The new transformers will likely require more frequent maintenance than the current models

Answer: b. The temporary shutdown could disrupt production and lead to additional costs. Explanation: While the recommendation focuses on energy savings, the report also mentions that part of the facility may need to be shut down during installation. This could result in production downtime, which would have a financial impact that should be considered alongside the long-term energy savings.

805. A large commercial building is advised to upgrade its HVAC control system to a more energy-efficient model that includes automated scheduling and remote monitoring. The recommendation notes that the new system will reduce energy consumption by 15% during peak usage times and improve overall system reliability. However, the system requires regular software updates and periodic recalibration to maintain optimal performance. What is the long-term implication of this recommendation that the building manager should keep in mind?
a. The new system will require more frequent repairs compared to the current system
b. The software updates and recalibrations will increase operational complexity and maintenance costs
c. The building will experience immediate energy savings with no additional costs
d. The new system will reduce the building's cooling capacity during summer months

Answer: b. The software updates and recalibrations will increase operational complexity and maintenance costs. Explanation: While the recommendation focuses on energy savings and reliability, the long-term implication is that the new system requires ongoing software updates and recalibrations, which could increase maintenance costs and operational complexity.

806. An energy audit for a manufacturing plant suggests that replacing standard lighting with LED fixtures will result in energy savings of up to 25%, as well as reduced maintenance costs due to the longer lifespan of LEDs. The audit also recommends installing occupancy sensors to further optimize energy use by automatically turning off lights in unoccupied areas. While the upfront cost is high, the audit claims that these upgrades will pay for themselves within five years. What broader effect of this recommendation should plant management consider?
a. The energy savings will likely be lower than projected due to the high upfront costs
b. The occupancy sensors may interfere with the operation of other automated systems in the plant
c. The reduction in maintenance costs may lead to decreased workload for the facility's electrical staff
d. The LED fixtures will require replacement more frequently than the current lighting system

Answer: c. The reduction in maintenance costs may lead to decreased workload for the facility's electrical staff. Explanation: While the audit focuses on energy and cost savings, the broader effect of reduced maintenance costs from longer-lasting LED fixtures is that the facility's maintenance staff may have less lighting-related work, potentially impacting staffing or resource allocation decisions.

807. A utility company recommends installing smart meters across all residential units in a housing complex to provide real-time energy usage data and improve billing accuracy. The smart meters will also allow for remote monitoring and faster outage detection. The report states that the installation process will cause minimal disruption and that the long-term savings from accurate billing will benefit both the utility and the residents. However, the report briefly mentions that the system may require network upgrades to ensure reliable communication between the meters and the utility's central system. What systemic impact should the complex's management consider before agreeing to the upgrade?
a. The installation will cause significant disruption to residents during the network upgrades
b. The smart meters will require regular recalibration to maintain accuracy
c. The network upgrades may increase the overall cost of the project beyond the initial estimates
d. The smart meters will result in higher energy bills for residents due to increased monitoring

Answer: c. The network upgrades may increase the overall cost of the project beyond the initial estimates.
Explanation: The report mentions the need for network upgrades, which could lead to higher costs than initially projected. Management should consider the potential for these upgrades to increase the overall cost of the project, beyond the immediate installation of the smart meters.

808. A technical report on a wind farm recommends replacing aging inverters with newer models that offer higher efficiency and lower maintenance requirements. The report claims that the new inverters will improve energy conversion rates by 5%, which will enhance overall power output. However, the new inverters also come with advanced monitoring systems that require integration with the farm's existing SCADA (Supervisory Control and Data Acquisition) system. The report briefly notes that this integration may require additional software updates and personnel training. What long-term implication should the wind farm's management consider based on this recommendation?
a. The higher efficiency of the new inverters will not justify the installation costs
b. The integration with the SCADA system may cause delays and increase training costs for the staff
c. The new inverters will have a shorter lifespan than the existing models
d. The advanced monitoring systems will reduce the need for human oversight, lowering operational costs

Answer: b. The integration with the SCADA system may cause delays and increase training costs for the staff.
Explanation: The need to integrate the new inverters with the existing SCADA system may require software updates and additional personnel training, which could lead to delays and increased costs. Management should weigh these factors when considering the upgrade.

809. A commercial building owner receives a recommendation to replace its aging electrical panels with newer models that include built-in surge protection and remote monitoring capabilities. The recommendation claims that the new panels will enhance safety by reducing the risk of electrical fires and will allow for real-time monitoring of power quality. However, the report also mentions that the installation of these panels may require a temporary shutdown of the building's power. What is the most significant short-term impact of this recommendation that the owner should consider?
a. The new panels will likely need more frequent maintenance than the current ones
b. The building's power may need to be shut down during installation, potentially disrupting operations
c. The surge protection features will not be as effective as standalone surge protectors
d. The remote monitoring capabilities may not be compatible with the building's existing systems

Answer: b. The building's power may need to be shut down during installation, potentially disrupting operations.
Explanation: The installation of new electrical panels often requires shutting down power temporarily, which could disrupt the building's operations. This is a significant short-term impact that the owner should carefully plan for.

810. A technical evaluation recommends upgrading an industrial facility's air compressors to energy-efficient models that can adjust output based on real-time demand. The report projects a 20% reduction in energy use and lower maintenance costs due to the compressors' variable-speed drives. However, it also notes that the new compressors may require adjustments to the facility's existing compressed air distribution system to ensure compatibility. What broader effect should the facility's management consider before implementing this recommendation?
a. The new compressors will require more frequent repairs than the current ones
b. The need for adjustments to the air distribution system could increase installation costs and downtime
c. The compressors' variable-speed drives will increase the facility's overall energy consumption
d. The new compressors will likely have a shorter lifespan due to the variable-speed drives

Answer: b. The need for adjustments to the air distribution system could increase installation costs and downtime.
Explanation: The report mentions that the facility's compressed air distribution system may need adjustments to work with the new compressors. These modifications could lead to higher installation costs and extended downtime, which the management should consider.

811. A facilities manager receives a recommendation to install power factor correction capacitors in an industrial plant to improve the power factor and reduce demand charges from the utility company. The recommendation explains that the capacitors will offset reactive power and improve the efficiency of the plant's electrical system. However, it also mentions that the capacitors will need regular maintenance to ensure they remain effective. What is the long-term implication of this recommendation that the facilities manager should consider?
a. The capacitors will eliminate all demand charges from the utility
b. The plant's electrical system will require more frequent shutdowns for capacitor maintenance
c. The capacitors will need regular monitoring and maintenance to maintain their effectiveness over time
d. The capacitors will not significantly improve the power factor and may not justify the cost

Answer: c. The capacitors will need regular monitoring and maintenance to maintain their effectiveness over time.
Explanation: While the recommendation emphasizes the immediate benefits of power factor correction, it also notes that the capacitors will require ongoing maintenance to remain effective. The facilities manager should plan for this long-term maintenance requirement.

812. A data center receives a recommendation to replace its backup diesel generators with new, more fuel-efficient models that have lower emissions. The report claims that the new generators will reduce fuel consumption by 10% and meet stricter environmental regulations. However, the report also mentions that the new models may require additional space for fuel storage and maintenance access. What systemic impact should the data center management consider before making this upgrade?
a. The fuel savings will not be significant enough to justify the cost of new generators
b. The additional space required for the new generators may lead to higher construction or retrofitting costs
c. The new generators will require less frequent maintenance than the existing models
d. The environmental regulations do not apply to the data center's operations, making the upgrade unnecessary

Answer: b. The additional space required for the new generators may lead to higher construction or retrofitting costs. Explanation: The new generators may require more space for fuel storage and maintenance access, which could increase construction or retrofitting costs. This is an important systemic impact that management should consider before proceeding with the upgrade.

813. A utility company suggests that a large industrial facility implement a demand-side management (DSM) program to reduce peak demand and lower energy costs. The DSM program would involve scheduling energy-intensive processes during off-peak hours and using energy storage systems to balance demand. The recommendation mentions potential savings on demand charges but also notes that the facility may need to invest in advanced monitoring systems to effectively manage energy use. What broader effect should the facility's management consider before adopting the DSM program?
a. The DSM program will lead to an overall increase in energy consumption due to the need for energy storage systems
b. The savings from reduced demand charges may be offset by the cost of installing and maintaining advanced monitoring systems
c. The DSM program will require significant changes to the facility's production schedule, leading to reduced productivity
d. The utility company will impose penalties for not participating in the DSM program

Answer: b. The savings from reduced demand charges may be offset by the cost of installing and maintaining advanced monitoring systems. Explanation: While the DSM program offers savings through reduced demand charges, the need for advanced monitoring systems could increase costs. Management should evaluate whether these upfront costs will offset the savings from reduced demand charges.

814. In a project report about implementing energy-efficient lighting systems, the introduction begins with a detailed overview of different lighting technologies and their energy consumption rates. It describes how LED, fluorescent, and incandescent lights perform under different conditions, focusing on the technical specifications. In the middle of the report, the tone shifts: "Considering the growing pressure to reduce energy costs, it's imperative that businesses take immediate action to upgrade their lighting systems. LEDs, in particular, offer the most cost-effective solution with an energy savings potential of up to 85% over traditional incandescent bulbs. Failing to make this transition not only impacts operational costs but also increases the company's carbon footprint." What kind of tone shift is present in this passage?
a. From descriptive to persuasive
b. From objective to informative
c. From specific to general
d. From prescriptive to cautionary

Answer: a. From descriptive to persuasive. Explanation: The passage begins with a descriptive overview of lighting technologies, focusing on their performance. The tone shifts to a persuasive argument urging businesses to adopt LED lighting, highlighting the benefits of cost savings and reduced carbon footprint.

815. In a technical manual for installing industrial generators, the first section details the types of generators available, focusing on their power outputs, fuel types, and efficiency ratings. Later in the document, the following

passage occurs: "It is critical that technicians adhere to all safety protocols when installing these units. Failure to properly ground the generator can lead to dangerous faults, posing severe risks to both personnel and equipment. Always verify that all connections are secure and up to code before operating the system." How does the tone shift in this document?
a. From prescriptive to descriptive
b. From general to specific
c. From objective to cautionary
d. From informative to persuasive

Answer: c. From objective to cautionary. Explanation: The document shifts from an objective discussion of generator types and specifications to a more cautionary tone, warning technicians of the risks associated with improper installation and emphasizing safety.

816. A comprehensive report on electrical grid modernization begins by outlining the historical development of power distribution systems, emphasizing the technological advancements over the past century. The report then transitions: "As energy demands rise and climate change accelerates, the need to modernize the grid has become urgent. Immediate investment in smart grid technologies is necessary to avoid widespread power outages and to integrate renewable energy sources. Without decisive action, the grid will be unable to support the growing population and their increasing energy needs." What tone shift occurs in this section of the report?
a. From historical to prescriptive
b. From neutral to urgent
c. From general to descriptive
d. From persuasive to cautionary

Answer: b. From neutral to urgent. Explanation: The report moves from a neutral, historical overview of the grid's development to an urgent tone, pressing for immediate investment in smart grid technologies to address rising energy demands and prevent outages.

817. A maintenance guide for solar inverters begins by providing a broad overview of the different types of inverters and their applications in various solar power systems. Later, the tone shifts: "To ensure optimal performance and longevity of your solar system, it is essential to perform regular maintenance checks. In particular, you must inspect the inverters every six months to detect any signs of wear or potential faults. Failure to do so can lead to reduced system efficiency and costly repairs." How would you describe the tone shift in this passage?
a. From specific to general
b. From descriptive to prescriptive
c. From cautionary to neutral
d. From persuasive to informative

Answer: b. From descriptive to prescriptive. Explanation: The passage starts by describing different types of inverters, then shifts to prescriptive language that instructs the reader on the importance of regular maintenance and outlines specific steps to avoid system inefficiencies.

818. An electrical safety document discusses general workplace hazards before transitioning: "In addition to standard safety protocols, employees must be aware of the specific risks associated with working in confined spaces. Electrical hazards in these environments can be deadly, and strict procedures must be followed. Always use lockout/tagout (LOTO) practices to ensure that equipment is properly de-energized before entering the space." What tone shift is present in this passage?
a. From general to specific
b. From prescriptive to descriptive
c. From cautionary to persuasive
d. From urgent to neutral

Answer: a. From general to specific. Explanation: The passage shifts from a general discussion of workplace hazards to focusing on the specific dangers and safety protocols related to confined spaces, providing more detailed instructions for managing these risks.

819. In a proposal for upgrading a manufacturing facility's electrical system, the document initially provides a cost-benefit analysis of various technologies: "Both systems offer comparable performance under standard operating conditions, but System A has a lower upfront cost, while System B provides long-term savings through reduced maintenance." Later, the proposal emphasizes: "Given the facility's long-term operational goals, it is strongly recommended to invest in System B. The initial cost will be offset by significant savings in future repairs and downtime." What shift in tone occurs here?
a. From neutral to descriptive
b. From informative to persuasive
c. From specific to general
d. From descriptive to cautionary

Answer: b. From informative to persuasive. Explanation: The proposal begins with an informative comparison of two systems but shifts to a persuasive tone as it argues in favor of investing in System B, emphasizing the long-term financial benefits despite the higher upfront cost.

820. A section of a technical specification document discusses various insulation materials for high-voltage cables, detailing their thermal properties and performance under stress. The document then shifts: "In environments with extreme temperature variations, it is recommended that technicians use cross-linked polyethylene (XLPE) insulation due to its superior heat resistance. Failing to choose the appropriate insulation for the application can result in premature cable failure and costly system downtime." How would you describe the tone shift?
a. From objective to prescriptive
b. From specific to general
c. From informative to persuasive
d. From neutral to cautionary

Answer: d. From neutral to cautionary. Explanation: The tone moves from a neutral, factual description of insulation materials to a cautionary warning about the consequences of selecting the wrong type of insulation, focusing on potential risks like cable failure.

821. An operations manual for electrical equipment begins by describing the basic functions of a circuit breaker. Later, the text becomes more urgent: "Circuit breakers must be inspected regularly to ensure that they are functioning correctly. A faulty breaker can fail to trip during an overload, leading to catastrophic equipment damage or even fire. Technicians must adhere strictly to the inspection schedule to prevent these dangerous outcomes." What type of tone shift occurs here?
a. From informative to descriptive
b. From general to specific
c. From neutral to urgent
d. From prescriptive to persuasive

Answer: c. From neutral to urgent. Explanation: The manual transitions from a neutral description of the circuit breaker's function to an urgent tone, emphasizing the critical importance of regular inspections and the potential hazards of neglecting them.

822. A training module for electrical apprentices begins with a section on wiring techniques, detailing the tools and materials needed for various types of installations. It then transitions: "Correct wiring is essential not only for the system's functionality but also for ensuring safety. If connections are not properly secured, the risk of short circuits or electrical fires increases dramatically. Therefore, always follow best practices for wire termination, and double-check connections before energizing any circuit." What tone shift is demonstrated in this passage?
a. From general to cautionary
b. From descriptive to prescriptive
c. From neutral to persuasive
d. From objective to specific

Answer: b. From descriptive to prescriptive. Explanation: The module shifts from a descriptive explanation of wiring techniques to a prescriptive tone, instructing the apprentices on best practices for ensuring safety and preventing dangerous conditions.

823. In a section of a report on electrical grid reliability, the tone is initially neutral: "Power outages can be caused by a variety of factors, including weather conditions, equipment failures, and human error." The tone shifts later: "To prevent outages, it is critical that utility companies invest in grid modernization efforts, including automation and real-time monitoring systems. Without these upgrades, the grid will continue to experience significant vulnerabilities, leading to increased outages and service interruptions." How does the tone shift?
a. From general to specific
b. From neutral to persuasive
c. From descriptive to informative
d. From prescriptive to cautionary

Answer: b. From neutral to persuasive. Explanation: The passage starts with a neutral discussion of power outage causes but shifts to a persuasive argument advocating for grid modernization, emphasizing the importance of investing in advanced technologies to prevent future outages.

824. A technical report on energy-efficient building design includes an example of a commercial office building in Chicago that reduced its energy consumption by 30% through the installation of high-performance insulation and energy-efficient windows. The report uses this example to suggest that similar measures could be applied to a wide range of buildings to achieve significant energy savings. However, the report also notes that the Chicago building had relatively mild winters compared to other regions. A building manager in a colder climate, like Minnesota, is considering implementing similar measures. How should the manager interpret the relevance of this example to their own situation?
a. The example directly applies to all climates, and similar energy savings can be expected.
b. The building in Chicago achieved energy savings that are irrelevant to buildings in colder climates.
c. The example suggests that energy savings may be possible, but the building manager should consider the more severe winters in Minnesota and adjust expectations.
d. The use of high-performance insulation will have no impact in colder climates, making the example irrelevant.

Answer: c. The example suggests that energy savings may be possible, but the building manager should consider the more severe winters in Minnesota and adjust expectations. Explanation: While the Chicago building's energy savings provide a useful case study, the milder winters there mean that the building manager in Minnesota should not expect the same level of savings. The example is relevant but must be adapted to account for regional climate differences.

825. An instructional manual for a photovoltaic (PV) system installer uses a hypothetical scenario where a homeowner installs a solar array in a location with high annual sunlight and achieves an average power output of 5 kW per day. The manual presents this scenario to illustrate the potential benefits of solar power but does not account for shading, panel orientation, or seasonal variations. A contractor using this manual to explain solar panel benefits to a customer in a region with less sunlight is trying to assess the value of this example. How should the contractor interpret this hypothetical scenario?
a. The example is universally applicable, and the customer should expect similar power output.
b. The scenario is irrelevant to any region with less sunlight than the one described.
c. The contractor should adjust the example to account for local factors like shading and reduced sunlight.
d. The hypothetical example proves that solar panels are ineffective in regions with low sunlight.

Answer: c. The contractor should adjust the example to account for local factors like shading and reduced sunlight. Explanation: The hypothetical scenario is meant to illustrate the potential of solar power under ideal conditions, but it should be adapted to reflect the specific conditions of the customer's location, including sunlight availability and shading, to provide a more realistic estimate.

826. A technical white paper on grounding practices in industrial facilities references a historical case from the 1970s, in which inadequate grounding caused a major equipment failure and safety hazard in a large factory. The white paper uses this case to emphasize the importance of adhering to modern grounding standards. However, the grounding technologies available today are significantly more advanced than those from the 1970s. How should a modern electrical engineer interpret the relevance of this historical example?
a. The example is outdated and irrelevant to current grounding practices.
b. The example serves as a cautionary tale, but modern grounding technologies reduce the likelihood of similar issues.
c. The example proves that all industrial facilities are still at risk for grounding-related failures.
d. The example suggests that grounding standards have not evolved, and current facilities face the same risks as those in the 1970s.

Answer: b. The example serves as a cautionary tale, but modern grounding technologies reduce the likelihood of similar issues. Explanation: The historical example is useful in highlighting the potential consequences of poor grounding practices, but advances in grounding technologies and standards since the 1970s mean that modern facilities have better safeguards in place. The engineer should view the example as a reminder of the importance of proper grounding, even though current risks are lower.

827. A case study on the use of smart grid technologies in rural communities presents the example of a small town that successfully reduced energy waste by implementing advanced metering infrastructure (AMI) and automated demand response systems. The case study suggests that similar outcomes could be achieved in other rural communities with limited infrastructure. A utility company considering smart grid upgrades in a rural area with a more dispersed population is evaluating the relevance of this example. How should the utility company interpret this case study?
a. The example is fully applicable, and similar results can be expected in any rural area.
b. The case study is only relevant to rural communities with the exact same population density and infrastructure.
c. The utility company should consider differences in population density and infrastructure when applying the case study's conclusions.
d. The use of AMI and demand response systems is irrelevant to rural areas with dispersed populations.

Answer: c. The utility company should consider differences in population density and infrastructure when applying the case study's conclusions. Explanation: While the case study provides valuable insight into the benefits of smart grid technologies, the utility company must adjust the conclusions to account for the differences in population density and existing infrastructure in their rural area, which may affect the implementation and outcomes.

828. A training manual for electricians includes a real-world example of a commercial building that reduced its overall electricity demand by 15% by implementing a load-shedding strategy during peak hours. The manual suggests that other buildings could achieve similar results by following the same approach. However, the example does not provide details on the specific load types or operational constraints of the building. An electrician working in a hospital is trying to determine whether this load-shedding strategy would be appropriate for their facility. How should the electrician evaluate this example?
a. The example can be directly applied to the hospital without modifications.
b. The load-shedding strategy is irrelevant to hospitals due to their unique operational requirements.
c. The electrician should evaluate the hospital's critical loads and operational constraints before considering a load-shedding strategy.
d. The example suggests that load-shedding is ineffective in any facility with critical loads.

Answer: c. The electrician should evaluate the hospital's critical loads and operational constraints before considering a load-shedding strategy. Explanation: While the load-shedding strategy worked in the example, hospitals have critical systems that cannot be interrupted. The electrician must assess whether load-shedding can be safely implemented without impacting critical operations before applying the example to the hospital.

829. An article on energy storage technologies includes a hypothetical scenario in which a utility company installs battery storage to balance supply and demand during peak energy use periods. The article explains that the battery system reduced peak load by 20% and resulted in significant savings for the utility. However, the scenario assumes

that the utility has an adequate budget for the initial installation and that local regulations allow for battery storage. A utility company in a region with strict regulations and budget constraints is evaluating this scenario. How should the company interpret the hypothetical example?

a. The scenario is fully applicable, and the company should install battery storage immediately.
b. The example is unrealistic due to budget constraints and regulatory hurdles in the company's region.
c. The company should explore battery storage but consider local regulations and budget limitations before proceeding.
d. The scenario proves that battery storage is not a viable solution in regions with strict regulations.

Answer: c. The company should explore battery storage but consider local regulations and budget limitations before proceeding. Explanation: The hypothetical scenario highlights the potential benefits of battery storage, but the utility company must account for its own regulatory environment and financial constraints before deciding whether this solution is feasible.

830. A technical presentation on electric vehicle (EV) charging infrastructure provides an example of a metropolitan area that installed fast-charging stations in multiple locations and saw a 50% increase in EV usage within two years. The presentation suggests that other cities could see similar increases in EV adoption by investing in fast-charging infrastructure. However, the example does not address whether the increase in EV usage was driven solely by the availability of charging stations or by other factors, such as local incentives for EV purchases. A city planner in a region without such incentives is considering this example. How should the planner interpret the example in the context of their region?

a. The planner should expect a 50% increase in EV usage regardless of local incentives.
b. The example is irrelevant because the planner's region does not offer incentives for EV purchases.
c. The planner should consider the role of incentives in the EV adoption rate and adjust expectations accordingly.
d. The installation of fast-charging stations will not impact EV adoption in regions without incentives.

Answer: c. The planner should consider the role of incentives in the EV adoption rate and adjust expectations accordingly. Explanation: While the example highlights the impact of fast-charging stations on EV adoption, the planner must also consider that local incentives likely contributed to the increase in EV usage. Without similar incentives, the planner should adjust expectations for their region.

831. A technical guide on power quality improvement in industrial facilities uses a case study of a factory that implemented harmonic filters to reduce total harmonic distortion (THD) and improve the lifespan of its electrical equipment. The case study reports a 25% reduction in maintenance costs after the filters were installed. The guide suggests that other industrial facilities could achieve similar improvements by installing harmonic filters. However, the case study does not specify the factory's initial THD levels or the type of equipment in use. How should an electrical engineer evaluating this guide for a different facility interpret the case study?

a. The case study is universally applicable, and the same improvements can be expected in any facility.
b. The engineer should assess the current THD levels and equipment in their facility before expecting similar improvements.
c. The installation of harmonic filters will reduce maintenance costs in all industrial facilities.
d. The case study suggests that harmonic filters are not effective in reducing maintenance costs.

Answer: b. The engineer should assess the current THD levels and equipment in their facility before expecting similar improvements. Explanation: The case study provides useful information about the benefits of harmonic filters, but the engineer should evaluate the specific conditions of their facility—such as existing THD levels and equipment—before assuming that similar improvements can be achieved.

832. A report on microgrid implementation includes a real-world example of a small island community that installed a microgrid powered by solar panels and battery storage. The report highlights that the microgrid allowed the community to become energy-independent and reduce reliance on imported diesel fuel. The example is used to suggest that microgrids could benefit other remote communities with limited access to traditional power sources. A town located in a mountainous region with frequent cloud cover is considering a microgrid. How should the town's planners interpret the relevance of this example?
a. The example is fully applicable, and the town should install a microgrid without considering local conditions.
b. The example is irrelevant because the town's location experiences frequent cloud cover, unlike the island community.
c. The planners should evaluate the impact of cloud cover on solar generation before deciding if a microgrid is feasible.
d. The installation of a microgrid will not be beneficial in any region with less sunlight than the island community.

Answer: c. The planners should evaluate the impact of cloud cover on solar generation before deciding if a microgrid is feasible. Explanation: While the example demonstrates the benefits of a microgrid, the town's planners must consider local factors, such as cloud cover, that could affect the microgrid's solar power generation capabilities. Adjustments may be necessary to ensure feasibility in their region.

833. A white paper on energy-efficient motors presents an example of a factory that replaced its standard motors with high-efficiency models, leading to a 10% reduction in energy consumption. The paper suggests that this example can be applied to most industrial facilities, but it does not address the specific operational conditions of the factory, such as load variation or duty cycle. A plant manager considering motor replacements is trying to assess whether the example applies to their facility, where motors often operate at varying loads. How should the manager interpret this example?
a. The example can be directly applied to any facility, and the manager should expect a 10% reduction in energy use.
b. The manager should evaluate their facility's specific motor loads and duty cycles before expecting similar energy savings.
c. The example proves that high-efficiency motors will not save energy in facilities with varying loads.
d. The manager should ignore the example because it is not applicable to facilities with different operating conditions.

Answer: b. The manager should evaluate their facility's specific motor loads and duty cycles before expecting similar energy savings. Explanation: The example highlights the potential benefits of high-efficiency motors, but the manager must assess the unique operating conditions of their facility—such as load variation and duty cycles—before assuming the same level of energy savings can be achieved.

You've made it to the end of this IBEW Exam Prep Study Guide, and that's no small feat. Along the way, you've tackled complex electrical concepts, honed your math and reading comprehension skills, and gained a deeper understanding of the tools, systems, and safety practices that will shape your career in the electrical industry. From understanding power calculations to diving deep into lockout/tagout procedures and electrical code nuances, you've equipped yourself with the knowledge needed to succeed.

It hasn't been easy—preparing for an exam like this takes effort, focus, and dedication. But the fact that you've stuck with it means you're already on the right track. Remember, every electrician was once where you are right now, studying and preparing, unsure of what would come next. And like them, you'll get through this and rise to the occasion.

The great thing about exams like this is that they don't just test your memory—they test your perseverance, your ability to learn from mistakes, and your willingness to put in the work. It's okay if you don't feel 100% ready. That's natural. But trust in the preparation you've done here, and take comfort in knowing you've worked hard to get to this point. Every practice question, every formula, and every real-world example you've absorbed has brought you one step closer to passing this exam and starting a career that offers endless opportunities.

Go into the exam with confidence. You've covered a lot of ground. Stay calm, take your time, and trust yourself—you've got what it takes. Best of luck as you take this next step toward your future!

Made in the USA
Columbia, SC
13 May 2025